The Islamization of the
Law in Pakistan

THE ISLAMIZATION OF THE LAW IN PAKISTAN

Rubya Mehdi

CURZON PRESS

Nordic Institute of Asian Studies
Monograph Series No. 60

First published 1994 by

Curzon Press Ltd.,
St John's Studios,
Church Road,
Richmond,
Surrey TW9 2QA

ISBN 0 7007 0236 9 : Paperback
ISBN 0 7007 0308 X : Hardback

British Library Cataloguing-in-Publication Data
A CIP catalogue record for this book is available from the British Library

Printed in the United Kingdom by
Antony Rowe Ltd., Chippenham

Table of Contents

Preface

This book provides information about the Islamization of the law in Pakistan. Special emphasis is laid on the period of Islamization, which started in 1977, until 1988 when most of the laws in Pakistan had been Islamized. Detailed information is provided on the Islamic aspects of constitutional, criminal and family law. The procedure adopted for Islamization is also dealt with in detail.

This critical study of Islamization focuses on the concept of instability and inconsistency in the Islamic laws of Pakistan.

A survey attached as Appendix I, though not representative in relation to the book, provides the general opinion of some of the lawyers and strengthens my assertions.

The legislative process, legislation and judicial actions are examined in this book, the purpose being to bring up questions capable of forming the basis for a more detailed study in the future.

Some time before this book went to press, a *Shari'ah* Bill became law in Pakistan. This is a major turning point in the legal history of Pakistan. The practical implications of this law will be a matter for the future. The text of the *Shari'ah* Act is attached at Appendix III.

Acknowledgements

I am thankful to Professor Ole Krarup for his constant support to me in all matters. He also cared for my personal welfare and had confidence in me even at stages when I lost confidence in myself.

I must acknowledge that this work would not have taken its present shape without the input of Dr Gordon R. Woodman of the Department of Law, University of Birmingham. He provided me with a close and continuous theoretical guidance.

My thanks to Michael Anderson (Department of Law, School of Oriental and African Studies, University of London) who, at the last stage, through his stimulating comments inspired me to reconsider some of my evaluations; and to Dr Werner F. Menski (also of the Department of Law, School of Oriental and African Studies, University of London) for his help and cooperation. I am grateful to have benefitted from the comments of Tove Lise Skov (lecturer at the Department of Political Science, University of Copenhagen) and of Professor Berl Kutchinski, Dr Annika Snare, Dr Margaretha Järvinen and Dr Jacob Winsløw (all of the Institute of Criminology and Criminal Law, University of Copenhagen).

I am also thankful to Kirsti Sparrevohn, Lone Jensen, Marie Stender and Jerry Justice for helping me to type the manuscript and other technical assistance, and to Lars Høg Jensen for the press clippings. I am in fact grateful to everybody in the Institute of Criminology and Criminal Law, University of Copenhagen, for facilitating my day to day work and for showing a lot of tolerance to me.

The Danish Research Academy provided me with the funds to spend three months at the School of Oriental and African Studies, London. G.E.C. Gads Fond provided me with funds for buying the material that was not available in Denmark. The Nordic Institute of Asian Studies (NIAS) and the Rehabilitation Centre for Torture Victims (RCT) funded my visit to Pakistan. Finally, contributions towards the publication of this book were gratefully received from Davids Samling and Margot and Thorvald Dreyers Fond.

My special thanks to my brother, Dr Mahboob Mehdi, who has

been helpful in sending me material from Pakistan. He also helped accomplish the survey attached at Appendix I.

I am deeply grateful to Dr Karl Reinhold Hællquist and Gerald Jackson of NIAS for striving to bring this manuscript into book form.

It is difficult to express in words my gratitude to my family, Marya Akhter and Pervaiz Akhter. Without their cooperation things would have been difficult for me; they showed tolerance even when I was using their time on the project. Pervaiz also helped prepare the glossary.

Rubya Mehdi

CHAPTER 1

Theoretical Framework:
Islamization and an Inconsistent and Unstable Legal System in a Peripheral Capitalist State

1.1 INTRODUCTION

It is difficult to understand the phenomenon of the Islamization of the law in Pakistan if we divorce it from political, economic and social processes. The inconsistency and instability in the law, which will be documented in the following chapters, is so obvious that it is difficult to consider the law simply as legal rules. In the last three decades it has been considered of great importance to relate legal systems to political, economic and social processes, especially with reference to developments in Third World countries (Dunn, 1971).

In analysing the Islamization of the law in Pakistan, and the phenomenon of inconsistency and instability in the country's Islamic legal system, some important aspects which are looked at in this chapter are the impact of British colonialism and the resultant legal pathology, the form of the post-colonial state, the role of ideology and the pluralistic legal structure which has always existed and still exists.

In Part 1.2, I will deal with the pluralistic legal and social structure of the Indian subcontinent before the advent of British colonialism. Part 1.3 deals with the British impact on Muslim law. Problems originating from British interference have been looked at from different points of view. The point is to show that all the negative points of Anglo-Muhammadan law continued even after the Islamization of the law. Part 1.4 deals with the post-colonial state structure and its relationship to the legal system. Part 1.5 deals with the role of ideology in a post colonial state and shows the lack of a consistent ideology. This part furthermore examines ideological differences and makes a general division of Muslims into Fundamentalists and Modernists. Part 1.6 is an account of Islamic revivalism, which began in Pakistan in 1977 with the imposition of martial law in the country and of how women became special victims of this law. Part 1.7 states the main theme of this book, i.e, inconsistency and instability in the laws of Pakistan. Part 1.8 shows how Islamization has not changed the Anglo-Muhammadan legal structure. Lawyers have played a significant role in preserving Anglo-Muhammadan values. In Part 1.9, I draw attention to an important aspect of the pluralistic legal structure in Pakistan and the limitations of different pluralistic legal systems. Part 1.10 deals with the extent to which the social effect of reformist legislation was limited. Part 1.11 deals with the development of Islamic State law with reference to the sources of Islamic law. Special attention is paid to custom as a source of Islamic law, because custom and a pluralistic legal structure are closely related to each other.

In order to obtain some data on the present status and on lawyers' opinions in regard to the legal phenomena studied, a survey was conducted in June 1990 among lawyers in the Punjab. A total number of twenty-six lawyers filled in a questionnaire. The results of the survey strengthen my claim that inconsistency and instability characterize Islamic law in Pakistan, as is demonstrated throughout the book. Respondents were selected by availability. The survey is therefore not representative but does show some general trends of thinking among lawyers. Some of the results will be mentioned at relevant places in the following.

The questionnaire and a note on field research is found at Appendix I.

1.2 PRE-BRITISH MUSLIM RULE IN INDIA

Islam came to India with Muhammad bin-Qasim in A.D. 712. No systematic work exists on the development of Islamic law or administration of justice in India. However a few attempts have been made to describe the administration of justice during Muslim rule in India.

Roughly speaking, the Muslim period in India can be divided into four periods. In the period from 712 to 991 there was no interference by the Muslim conquerors in the administration of justice. It was therefore carried out by the Indians themselves. For the second period, which lasted from 991 until 1206, there is little record about the administration of justice. The third period (1206-1526), which includes the slave dynasties, the *Khalji* dynasty, the *Tughlaq* dynasty, the *Lodi* dynasty and the *Sur* dynasty, was the period when the Muslims permanently settled in

India. The fourth period was that of the Mughals (1526-1757), which came to an end when the British defeated Siraj-al-Dawla and established their power.

Throughout the history of India, Indian villages have maintained an important degree of autonomy. The rule of the king or emperor was felt mainly in the form of local grants, taxes, conscription and the improvement of public facilities such as roads and canals. Justice was nominally administered by the king, but the administration of justice was not centralized in the vast land of India. Justice was administered in practice by village tribunals, which applied local customary law. 'Law in the modern sense was only represented by the liability to pay certain taxes and to abstain from certain acts which were contrary to the interests of the state' (Lipstein, 1957: 85-6; Ahmad, M.B, 1951: 62-3). Even under the highly centralized and well established Mughal government of the seventeenth century, with its extensive judicial machinery, law enforcement seldom reached the village level.

> Only in cases where there had been a very considerable breach of the peace, or where the revenue of the village had not been paid, were villagers likely to come into contact with Mughal law enforcement officials (Calkins, 1968/9).

The scope of Islamic law was limited, leaving the ancient village organization with all its Hindu institutions intact.

Another writer explains the situation like this:
> Accordingly no effort was made by the Mughals to disturb the corporate life of the villages or encroach upon their ancient institutions or to bring them in line with other centralizing agencies; as a result of this they retained their autonomy ... (Hasan, Ibn, 1936: 309).

What this means is that while the Muslim administration of justice was centralized, traditional local units remained independent and undisturbed. Muslim courts were located in towns and the proportion of Muslims was also much larger in towns. Communications were primitive and expansion of the system was not desired at the cost of disturbing the peace of the independent units of justice known as *Panchayats* (local courts) (Husain, Wahed, 1977: 83-5; Ahmad, M.B., 1951: 168-9).

Even *shariah* (Islamic law) was not applied in its rigid form. In the application of *shariah* there was place for custom

(Galanter, 1968: 67).

Muslim kings were tolerant towards their non-Muslim Hindu subjects. King Akbar (1542-1605) was an extreme example of this tolerance (Jain, 1970). In some cases, Muslim kings are also reported to have practiced the old Hindu system of trial by ordeals (instances are Sultan Jalal 'uddin Khilji (1290-96) and King Akbar).

> Trials by ordeal were frequently resorted to. In some cases the accused was made to take a caustic drink (*Bish*). It was believed that if he spoke the truth the drink would do no harm to him. Similarly an accused person was often thrown into water. If he was innocent, he would not drown. There was a still more drastic form of ordeal. An accused was required to hold in his hand a red hot iron wrapped in a leaf in order to establish his defence (Ahmad, M.B., 1951: 59-60).

Hamilton mentioned such a trial in South India during the reign of Aurangzeb (1658-1707) where the accused person was made to put his hand in a pan of boiling oil (Kulshreshtha, 1981: 33). Even if the Muslim rulers did not adopt trial by ordeal themselves, they did not interfere with the non-Muslim states in order to stop it. Therefore, the system continued under the protection of the Sultans and Mughals.

Though a pattern of political centralization was established under British rule and later in independent India and Pakistan, the local political and legal structure still remained strong.

1.3 ANGLO-MUHAMMADAN LAW

British colonialism, represented by the East India Company, started its penetration of India as early as 1601 and continued under different charters. The British brought to India the legal rules known as Common Law. With Common Law they also brought their traditions, outlook and techniques in establishing, maintaining and developing the judicial system. But the common law they introduced was not pure Common Law; it was intermixed with Islamic law and came to be known as Anglo-Muhammadan law.

Centralization and unification of the legal system was important for British rule. This was seen as a condition of progress toward modern nationhood, and law and legal institutions were seen as the best means to achieve this end.

The confrontation with myriad forms of legal authority and variegated local practices highlighted one of the foremost problems of colonial control: how to obtain simple, reliable, and reasonably accurate understanding of indigenous social life without sacrificing great labour and capital? Law and legal institutions provided a solution (Anderson, Michael R., 1989: 12).

In the beginning, the British looked upon the laws of the natives with strict neutrality, since their basic purpose was the collection of revenue. British penetration of Islamic law was slow.

During the latter part of the eighteenth century Islamic criminal justice was replaced by British (Fisch, 1983). But Hindu and Islamic law continued to be applied as the personal law of Indian litigants in such matters as inheritance, succession and religious endowments.[1] This was the first time that Islamic law became the object of a systematic and constitutional legislation.

In 1726, letters patent of George I enabled the courts to give judgment 'according to justice and right' and this naturally came to mean British notions of justice and right. According to later directives, where no specific rules were laid down in Islamic or Hindu holy books, the judges were to act 'according to justice, equity, and good conscience'. The expression was 'generally interpreted to mean the rules of English law if found applicable to Indian society and circumstances'.[2]

In this way, Western legal thought in India came primarily through British sources. Islamic legal rules were retained in personal status cases involving Muslims. However, these rules were in many instances interpreted by British judges or by indigenous judges with British training. Islamic law was interpreted along the lines of British legal thinking (Liebesny, 1953: 502-3).

The uniformity provided by the British had been produced neither by Hindu nor Muslim law in India. But this uniformity and centrality were provided at the cost of imposing rigid Islamic rules. The British acted as if Islam consisted of universal rules disregarding the diversity of Islamic law.

Michael Anderson criticizes British policy in the following words:

> The presumption that a single set of legal rules could apply to all persons professing adherence to Islam violated both Islamic theory and South Asian practice. Hastings had subsumed all indigenous legal arrangements under two categories: Hindu

(earlier, Gentoo) and Muslim (Muhammadan). From the outset, this binary categorization was inadequate to contain the diversity of legal life on the subcontinent. Not only did it fail to acknowledge the distinction between *shi'i* and *sunni* -- and the differences among the schools within each. It also failed to address adequately the practice of the many groups that adopted an eclectic approach to Islam ... (Anderson, Michael R., 1989: 13).

The Islamic law relied upon by the British was inadequate. Until Anglo-Muhammadan law was consolidated in textbooks and precedent, courts appointed *maulavis* to advise British judges. Michael Anderson has criticized this practice. He says that the practice was to present the *maulavi* with a question formulated in an abstract and hypothetical manner, often shorn of relevant details. The answer was necessarily in an abstract form which was applied to the case at hand. Anderson rightly concludes that 'this procedure resulted in a highly formalized and rigid application of legal rules' (*ibid*: 15).

Moreover the British approach towards Islamic law was a text-book approach. They were interested in translating the Islamic text into English so that it could be applied directly by British judges. Anderson says that the British understanding of Islam was that of an essentialist, static Islam incapable of change from within.

The translations had greater legal effect as judges began to rely upon them more directly. Although produced in haste, and with imperfect language skills, the unrevised eighteenth century translations remained authoritative (*ibid*: 17).

Other problems with the text-book approach were that the British made the mistake of treating certain classical Islamic texts as binding legal texts. Islamic texts were applied in ignorance of social circumstances (*ibid*: 14). In spite of all the British policies of centralization and unification, the independence of the local autonomous units was not fully destroyed.

British policy in India engendered a special relationship between State law and folk law. What effect did this have on local autonomous legal life? This is discussed in the next part.

1.3.1 Social Effect of Anglo-Muhammadan Law

It is important to look at the relationship between 'British State law' and people's reaction towards it because this will help us to understand the current relationship of 'Islamic formal state law' to Pakistani society, which is very much a continuation of the former relationship.

A great deal of work has been done on this relationship in India, but no work has been done on it in Pakistan. The work done on India is also relevant for Pakistan, because the inherited British pattern of legal system is the same in both countries, though the phenomenon of Islam as state religion is unique to Pakistan.

Let us look at what different writers have said about this relationship. Cohn contends that English legal culture did not suit Indian situations. For example British legal culture contains values such as equality in law, the judicial ignorance of litigants, the idea that economic relations are based on contract not status, the goal of settling the case at hand, and the necessity of a clear-cut decision rather than a compromise all of, which were at odds with the wide range of adjudication procedures followed in the villages of India. Therefore the results were legal ineffectiveness, voluminous litigation, etc. Cohn says:

> It is my thesis that the present attitude of the Indian peasants was an inevitable consequence of the British decision to establish courts in India patterned on British procedural law. The way a people settles disputes is part of its social structure and value system. In attempting to introduce British procedural law into their India courts, the British confronted the Indian with a situation in which there was a direct clash of the values of the two societies, and the Indians in response thought only of manipulating the new situation and did not use the courts to settle disputes but only to further them (Cohn, 1959: 90).

In another article he says:

> The use of the courts for settlement of local disputes seems in most villages to be almost a minor one. In Senapur, courts were and are used as an arena in the competition for social status, and for political and economic dominance in the village. Cases are brought to court to harass one's opponents, as a punishment, as a form of land speculation and profit making, to satisfy insulted pride, and to maintain local political dominance over one's

followers. The litigants do not expect a settlement that will end the dipute to eventuate from recourse to the state courts (*op.cit.* 1965: 105).

R.S Khare explains 'lawyers law' as being different from 'religious immutable law'. There is no acceptance of court law as the just law. He describes it like this:

> The ways of the courts are regarded as 'foreign and deceptive at every step, unless there is someone acquainted who can help find the way'. The procedures are never completely known to an outsider; new manipulations by *babus* (clerks, typists, legal assistants, lawyers, etc.) are always cropping up, making previous experiences of limited guidance" (Khare, 1972: 77).

> Lawyers law is undesirable not only because of several practical difficulties but also... because of several negative cultural 'images' or meaning associations that it popularly carries under the sacred scheme (*ibid.*, 78).

But he says:

> ... it has strong and effective informal organizations at both the village and city levels, and that both functionally interrelate for making lawyer's law effective in socioeconomic controls, despite its enormous bureaucratic complexity and continuing 'strangeness' to a common villager (ibid., 94).

The Rudolphs have mentioned some reasons for ineffectiveness and the large gap between state law and popular practice. They think that the two systems represent different values. For example universalism and impersonality are the values of modern western legal systems, while for Indians the social differences among men are central to their legal identity. In the same way Indians do not think of impartiality in terms of 'anonymity'. Western procedure makes the decision in a case by declaring that one side has won and the other lost, while village tribunals try to compromise differences (Rudolph, L. & S., 1965).

Whatever different writers might have said about the relationship of British and local law, generally all agree that the pathology of the state legal system, contains a great many problems. As has been mentioned, in spite of all British efforts to create a centralized legal system the pattern of diversified or plural legal practices were never fully broken. After independence in 1947, India was divided into India and Pakistan, because of the demand of Indian Muslims for a separate homeland. Anglo-Muhammadan law became the state law of Pakistan. All the defects of Anglo-Muhammadan law continued in the new state of Pakistan.

1.4 THE STRUCTURE OF THE PAKISTANI STATE

To understand the peculiar nature of the instability and inconsistency of the Pakistani legal system, it is important to look at the nature of the post-colonial peripheral state in Pakistan, since this seems to directly affect its formal legal system.

If we look at the political history of Pakistan we can easily see the dominant role of the military in its politics (Haque, Ahmed Shafiqul, 1982). Pakistan has been under military dictatorship for more than half of its history, while the military/bureaucracy has exercised indirect political influence the rest of the time. On 8 October 1958, General Ayub Khan (1907-74) imposed martial law in the country. He abrogated the Constitution and concentrated all State power in himself. In May 1962, after almost four years, the General promulgated Pakistan's second constitution and ruled Pakistan until nearly the end of the decade. He was replaced by another military dictator, General Yahya Khan, in 1969, who abrogated the Ayub Constitution and promulgated his own 'legal framework', which was in fact a third constitution.

Under this constitution the first general elections in the history of Pakistan were held in 1970. Zulfikar Ali Bhutto's Pakistan People's Party won a majority of the seats in West Pakistan while Sheikh Mujibur Rahman's party won in East Pakistan. The conflict between the two parties worsened and finally turned into a civil war. India became involved in this situation, which ended up by East Pakistan becoming the independent state of Bangladesh. On 21 April 1972 Bhutto convened the National Assembly. In 1973 a new constitution was adopted. But people lost confidence in Bhutto because of his many unfulfilled promises. He was also distrusted by the bureaucrats and the army. He rigged the elections and managed to obtain an overwhelming majority for his People's Party both in the centre and in the provinces. The outcome of the elections enraged the people who rose in revolt. The Pakistan National Alliance (PNA), a united front of numerous political parties, adopted the defence of Islam as its central theme. It gradually consolidated power and announced its aim of transforming Pakistan into a model Islamic state. Once again the army stepped in and arrested Bhutto in a military coup in 1977. General Zia ul Haque took over power and imposed martial law. The General promised elections within three months, but kept postponing them on one pretext or the other. He executed Bhutto by bringing a capital charge against him in court and finding him guilty.

During his rule, General Zia promulgated many Islamic laws in the form of Presidential Orders. The eighth amendment to the Constitution, made in 1985, validates all laws made during the period of martial law. They cannot be challenged in any court of law.

How are we to account for the central position of the military in the politics of Pakistan? A great deal of work has been done about the 'peculiar nature of state structure and the special role of military in the countries which were colonies and now are complementary and subsidiary attached to world capitalism'. Kirsten Westergaard has written a good chapter on different notions of post colonial peripheral state structure (Westergaard, 1985). John Martinussen, while analysing the post-colonial state, has laid more emphasis on the mode of production in these countries (Martinussen, 1980). Alavi has provided a most acceptable explanation of military dominance in politics, especially with reference to Pakistan. Ove K. Pedersen, like Alavi, looks at the state as the coordinator, i.e., he sees a multicentral system. This idea of a multicentral state is analogous to Alavi's idea of an industrial society. There is a movement away from a monolithic to a heterogeneous structure (Pedersen, 1990). John S. Saul has worked with reference to Tanzania and given another perspective to Alavi's work. W. Ziemann and M. Lanzendorfer, while basically criticising Saul, have provided yet another perspective to Alavi's work, laying more stress on the economic basis of the state. Colin Leys, however, is critical of the Alavi's total concept.

The relevance of these theories is that they deal with the concentration of power in the state apparatus, which further explains the reasons for frequent military takeovers, abrogation of constitutions, ad hoc legislation, etc., that make these states unstable, with limited legitimacy and in states of permanent crisis. Ideological manipulation is another main feature of authoritarian governments. In Pakistan non-consensus on the issue of Islam is complementary to instability and will be discussed under law and ideology.

Hamza Alavi's contribution, as has been mentioned, refers particularly to Pakistan. The general features of the Pakistani state structure, he says, are, firstly the special role of the military bureaucratic oligarchy. From the inception of the state, state structure lay in their hands rather than with the political leadership.

> There is a widespread tendency of regimes in a peripheral capitalist society, such as Pakistan, to acquire an authoritarian character and to proliferate military dictatorships (Alavi, 1983: 42).

From the special role of the military bureaucratic oligarchy, Alavi comes to the second feature of an overdeveloped superstructure or state apparatus. These are the creations of the colonial regime, he says, as it was necessary for the colonial power to have a powerful state apparatus to subordinate the native social classes. 'The colonial state is therefore equipped with a powerful bureaucratic-military apparatus and mechanisms of government which enable it through its routine operations to subordinate the native social classes'. Pakistan inherited that over-developed state structure and its institutionalized practices from the colonial period (*ibid.*, 1972: 61).

A third feature is the existence of several economically dominant classes, namely the metropolitan and indigenous bourgeoisies and the landowning class, whose rival interests and competing demands are mediated by the state (*ibid.*, 1972: 62; 1971: 55-6; 1982).

This has given a fourth feature to the Pakistani state structure, i.e., its relative autonomy, which means that the state apparatus is not the instrument of any one single class; it mediates the competing interests of the three propertied classes. I quote from Alavi:

> ...the apparatus of the state furthermore assume also a new and relatively autonomous economic role, which is not paralleled in the classical bourgeois state. The state in the post-colonial society directly appropriates a very large part of the economic surplus and deploys it in bureaucratically directed economic activity in the name of promoting economic development (Alavi: 1972: 62).

This constitutes an independent material basis for the autonomy of the bureaucratic military oligarchy.

A fifth feature is the concept of the structural imperatives of peripheral capitalism, which Alavi explains like this:

> Post colonial states function within the structural framework of peripheral capitalism. It is subject to the collective interest of the three economically dominant classes, which together thus constitute the ruling bloc in power. The post colonial state, as well as these classes, is subject to the imperatives of peripheral capitalism and must act in accordance with its demands (*ibid.*, 1983: 43-4).

The expression 'structural imperative' Alavi explains thus:

> ... the concept, as I have articulated it, opens up the analytical framework to take account of structural conditions on the one hand and, simultaneously and dialectically, the conscious and purposive actions of the guardians of the state or individual capitalists on the other. Structural conditions do not determine the actions of social agents but, rather, the outcomes of their actions, which in turn become points of departure for subsequent conscious and purposive actions designed to secure their objectives. In the light of such a theoretical framework, we grasp the development of courses of action over time in relation to objective conditions, in dialectical reciprocity of mutual determination of purposive actions and structural conditions (*ibid.*, 1983: 63).

The institution of private property and the capitalist mode of production is dominant within the above mentioned framework.

Finally, Alavi concentrates on the role of the politicians. The relationship of the state and political parties is competitive and complementary. If politicians respect the autonomous role of the state, it becomes a partner. But if they challenge its relatively autonomous role, than they are overthrown. It is the desire of the ruling classes, though, that the politicians and legal institutions are there to keep a facade of democracy.

> Politicians and political parties stand at the centre of a complex set of relationships. On the one hand, they are expected (ideally) to articulate the demands of those from whom they seek support; they are supposed to attempt to realize those demands by their participation in the working of government. On the other hand, they also play a key role in manipulating public relations on behalf of those who do make public policy, to make it acceptable

to the community at large. For that they channel public grievances and seek to promote an understanding' of the situation concerning public issues which would diminish potential opposition (*ibid.*, 1972: 62).

With some reservations, Saul supports Alavi's notion of an over-developed state structure with relative autonomy. Saul draws two points of crucial significance from Alavi, first, the over-developed state apparatus and second, its relatively autonomous economic role. He adds a third feature to the two, that is, the special ideological function of the state, which will be discussed in Part 1.5. However, Saul has criticized Alavi for his concept of class determination and state mediation of their interests, with special reference to Tanzania.

Colin Leys rejects the notion of an overdeveloped state structure. He is also critical of the 'centrality' of the state. He is in fact against the total concept. He criticizes Alavi for laying too much emphasis on superstructure. He says:

> But the important point is not so much that the idea of the 'overdeveloped' state is empty; it is really that this whole way of approaching the question of the significance of any state, i.e., of starting out from its structure or scope, whether inherited from an earlier situation or not, is a mistake. In order to understand the significance of any state for the class struggle we must start out from the class struggle, not the state. The idea of the 'overdeveloped state' functions, in both Alavi's and Saul's accounts, as an apparent reason for reversing the proper order of procedure: the inherited state is said to be 'overdeveloped', therefore it has exceptional significance in post colonial societies, therefore the class character of the bureacracy of this overdeveloped state is the key issue. This leads to formulations about the state bureaucracy which seem as questionable as the idea of the 'overdeveloped state' (Leys, 1981: 43).

But Leys' rejection of the centrality of the state provides no explanation of the special role played by the military, while Alavi's account does provide an explanation for this phenomenon.

Ziemann and Lanzendorfer (1977), while criticising Saul, have provided useful analyses for explaining the concentration of political power in the state apparatus. They have laid more stress on the economic structure as opposed to the superstructure. They have used the term 'peripheral state structure', which means complementary and subsidiary systems attached to the metropolitan system. They have attributed three features to peripheral reproduction of a capitalist structure: (a) structural distortion of economic development (b) structural dependency of the peripheral economy (c) the heterogeneity of the economic structure, in particular heterogeneous relations of production.

They agree with Alavi about the state's relative autonomy, but attribute it to the classical Marxist view of the capitalist state, denying that it is peculiar to the post-colonial state.

The three features of peripheral reproduction weaken the class structure and therefore the state takes over the mediating role. The conclusions drawn by Ziemann and Lanzendorfer are relevant as they discuss the weakness of peripheral states in the sense of their political instability, regional disintegration and the restricted effectiveness of their government resources.

In the light of the above discussion let us look at the political economy of the legal system in Pakistan. Alavi provides the best analytical framework to analyse the pathology of legal system in Pakistan.

1.5 LAW AND IDEOLOGY IN PAKISTAN

As Islam has played a central role in the formation of laws and legal institutions in Pakistan it is important to understand the nature of Islamic ideology.

The word ideology is used in the sense provided by Fred Halliday and Hamza Alavi in an introduction to a jointly edited book:

> Vital to the project of states, and to any legitimation of power within them, are ideologies, the third major theme of this study. We use ideology in a broad sense, to denote sets of beliefs concerning social and political issues, which are both explanatory and normative, that is, which purport to explain why the world is as it is, how it came to be so, and what the goals of political action should be" (Halliday & Alavi, 1988: 5).

1.5.1 The Relationship of Law and Ideology

There are different theories about the relationship of law and ideology to the state. According to traditional Marxist theory, law and ideology are both part of a superstructure. Law is regarded as an instrument of oppression of one class by another, while ideology is a mode of convincing people *inter alia* that the ownership of the means of production is in the right hands. Superstructure and base influence each other. This view of the relationship of law and ideology is criticized by many people from a neo-Marxist point of view. This is considered by them as a crudely instrumentalist approach, in which law is not recognized as independent and autonomous (Collins, 1984).

Here it would be interesting to look at the different attempts being made to find a direct relationship between law and economic base. In Scandinavia such an attempt has been made by one scholar, Agnete Weiss Bentzon. Based on her experience in Greenland, she finds a dependence of law on the economic basis of society, i.e., on the introduction of private capitalism in Greenland and its conflict with traditional law there. For example, she says, the continued existence of lay judges in order to secure a place for Greenlandic customary law is not very functional for capitalism. She maintains that there is a possibility of the 'co-existence of more sets of conceptions of law connected to the contemporaneous existence within the formation of society of different bases for the procurement of the necessities of life' (Bentzon, 1982).

Her main concern remains the problem of adapting the law to changing material conditions. Jørgen Dalberg Larsen, another Danish writer, has also mentioned the necessity of introducing the modern Danish legal system in place of Greenland's traditional law because of economic development. His argument is that law is not a empty symbol for society but should be compatible with the surrounding realities of life (Dalberg-Larsen, 1989: 290-1).

Ziaul Haque says about the Islamic ideology in Pakistan:

> From this viewpoint, our assumption is that the religious Islamic ideology of the modern state of Pakistan (or more precisely, of the ruling social strata) forms an important part of the general social, legal and political superstructure which has been constructed to justify and preserve the existing social relationships between feudal lords and serfs, capitalists and wage-labourers, based on the semi-feudal and capitalist mode of production which, in itself, is multilaterally linked to international monopoly Capitalism (Haque, Ziaul, 1983: 368).

In the situation of Pakistan there are differences of opinion about the economic base of the country, i.e., if the economic base is capitalist, feudal, semi-capitalist or semi-feudal (Martinussen, 1980). However, it is difficult to find any direct relationship between the economic base and state law in Pakistan, though a direct relationship between the state structure and the law are visible.

With the state structure inherited from the colonial period in an over-developed form, as described in the previous Part, the law becomes an instrument in the hands of the state. In some situations the state does not even hesitate to implement martial law and abrogate the constitution of the country. In Chapter 4, it is shown that Shariat courts were established by the martial law administrator and judges were appointed by him and, if any decision was not liked by the military regime, it had the power to reconstruct the court, appoint new judges and achieve the results it desired.

1.5.2 The Need for Ideology in a Post-Colonial State

Few writers have described the special role of ideology in Third World countries in comparison to capitalist countries. According to these writers, the role of ideology to justify the state system and to maintain the socio-economic system is a matter of priority in the developing countries because their national cohesion is weak and the socio-economic formations are not well defined. Ideology serves to hide the underlying realities of the state system (Ghai, 1976: 31).

John Saul has developed Hamza Alavi's arguments. He says that three points define the crucial significance of the state in post-colonial societies. Two of them can be drawn from Alavi and about the third feature Saul says:

> There is a third feature, about which Alavi says little. In advanced capitalist countries, the state is the 'dominant classes' political power centre' and, in this respect, comes to have an important ideological function. For in fact it symbolizes the unity of the social formation, seeming to transcend any narrow class or sectional interest and thus helping to legitimize the status quo. It is for this reason that Poulantzas has conceived the state as being 'not a class construct but rather the state of a society divided into classes', a fact which does not negate the further reality that such a capitalist state 'aims precisely at the political disorganization of the dominant classes'. But the state function of providing an ideological cement for the capitalist system is one

which has evolved slowly and surely in the imperial centres, in step with the latter's economic transformation. In post-colonial societies, on the other hand and particularly in Africa, this hegemonic position must be created, and created within territorial boundaries which often appear as quite artificial entities once the powerful force of direct colonial fiat has been removed (Saul, 1974: 351).

Saul's view has been criticized by Ziemann and Lanzendorfer on the grounds that the ideological apparatus tries to cover up peripheral capitalism's lack of legitimacy. But in fact the legitimacy difficulties do not lie primarily on the political level. The ideological function derives more from the fact that capitalist commodity relations have not been generalized. They explain this in the following terms:

> On the one hand there is the semblance of formal freedom and equality for all commodity owners which derives from the mystification inherent in the capitalist production, on the other, the social integration by means of commodity and financial ramification is incomplete (Ziemann & Lanzendorfer, 1977: 148).

Recently Halliday and Alavi have compared the need for ideology in advanced capitalist countries to the need for ideology in developing countries. They explain it this way:

> In advanced capitalist societies the importance of values as social bonds and political legitimisers and as constituents of any stable system of authority has long been recognised by thinkers as diverse as Weber and Gramsci. In developing societies, where the very name, language and identity of the community may be a recent creation, where no previously recognised territory or political system may have existed, ideologies have an enhanced role as the articulators of uncertainty and of contesting demands, both internally and internationally, as well as serving to instil acceptance of new and apparently arbitrary political entities (Halliday & Alavi, 1988: 5).

Ziaul Haque has mentioned another reason for the use of ideology in Pakistan.

> This distortion of reality and deliberate confusion of the social problem by the ruling elites through the political use of religion

is characteristic of those developing societies of Africa, Asia and Latin America which have been annexed by world capitalism as its periphery and its proper area of control. The loot of the natural and human resources of underdeveloped societies under ideological camouflage is made possible with the help of the indigenous upper classes. As custodians of ideology, these elites, as part of the international capitalist system, formulate and develop religio-political ideas, concepts and theories which conserve the existing neo-colonial economic structures of these societies (Haque, Ziaul, 1983: 369).

1.5.3 Ideological inconsistencies and conflicts in post-colonial Pakistan as reflected in the law

The need for ideology led the rulers of Pakistan to resort to Islam, as this was the best possibility. This was understandable because it is commonly known that Pakistan's *raison d'être* was and is to constitute a homeland for Muslims. Islam has become the foundation of state legitimacy.

Though Pakistan was created in the name of Islam, it was the result of various conflicts between different groups in society, which were resolved by making a separate state for the Muslims. Hamza Alavi outright denies that Pakistan was made to fulfill the millenarian religious aspirations of Indian Muslims, because the principal bearers of the Islamic religion were alienated from the Pakistan movement and the leaders of the movement were committed to secular politics (Alavi, 1986; 1988). The Muslim league stressed the existence of two nations within the subcontinent and insisted that there was no solution to the problems of the two nations other than the creation of a separate homeland for the Muslims (Ziring, 1984: 933).

But the person responsible for the creation of Pakistan, M.A. Jinnah,

discounted the notion of Pakistan as a theocratic state and by his actions promoted and encouraged the idea of secular nationalism. ... In effect, Jinnah, as a spokesman for the Muslim league, practised a strict separation between religious experience and political development (*ibid.,* 933-4).

Jinnah was interpreted differently by Fundamentalists and Modernists. In fact Muslim fundamentalist parties opposed the creation of Pakistan, their argument being that Islam knows no boundaries. It was only after the country was created that they moved to Pakistan.

Islam in itself does not provide a concept of an Islamic state; it defines the concept of a society (Engineer, 1980; 1984). With the development of national states it became important for Muslims to define 'Islam' as the ideology of the state (Zubaida, 1987).

The rulers of Pakistan have always wanted to have one dominant ideology to provide the justification for the creation of Pakistan. They were in fact in need of such ideology to hold together the various ethnic groups. This need of ideology became stronger when Islam as a common factor was shaken with the separation of Bangladesh. It increased still more with the added need to legitimize the military takeover in 1977. Such a need can be seen in actions like changing the educational syllabus during Islamization. School, college and university syllabuses were changed to make Islamic studies and Pakistani ideology compulsory. This was also made compulsory for medical students and students of engineering. The media were also used intensively to project the Islamic version of state ideology.

The question arises as to whether the dominant classes in Pakistan share a well-defined and coherent ideology. Though there is need for an ideology, there is still a lack of any that are consistent and coherent. There are continuing efforts to create a dominant ideology. James Scott has discussed the issue of hegemony and ideological dominance with reference to Gramsci. His main purpose is to see how complete this 'hegemony' is. He says 'what is certain however is that, while domination may be inevitable as a social fact, it is unlikely also to be hegemonic as an ideology within that small social sphere where the powerless may speak freely' (Scott, James C., 1985: 330). His main concern being to negate the total hegemonic situation, he further says 'properly understood, any hegemonic ideology provides, within itself, the raw material for contradictions and conflict' and he outrightly concludes that ideological coherence is quite rare.

The writers of the book *The Dominant Ideology Thesis* have also questioned whether dominant ideologies are clear, coherent and effective. They have tried to prove that on the contrary, they are incoherent and even contradictory in most historical periods - this is especially true about late capitalism (Abercrombie, Hill & Turner, 1980).

Although the post-colonial state in Pakistan made an effort to create one dominant unitary ideology, ideological coherence does not exist. It is a matter for further research to establish if the need for ideology on the one hand and its incoherence on the other is a specific feature of a peripheral capitalist state.

Ideologically Islam is capable of being interpreted in many ways and every interpretation regards the other as 'deviant' or not truly Muslim. To the people of Pakistan, Islam means justice, equality and universal brotherhood. Ziaul Haque argues that the Islamic ideology presented by the ruling class in Pakistan has remained vague (Haque, Ziaul, 1983).

'The rhetoric of an Islamic state has been widely used and debated in Pakistan since its inception in 1947... for as soon as one Islamic principle is proved worthless, back comes the justification that it is not true Islam' (Verinder, 1984: 113). From the very beginning, nobody was sure what type of state Pakistan would be. Apart from the major division between *Shiites* and *Sunnis*, there are various schools of thought among *Sunnis* themselves which differ widely in matters of legislation. After the creation of Pakistan, this controversy led to broadly speaking two tendencies, Modernism and Traditionalism or Fundamentalism (Abbott, 1966: 368-9; Rahman, Fazlur, 1971: 5; Verinder, 111).

The Traditionalist concept of the Islamic state is that *shariah* encompasses the whole sphere of life. Islam regulates not only general social relationships but the whole area of criminal and civil law. The purpose of the state is not to make laws but to enforce laws, since the law is already complete, enshrined in the sacred texts and in immemorial custom. Therefore there is nothing like a modern legislature. *Shariah*, being divine law, is immutable. It is the responsibility of the *ulema* (religious scholars) to decide how the Islamic state should function.

The modern concepts of democracy and secularism are out of the question. All non-Muslims are *dhimmis* and should pay *jizya* (Ahmed, Ishtiaq, 1987). Maulana Maududi is the pioneer of this concept in Pakistan (Ahmad, Sayed Riaz, 1976; Maududi, 1980). Moreover, according to Traditionalists, political parties are non- Islamic and only exaggerate political division, while the Modernist view is that elections are a democratic process and demonstrate the solidarity of Muslims not their differences. The Modernist concept of the state admits the existence of human will and is very similar to that of a modern democratic state (Rosenthal, 1964; 1965; 1970).

Ishtiaq Ahmed claims that, if the Traditionalist concept of state were implemented, it would result in an oppressive sectarian polity and not in an Islamic state for the entire Muslim community. The division between the Traditionalist and

Modernist is very wide although there are many different positions on both the Traditionalist and the Modernist sides. Traditionalism ranges from absolutist positions to comparatively reformist positions. Ishtiaq Ahmad has classified different ideological positions: a theocratic position seeking adjustment with Modernism (example Muhammad Asad), a theocratic position seeking severance with tradition (Ghulam Ahmed Perwez), a position of cohabitation between theocracy and secularism (Khalifa Abdul Hakim) a moderate version, a radical version (Javid Iqbal), a secular state admitting divine will (S.M. Zafar, with a socialist version supported by Professor Muhammad Usman), and a secular state excluding divine will (Muhammad Munir). Under the classification of 'the secular state admitting divine will' and 'the secular state excluding divine will', Ishtiaq Ahamed has given nine different positions predominating in Pakistan about the concept of an Islamic state in Pakistan. This shows the variety and diversity in viewpoints (Ahmed, Ishtiaq).

The controversy between the Traditionalists and the Modernists affected the framing of Pakistan's constitution (1947-1956). The framers of the Constitution had the difficult task of producing a document which would satisfy different groups with divergent views on the concept of an Islamic state.

Vagueness is obvious in the legislation. Because of conflicting ideas, vague compromises were made. An example of this is the ambiguity of the Objectives Resolution and the Islamic clauses of the constitutions of Pakistan. The first expression of the Islamic state was found in the Objectives Resolution of March 1949, where Pakistan is conceived of as a state with the purpose of enabling Muslims to order their lives in accordance with the teachings of Islam. Compromise clauses were made because it was difficult for Traditionalists and Modernists to agree on various Islamic clauses. It satisfied the Modernists, as it included a parliamentary form of government, and it satisfied the Traditionalists because of the presence of the Islamic provisions. This ended up in vague compromised provisions so an agreement could be reached without looking at the practical problems of implementing it. For example, the general and abstract notions of social justice, equality and freedom in the constitutions meant nothing as no corresponding institutions were created (see Chapter 2).

Fazrul Rahman says that such ambiguity in legislation is dangerous in its consequences 'because it affects the entire concept of "Islamic law" which is to govern the lives of all citizens' (Rahman, Fazlur, 1971: 7).

In the formal state legal system one can clearly see the conflict of ideologies. There is no unanimity of opinion about various aspects of Islam. Another example is when in 1953 the *Jamaat-i-Islami* (Traditionalist party) started a protest movement to establish that the *Ahmadis* be declared non-Muslims. (Muslim fundamentalists had long maintained that the *Ahmadis* recognized their founder, Ghulam Ahmad, as a prophet, this being against the cardinal teachings of Islam, according to which Muhammad was the last prophet of God). In Islam there is a fundamental distinction between the rights of Muslims and non-Muslims. If the *Ahmadis* were declared non-Muslims, they would not be able to occupy high offices in the state. On the refusal of the government to declare them non-Muslims, the Traditionalists took to killing *Ahmadis* in the streets and looting their property. An enquiry commission under the chairmanship of Muhammad Munir, Chief Justice of the Supreme Court of Pakistan, was appointed. The report of the commission showed that there was no agreement among the *ulema* even on the fundamental question of who is a Muslim.[3]

The complexities of both Modernism and Traditionalism were again visible in the activity of the commission appointed on 4 August 1955 to study family law. On issues like divorce and polygamy there was a large gap between the Modernists and Traditionalists (Abbott, 1968).

A long debate between the proponents of modernity and those of traditionalism ensued. Five years passed before the recommendations of the commission were acted upon. While the Muslim Family Laws Ordinance (MFLO) of 1961 incorporated many of the commission's recommendations for reform, the strength of the traditionalist opposition is reflected in certain omissions and also in relatively mild punishments for offenders (Esposito, 1980a: 224-5). One of the reasons for the ineffectiveness of the MFLO is that the sections were formed as a compromise (Rahman, Fazlur, 1971).

The Modernist stand on family law reforms is clearly reflected in the Family Law Commission Report, and the Traditionalist stand is reflected in the answer to that report.

Under the Modernists, Pakistan made a great many reforms in the formal state law of the country especially in family law. These reforms are discussed in Chapter 4.

Furthermore there are so many disagreements among the ruling ideologies that they pose a threat to each other, resulting in the instability of the MFLO because it is under constant threat from the opposing faction (see Chapter 4).

Traditionalists had always insisted that *shariah* should be the law of the land. Modernists tended to accept the idea that the legal system, which was already patterned after the British one, should be continued and other reforms in the same direction should be introduced.

President Ayub Khan was a Modernist who went as far as to speak of the separation of religion and politics. But at one stage he had to compromise with the Traditionalists because of growing pressure. With the coming of General Zia, a Traditionalist period began in the history of Pakistan, when most of the Islamization took place.

The ideology of the state was reflected in the attitudes of the courts. In Ayub's time, liberal legislation was passed and the attitude of the courts was more liberal in interpreting the laws. Judicial khula (women's right to divorce) was in fact developed by the judiciary in that period. In General Zia's period, orthodox legislation was made and courts became very conservative in interpreting family law. Every time the government changes, the dominant ideology is changed and this results in a different attitude of the courts (Hoebel, 1965).

Ideological conflict is also reflected in criminal law. Islamic criminal law has been interpreted in various ways in the courts. There is much disagreement as to whether severe punishments are Islamic or un-Islamic. There has been controversy among the Modernists about the implementation of punishments like the loss of life or limb for sexual crimes or theft (Engineer, 1980). Muslim conservatives have demanded the traditional *Quranic* criminal penalities as the law of the land. Their argument is that the threat of punishments such as amputation and flogging can prevent crimes (Mayer, 1984). The Modernist viewpoint is that the amputation of limbs could be justified only in a society where everybody had the basic necessities of life. The same is true of other punishments. Asma Jahangir and Hina Jilani have argued that since *hadd* punishments have never been executed, these punishments are kept on the statute book merely in order to appease the Traditionalist lobby (Jahangir & Hina, 1990) (see Chapter 3). Weiss argues that there is no consensus among the many Muslim states as to how Islamic laws should fit into a contemporary institutional framework (Weiss, Anita M., 1986a).

The rulers of Pakistan who needed an ideology looked to Islam but could not present a consistent ideology. What was the reason for that? As mentioned before, Islam is capable of being interpreted in different ways, so that the government's failure to recognize this diversity by coming up with 'one ideology' also created problems with different Muslim sects in Pakistan. One of the main problems of Islamization faced by Zia's regime was that Islamization could not handle controversies between Muslim sects (Weiss, Anita M., 1985: 6). *Shiites* and *Sunnis* differ on the question whether *zakat* and *ushr* (charity tax which Muslims are obliged to pay) should be voluntary or be enforced by the state (Lodhi, 1988; Keddie, 1988: 27). The government ordinance provided for compulsary *zakat*. Due to protest from *Shiites*, the government had to amend it (Ordinance 52 of 1980). The *Ahmadi* controversy is another example.

Concerning the lack of a consistent ideology, John Esposito argues that the reason for Pakistan's ideological difficulties is the failure to move beyond the use of Islam in an *ad hoc* piecemeal fashion.

> While an ad hoc approach may seem the most expedient and least troublesome path in the short run, long term it does not provide a clear substantive ideology upon which to base a sense of national identity and some sense of unity amidst Pakistan's significant linguistic and regional differences. Failure to face head on and to resolve fundamental differences of interpretation has perpetuated the still present problem that beneath Pakistan's Islamic and nationalist rhetoric and terminology is a vacuum, an unresolved identity crisis which promises to be a source of continued unrest (Esposito, 1980b: 160).

The competing ideologies were the result of competition between the *ulema* and the state bureaucrats on the one hand and between the feudalists and capitalists on the other. It is however a matter of investigation which version of Islam suited which class interests in different periods of history in Pakistan.

1.6 ISLAMIC REVIVALISM IN PAKISTAN

In this Part an account will be given of the movements to amend Anglo-Muhammadan law for the purpose of making it more Islamic.

Because of Pakistan's commitment to Islam, the authorities in Pakistan promised that the law of the land would be in accordance with the tenets of Islam. Each of the constitutions of Pakistan contained provisions for Islamizing laws but only a few attempts were made in this direction. In 1961 Pakistan enacted a new family law, the MFLO, somewhat influenced by Traditionalist ideas. But it was only in 1977 after a military takeover, that Pakistan faced a wave of Islamic revivalism and a great many changes were made in the criminal law.

The laws made by the British before the creation of Pakistan continued to be the laws of Pakistan. From the very beginning it was the plan of *ulema* that Islamic law would be the law of Pakistan. This was the reason why all three constitutions of Pakistan have contained clauses to the effect that the laws of Pakistan would be in accordance with the *Quran* and *Sunna*. But no concrete steps were taken in this direction in the first thirty years of Pakistan's history. The first constitution of 1956 did not last long. The second constitution of 1962, which was created by a Modernist, created two institutions appearing to promote Islamization, i.e., the Council of Islamic Ideology and the Islamic Research Institute, but both bodies only had an advisory function.

After Ayub's period, Bhutto, himself a modern secular politician, never encouraged any attempt to include specific Islamic laws in the legal system. But at the end of his period, it became 'politically expedient' for him to do so. (Sayeed, 1980; Burki, 1980, Weiss, Anita M., 1986a). David Taylor calls it 'Islamic symbolism' (Taylor, 1983: 181), while William L. Richter calls this 'defensive Islamization' (Richter, 1986: 131). In 1974, during Bhutto's era, *Ahmadis* were declared non-Muslims. The Constitution of 1973 required that both the president and prime minister be Muslims and take an oath affirming the finality of the prophet Muhammed. In 1977 Bhutto outlawed drinking, gambling (betting on horse races was banned) and night clubs, and declared that within six months *shariah* law would be established and enforced.[4] Moreover, Friday, the traditional Islamic holiday, replaced Sunday. Despite all the Islamic steps he took, he was accused by the PNA (Pakistan National Alliance) of un-Islamic behaviour.

The period of Islamic revivalism, popularly known as Islamization, started in 1977. Most of it was carried out by one man, General Zia-ul-Haque, who took over in 1977 and promised elections within three months. In 1984 he held controlled elections and became President.

Islamization included steps like compulsory prayers in Government offices during working hours; the review of text books to conform to Islamic teachings; emphasizing Pakistan's national Islamic ideology; making Urdu the official language and medium of instruction; and the compulsory wearing of national dress at Government functions, feasts and banquets and even - in theory - by judges in court. Under a Presidential order the month of fasting was legally enforced by prescribing punishment, if violated publicly; radio and television were made to change their programmes to conform with Islamic teachings; in order to encourage the observance of Islamic ethical standards, measures were taken to eliminate obscenity and vulgarity from audio-visual media, art galleries, newspapers, journals, magazines and films.

Islamic penal laws were introduced. *Shariat* courts were given the authority to determine whether or not the laws of the country were in accordance with Islam (Khan, Gul Muhammad, 1986a; Ahmed, Ali Khan, 1985).

To solve the country's economic problems Zia promised to implement a true 'Islamic Economy', and consequently the Zakat and Ushr Ordinance, 1980, was promulgated.

> The philosophy behind *zakat* is that whatever remains surplus with a Muslim after a year, a portion of the same must be contributed towards the betterment of the community. Thus, those who possess more that the prescribed minimum, the surplus of the liquid assets, to the extent of 2.5 per cent of the same, shall pay as *zakat* i.e., contribution towards looking after the needy, orphans, widows, wayfarer and other public welfare purposes sanctioned by Islam. On the other hand, *ushr* is to be used for the betterment of the rural community" (Iqbal, Javid, 1984: 72).

But it seems that to achieve economic justice from the above mentioned Ordinance was not the purpose. There have been a lot of complaints of corruption in handling *zakat*.

In 1981 General Zia inaugurated the *Majlis-i-Shura*, an appointed advisory body to replace the dissolved elected National Assembly. On 19 December 1984, he held a national referendum to determine whether the electorate supported his program of Islamization. General Zia claimed the vote was a 'mandate' for the continuation of his Islamization programe and assumed the presidency for a five-year term. On 12 January 1985 General Zia announced elections to the National and Provincial Assemblies. It was also announced that the elections would be held on a non-party, adult franchise basis, with separate electoral arrangements for Muslims and non-Muslims. The media were barred from making any reference to the political parties. Meanwhile the arrests of the political parties' leaders continued.

1.6.1 Women and Islamization

Islamic revivalism specially affected the legal status of women, which I will deal with in Chapters 3 and 4. Women are specially affected by the Islamization of the law in Pakistan. Besides the Islamization of laws which directly affect women, other rules and regulations have also been made for women; for example, women in jobs and in the educational institutions are supposed to wear the chader. Women newsreaders on television were supposed to cover their heads and were not to wear make-up. Government directives curtailed unmarried women's opportunities in the foreign service. Women were banned from appearing in public sports. Approval was given for the establishment of a separate university for women. This was deplored because it would lower the standards of women's education in Pakistan due to limited financial resources (Carroll, 1982: 75).

Women were no longer allowed to appear as witnesses in *hadd* cases and the law of evidence made their testimony worth half a man's. The Council of Islamic ideology recommended that in the case of *diyat*, if the murdered person was a woman (or a non-Muslim) the compensation paid to the victim's family was to be one-half that paid to the family of a male Muslim victim.

It has been noticed that there was inconsistency in government policy concerning women. Carroll maintains that Zia also stood for the equality of women. She counts the positive steps taken in this direction, for example the appointment of the first woman Cabinet Secretary and the creation of the Women's Division in the Zia government in 1979 (*ibid.*, 1982: 75).

> There is an apparent contradiction in policy as well as in thought regarding women's ideal and objective position and role since their status has been simultaneously uplifted by the establishment of the women's division, and diminished by the incorporation of some Islamic laws (Weiss, Anita M., 1985: 5).

> The conflict that has emerged throughout the Muslim world has developed in Pakistan: the push of modernity (i.e., industrialization and emphasis on the realization of human potential) versus the pull of redefined tradition (i.e., Islamization) (*ibid*, 1985: 5).

Weiss argues further that the government has been inconsistent regarding when to appeal to *ijtihad* and when to apply a strict traditional Hanafi interpretation of the law.

Nikki R. Keddie, on the other hand believes that militant and effective opposition to Islamization by women and their continued activism was largely responsible for making Zia set up an activist 'Women's Division' in his government and creating a commission on women (Keddie, 1988: 27).

1.6.3 Why specially against women?

Islamization especially affected urban educated women. Rural women were not affected by the Islamic laws in the same way. For example, the banning of women from public sports affected the urban women who participated in them. The same is true of suggestions for a separate women's university (Mazari, 1983: 79).

> Educated Muslim women are primarily the ones who have enjoyed the individual civil rights that are being curtailed or at least threatened by Islamization. They have generally been aware of the legal protections for women built into the Muslim Family laws of the 1960s (Korson & Maskiell, 1985: 603).

Korson and Maskiell's analysis is as follows. In 1968 the percentage of women in Pakistan's labour force was one of the smallest in the world, and the same was also true in 1985. Rural women still comprise the majority of working women in Pakistan. The majority of women professionals continue to work in gender-segregated environments. He says that Zia's Islamization policies toward educated working women dealt with fairly superficial issues, for example covering the heads of TV newsreaders and changing the dress of women employees in Pakistan International Airlines. In a society such as Pakistan, where strong traditions of gender segregation are coupled with limited respectably paid employment opportunities for women, informal processes would keep women out of the majority of public jobs without directives from the government.

> The Zia government has not yet developed a consistent policy on enforcement of proper public behaviour for Muslim women, nor has it developed a wide-ranging policy on gender-segregated employment. This is at least partially due to disagreements within the government itself as to how women should be treated. The government has moved toward institutionalizing gender discrimination in civil law as well as in a few directives

concerning professional working women. It has committed itself to gender segregation in education - the separate women's university issue and the virtual cancellation of women's sports outside of women's colleges only affect a small minority of Pakistani women. However, government policies have indirectly affected all women through the paucity of government resources committed to women's economic development (Korson & Maskiell, 1985: 610-611).

Weiss holds the view that Islamic law as applied in South Asia has favored the maintenance of extended patrilineal kinship networks and the control of women by male members of these networks. She says that one of the reasons behind government proposals on women is that a certain type of economy is sustained by enforcing traditional law. This argument relies on the supposition that the secularization of society is an indicator of the transformation from feudal conditions to capitalist ones. She finds Pakistan in incomplete transition to a capitalist economy and links this to the fact that Pakistan does not favour secular laws for women (Weiss, Anita M., 1986: 108-9). Another reason Weiss has given for the laws against women is that the government is trying to appease the Traditionalists (ibid: 108).

> By proposing laws based on religion yet not enforcing them, the Fundamentalists are appeased but other powerful groups (consisting of men) in the society are not challenged. The government could have focused on so many other areas (e.g., redistribution of wealth, especially of rural land-holdings; establishment of an Islamic-based political decision-making process; social programs stressing man's obligations to God's creation), that the fact that women have been singled out is significant (Weiss, Anita M., 1985: 14).

The transformation of economic conditions (i.e., the capitalization of the economy) would recognize the economic importance of women, but

> ... this is not been done in Pakistan, perhaps because of the as yet incomplete transition to a capitalist economy which has meant that Pakistan's greatest export and source of foreign exchange is migrant laborers to the Gulf States. Therefore, favoring secular laws that promote capitalist relations would be difficult in an envirnoment where few are benefitting from them (Weiss, Anita M., 1985: 15).

On the other hand women's participation in the economic field in Pakistan should not be underestimated, as Korson has done. Farida Shaheed and Khawar Mumtaz have observed that 'national statistics indicate negligible participation of women in the organized sector of the labour force. Many more women however are found working on piece rate in the unorganized sector. These are invisible workers'. Moreover, national statistics themselves differ vastly (Mumtaz and Shaheed, 1987). Two other writers have analysed the same type of situation with reference to the Third World. Elson and Pearson:

> ... suggest that this process of subordination of women as a gender can be understood in terms of the exclusion of women as a gender from certain activities, and their confinement to others; where the activities from which women as a gender are excluded are some of those which are constituted as public, overtly social activities to which women as a gender are confined are some of those which are constituted as private, seemingly purely individual activities (Elson and Pearson, 1981: 94).

In the late 1980s women have produced a few works in Pakistan to expose the Census Reports and Labour Force surveys which 'depict an extremely low profile of women as workers with small percentage of women in the labour force'. Of course this is because of male domination and the desire to exploit female labour (Patel, 1991; Khan, Nighat Said, 1989; Mitha, Y., Anwar, M., Khan, N.S., & Asmaa, J. Pal., 1989; Jahan, 1990; Zareen, Humaira, 1989).

1.6.3 The women's movement

It is interesting to note that most resistance to the Islamization of the law has been shown by women. The response to Islamization is that a group of Muslim women have come forward to make new interpretations of Islam. Most of the books produced on this subject have been written by women.

For the first time in the history of Pakistan there has been a nationwide feminist movement (Mumtaz and Shaheed, 1987). Hamza Alavi explains that Islamic Traditionalism does not suit women of the urban white-collar middle classes.

> To be able to carry on with their new found professional careers women also need to be able to move about freely. All this calls

for a much more liberal ideology and definition of values than is allowed in the fundamentalist interpretations of Islam. The situation has, therefore, favored the growth of secular or Islamic modernist attitudes. The heavy pressure of state orchestrated propaganda for obscurantist mullah ideology or Islamic fundamentalism can all too easily obscure the actual extent of secular thinking in Pakistan. The changing role of women in our society is a major force behind the survival and growth of secularist and rational ideas (Alavi, 1985: 5).

The lower middle class, on the other hand, where men control and isolate their women folk, 'find Islamic fundamentalism very congenial, for thereby they glorify, with a sense of self-righteousness their otherwise humiliating and inferior place in society' (Alavi, 1985: 5).

1.6.5 *Islamic Revivalism and the Reasons behind Islamization*

The role of Islam as the ideology of the state of Pakistan has been discussed in detail. Here it would be relevant to discuss the reasons for the wave of Islamization, which started in the late seventies under General Zia-ul-Haque.

Different writers have provided different reasons for the wave of Islamization in Pakistan. A brief review of the opinions would help to appreciate the situation. Richter does not think that Islamization was the simple planning of a military government to appease a hostile populace. He draws attention to a variety of factors. The post-Bangladesh search for national identity was one reason. Other reasons were people's frustration and disappointment with foreign ideologies, first capitalism under Ayub and later socialism as used by Bhutto and, lastly, the increased prominence and power of the Islamic countries of the Middle East during the 1970s. Therefore there was an appeal in the revival of Islam.

> Pakistan has not only moved closer to its Middle Eastern neighbors through its loss of Bangladesh and consequent westward shift of attention, but the Islamic countries of that region also enjoyed during the same period a dramatic increase in power and prestige. The consciousness and use of their bargining power over their oil resources brought vast new wealth to the region. Pakistan has participated in this boom in a number of ways, most notably by exporting large numbers of

skilled and unskilled laborers to Saudi Arabia and the Persian Gulf States. This 'brawn drain' has become in a very short time Pakistan's top foreign exchange earner (Richter, 1979: 556).

Pakistan was also influenced by neighboring Iran and Afghanistan. Another reason Richter mentions is that Islam is a useful slogan, sufficently potent to elicit public support, as Bhutto attempted to do, recognising the public appeal of Islamic issues. Richter sees Islamization as one function of a political dynamic, with military exploitation of the Islamic issue as only one aspect (Richter, 1986).

Another reason stated by many writers is the legitimization of the illegal takeover by the martial law regime (Gardezi, 1982; Weinbaum & Cohen, 1983; Kennedy, 1990). 'Zia ul Haq from the inception of his regime has legitimated his coup and subsequent rule through demands for *Nizam-i-Mustapha* or, as it is more commonly called, *Nizam-i-Islam*' (Esposito, 1982: 201). Another writer says:

> Initially, General Zia obviously saw Islam, Islamisation, and an emphasis on the Islamic ideology of Pakistan as the basis for unification and integration of a state wracked by political and regional conflicts, and as a vehicle for securing popular support for his illegal regime. Instead, Islamisation, when taken beyond the level of mere sloganising, has brought into prominence new areas of conflict that will not be easily resolved - that are perhaps incapable of resolution because they involve fundamental questions beyond the scope of political compromise (Carroll, 1982b: 86).

Weiss says that a major challenge facing the Zia government was one of legitimacy. After having held control of the state, the Army was hesitant to relinquish it. General Zia had neither religious nor legal grounds for usurping power. The reason he used was the establishment of an Islamic state (Weiss, Anita M., 1986b). Alavi contends that the purpose of Islamization was to legitimize power.

> With the assumption of power by the Zia regime another factor has come into play, namely the legitimacy of power. Afraid to face a free electorate and having no mandate to govern, Zia has turned to Allah. He has been forced to go far beyond the worn out old rhetoric and show to a cynical public that he actually means business. There is not much that he can do in practice, at

least with regard to the economy; he must run a peripheral capitalist economy which has its own rules, logic, and imperatives that he can not afford to disregard or interfere with. So he has drawn the line clearly. He will make symbolic changes instead (Alavi, 1986: 45).

Recently Ayesha Jalal in her analysis of Zia's period also states that Zia's state-sponsored 'Islamization' was no more than a token effort to establish his own legitimacy (Jalal, 1990: 324).

The reasons provided by different writers give us an insight into the wave of Islamization not inspired by sheer Islamic spirit but related to other powerful interests.

1.7 THE ISLAMIZATION OF THE LAW IN PAKISTAN: *Instability and Inconsistency and Other General Features*

Throughout this book it will be shown that Islamization was an attempt to infuse more *shariah* into the Anglo-Muhammadan laws created in the colonial era. There was inconsistency and instability in the formal state law called Islamic law. An attempt will be made to bring examples of these. However, Islamization has not made any qualitative change; all the features of Anglo-Muhammadan law are still there.

Before I proceed to explain the concept of inconsistency and instability, it would be interesting to refer to the models of litigation provided by Richard L. Abel. He provides four models of institutional forms with reference to litigation, i.e., disputes in tribal society, in colonial and neo-colonial society, in reformist, utopian and revolutionary society, and in modern society. The litigation pattern Abel has described for modern society and the imposition of that on colonies is interesting because colonial societies do not borrow the total pattern of imposed law. My contention is that it gives a morbidity to colonial state law which post-colonial states carry with them and I look at it in terms of inconsistency and instability (Abel, 1979). Inconsistency implies instances of contradictions. There are different types of contradiction:

(a) between formal legal norms and socially observed norms e.g., the prohibition of prostitution and homosexual practices in both the PPC (Pakistan Penal Code) and the 1979 statutes but their existence in society; and the prohibition of child marriage and restriction on polygamy but their uncontrolled presence in society. People practice law according to their traditions and customs widely disregarding the formal state legal system.

(b) between statutory legal norms and the norms applied in practice in the courts, e.g., the existence of *hadd* punishments in the 1979 statute but their complete absence in practical application. Though *hadd* punishments are sometimes prescribed by the courts they have always been turned down on appeal. In family law, non-compliance with the MFLO, which is overlooked in family cases by the courts, is punished under the *zina* Ordinance. Examples of this are given in Chapters 3 and 4.

(c) between different formal legal norms, e.g., where the law of evidence prevents the substantive law from being carried out, as where the requirements for proof of an offence subject to *hadd* punishment are virtually impossible to satisfy in practice. According to one Muslim criminologist, the last contradiction is desired and the aim of Islamic criminal law:

> The tendency of the Muslim law is not to inflict the punishment of *hadd* as far as possible, with a view to attain this object they have made the laws of evidence strict to be complied with for instance evidence of four male eye-witnesses is required to prove an instance of whoredom, and as such an act is committed in secret, it is usually impossible to prove even an actual instance. At the same time the witnesses deter in giving evidence, because of the law of slander, which makes them liable to receive 80 stripes for falsely accusing the persons (Muhammed, 1986: 83).

In the interviews with lawyers a great number of lawyers agreed that *hadd* punishments were symbolic and not intended to be carried out. In other words, punishments are impossible to implement because of the high standard of proof required, their only purpose being to affirm the principles of traditional Islam. Some of the lawyers took the stand that Islamization is real in its effects.

This type of inconsistency has given rise to other problems. Thus the *zina* Ordinance requires a rapist to be punished, but the requirement upon witnesses cause the offender to be released and the victim to be convicted. Her pregnancy and coming to the court was considered tantamount to a confession, confession being another form of evidence required for the implementation of *hadd* in *zina* cases. This problem will be dealt with in detail in Chapter 3.

In constitutional law, commitment is shown to implement Islamic law but, on the other hand, such institutions as are established to implement Islamic law are given no powers.

Another example is provided by the fact that the institutions on which the MFLO is dependent do not exist. After the repeal of the Basic Democracies Order, 1959, powers were not delegated to any other authority and neither the Ordinance nor the Rules are being enforced.

The reasons for inconsistency have been dealt with elsewhere. Briefly, inconsistency type (a) exists because of the presence of a plurality of legal practices. People have over many years evolved a network for mediating their conflicts and thus there is a large gap between formal state law and popular practice. This I will discuss in the Part on legal pluralism. Another aspect of this inconsistency will be dealt with in Part 1.10. Inconsistency type (b) exists because courts are influenced by the ruling factions and fluctuate in their interpretations. Courts in Pakistan have played an important role in interpreting the Islamic principles of the legislature. The first contradiction regarding inconsistency type (c) means, in other words the ineffectiveness of state law. This exists - as will be demonstrated in Chapters 2 and 4 - because most of the provisions were a compromise between Modernists and Traditionalists, which made the laws ineffective. In Chapter 4, I mention several instances where legislation against abuses is weakened by the fact that although it makes certain acts illegal, they are not rendered invalid. However I would not assume that legislation to invalidate such acts, while perhaps desirable, would necessarily have a decisive effect in deterring people from committing them. Furthermore, in the case of polygamous marriages (although not necessarily in any other of these cases), it might possibly do more harm than good to the interests of women to invalidate them. Some women might find that their marriages, which they had believed to be valid, were legally void. This raises an important question as to whether it is possible to make the existing provisions more effective by adjusting the law to remove the specific weaknesses and lacunae which I have identified. Can we attribute inconsistency to the lack of unanimity among policy makers which results in the law being only a series of formulas for compromise?

The interviews with the lawyers show that more then half of them agreed that the state laws show inconsistency. Only a few maintained that the legal system had a consistent pattern.

By instability in the Islamic law in Pakistan is meant frequent change or threatened change, not following a consistent pattern. Of course, stability is not to be advocated at the cost of change. But changes in legislation can occur in a more harmonious way and less frequently. There is instability even in the constitution which is changed at the whim of army generals. In one case, General Zia even inserted in the constitution a provision that he would be the President of Pakistan for the next five years (Revival of the Constitution of 1973 Order, 1985).

The reasons for instability are, first the special nature of the post-colonial structure of Pakistan which has been discussed in Part 1.3. The state is in a position to manipulate the legal system directly, e.g., all Islamization is one man Islamization and statutes and courts can be manipulated by the will of one man. Another source of this instability is again the conflict of ideology discussed in Part 1.4. One example of this is the constant challenge to the MFLO of 1961. Threats of change have been so severe that, time and time again, women demonstrating against amendments to the MFLO have been tear-gassed and beaten up by the police.

It would be relevant here to look at the opinions of lawyers on Islamization and instability. When asked about the stability or instability of the legal system, little more than half said it was unstable, while others held that it was stable.

In answer to the question whether Islamization would last long, twelve said that it would, while fourteen thought it would not.

There are other features of the legal system in Pakistan which are relevant to the concept of inconsistency and instability. These are discussed below.

1.7.1 Discrimination

Anglo-Muhammadan law was not the same thing for poor people as for rich, because it was expensive, dilatory and couched in an incomprehensible language. Similarly Islamic state law has also not abolished a major class distinction. In the *hadd* cases of *zina*, some women were found to have been in prison for up to five years awaiting trial. It was specially marked that all the women in prison for *zina* were from a low income social background. It has been said:

> ... although many in the government do realize that the majority

of the female defendents in adultery/rape cases brought to the court have been poor, rural women or members of destitute families unable to hire lawyers and without political influence, no one in power appears to recognise which segments of the female population are most affected by the new laws; in fact, they are upholding class distinction as well as gender distinction (Weiss, Anita M., 1986: 108).

Asma Jahangir found a tremendous increase in the number of female convicts. She found that, in 1978, the number of female convicts in the Punjab was twenty-nine and that of prisoners under trial was 267. In 1988, the figure of those under trial rose to 501 of which 76 were convicted. Seventy percent of women on trial were accused of *zina*, which also accounted for forty percent of all convictions. Many of these were mere girls - eighteen percent were between the ages of fifteen and twenty-one years. Eighty percent of them were married. They belonged to low-income families (out of thirty-seven women interviewed in Multan prison, sixteen had a family income of only Rs 500 and no one had a family income of over Rs 3000 (Jahangir, 1988: 30).

In answer to the question as to whether laws are different for the rich and the poor almost all the lawyers interviewed agreed that they were. Only a small number said that the laws are the same for rich and poor (see Appendix I).

In answer to the question as to whether the law is effective in achieving social reforms in Pakistan, of the lawyers interviewed, a few said that it has some effect. But the great majority said the law is not effective. They described different reasons for this. One said that because people with resources can purchase the law or even the law makers, these are not effective. Another said the same thing and used the expression 'money makes the mare go' and 'might is right'. One lawyer blamed the men in power. One said that the reason for the ineffectuality of Islamic laws was that the laws - such as family law and the *hudood* ordinance - are defective. One said that poor people could not claim their rights easily because of procedure and corruption. One said that laws in general were effective but not for law enforcing agencies. One said that they were ineffective because most of the laws were made 100 years ago.

1.7.2 Manipulation by Individuals

People use the Islamic laws in Pakistan, just as Anglo-

Muhammadan law was used, not for solving their problems but for taking revenge or creating trouble for the opposing party (Cohn, 1959: 90). Hundreds of women are arrested in Pakistan under the *zina* ordinance on complaints filed by husbands (Patel, 1991: 27).

Asma Jahangir, a practising lawyer in Pakistan, describes how, if a women files for divorce against her husband and leaves her home (as required in law), her husband may prefer an allegation of *zina* against his wife, on the ground that she has moved into a household which has a man other than her blood relative. At times a husband applies for bail and the woman has no choice but to return to her marital home, otherwise he could cancel the bail (Jahangir, 1988: 29). Jahangir also tells of cases where married couples have been arrested owing to enmity or because they have been married by their own free will. She has further pinpointed that one of the frequent circumstances under which *zina* is alleged to have occurred is in cases of elopement. Of the forty-four women in Karachi prison charged with *zina*, over half are accused of having committed *zina* due to abduction. It is assumed that any couple who elopes must have engaged in extra marital sex and is therefore liable to prosecution for *zina* (Jahangir, 1988: 29).

Moreover, the MFLO requires the registration of marriages and divorces, the responsibility for which rests with the husband. Quite frequently divorce is pronounced on the wife and the husband deliberately does not get the divorce deed registered. If a divorced wife marries again her first husband can charge her for *zina*. Sahida Parveen's famous case is an example of this (Kumar & Nadvi, 1987: 4; Jahangir & Jilani, 1990).

Bushra Ahsan says quite clearly:

> A husband wants to marry again and would like his first wife out of the way; or relatives wish to deprive a women of her property. Charged with *zina* under the *Haddood* Ordinance she can be locked up for up to three years before her case comes up for hearing (Ahsan, 1987).

The misuse of the *zina* ordinance has become so notorious that it became the subject of plays and stories. This issue will be dealt with in detail in the Chapter 3.

Family law is also such that it is manipulated by men to create problems for women who dare to bring their grivences to the courts. In a recent conference in Lahore a female lawyer mentioned the problem arising from what she called 'nasty tactics'. When a wife filed a case for dissolution of marriage in one city her husband would file a case in another province in Pakistan for the restitution of conjugal rights to harass her.[5]

1.7.3 Excessive litigation

This is a vast topic in itself. Again this needs detailed research. Excessive litigation was a well-known feature of the British influence on India and Pakistan. Here my purpose is only to pinpoint that it has fully continued even after Islamization. Too many lawyers are preoccupied with litigation (Qureshi, 1988). There has been a lot of long discussion on the petitions brought in the FSC (Federal *Shariat* Court).[6]

Not everyone is happy with this situation. In a letter to a newspaper editor, the writer suggests first that the standard of legal education must be improved. Second, he contends that lawyers should try their utmost to resolve disputes outside court. He refers to a hadith which says 'May I tell you what is even better than prayers, fasting and charity; it is reconciling the differences and disputes among men. Sowing discord wipes off all virtues'.[7]

The Chief Justice of the Supreme Court of Pakistan, Justice Mohammad Haleem, was reported to have said in 1987 that Pakistan's system of justice is time consuming, expensive and complicated. He suggested the need for the introduction of a conciliation system to settle cases regarding mutual quarrels disputes and differences. He said that this would help to curb the tendency towards litigation and lessen the case-load on the courts. He added:

> For the success of the conciliation system, it is necessary to set up whole time *'punchayats'* on *mohallah* basis comprising of honest and god-fearing persons and the members of the *punchayat* should be empowered to enforce their decision.

Explaining the problem of litigation, he says:

> No specific time limit is pescribed to dispose of judicial and official work, but hundreds of technical matters have been included in the legal procedure, to delay the final disposal of cases. As such, litigation continues for many years - even for generations - and work in offices remains pending indefinitely.[8]

1.7.4 Dualism and a tendency towards anarchy

With the introduction of Islamization, a duality has appeared in state formal law. Lawyers who were trained in the western way to practice Anglo-Muhammedan law have lost some power or have had to share power with *ulemas*. They have had to be re-trained in the Islamic way. Lawyers did not support Islamization of the law wholeheartedly, their stand being that the Anglo-Muhammadan system was Islamic enough.

At the time when martial law was imposed, there were three sets of legal systems operating simultaneously: military courts, shariat courts and civil courts. General Zia ruled through martial law regulations, orders and ordinances. In spite of all his claim of devotion to Islam, he did not allow the decisions of military courts to be challenged in shariat courts or civil courts.

In the military courts, military personel were not trained as lawyers. There was a case where certain boys were tried by a summary military court, and a petition was moved in the High Court requesting that the sentence awarded by the court be set aside and the boys saved from whipping as they were below eighteen years of age. However, while the petition was being heard, it was learnt that the boys had already been flogged a few hours after the sentence had been announced. Later Justice Dilawar Mahmood held that the prosecution has failed to prove any of the four charges against the convicts. There was nothing on the record to suggest that they took part in a procession of a political nature, damaged property, or attacked or injured any member of the police force.[9]

There were also examples in which the wrong men were arrested and convicted under the military court.

1.7.5 Corruption

There is corruption in the legal system in Pakistan. One example will be provided in Chapter 5, where one court decided that stoning to death was not Islamic. The government did not like the decision and changed the judges. The new judges decided that stoning to death is in accordance with Islam. This is one form of corruption.

Other examples of corruption such as bribery and contact with influential people are widely used in the Pakistani legal system. A famous writer describes corruption in the profession, he quotes a Pakistani lawyer:

Below the level of the High Court all is corruption. Neither the fact nor the law on the case have any real bearing on the outcome. It all depends on who you know who has influence and where you put your money (anonymous oral communication, Lahore, March 1961) (Hoebel, 1965: 45).

Hoebel further describes from the National Law Reform Commission, which states:

> There are complaints that subordinate Court officials who have to deal with the public, extort illegal gratification from the litigants before condescending... to take any steps which are necessary in the progress of a case in Court and "It is said that papers move only on golden or silver wheels..." the problem is so great that this kind of action (prosecution for corruption) hardly touches its fringe (1959: 101). (Hoebel, 1965: 45-46).

However, Braibanti holds the view that the High Court and Supreme Court are highly respected and revered as staunch and objective protectors of fundamental rights and liberties (Braibanti, 1966).

When asked about corruption, all the lawyers interviewed, with minor exceptions, agreed straightforwardly that corruption prevailed, totally or partially. Different examples of corruption were given. For example, bribes taken by state attorneys in the lower courts is a daily practice. Filing of cases, getting cases fixed for hearing, obtaining copies of court orders or inspecting the files are matters which never proceed without bribes. Readers of the courts always take money for giving suitable dates for cases and Bail Bonds. The daily work cannot be accelerated without paying to the staff. They thought that bribes were taken as of right and bribes are not not even considered by many to be corruption. In answer to the question if corruption is increasing or decreasing, all agreed that that corruption is increasing (see Appendix I).

Hoebel Adamson however thinks that the behaviour of the petty courts officer is 'corrupt' only in terms of an abstract ideal of justice embodied in the Islamic and English legal system. He quotes from the *Quran* a warning against corruption. But in reality he says:

> Structurally and functionally viewed in terms of the folk law, the courts and the police do not exist for the purpose of justice, but are to be used to equalize a relationship of opposition that

has become uncontrollably out of balance in the folk system. The officials are outside the normal system of reciprocal relations. Since a personal relationship other than a kinship or clientship is almost inconceivable, a tangible equivalent of reciprocal compensation for personal services rendered is taken for granted (Hoebel, 1965: 46).

More detailed investigation is required to understand the frequent existence of corruption in the legal system of Pakistan.

1.8 ISLAMIZATION OF THE LAW & ANGLO-MUHAMMADAN LAW

Another important aspect to which attention must be drawn, is that Islamization has not destroyed Anglo-Muhammadan law in Pakistan. The Anglo-Muhammadan framework is still there.

In the post-colonial peripheral state of Pakistan, Islamic law is the further development of the Anglo-Muhammadan colonial law. In Part 1.2, the result of the interaction of Anglo-Muhammadan law with local law was discussed, along with the reactions people developed towards it. Here I want to show that Islamic law has not made any difference to the legal system of Pakistan. While there has been a great deal of legislative activity since 1947 to repeal or modify the colonial law, much of the latter is still intact, e.g., the penal code, commercial law and the law of torts. Whenever any change is made, however Islamic, it is often a reproduction of English law. The rules and assumptions of interpretation that the Pakistani courts follow are those of Common Law and its ethos. Thus the legal system, besides embodying much of the law of England, is still a significant carrier of values, assumptions and procedure - the ideology - of the Common Law. The essence of the legal system is still Anglo-Muhammadan, especially so far as procedure is concerned and, to a great extent, also substantive law. One example of this is the system of judicial precedent, which is fully preserved even when the claim has been to implement classical Islamic law.

Judicial *khula* is an example of a doctrine which was developed by the courts, a practice of Common Law different from Islamic law. Esposito says that judicial reforms in Pakistan follow from Anglo-Muhammadan law as opposed to classical Islamic jurisprudence, according to which the function of the courts was simply to apply or follow and not to create (Esposito, 1980a: 237-8).

In the same way changes made in the law of evidence to Islamize it are very minor. It is only the numbers of the sections which have been changed. This has not made any difference to the law, but did, of course, cause problems for the lawyers who were used to the old system.

It is interesting that when a classical concept of Islamic criminal law is adopted in Pakistan, *hudood* ordinances are set out in 'modern statutory fashion' (Faruki, 1983). Moreover, definitions of different crimes like *qazf*, etc., are taken from the PPC (Pakistan Penal Code (XLV of 1860) with minor changes. The law of theft is changed into classical *shariah* law, but it is not applied because of the high standard of proof demanded. So, for practical purposes, it is still the law of theft as laid down in the PPC which applies.

Another interesting point is that the courts under the military regime, which mostly claimed to be upholding Islamic laws, used theories from western jurisprudence. Kelsen, for example, was widely used to justify the extra-constitutional step of military takeover.[10]

All the negative aspects of Anglo-Muhammadan law are present in Pakistan. The law was alienated from the legal culture of the villages. In this situation, a new element in the state law was introduced, that of Islamic law. This was again alienated from the people's culture. There is inconsistency and instability in it and it has preserved all the evils of Anglo-Muhammedan law. Islamization has merely increased the inconsistency and instability of the system.

The next question is, how good are the possibilities of getting rid of the colonial pattern of law, inherited by the post-colonial states? Anglo-Muhammadan law, which fulfilled the needs of a colonial system, also came to fulfill the needs of a peripheral state. After having been the law of the country for so many years, people have also become used to it. They have started thinking in so-called modern democratic terms. One example of this is that people in Pakistan believe in the modern democratic principle and react strongly if their rights are not guaranteed. *Shariah* in its conservative form does not suit. There have been disputes in Pakistan about the nature of Anglo-Muhammadan law, whether it was Islamic or whether it needed some changes in it to make it compatible with the *Quran* and *Sunna*. Modernists in Pakistan did not find Anglo-Muhammadan law contradictory to Islamic law and this is why no attempt was made to change the state legal system until the great wave of Islamization in 1977. Whatever changes were made were made under the Modernist influence and were not in contradiction to the spirit of Anglo-Muhammadan law. The important question is whether it is possible to get rid of Anglo-Muhammadan law or whether it is already fulfilling the needs of the post-colonial state.

Marc Galanter maintains that official law competes with traditional law. He maintains that after a foreign legal system has been transplanted into a country and has been in use for so many years, it becomes the law of that country, not foreign to it (Galanter, 1978: 43). Throughout his article, Marc Galanter has tried to look at the possibilities of replacing the present Indian legal system with revived indigenous law. He says:

> The borrowed elements underwent more than a century and a half of pruning in which British localisms and anomalies were discarded and rules elaborated to deal with new kinds of persons, property and transactions. By omission, substitution, simplification, elaboration, the law was modified to make it 'suitable to Indian conditions' (Galanter, 1972: 63).

Thus Marc Galanter observes that in India no such need was felt to change the formal legal system inherited from the colonial period. Marc Galanter maintains:

> Strangely, the law seems more separable from its origin, relatively easy to borrow and hard to discard (Galanter, 1968: 86).

He further says:

> Both intellectually and institutionally, there seemed an acceptance of the mid 20th century system as something fully Indian (Galanter, 1978: 42).

Agnete Weiss Bentzon also believes that the unification of colonial law and local law is possible. She says:

> The unification of the system of law follows two main roads: the legislation and the practice of the courts. The result of the unifications seems generally to be an amalgamation of the customary law (folk law) and the state law of the colonial power. The product of this amalgamation might be called: local law. This term indicates, that it is a local variation of the state law and the colonial power. After the abolition of the colonial government and the establishment of self-government, the local

law develops into national law (Bentzon, 1983: 4).

A good number of lawyers, when asked whether the prestige of the law in Pakistan today is very much below what it was 30 years ago and if the legal profession has improved in quality since independence, said that the prestige of the law in Pakistan is less than what it was thirty years ago, although some disagreed (Appendix 1) Further examples of preservation of the Anglo-Muhammedan pattern will be demonstrated in later chapters.

1.8.1 Lawyers' Resistance to the Islamization of the law

Having looked at inconsistency and instability and at Islamic law as a continuation of Anglo-Muhammadan law, it would be interesting to look at the attitude of lawyers towards the Islamization of the law. As we shall see, lawyers have played an important role in preserving the values of Anglo-Muhammadan law in Pakistan.

Lawyers and the law in Pakistan are characterised by the following features. Well-established lawyers usually belong to the upper class; they are sometimes qualified as barristers in England. Usually the majority of lawyers come from the middle and lower middle classes. Law is not communicated to the people, it is the monopoly of lawyers. Lawyers are visualized as persons whose principal function is to argue in court. Practicing lawyers sit in wooden boxes outside the courts and the atmosphere is like a fish market.

Legal training is of a formal nature. Lawyers are not trained to think in terms of process. There is a wide gap between legal theory and practice. As such, the legal system as a whole is weak and the legal profession inadequately trained. There is a lack of analytical skills and process learning as distinct from rule learning. Lawyers are poorly trained and narrow in outlook, perhaps, but nevertheless locally regarded as qualified (Merillat, 1966). The law is taken as a body of relatively sacred and immutable principle which are applied to social life through formal and ritualistic techniques. The standard of legal education in Pakistan is comparable to the standard of legal education in India (Mehren, 1965; Braibanti, 1966).

A great number of lawyers interviewed held the view that the standard of legal training was low in Pakistan and there was a big gap between theory and practice. Four said that legal training was satisfactory in Pakistan. Two said it needed improvement.

One said that there was a gap between education and practice all over the world and Pakistan was no exception (see Appendix 1).

It is generally held that the legal profession is overcrowded in Pakistan (Braibanti, 1966). 'Many fresh graduates took to the law because no other avenue of gainful employment was open to them. This fact was borne out by the high rate of "dropouts"'. S.M. Zafar pleaded for checks on new entries to the legal profession as it had become overcrowded.[11] Braibanti disagrees, saying:

> It is common to assume that developing states in the British imperial tradition have too many lawyers and that the consequent disproportionate emphasis on legal modes of thought is antithetical to the needs of development (Braibanti, 1966: 254).

Braibanti argues that it is only the number of lawyers that has made the legal community in Pakistan strong. He says that the legal community was successful in persistently challenging governmental policy during and after martial law, and was successful primarily because of its size and consequent network of influence throughout the country. In short, the legal community is of some magnitude and is a power to be reckoned with. He says that the legal profession in Pakistan is an influential, articulate group and indeed is probably the most important group in national politics. Bar Associations have commonly been unusually vigorous in taking stands on political issues (Braibanti, 1966).

Abid Hassan Minto, a famous Pakistani lawyer has shown that lawyers were in the forefront of democratic compaigns. He has given a detailed account of the struggle of the lawyers against the martial law regimes (Minto, 1986). The Women Lawyers Association played a special role.

When asked about the role of Bar Councils in politics, twenty of the lawyers interviewed said that Bar Councils played a positive role in the struggle for democracy in Pakistan, some even said to the extent that politics cannot grow without Bar Councils. Three however said that Bar Councils have played a negative role and they should not indulge themselves in politics. Two did not answer the question and one misunderstood (see Appendix I).

Keeping in view the lawyers' background, let us look at the role which they played in the process of Islamization. Generally lawyers resisted Islamization and for a long time did not even knew that it had occurred. The Law Reform Committee of the Pakistan Bar Council, in reply to the questionnaire issued by the Council of Islamic Ideology, has held that the present system of the administration of justice is 'not in conflict with the basic principles of Islam' and that there is 'no need for basically changing the present judicial stucture'. As for the proposal made about the appearance of *"alims"* in the *qazi* courts, the report suggested that it would cause complications on account of their lack of professional and specialized knowledge.[12]

Eberhard says that the question as to what the law of Pakistan should be is not easy to answer for the lawyers because

> Many of them were trained in law, and the law of undivided India was in general British-Indian law, based, philosophically, upon western tradition. At least in its application modern Pakistani law is influenced by modern psychology and sociology. Jurists often had no or little knowledge of *shari'ah* law, and a return to *shari'ah* law would have made the *mullahs* to judges and the judges unemployed (Eberhard, 1959/60: 144).

He further says:

> Over centuries, a local 'customary Muslim law' had developed which was adjusted to the special conditions of the country. Although many intellectuals were in favor of changing away from British-Indian law, the idea to build a new law on the basis of customary law seemed to them more acceptable than a return to the original *shari'ah* law (*ibid*: 144-5).

Thirty years ago, Eberhard asked the question whether such laws as stoning an adulteress to death and to cutting off the hand of a thief should be introduced into a modern and modernising society (*ibid*: 144-5).

When asked about the role of lawyers in politics, the lawyers interviewed were very clear and positive that they had always been in the forefront of the fight for democracy but when asked about lawyers' role in the Islamization of the law, it is my impression that they were not very sure. On the one hand, they know that some laws have been Islamized and they should take part in it otherwise they would be left behind. On the other hand, they feel threatened by the Islamic laws. Some of them said that lawyers resisted so-called Islamization in Pakistan. In this regard they appreciated the role of women. Some held the view that lawyers could have played a more positive role against so-called

Islamization. A small number however felt helpless against the movement of Islamization. Few appreciated Islamization.

The attitude of the woman lawyers was different. They openly took a strong stand against the Islamic laws while at the same time practicing in the Islamic courts. I observed in 1991 that students trained at an Islamic university do not have any trouble adjusting themselves to the ordinary type of courts. In a particular example of a women lawyer, I was told that people in the Islamic University were not very happy with her as she sat outside the courts with other advocates without covering her head and practising as a 'liberated' woman, against her training in the Islamic university.

It would be interesting to mention Marc Galanter's remarks from his experience of lawyers in India where he says that, to the lawyer, the legal system, in spite of its foreign roots, is Indian. They have no sentiments for the revival of 'indigenous law'; in fact they would like to ignore the very existence of it. They may be critical towards the present system but they are also committed to it. He says, 'lawyers are quite unable to visualize any basic change in either the legal system or the organization of professional services' (Galanter: 1969: 215-16).

My own observations confirm the same type of impression from Pakistan.

1.9 LEGAL PLURALISM

So far my purpose in the preceding parts has been to negate the state's claim that Islamic state law is the only law in the legal arena. Inconsistency, instability and other features of Islamic state law show that it not only creates problems; it is also generally distrusted by the people.

The purpose of this Part is to emphasize that there is more than one type of legal norm practised in Pakistan. The Islamic legal order presented by the formal state law is not the only law of the country.

With reference to the Islamization of the law, it is important to point out the pluralistic legal social order in Pakistan, because orthodox jurisprudence has first established the universality of the western transplanted law on the pretext of modernity, equality of law, impartiality, etc., later replacing it with the concept of 'Universal *Shariah*', thus provoking religious feelings. While stressing the universality of the above mentioned orders, they completely ignore the presence of other legal social orders, which are in fact social reality, while the concept of unified and exclusive *shariah* has no roots.

Before we proceed to the pluralistic legal situation in Pakistan we can look at some of the theories of legal pluralism. This would help in understanding the definition we are employing about pluralistic legal systems in Pakistan. Some other social phenomena which might somewhat resemble legal pluralism should be differentiated from pluralism.

A few words about legal centralism - which is opposite to legal pluralism - are important to understand legal pluralism. According to the ideology of legal centralism:

> Law is and should be the law of the state, uniform for all persons, exclusive of all other law, and administered by a single set of state institutions (Griffiths, 1986: 3).

The ideology of legal centralism is so strong that it dominates the western as well as the non-western world. The exponents of the theory of legal pluralism speak of its existence everywhere in the world. Because of inconsistency and instability in the formal state law in Pakistan, the legal centralist claim may be easy to expose in comparison to societies with more sophisticated state laws.

One view of legal pluralism (in the weak sense) is:

> ... a legal system is 'pluralistic' when the sovereign (implicitly) commands (or the *grundnorm* validates, and so on) different bodies of law for different groups in the population. In general the groups concerned are defined in terms of features such as ethnicity, religion, and nationality or geography, and legal pluralism is justified as a technique of governance on pragmatic grounds (*ibid*: 5).

Hooker's definition of legal pluralism is close to the above mentioned concept. For him, law is a set of consistent principles, valid for and binding upon the whole population and emanating from a single source (Hooker, 1975). Bentzon, who has worked mainly on the legal system in Greenland, writes:

> Pluralistic legal systems are spoken of when substantial law and procedural law are different for various social groups within the same territory. This usage is especially adopted to describe the legal situation in regions with colonial or similar status where the plurality of laws consists of one formalized and more non-formalized law systems (Bentzon, 1982: 2).

J. Griffiths calls this concept 'legal pluralism in the weak sense'. One of the best examples of this is when the East India Company provided that in 'suits regarding inheritance, marriages, caste and other religious usages and institutions, the laws of the *Quran* with respect to the Muhammadans and those of the Shaster with respect to the Gentoos shall invariably be adhered to'.[13] Another example of this is the recognition of customary law in Greenland by the Danish authorities (Bentzon, 1983).

Griffiths says that the idea behind recognition of the customs of the various groups is to supplant the uniform general law. The eventual goal is unification which is considered inevitable, necessary, normal and modern. Therefore a choice is made and rules are set. Griffiths' contention is that the concept is not inconsistent with the ideology of legal centralism. He says 'it is merely a particular arrangement in a system whose basic ideology is centralist'. It is worth quoting from Griffiths:

> The very notion of recognition and all the doctrinal paraphernalia which it brings with it are typical reflections of the idea that 'law' must ultimately depend on a single validating source. Legal pluralism is thus but one of the forms in which the ideology of legal centralism can manifest itself. It is, to be sure, by the terms of that ideology an inferior form of law, a necessary accomodation to a social situation perceived as problematic (Griffiths, 1986: 8).

Among the other descriptive concepts of legal pluralism, Griffiths has provided an interesting and useful criticism of Gilissen's and Vanderlinden's concepts of legal pluralism. He thinks that Gilissen confuses legal diversity with legal pluralism, i.e., different rules for different classes of the population (soldiers, doctors, etc.) does not constitute legal pluralism. While Vanderlinden confuses different legal mechanisms applicable to the same situation. 'These are different features of the arrangement of the state law therefore are a centralist conception of legal pluralism', says Griffiths.

Griffiths has also looked at the theories of a legally pluralistic social structure, among which he names Pospisil's, Smith's and Ehrlich's theories. Pospisil's theory seems to be dominated by the whole society perspective where subgroups are like building blocks within that structure. This suggests a static structural neatness (Pospisil, 1971). Griffiths expresses more appreciation for Ehrlich (Ehrlich, 1936) and Sally Moore, (Moore, 1973; 1978) though with some reservations. In the end we can look at the definition of legal pluralism provided by Griffiths with the help of the Ehrlich and Moore theories. He says:

> Legal pluralism is a concomitant of social pluralism: *the legal organization of society is congruent with its social organization.* 'Legal pluralism' refers to the normative heterogeneity attendant upon the fact that social action always takes place in a context of multiple, overlapping 'semi-autonomous social fields', which, it may be added, is in practice a dynamic condition. A situation of legal pluralism - the omnipresent, normal situation in human society - is one in which law and legal institutions are not all subsumable within one 'system' but have their sources in the self-regulatory activities of all the multifarious social fields present, activities which may support, complement, ignore or frustrate one another, so that the 'law' which is actually effective on the 'ground floor' of society is the result of enormously complex and usually in practice unpredictable patterns of competition, interaction, negotiation, isolationism, and the like (Griffiths, 1986: 38-9).

In the light of Griffiths' formulation of the concept of legal pluralism we can look at the pluralistic legal structure in Pakistan. From this concept, we can deduce no more than that there is more than one legal way of solving conflicts. Which means that besides state legal order there are local legal alternatives. We can call them by different names: for example, folk law, people's law, customary law, unofficial law and indigenous law (Allot and Woodman, 1985).

But a simple agreement about the concept of legal pluralism is only the first step, which brings us to the relativity of 'truth' and it does not necessarily means that legal pluralists are always in favour of people's law and opposed to state law (Sack, 1986).

Baxi says that some people 'celebrate people's law as a constant reminder of social limits on the sovereign power of the state; and as a promise of the human potential to transcend the state and its repressive ideological apparatuses' - in Baxi's words 'Millenarian approaches'. Baxi has drawn attention to the fact that people's law, too, can be repressive, exploitative and aggressive, though state power is blamed for this deformation in people's law, which 'arrests, deflects, distorts and denatures people's capabilities and potential for self-regulation'. Baxi gives examples of Muslim personal law which 'even till today, preserves unilateral talaq (divorce), polygamy, differential inheritance rights, and no maintenance rights beyond customary *mahr*' (Baxi, 1986: 54).

Baxi observes that there is a deep-seated conflict between legal pluralism and feminism.

> Pluralist social reality is, it appears, overwhelmingly oppressive of women. It is therefore likely that the state and its law currently offer, at a pinch, a more promising arena of struggle for the emancipation of women than is offered in the domain of the people's law (*ibid*: 54).

Baxi says that the next question is to what extent the repressive (and terrorist) repertoire of NSLS (Non State Legal Systems) can be explained as a 'deformation' induced by dominant classes and to what extent this 'deformation' may be perceived as coded within their very structure which requires searching analysis in the study of legal pluralism (*ibid*: 56). Baxi suggests a plurality of power structures as a subject of legal pluralism. Baxi refers to Foucault, who identifies this as disciplinary power which constitutes 'counter-law'. I agree with Baix when he says:

> But at least legal pluralism can be explained in such a manner as would facilitate the gradual development of insurrectionary jurisprudence, of alternative forms of legality, based on an imaginative, strategic and tactical inversion of the structure and ideologies of both sovereign and non-sovereign types of power and law (*ibid*: 60).

1.9.1 Legally Pluralistic Social Structures in Pakistan

Very little has been written about the nature of the legal pluralist social structure in Pakistan. In fact not much literature exists about legal pluralism in Islamic countries. Since different social structures having an Islamic framework are legally pluralistic, it is a vast field for research.

One factor which Pakistan shares with India is the plurality of the legal system. Pakistan does not have only one legal system. The system which we can call the 'formal state legal system' is the law which is state law while on the other hand there are the different legal norms which are practised by people. E. Adamson Hoebel writes:

> The legal system of Pakistan does not constitute a neatly

integrated whole; it is made up of an undetermined multiplicity of subsystems. Many of these are disjunctive in their relations to others. Most obvious among these systems is the formal national law which arches as an ethereal dome above all the lesser systems. It is the law inherited from the imperial rule of British India. It is founded upon a series of codes enacted through hundreds of enactments before and since partition.

Deeply imbedded in the village and tribal areas of Pakistan is a vast array of local folk systems of law varying from village to village and area to area. This is the folk law of the people, nine-tenths of whom live in the villages and who rarely have contact with government courts, civil or criminal. Folk law too, is a relatively uncharted universe (Hoebel, 1965: 44).

The next question that is relevant for our purpose is the nature of folk law. Is it Islamic in its nature?

... Ideologically, it incorporates Islamic law, but the folk ignorance of Islam is in fact profound. The great tradition and the little tradition are, as is to be expected, two different things (*ibid*: 44).

Coulson also recognizes the gulf that exists between *shariah* doctrine on the one hand and actual Muslim legal practice on the other (Coulson, 1959-1961: 23).

Some literature exists on the aspect of how the practice of Islam differs from what is written and practised as Islam. Gordan P. Means, for instance, describes a situation in Malaysia which is very close to the situation in Pakistan (Means, 1969). Eberhard describes the big gap between written Islam and Islam as practised specially in the villages of Pakistan:

In villages we find what R. Redfield called 'the little tradition'. Thus far this 'little tradition' has not yet changed much, as the village society has not yet undergone great changes. Pakistani farmers are proud to call themselves Muslims and, if they feel themselves attacked, will defend this religion, as they understand it, to the last. But actually, Islam does not constitute a strong force in their daily life. Their religious leaders, the *Maulvis* and *Mullahs* have a low social status: they are regarded as 'servants' to the farmers and are paid by them. They have only superficial training in Islam, have memorized the *Quran* but not really studied its meaning. Their sermons as we found in our village research, stress only the punitive aspects of Islam, they are more or less exclusively 'hell-fire talks'. These ill-educated *Mullahs* believe that the present time is a time of degeneration and people should return to the behavior of the people of early Islam as they see it. They are, therefore, against modernization of any kind. The farmers, by themselves conservative too, are nevertheless lax in their participation in religious practice: we found that only few farmers performed regularly the minimum of daily prayers required of a Muslim (Eberhard, 1959-60: 140-1).

Hoebel cites a university student in Pakistan as saying that the law of the police and courts is not the law of the people. He says

It appears in Pakistan that most disputes within a village (in the absence of factions) are settled by the landlord with counsel from the Council. Factional disputes run their courses with annoying harassment, kidnapping of women, armed assault, and homicide. In most villages there are no police and, even if there are, they are not called in ordinary homicides, but only when one faction is so overwhelmingly bested that it despairs of successful retaliation. Then it surmounts its 'apprehension of being subjected to harassment and ill-treatment at the hands of police officers themselves' (Law Reform Commission 1959: 50) in order to force the opposing party to suffer with it. Involvement with the police and the courts can mean physical discomfort and nearly endless expenditures to both parties (Hoebel, 1965: 45).

Recently Richard Kurin has done some very interesting work describing the impact of Islamization on a village in Pakistan and shows that people's practice of Islam is different from what the state prescribes and that there is a large gap between the state Islamic law and the legal norms practised by the people (Kurin, 1986: 115-28). It is very true what Kurin said in his survey of the village of Chakpur:

The central government institution of *shariat* law has yet to affect villagers in a direct way. *Hudud* ordinances, discussed by villagers, have yet to be applied to villagers themselves. Generally, Chakpuris have been quite reluctant to adjudicate conflicts through the court system. Seeking the police, using lawyers, and being called before the court bring forth all sorts of intrusions most Chakpuris regard as undesirable. Most conflict resolution among villagers is handled informally through clan leaders (*biradari*, heads), or by public argument. Using the courts is really a last resort, done only when the local machinery for resolving a disagreement has broken down. This happened the first time I was in the village, when a murder was committed. Often, though, relatively severe conflicts never reach the courts. For example, one villager having a long-term affair with the wife of a fellow clansman was continually upbraided by delegations of influential intermediaries, but was never the subject of an official police complaint, even though he freely acknowledged the affair (Kurin, 1986: 120-1).

A similar type of situation was noted in India by R.S Khare where he says that culturally it is not natural for an Indian to turn at once to lawyer's law for redress his grievance. It is either the last or inescapable resort (Khare, 1972: 85).

Disputes are sorted out on the local level. Sometime the legal mechanism used might be close to the official law, in other situations they might be very different.

In answer to the question about whether the *panchayat* system or local systems to solve conflicts exist in Pakistan, all lawyers interviewed (see Appendix I) acknowledged that the *panchayat* system is used though two said that it exists but does not fulfil the requirements of justice. Two said it is popular only for small disputes. But few lawyers denied the existence of such a system. The reason for this denial could be that one is so much used to the state legal system that one can even easily overlook the existence of local ways of solving disputes. Lawyers also tend to deny it as they are prone to preserve Anglo-Muhammadan values. In answer to the question that courts are only the last resort, twenty of the lawyers agreed. Six disagreed. (See Appendix I). In answer to the question, 'Is the law of the police and courts not the law of the people?', more then half agreed with the statement. Only a few disagreed.

A human rights activist, the woman lawyer Asma Jahangir, told me that customary laws are very oppressive for women. She said, 'Tell me one tradition starting from bangles to ear-rings which favours women'. Baxi is right. We cannot glorify customary law against state law (Baxi, 1986).

There is a large gap between the Islamic formal state law of Pakistan and the Islamic law practised by the people. More details have been provided in Part 1.11.1 to examine the effect of custom on Islamic law, resulting in a pluralistic Islamic legal structure.

1.10 SOCIAL REFORMS THROUGH LAW

One of the inconsistencies discussed is the wide gap between the state legal norms and the norms applied in practice. Here I would like to go into more detail about the effect of legislation created for social reforms. In the following chapters I have documented a series of attempts to effect social change through legislation. Such changes have been extremely difficult to achieve. It is extremely difficult for the state to change the accepted, socially observed laws of its subjects.

The effect of British reform law on the social institutions was limited. For example a number of measures were introduced to improve the status of women, but these reforms often remained dead letters. Of course, many of the urban elite appreciated these reforms as they were critical towards their customary practices.

During the British *raj*, reforms were made in keeping with British standards, for example emphasis on the equality of women and on the nuclear family, etc. Joanna Liddle and Rama Joshi argue that it is important to look at the intentions of the British claim that the reforms were a liberating force in British India and that India was not fit for self-rule. The reforms claimed by the British were not intended to be implemented in their spirit. This was the reason that even the most emphasized reform of banning *sati* was ambiguous and their actions on other questions contradicted their claim (Liddle and Rama, 1986; Kamal, 1987).

One of the papers presented by the SIMORGH organization drew attention towards British reforms in a different way that is very relevant:

> ... motivating impulses behind their intervention in the life patterns of the subcontinent were linked to British interests as colonizers. Even in the case of laws which benefited women directly such as the Child Marriage Restraint Act for example, it would be difficult to accuse them of altruism, as these laws were politically strategic gestures brought about in response to pressure from the more progressive sections of the 'native elite'. As mentioned earlier, the British consolidated their position in the subcontinent by creating a Europeanized native elite. For obvious reasons women were not excluded from this category. A system of education, which disseminated Eurocentric ideas in the garb of great universal truths was a major tool employed by the British to bring about this eventuality.

The paper further stated:

Although this strategy succeeded in creating a class of women alienated from their own culture, paradoxically enough in the long term it also benefited wider sections of women in the subcontinent. Exposure to an alien and avowedly 'superior' culture enabled the women to question the contradictions and injustices in their own systems of belief.[14]

The educated urban elite benefited most from these reforms. They appreciated uniformity, modernity and individualism. The same was true after independence. Social reformative state law was mostly for the service of the educated urban elite.

It is interesting that reforms in Pakistani family law did not initially stem from any popular demand but were imposed on people from above in the interests of administrative efficiency and in deference to foreign opinion. It was only a group of westernized urban women who demanded these reforms. It was not very long, however, before they began to gain considerable support among those elements in the population which had received a modern education (Anderson, J.N.D., 1971: 3).

On the other hand, the villagers never gave up their traditional ways of solving disputes and also upheld the norms they believed in. This is why reforms intended as social reforms were largely ineffective both before and after independence.

While looking at the social effect of the law, it is important to keep in mind the high illiteracy rate in Pakistan. Some customs exist because of poverty and illiteracy in the country. Other customs, like arranged marriages and child marriage, are related to social institutions like the joint family and to the interests of keeping land within the family, etc. If economic opportunities were available outside rural areas, the power of parents over their children would be circumscribed.

June Starr has published an article on the social effect of a similar law in Turkey. She explains that the effectiveness of laws in Turkey is related to structural and social changes. In other words, she shows that changes in legislation have to be related to economic and social changes (Starr, 1989).

How much has state law affected social practice? Little research has been done on this aspect in Pakistan. Some of the research available has been mentioned in the relevant places.

It is important to mention that, though the laws meant as social reforms are ineffective and do not serve the purpose for which they are made, they do have a general effect on the people. It has been argued that the changes in criminal law under *hadd* are symbolic. They are comparable to the temperance movement in America, which was an attempt by abstainers to correct the behaviour of immoral people. The issues they took were symbolic rather than instrumental or pragmatic issues (Gusfield, 1976). One can question whether it was the object of legislation to change sexual behaviour, as sexual behaviour in Pakistan was already generally in accord with Islamic moral precepts. The object of much of this legislation was simply to make moral statements - to affirm an acceptance of the principles of traditionalist Islam. This might have been done to promote a political ideology, or out of religious conviction. Perhaps there was not much concern as to whether people would obey, or the law would actually be used (Aubert, 1966).

Generally, the legislation on sexual morality has not produced the desired results but has still indirectly created an effect. For example, though punishments like stoning to death for *zina* have not been executed officially, their very existence in law has caused some people to carry out this punishment after the decision of a local *mullah*. Moreover while the law exists, there is always the possibility of its execution - it is like a hanging sword. In cases where *hudood* punishments are applicable, the lower courts have on many occasions sentenced people to amputation and death by stoning.

On the other hand, in family law, the existence of social reforms - although not effective - still give women a protection in general, which, if taken away, would detrimentally affect the situation of women in Pakistan.

In answer to the question put to lawyers if social reform legislation is effective, only some of them said that social reform legislation was effective, while a great number deplored its ineffectivness (see Appendix I).

The conclusion is that the laws are relatively ineffective but that is not the same as saying that they are not necessary. Their ineffectiveness could be for different reasons, as most of the lawyers blamed corruption as the reason for the ineffectiveness of the laws. On the other hand, there is also the plural legal structure, i.e., people's faith in their own way of solving disputes, which makes them less likely to contact the legal agencies and which makes laws ineffective in that sense. But the social reform laws are also effective or necessary in the sense that women's movements and human rights organizations stand for those reforms, for example laws against child marriage and women's right to divorce, etc. These laws have become symbols of progress. Their abolition would strengthen reactionary forces.

1.11 DEVELOPMENT OF ISLAMIC LAW IN PAKISTAN

Let us come back to the Islamic state law of Pakistan. The question arises as to whether classical Islamic law is flexible. What are the possibilities of development in Islamic law? This is a vast study and not the subject of this book. The only purpose here is to show the struggle of the Modernist in the legal arena of Pakistan. The issue is looked at with reference to the sources of Islamic law.

It is important, firstly to show how these sources have been used by the legislature and judiciary in Pakistan in different periods. In some periods, the sources of Islamic laws have been interpreted liberally by the legislature, while other times they have been interpreted very rigidly. The second important aspect of this is that, from a legal pluralist viewpoint, Islamic law is not the law in the *shariah* books but what Muslim people use in their everyday life. In real life people take Islam as a way of living or as their culture, not something outside them. In this respect, it is important to look at the relevance of the sources of Islamic law, in the manner Lawrence Rosen has done in Morocco. Rosen has given interesting examples from Moroccan society to show that the sources of Islamic law have also been applied by people in a more flexible way (Rosen, 1989a; 1989b). This is an important aspect, but not the main subject of this book. The third important aspect in this part is related to the second and concerns the question, can we say that a flexible interpretation of these sources also allows room for custom?

Islamic law is one of the most important legal systems in the world. Åke Malmström and Ole Lando's classifications of legal systems outside Europe include Islamic law among the religiously motivated legal systems (Malmström, 1969; Lando, 1965). There is no doubt that religion has played an important role in evolving the Islamic legal system.

Islamic law is sacred religious law, as it is given by God. Does this mean that it is immutable? Muslims have made efforts to expand it, keeping in view the principle that it is in fact immutable and therefore every change should be explained and related to the original sources. This is the reason why it is important to look at the sources of Islamic law (Anderson J.N.D., 1966; 1971).

To build a system of Islamic law, responsibility fell on the jurists. This is the reason that it is also called 'jurists' law.' In the second and third centuries of the *Hegira*, four Muslim jurists made efforts to build an Islamic legal system. Four schools of jurisprudence were established, named after their founders *Abu Hanifa (Hanifite), Ibn Malik (Malikite), Ash-Shafi'i (Shafi'ite)* and *Ibn Hanbal (Hanbalite)*. Moreover, on the basis of theological and political differences, several heterodox groups like the *Shiites* developed. According to orthodox doctrine, after the establishment of these schools the gates of independent reasoning or *ijtihad* were closed in the 9th century A.D (4th century, A.H.) But modernists in the Muslim world have propounded the view that the right to *ijtihad* could be invoked by modern legislators.

Another way Islamic law developed was through the methodologies of change employed. Methodologies include borrowing one rule from one school and another from another.[15] Another means of change in Islamic law was the influence of Western law. This Westernization was basically the result of colonial rule. Islamic law was replaced by western law, though family law was codified on the basis of *shariah*.

The application of Islamic law in most Muslim countries today is limited to family law and, even in this field, a lot of modifications or reforms have been made. Pakistan, under the rule of the Modernists, experienced considerable development in state Islamic family law.

The sources of Islamic law are considered to be the following.

Quran
The book of Muslims, the *Quran* is not a law code. It is a religious book which in various places provides some rules of a legal type (Mahmood, Tahir, 1987).[16] Therefore Muslims have applied other means to develop Islamic law.

Sunna and Hadith
In the earlier times of Islam the 'sayings' and 'doings' of the prophet became the guidelines, if explanation of Islamic deeds were required in practical problems. These came to be known as *Hadith* and *Sunna*. An elaborate system of *Hadith* and *Sunna* was built up by Muslim jurists. A group among the Indian Muslims deny the authority and significance of the prophetic sayings. There are many differences of opinion among Muslims about the authenticity of the *Sunna* and *Hadith*. But these two sources have contributed much to building up Islamic law.

Qiyas
Qiyas (analogy) is the derivative source of law. An example of

this type of law-making is fixing the same compensation for injury to teeth as for injury to fingers. Another example is the fixing of the minimum value of dower by drawing an analogy with the minimum value of stolen goods for *hadd* punishment (Hasan, Ahmed, 1976). Let us consider some of the opinions concerning *qiyas* to understand the type of problem faced in employing analogy in expanding to sphere of Muslim legal activity.

Ahmed Zaki Yamani has explained the application of *qiyas* with reference to the two concepts of *illa* and *hikma*. *Illa* is what can be objectively ascertained and measured, while *hikma* is the value judgement and the underlying reason for the principle. An example of this is the breaking of the fast by a man on a journey. The hardship of the journey is *illa*. Now another situation is where a person is travelling in such luxury that the idea of hardship, due to which this concession was granted, is not present. On the other hand, a labourer who is working hard could be more deserving of a concession in fasting. According to the opinion of Ahmed Zaki Yamani, the differentiation between *illa* and *hikma* is relevant only in matters of devotional rituals. In matters of secular and commercial transactions, it could be said that a judgement is dependent on its *hikma*, i.e., underlying subjective reason. This avoids the mechanical application of *qiyas* (Yamani, 1979). He further says that, faced with this possibility, Muslim jurists decided to foresake analogy and employ custom, welfare or benefit and the elimination of hardship as guiding principles in their derivation of new judgments. Fazlur Rahman has, however, criticized Sheikh Yamani's differention between devotional rites and the secular and commercial. He says that that the distinction between the religious and the secular does not exist in Islam (Rahman, Fazlur, 1979).

Ijma
Ijma is another way Muslims have used to expand Islamic law. It means that if all the jurists of a generation reach a decision on a point of law, it should be accepted. The basis of this is derived from a well quoted saying of the Prophet Muhammed that 'My people never agree on whoever leads them astray' or 'My community would never unite on error'. Muslims differ in explaining the word 'My Community'. The question is whether it refers to the collective consensus of the community or of the legal experts. According to one view it should be the unamious opinion of the *mujtahidun* (legal experts). There is also great

diversity of opinion as to until what period in the history of Islam *ijma* can be accepted.

A leading Muslim philosopher who is considered to be the national poet of Pakistan, Muhammed Iqbal, stressed the dynamic nature of Islamic law. He saw *ijma* as the most important legal doctrine in Islam; in modern times, the only place it can be exercised is through a representative assembly (Iqbal, Muhammad, 1977: 155-60). This shows how Modernists have used the concept to demonstrate its democratic character. Richard H. Nolte has noted:

> The principle of consensus might have provided Muslim law as indeed it did for a time with a powerful means of growth and adaptation to changing circumstances. Instead, it became the great obstacle to adaptation and change, a principle of rigidity. A consensus once reached on a given point was considered to be forever binding beyond any chance of reconsideration - a sort of canonical stare decisis. Muslim scholars of a later day did not have the power to reopen questions answered by their predecessors; and instead of a flexible instrument of progress, *Ijma* became the mighty anchor of the status quo, the status quo of the 10th century A.D. (Nolte, 1958: 302).

Ijtihad

Ijtihad means powers of interpretation, in keeping with the spirit of Islam. Traditionalists do not believe in taqlid which is the opposite of *ijtihad*. According to them the gates of *ijtihad* are closed, so *ijtihad* should be replaced by the duty of accepting the teaching of one's school and its leading jurists as authoritative. Modernists on the other hand consider it important to revivify Islam in the face of new questions and issues that arise with new conditions.

Bernard Weiss says that *ijtihad* roughly corresponds to what in western jurisprudence is called interpretation. It is not the laws which are interpreted but the sources of law.

> In principle, the Muslim jurist never invents rules; he formulates, or attempts to formulate, rules which God has already decreed and which are concealed in the sources. These rules, which constitute the ideal law of God, exist objectively above and beyond all juristic endeavor (Weiss, Bernard, 1978; 200).

A Pakistani Muslim scholar says:

The claim of the present generation of Muslim liberals to re-interpret the foundational legal principles, in the light of their own experience and the altered conditions of modern life is, in my opinion, perfectly justified. The teaching of the *Quran* that life is a process of progressive creation necessitates that each generation, guided but unhampered by the work of its predecessors, should be permitted to solve its own problems" (Iqbal, Muhammad, 1977: 168).

One example of *ijtihad* in Pakistan was in 1955 when the government appointed a commission on marriage and family laws (Pearl, 1979: 167). The Commission presented a report which was Modernist and was very much opposed by the Traditionalists. In the report stress was laid on the progressive and dynamic nature of Islam. The commission claimed *ijtihad* as the key to reforms in Islamic law. Maulana Ihtisham-ul-Haq challenged the Modernist majority and also challenged their capacity of *ijtihad* and *ijma* (Smith, 1971: 67-79).

The commission maintained that the *Quran* must be read with the requirements of social justice in mind and that the laws and injunctions of Islam were not inflexible and unchangeable and that distinctions might be drawn between them 'on the basis of their universality or applicability to a particular structure of society in a particular epoch and in a particular region'.

The commission, strongly asserting the right of independent judgement, is concerned, under its terms of reference, to determine whether Muslim women under existing laws 'achieve their proper place in society according to the fundamentals of Islam'. Their emphasis is on the individual women. Is quick divorce fair to the women? How does one stop the abuses of polygamy? This primary stress on the individual perhaps represents some absorption of eighteenth-century humanitarian ideas (Abbott, 1968: 202).

The judiciary in Pakistan has in different times exercised *ijtihad* (Khan, Gul Muhammad, 1986b). Hoebel has cited two cases to show that: *Balquis Fatima v. Najm-ul-Ikram Quereshi*[17] and *Rashida Begum v. Shahab Din and others*[18]. The latter was an appeal from a widow, custody of whose child was given to its paternal uncle. Hoebel says:

The decision in Rashida Begum sweeps aside Familism and establishes individual well-being as the sole criterion. The court implicitly accepts Maine's proposition, albeit without reference to it, that 'the movement of the progressive societies has hitherto been a movement from status to contract ... wherein "contract" means individual obligation arising from the free agreement of individual.' The court seems implicitly to accept the idea that social systems based on strong corporate families are incompatible with 'modernization' ... At any rate, the court's intent is to reform Muslim law in Pakistan on this unstated proposition (Hoebel, 1965: 51-52).

He says about *Balquis Fatima v. Najm-ul-Ikram Quereshi* that it throws the gate of *ijtihad* wide open once again. In this case the court held that the wife is entitled to dissolution of the marriage if the judges apprehend that the parties will not observe the limits of God. The court's right to *ijtihad* was established.

N.J. Coulsen, an eminent writer, remarked about *Khurshid Jan v. Fazal Dad*[19] that it was a clear renunciation of the doctrine of *taqlid* in the widest possible sense (Coulson, 1969: 107). More details about this aspect will be provided in the chapter on family law.

Istihsan, Masalih al-Mursalah or Istislah

These are related concepts. *Istihsan* is 'the equitable preference to find a just solution'; *Masalih al-Mursalah* is 'the public interest; and *Istislah* is 'seeking the best solution for the general interest'. Public interest is also regarded by some Muslim jurists as one of the sources of law. Jurists have, however, used different terms to describe it. An example of this is that, according to one of the Islamic instructions, no man should see certain parts of the body of a woman. But, out of necessity, a physician may be allowed to examine and diagnose a women in the interest of saving her life. Another example is that punishment of theft by the amputation of a hand does not apply if the theft is committed during a famine. Meat which is not slaughtered according to Islamic ritual is not normally permissible, but it is when no lawful food is available. From these examples it is also clear that the sources of Islamic law overlap, which means that these examples could also be deduced from *qiyas*.

Esposito says about the application of *istihsan* and *istislah* in Pakistan:

> The employment of this principle by justices in courts of law can do much to facilitate the equitable application of Islamic law to the needs of Muslims. For all practical purposes, such an

application has existed in one area of the Muslim world-India-Pakistan. Here the justices, while acknowledging their obligation to apply Islamic law in family law cases, have asserted their right to depart from the letter of the law where justice and equity warrant (Esposito, 1976: 35).

Fatwas

Fatwas are the opinions of *muftis* who provide authoritative opinions in specific cases which were consulted for new kinds of problems. Liebesny compares *fatwas* with the opinions of the Roman jurists (Liebesny, 1967: 18).

Some Muslim countries have used a procedural device, leaving the substantive law intact and unchanged. In Egypt this method was used to discourage child marriage. Some reforms were made by means of an eclectic choice between the wide variety of opinions advocated, at one time or another, by eminent jurists of the past.

J.N.D. Anderson has provided a full list of reforms accomplished in the Muslim countries, for example the wife's right of judicial divorce, restriction on the man's power of divorce, elimination of child marriage, restriction or abolition of polygamy, and several reforms in law of intestate succession. Pakistan was ahead of many Muslim countries in these reforms (Anderson, J.N.D., 1960; 1966).

Modernists in Pakistan have achieved a lot, struggling with the sources of Islamic law and relating them to contemporary needs. However, the Islamization carried out in the seventies applied the sources of Islamic law rigidly.

1.11.1 Custom as a Source of Islamic Law

Traditionalists undermine the effect of customary law on Islam, claiming it provides one unified law. But Islamic customary law has not died. This is why there is a culture gap separating the inhabitants of the cities from those of the villages.

Custom as a source of Islamic law is very much related to the discussion of legal pluralism. The existence of a pluralist legal structure is also evidence of the influence of customary laws on Muslims. There is no doubt that custom has played an important role in the development of Islamic law. There is however a difference of opinion in classical Islamic law about custom as a source of law. According to one opinion, custom is not recognized as a formal and independent source of law, but, according to others, custom is recognized as an important source of law, on condition that it does not contravene the basic tenets of Islam (Mahammadi, 1977). Under the names of *adah* and *urf*, Islamic legal authorities have long recognized the existence of local custom which can sometimes run counter to the details of the *shariah*. The problem arises when custom is at variance with what the text-books say.

One of the arguments put forward in allowing custom as a source is that the prophet Muhammad himself did not abolish all pre-Islamic customs (Mahmood, Tahir, 1965; Leavy, 1957). *Shariah* never covered all areas of the law and customary law remained an important factor:

> ...yet, while reognizing the introduction of new beliefs, regulations and institutions, a good deal of the Islamic way consisted of a reform of existing customs and a continuance of that which was not in need of specific reform (Esposito, 1976: 43).

Esposito has mentioned different avenues through which custom became one of the source of Islamic law. He has drawn attention to the early courts of the Umayyad and early 'Abbasid period, where a *qadi* in rendering a decision would look to the *Quran* and *Sunna* for guidance, but employ custom where no relevant texts were found. An example of this from family law is in the situation of dower when a specific amount is not stipulated in the contract. The allotment was usually determined on the basis of local custom following the maxim 'custom ranks as a stipulation'. A second avenue through which custom entered Islamic law is the *hadith*, i.e., tradition. The usual classification of *Sunna* is *al-sunnah al-qawliyah* (saying of the prophet), *al-sunnah al fi' liyah* (deeds of the prophet) and *al-sunnah al-taqririyah* (actions performed without his disapproval). This last category represented largely the original customs and usages of the pre-Islamic Arabs.

One other historical source of custom was the *ijma* of Malik, which was restricted to that of the Medinan community.

> Where no explicit text existed, the customs of the *Medinese* were regarded as a legal source. Besides the importance of the Prophet's community, this *maliki* concept also reflects the early tendency for the *ijma* 'to be a local geographical consensus (the *ijma* of *Kufah*, *Basra*, or *Madinah*) which became the *sunnah*, ideal pattern of behaviour of each local school (Esposito, 1976: 44).

A final historical source, mentioned by Esposito for the incorporation of custom in law was the *fatwas* (opinions) of *muftis*. The influence of custom on Islamic law is so great that it cannot be denied.

Coulson maintains that, in theory, a limited function is assigned to custom by *shariah* but in practice, especially in the field of commerce, the *shariah* was forced to give ground to customary law and practice. He gives the example of Berber customary law in Morocco, Muslim Africa and the fact that the *Shariat* Act of 1937, which sought to impose *shariah* law upon certain Muslim communities previously governed by custom, specifically excepted matters relating to agricultural land.²⁰ He further gives the example of Muslim communities of the *Ismai'li Khojas*, the *Bohars* and the *Cutchi Memons*, in the Indian sub-continent, who originally converted from Hinduism and, until comparatively recently, were governed by the Hindu law of testate and intestate succession. Coulson also shows how case law (binding judicial precedent) has entered into the application of *shariah* law through the influence of foreign legal systems. The same is true about systems of appeal (Coulson, 1959-61: 21). Coulson concludes:

> Externally and objectively doctrine and practice can only appear as component parts of a single entity - namely the law that governs the lives of Muslims; and it is, indeed, not so much the moribund *shariah* doctrine of the mediaeval texts, but rather the whole complex living reality of Muslim law - in the development of which a rich varity of stimuli, both indigenous and foreign, have been and are today at work - that provides such a wealth of fascinating material for the comparative lawyer (*ibid*: 24).

The gulf that exists between *shariah* doctrine on the one hand and actual Muslim legal practice on the other and a compromise between the two is provided with many examples by I.M. Lewis (Lewis, 1966). Leavy, while examining the role of custom in different countries, has also shown examples of how in the case of India custom has influenced the Islamic law. He observes that because of the influence of Hinduism in some Muslim communities in India, divorce is an occurrence of considerable rarity. Another reason for this could be that people are often married to their own relations. 'A wife who is divorced brings the greatest possible shame on all her people who happen to be also the people of her husband'. Again he says that the *shariah* laws of inheritance, which are based upon the rules of tribes owning easily divisible property consisting of flocks and herds and movables of other kinds, cannot be successfully applied amongst peoples whose property is chiefly or partly in land. Such laws are therefore disregarded in India, and he says it is seldom that a *qadi* is called upon, should there be any dispute, to determine 'shares' in accordance with the *shariah*. He says also:

> There is evidence for believing that, in one of the lesser and obscurer tribes living in Baluchistan, until recently a host might provide an unmarried, but nubile, girl for the better entertainment of a guest (Leavy, 1979: 247).

The *Zikris* of Baluchistan also, instead of performing the *haj*, go on the ninth day of the pilgrimage month to *koh Murad*, a hill in Kech (Leavy, 1979: 250). The custom of circumcising women, about which official Islam says nothing, is still widespread, being found in Islamic lands from India to Morocco (Leavy, 1979: 252).

During pre-British Muslim rule, some of the punishments prevalent among the Muslims were such as were not provided by the *shariah* (see Part 1.2). Recently a journalist travelling in Baluchistan wrote of her experience watching a person accused of murdering a cousin in a land dispute, 'walk the fire', a tribal ritual according to which if the person walked the fire and and was not burned, his accuser would have to pay him compensation, including the cost of firewood, and could never accuse him of this crime again. This resembles the trial by ordeal practised by the Hindus (Weaver, 1990).

In the survey conducted, the lawyers were asked about the role of customary law. In answer to the question whether disputes are settled according to customary law which is contrary to modern law, eighteen said yes, eight said no. Two accepted the existence of such custom in tribal areas and the interior of Sind (see Appendix I).

The future depends on how much Islamic law is interpreted in the light of changing circumstances and on the strength of modernism in Pakistan. As we have seen, even the classical sources of Islamic law could be used by Modernists to determine future development. The second important aspect is how much the Modernists will open themselves to the plurality of legal norms practised by the vast majority of people in Pakistan, of course keeping in view a certain standard of human rights.

Rashida Patel rightly says that the misinterpreted Islamic state laws, on the one hand, and old customs, on the other, are both repressive to women (Patel, 1991: 110).

1.12 CONCLUSION

This chapter has mentioned that the centralization of law was weaker before the British period. It became strong during the British period and a pattern was built by the British which Pakistan inherited along with an overdeveloped state structure. Classical concepts of ideology, such as superstructure and dominant ideology do not really altogether fit the situation of Pakistan. In Pakistan there is no coherent dominant and legal ideology, as has been documented with examples. Incoherence in ideology is due to different factors but the basic one has been the wide divergence of opinions. The classical concept of law, i.e., a myth of uniformity, is not helpful in providing an analysis of Pakistan. Legal pluralism helps against the mythology of legal centralism as pluralistic legal practices provide the other side of the picture. But legal pluralism, in my understanding, is only a way of thinking which does not really mean that local legal practices are a better alternative to the State legal order. Both systems have their own good and bad points.

Islamic revivalism started with the coming of dictatorship in Pakistan, basically to legitimize the illegal usurpation of power. Women were made the special target of Islamization, being used as scapegoats. This has not, however, succeeded, the strongest resistance against Islamization being provided by women.

The Pakistani legal system is inconsistent and unstable. This inconsistency and instability occurs in every country to some extent but, in the case of Pakistan, the degree is so high that it must be differentiated from that in other countries. Some other features added to this are discrimination, manipulation and corruption, etc.

Muslims' references to the sources of Islamic law have been used by the Modernist state for the development of Islamic law, though it also needs to be investigated how people use the reference of Islam when they are making changes and development in their legal practices. The influence of custom on Islam has been specially noticed.

It is very important that research be conducted in Pakistan to see how customary law has influenced people's practice of Islam. The pluralistic legal structure of Pakistan should be respected. It is appreciated that people should want to resolve their conflicts within the community in accordance with the custom and usage of the community. Of course customary law should only be given limited consideration on matters infringing human rights. This is specially true in family matters where it is considered to be a disgrace to bring the matter to court. Courts, for people in Pakistan, are external authorities to make final decisions, something that is also against the nature of the community, where mediation is preferred to the system where courts offer decisions in the form of guilty and not guilty.

The effect of custom on family law is wide. Sometime these customs are good and for the welfare of the community, and other times they are harmful for some individuals like child marriage and other customs dealing with the subordination of women. But because of these customs, laws meant as social reforms are not effective, as we have seen. The eradiction of illiteracy is fundamental and then the power of conflict solving should be distributed to the local units.

An organized study is required on pluralistic legal practices in Muslim countries or on the influence of custom on Islam.

Positive measures such as 'clarification, reform and systematization of the custom' would make some positive change in filling the gap between the law and practice.

These steps are difficult to take for a state which employs the law in its own interest. The Islamization of the law has been repressive and is ineffective. The MFLO, made by a more liberal government purporting to reform the whole fabric of the family structure, does not really affect the general population. It have not changed the traditional Muslim way of life. Behind the facade of Islamization, the majority of Pakistanis living in rural areas live the life of their ancestors, unaware of the laws of the cities. In the villages state laws are bypassed in favour of arbitration or, even more frequently, conciliation according to traditional procedure. The state law would only be effective if people found it was not too different from their own system. State laws involve them in too much litigation, long proceedings, bribery and corruption. But this is all related to the total development of society. Making the country more democratic, and recognising the plurality of Islamic beliefs, would prevent the law being used for the profit of the special element of society whose already privileged position is reinforced.

People have come to know about Islamization as a system of punishment, though the real effect of Islamization in the vast number of isolated villages in Pakistan remains to be seen. But we know from specific research that the reform laws did not make a considerable impact on the villagers who constitute the vast majority of the population of Pakistan. Reformative laws are only used by a small percentage of people living mostly in the cities.

CHAPTER 2

Islamic Provisions in the Constitutions of Pakistan

2.1 INTRODUCTION

The first Constituent Assembly of Pakistan was set up by the Indian Independence Act of 1947. Its principal task was to frame the new constitution and to act as a central legislature during the interim period. Until the framing of the constitution Pakistan was to be governed in accordance with the Government of India Act, 1935, suitably amended. Pakistan had no constitution of its own for the nine years from 1947 till 1956. During that period the country was basically governed by legislation passed during the colonial period.

Besides other controversial issues, one difficult task for the framers of the constitution was to decide the exact role of Islam in the newly created state. It was difficult to reach unanimity of opinion as to how the new constitution was to incorporate Islam because of controversy between Traditionalists and Modernists on this issue. The views of M.A. Jinnah, the architect of Pakistan, were not helpful because of his ambiguous, vague, contradictory and imprecise description of the Islamic state. His views were interpreted differently by the *ulema* and the politicians - the Modernists interpreted them to mean the creation of a modern national state, while the Traditionalists interpreted them to mean a 'traditional' Islamic state.

The constitution eventually enacted in 1956 was abrogated in 1958. The second was promulgated in 1962 and abrogated in 1969. The third constitution was enacted in 1973. This, though not abrogated by the next martial law regime, was amended so much during the period of rule by martial law in the 1980s that it became in fact a new constitution.

2.2 THE OBJECTIVES RESOLUTION

The Objectives Resolution was the first important document in the procedure of creating the Constitution of Pakistan. It was presented to the constituent Assembly by Liaquat Ali Khan, the Prime Minister, on 7 March, 1949. It was not a constitution, but merely a document outlining the aims and objects or general principles of a constitution to be drawn up in the future - in other words, one could call it 'a statement of intent' on which the future constitution was to be based. Binder described it as:

> merely a deposit on account, to be accepted as an indication of good faith' (Binder, 1963: 144).

Keith Callard explained it as a document 'to provide a declaration of national objectives, but certain aspects of the form of the future state are outlined in its provisions' (Callard, 1957: 90). The Resolution was debated for five days before adoption. The Preamble to the Resolution was retained by a vote of twenty-one to ten. All the amendments suggested by the opposition were defeated.

With the passage of time, this document became very important in the constitutional history of Pakistan. It was made the Preamble of the three constitutions of Pakistan. With the Zia regime's amendments to the constitution in 1986, it was made part of the Constitution of Pakistan itself. Justice Javid Iqbal, Chief Justice of the High Court at the time, describes the importance of the Objectives Resolution in these words:

> The *grundnorm* of Pakistan is enshrined in the Objectives Resolution which clearly states, among other things, that the Muslims in Pakistan would be enabled, individually and collectively, to order their lives in accordance with the teachings and requirements of Islam as set out in the *Quran* and *Sunna*. The principles contained in the Objectives Resolution have not been abrogated by anyone so far, nor have these been departed or deviated from by any regime, military or civil (Iqbal, Javid, 1984: 65).

The sections of the Resolution dealing with the role of religion are the following:[1]

> Whereas sovereignty over the entire universe belongs to God Almighty alone, and the authority which He has delegated to the

State of Pakistan through its people for being exercised within the limits prescribed by Him is a sacred trust;

This Constituent Assembly representing the people of Pakistan resolves to frame a Constitution for the sovereign independent State of Pakistan;

Wherein the State shall exercise its powers and authority through the chosen representatives of the people;

Wherein the principles of democracy, freedom, equality, tolerance and social justice, as enunciated by Islam shall be fully observed;

Wherein the Muslims shall be enabled to order their lives in the individual and collective spheres in accord with the teaching and requirements of Islam as set out in the Holy Quran and the Sunna;

Wherein adequate provision shall be made for the minorities freely to profess and practice their religions and develop their cultures;

Wherein shall be guaranteed fundamental rights including equality of status, of opportunity and before law, social, economic and political justice, and freedom of thought, expression, belief, faith, worship and association, subject to law and public morality;

Wherein adequate provision shall be made to safeguard the legitimate interests of minorities and backward and depressed classes;

Introducing the Resolution, Liaquat Ali Khan emphasized that the Islamic state of Pakistan would not be a theocratic state, because the idea of priesthood or any sacerdotal authority was absolutely foreign to Islam. He referred to those parts of the Resolution which speak of the authority of the people and the state's exercise of all power and authority through the chosen representatives of the people.[2]

Let us look, separately, at different parts of the Objectives Resolution and see what they meant in the eyes of different members of the Constituent Assembly and different scholars.

The clause 'sovereignty over the entire universe belongs to God Almighty alone, and the authority which he has delegated to the state of Pakistan through its people for being exercised within the limits prescribed by Him', was much debated in the Constituent Assembly. B.K. Datta and S.C. Chattopad, two non-Muslim members of the Assembly, asserted that, if sovereignty belongs to God, then it does not belong to the people and thus Pakistan could not be a democratic state.[3] They insisted on the separation of politics and religion; the Objectives Resolution intermingled the two, they said.

All the Muslim members of the Assembly approved the clause, with the exception of Mian Iftikharuddin who said that, by giving sovereignty to God, it had not done anything extraordinary. He assured the non-Muslim members:

> The objection that has been raised by the members of the Congress Party on this Resolution relates to the statement that power is derived from God. It has been said that it gives the Constitution a theocratic approach. Sir, I assure the members of the Congress Party that the wording of the preamble does not in any way make this Objectives Resolution any more theocratic, any more religious, than the resolution or the statement of the fundamental principles of some of the modern countries of the world - Ireland is not the only country that I know of - the Constitution of which starts with somewhat similar words about God.

Moreover, he said:

> As a matter of fact it amused me how the people of our country have hailed this preamble, this statement of objectives, as a new discovery. I see that a section of the press gave it out as if they had scored a journalistic scoop by reporting that the authority is derived from the higher power. Sir, the authority, whether we say it or not, is derived from that power. It does not lie within our power to change the laws of nature or to add to or detract from the power of nature's God. Therefore, in having stated that, we have not done anything very extraordinary, and the members of the Congress Party may rest assured that the God of the Muslims, the conception of *Allah* in the Muslim religion, is in no way less merciful than the conception of the Almighty in other religions, the objection from the party opposite is not an important objection at all.[4]

He also objected to the expression '...authority delegated to the state of Pakistan through its people'. He said that the state should not have been mentioned separately.

> We know that the final authority to decide about the limits, the final authority to interpret the rights of the people, is the people themselves. To bring in, therefore, the agency of the state is to confuse the issue (*ibid:* 366).

What Mian Iftikharuddin meant by the expression 'sovereignty of God' was absolutely different from what the *ulema* meant by this expression. To the *ulema* this expression was crucial, because it meant that *shariah* (Islamic law) would be the law of the land. Sovereignty of Allah meant that the law (*shariah*) prescribed by Allah would be implemented. With reference to this it should be remembered that *shariah* is seen as immutable law because it is God-made, not man-made, and the expression 'within the limits prescribed by God' was also interpreted by the Traditionalists as limits prescribed by *shariah*.[5]

As far as the analysis of different writers on this issue is concerned, one opinion is that the sovereignty of Allah is, in any case, of spiritual and not political relevance. According to another opinion the sovereignty of Allah in the Objectives Resolution is not only of spiritual value, but of political importance (Sandeela, 1978). According to Rosenthal, the expression that 'the entire universe belongs to God' stresses the fact that the delegation of authority to the people by God is limited. This clearly implies the establishment of Islamic law (Rosenthal, 1965: 210). Rosenthal does not find any popular sovereignty contained in the Objectives Resolution. On the other hand G.W. Choudhury holds that the sovereignty of God is not in conflict with popular sovereignty, which is one of the ingredients of democracy. He says:

> In such a conformation of the state, there is nothing that may be incompatible or out of tune with the spirit and tradition of democracy or of rule by the people (Choudhury, G.W., 1971: 37).

It is interesting to compare that with Rosenthal's view that the expression 'sovereign independent state of Pakistan' is no more than an 'expression taken over from Western Constitutions by those who drafted the Resolution in an attempt to please both sides' (Rosenthal, 1965: 210), because it is absolutely irreconcilable with the concept of the sovereignty of God. As far as the sovereignty clause is concerned, Binder's remarks are very interesting. He says:

> The Objectives Resolution acknowledged the sovereignty of God, recognized the authority of the people derived from their creator, and vested the authority delegated by the people in the Constituent Assembly for the purpose of making a constitution for the sovereign state of Pakistan. Thus is God sovereign, the people sovereign, Parliament sovereign, and the state sovereign in Pakistan. It would indeed be a narrow-minded people who was not satisfied with such a compromise" (Binder, 1963: 149).

We should also look at the remarks of Afzal Iqbal, a Modernist, about the sovereignty clause. He says:

> The Objectives Resolution talked of the people's resolve 'to frame a Constitution for the sovereign, independent state of Pakistan'. The State and God are both sovereign, and so perhaps was the Constituent Assembly which was to 'frame a Constitution'. The recital of such simultaneous sovereignty is misleading. Does it not deny the Ulama's claim that the divine law is already there; It has only to be elaborated and applied, not 'framed', as the Resolution suggested (Iqbal, Afzal, 1986: 46).

The sovereignty clause was in fact set out as a compromise. It satisfied everyone as it could be taken differently by different people. Manzooruddin Ahmed illustrates it like this:

> The liberals admitted the idea of divine sovereignty over the entire universe as a general moral precept, while the theologians were keen to apply this principle in such a way that it enveloped the whole constitutional set up of Pakistan. They wanted to make it an active principle in determining the Islamic character of the government (Ahmed, 1965: 210).

In the fourth paragraph of the Resolution, the assertion that democracy, freedom, equality, tolerance and social justice 'as enunciated by Islam' shall be observed, was again criticized by the non-Muslim members of the Constituent Assembly. One of these members B.K. Datta, in stating the objections said of the clause 'as enunciated by Islam' that it

> ... at once created a ruling race, the patricians of Pakistan, and condemned the minorities to an inferior status. The nation would

remain communally divided into two distinct houses, the minorities tasting neither democracy, nor freedom, nor equality, nor social justice, but being merely tolerated. Non-Muslim members felt that democracy 'as enunciated by Islam' would condemn them forever to an inferior status".[6]

G.W. Choudhury argued that the problem of the non-Muslim religious minorities was further complicated with the passing of the Objectives Resolution. It proposed a Islamic state wherein 'the principles like democracy, freedom, equality, tolerance and social justice have been qualified to give a well understood meaning. This puts the non-Muslim minorities in a difficult position. In spite of all tolerance for non-Muslims in Islam they have definitely inferior status' (Choudhury, G.W., 1956: 315-16).

The Pakistan Times wrote:

> It was not clear whether the principles of democracy, freedom, etc. were to be fully observed because all these principles had been enunciated by Islam, or whether some special brand of these principles had yet to be evolved in accordance with some particular individual's enunciation of Islam; if the former, the formula would be progressive and straight-forward; if the latter, it might easily open the door to disruptionist and sectarian tendencies.[7]

J.N.D Anderson has asked:

> One wonders what, precisely, the phrase 'Islamic principles of social justice' really means. No doubt there are many principles of social justice which are enunciated in the sacred texts of Islam; but a non-Muslim can not help wondering, first, whether Muslims in Pakistan or elsewhere would claim that these are in any way distinctively or peculiarly 'Islamic'. Do they really differ in any material respect from principles of social justice accepted in non-Muslim countries? Secondly, one wonders what Muslims would say in this context of the classical Islamic attitude to such matters as slavery, the position of women, and the rights of non-Muslims in a Muslim state (Anderson, J.N.D., 1967: 128-29).

Paragraph Five of the Objectives Resolution promises a society where 'Muslims shall be enabled to order their lives in the individual and collective spheres in accord with the teachings and requirements of Islam as set out in the *Holy Quran* and the *Sunna*'. G.W. Choudhury says that the clause implies that the state would create conditions conducive to the building up of a truly Islamic state. However, he sees a danger if Islamic ideology is not given a progressive and dynamic interpretation. He says that otherwise such a clause might prove to be an excellent tool in the hands of reactionary *ulemas* (Choudhury, G.W., 1971: 38).

Three paragraphs of the Resolution deal with the rights of minorities; non-Muslim members were the only members who were dissatisfied with the Resolution and did not take part in praising it (Calder, 1956). Full assurance to the non-Muslims that they would be free to profess their religion and culture, and the three assurance clauses did not initially satisfy them (Khel, 1984: 48). The Traditionalists, though, thought that the Resolution placed unnecessary emphasis on the rights of non-Muslims. Prime Minister Liaquat Ali and Foreign Minister Mohammad Zafrullah Khan and others, however, assured non-Muslims of protection.

Non-Muslims had grounds for apprehension and in fact the assurances given were not in accordance with the traditional Muslim concept of *Dhimmis*. The statements of Maulana Shabbir Ahmad Osmani, one of the *ulema* of Deoband, added to the apprehensions of the non-Muslims. He said that non-Muslims could not be entrusted with the responsibility of framing the general policy of the state, or dealing with matters vital to its safety and integrity.[8] A long discussion then ensued to assure Congress and the minorities in general that their rights would be guaranteed. Ishtiaq Hussain Qureshi explained that Islamic principles were not in conflict with the United Nations Charter on Human Rights.[9] Liaquat Ali Khan said that Islamic democracy was 'distinguished from both the democracy of the West and the democracy of the Soviet Union; it was in fact more democratic than both'.[10] A number of assurances and explanations came from other Muslim leaders. The foreign Minister, Zafrullah Khan, and Sardar A.R. Nishtar also reassured the minority members. S.E. Chattopadhyaya protested vigorously: 'You are determined to create a Herrenvolk ... This resolution in its present form epitomizes the spirit of reaction'. For the minorities, 'a thick curtain is drawn against all rays of hope, all prospects of an honourable life'.

To conclude, the non-Muslim members showed great dissatisfaction with the Objectives Resolution, as they feared future second-class status. They thought that the Resolution would set aside Jinnah's concept of a secular democratic state.[11] However, both Modernists and Traditionalists among the Muslims were satisfied as 'the words of the Resolution spoke differently to different people', thus 'the Resolution was in a way a compromise', i.e., it:

... represented a compromise between the two main strands of opinion: the *Mullah* element, who would like to see Pakistan a true Islamic State and who considers that politics must derive inspiration from *Shariat*, and the westernized elements, who, inspired by westernized ideas and institutions, consider that politics and religion should be divorced from each other (Rashiduzzaman, 1967: 86).

Traditionalists felt happy with the Resolution, because it was a matter of great satisfaction for them that the principle of the supremacy of God in matters of state had been established and that the government stood committed to give effect to this principle (Rahman, Fazlur, 1974: 31). Khurshid Ahmad, a Traditionalist, remarked that with the passing of the Objectives Resolution, the purpose of the state of Pakistan was clearly defined and thus the first round of the fight between the people and their rulers was won by the people. By 'rulers' he meant the westernized, ruling group (Ahmad, Khurshid, 1980: 28).

The Modernists felt content because the Resolution laid down, in highly imprecise terms, the broad Islamic objectives of the future constitution without even bringing in the word Shariat (Rehman, 1982). But later developments showed that the compromise was only temporary. Rashiduzzaman illustrates the dissatisfaction of the traditionalist.

Neither the Westernized intellectuals, nor the *Mullah* elements could really be satisfied. The *Mullah* elements felt that the democratic institutions of Western style which the proposed constitution would bring and make room only for the lawyer-politicians who have little respect for the orthodox views inspired by *Quran* and *Sunnah* (Rashiduzzaman, 1967: 86).

The compromise Resolution was a confused document; it shows the uncertainty of the members as to the concept of the Islamic state. Inamur Rehman says:

Being a general formulation, however, the Resolution lay open to different interpretation by both sides who, in subsequent months, did not fail to invoke its clauses to press for the acceptance of their respective concepts of an Islamic state (Rehman, 1982: 8).

The Objectives Resolution did not have any practical effect.

2.3 THE CONSTITUTION OF 1956 AND ITS ISLAMIC PROVISIONS

2.3.1 The Constitution of 1956 and the Objectives Resolution

The period in between the passing of the Objectives Resolution and that of the Constitution of 1956, was a long period of struggle between Modernists and Traditionalists.

The Objectives Resolution was made the preamble of the Constitution with few changes. After the clause dealing with the sovereignty of *Allah*, a new clause was added reading 'Whereas the founder of Pakistan, Quaid-i-Azam Mohamed Ali Jinnah, declared that Pakistan would be a democratic state based on Islamic principles of social justice'. From the clause dealing with the sovereignty of God the reference to the delegation of authority was taken away. The new form of the clause read: 'Whereas sovereignty over the entire Universe belongs to Allah Àlmighty alone, and the authority to be exercised by the people of Pakistan within the limits prescribed by him is a sacred trust'. This did not make any difference to the meaning of the clause.

Law Minister Chundrigar explained the reason for deletion of the word 'delegate'; he explained that 'delegate' was likely to create more than one apprehension. 'How was one to say the delegation had been made? Why had it been made to one people and not to others? And through whom was such delegation conveyed?' (Choudhury, G.W., 1971: 180).

Parmatma Sharan, an Indian writer, thinks that recognizing the sovereignty of God gave a spiritual basis to the Constitution (Sharan, 1968: 49). Fazlur Rahman has a very interesting evaluation of the 'God's sovereignty' clause in the Constitution - he does not interpret it as Maududi does in the preamble: that this is political sovereignty which is transferred to God. He says:

> The truth, however, is that the sovereignty clause, as it was actually adopted in these Constitutions, represents a compromise between the Ulama (led in this respect by Mawdudi) on the one hand and the Modernists on the other. For the *Ulama* wanted this clause to mean explicitly that the *Shariah* as expressive of God's Will be sovereign. This would have meant subjugation of the present legislature to the entire gamut of historic Islam's experience. The Modernists, therefore, found it expedient to accept the sovereignty of God in general terms, even though the concept of sovereignty of God had no meaning at all in the political context and, in fact, leads to ludicrous consequences.

While, therefore, making a compromise under pressure from the rightists, the Modernists in reality succumbed to the conceptual framework of the rightists inasmuch as they accepted 'God's Sovereignty' rather than asserting, as they should have done in honesty, that sovereignty belongs to the people of Pakistan, who, being consciously Muslims, willed that Islam be implemented in Pakistani society both at the individual and the collective levels (Rahman, Fazlur, 1970: 277-8).

Fazlur Rahman further criticizes the insertion of the statement in the Objectives Resolution: 'Whereas the founder of Pakistan, Qaid-i-Azam Muhammed Ali Jinnah, declared that Pakistan would be a democratic state based on Islamic principles of social justice...' it is unclear how sovereignty of God is immediately expressed by the authority of Muhammed Ali Jinnah. Fazlur Rahman is very open in his criticism, asking why concepts like social justice, freedom, equality and tolerance, etc. should be described as 'Islamic' and, if this is so, why the expression 'Islamic' is not used in connection with concepts like the representative form of government, safeguarding minorities' rights, etc. Fazlur Rahman finds this lacuna in the whole Constitution: 'where, that is to say, positive values are involved as distinguished from the purely technical side of statecraft'. The reason he gives for this state of affairs is the bitter struggle between 'rightists' (i.e., Traditionalists) and Modernists over the meaning of an Islamic state. While describing this struggle, he says the Traditionalists meant by the sovereignty of God the implementation of *shariah,* which further meant the revival and resuscitation of the past, but that their demands would boil down in particular to a few specific institutions. For example, public prayers, fasting, the *zakat* tax and pilgrimage were the positive demands while, on the negative side, were demands for the implementation of legal penalities for theft, adultery and drinking of alcohol, etc. This is considered by Rahman as misuse of the *shariah* which entered Islam in the middle ages.

On the other hand, the Modernists reinterpreted Islam in response to Western domination but, while seeking to prove the 'superiority' of Islamic teachings to Westerners, their aggressive revivalism gave it a reactionary, revivalist or negative content. Traditionalists were satisfied with 'minimal' and 'negative' Islam (*ibid*: 281-2). A third group, Secularists, came close to the *ulema* and the Traditionalists since they allegedly represented an individual's private duties to God, claims Fazlur Rahman. Neither the Secularists nor the Modernists included a complete separation of state and religion in their programme on the pattern of Turkish secularism. He concludes:

> We are now able to understand the constitutional dilemma of the Modernist. Under pressure from the revivalist on the one side, the secularist on the other, continuously harassed by the *Ulema* (who, mainly because of the faintheartedness of the Modernist, do wield considerable influence on the masses) and, above all, by his lack of a strong faith in his own Modernism, he cannot find a firm *locus standi*. Even thus emerges the constitution as a truly Islamic fetish: a mere ad hoc and mechanical application of the term "Islamic" to certain concepts, to the exclusion of others. 'Islamic justice and tolerance'... Why are not human rights Islamic? What about education and health? And above all, is not the eradication of poverty - the removal of poverty being the *sine qua non* of 'enabling the Muslims of Pakistan individually and collectively to order their lives in accordance with the principles and concepts of Islam' - a fundamental Islamic duty? (*ibid*: 285).

Fazlur Rahman believes that the constitutions of Pakistan have failed in their ideological target and calls them an 'Islamic fetish' (Rahman, Fazlur, 1970: 280-5).

2.3.2 Islamic Provisions in the Constitution of 1956

Pakistan was defined as the 'Islamic Republic of Pakistan' in Part I, Art. 1(1) of the 1956 constitution. Naming the federal republic thus was not held to be equivalent to making Islam the state religion of Pakistan, according to different writers on the subject (Choudhury, G.W., 1971: 103). Very few showed dissatisfaction with this article.[12]
  Part II, dealing with fundamental rights, provided safeguards for educational institutions in respect of religion, etc. (Art. 13); guarantees of non-discrimination in respect of access to public places (Art. 14); safeguards against discrimination in services (Art. 17); guarantees freedom to profess any religion and to manage religious institutions (Art. 18); and safeguards against taxation to support any particular religion (Art. 21).
  Part III, named 'Directive Principles of State Policy', was declared to be not enforceable in any court (Art. 23(2)); it was only to be the guiding principles for the state authority. It continued with religious statements. It laid down that the state

was to strengthen the bonds of unity among Muslim countries (Art. 24). G.W. Choudhury says the clause 'to strengthen the bonds of unity among Muslim countries' should not be interpreted as pan-Islamic (Choudhury, G.W., 1971: 103). The state was further to enable the Muslims of Pakistan to order their lives according to the *Quran* and the *Sunna* by providing facilities to understand the Islamic philosophy of life (Art. 25(2),(a)); by making teaching of the *Quran* compulsory, (Art. 25(2),(b)); by promoting Islamic moral standards (Art. 25(2),(c)); and by securing the proper organization of *zakat, waqfs* and mosques (Art. 25(2)(d)). It further provided that minorities would not be discriminated against, 'including their due representation in the Federal and Provincial Services' (Art. 27). Prevention of prostitution, gambling and taking of injurious drugs is also promised (Art. 28(e)) while, regarding the prohibition of alcoholic liquor, it is stated that it would be allowed for medical purposes and for consumption by non-Muslims (Art. 28(f)). *Riba* (usury) would be eliminated 'as early as possible' (Art. 29(f)).

The Constitution of 1956 stipulated that the President of Pakistan (the head of state) must be a Muslim (part IV, Art. 32(2)). In the absence of the President, the Speaker of the National Assembly would exercise the function of the President. The Speaker could be a non-Muslim (Art. 36). The provision that only a Muslim could be the President of Pakistan, was held to be the only discriminatory provision in the whole Constitution. It is important to note that this condition is not obligatory on the acting head of state or on the working head of state. This means that in some situations the temporary head of state could be a non-Muslim. G.W. Choudhury provides justification for this discriminatory clause by saying that:

> Pakistan was founded on the basis of Islamic philosophy and it was therefore logical that the president as symbolic Head should be amongst those believing in that philosophy (*ibid:* 104).

But elsewhere he also says:

> This clause seems to have done considerable harm to the liberal interpretation of the 'Islamic state' in Pakistan. The sooner it is amended the better (*op.cit.*, 1956: 319).

Part XII of the Constitution was entitled 'General Provisions' and contained among others the subtitle 'Islamic Provisions'. This part of the Constitution provided for the setting up by the President of an organization for Islamic research and instruction in advanced studies to assist in the reconstruction of Muslim society (Art. 197(1)).

Article 198(1) is very important. It says: 'No law shall be enacted which is repugnant to the injunctions of Islam as laid down in the *Holy Quran* and *Sunna* ... and existing law shall be brought into conformity with such injunctions'. There is a note at the end of Article 198 which says: 'In the application of this Article to the personal law of any Muslim sect, the expression *Quran* and *Sunna* shall mean the *Quran* and *Sunna* as interpreted by that sect'. This note clearly implies the recognition of different sects. It also provided that the President should appoint a Commission to advise on the enactment of Islamic law (Art. 198 (3)).[13] The Commission would give a report which finally would come before the National Assembly which 'after considering the report shall enact laws in respect thereof' (Art. 198 (3)(a)(b)). It is, however, assured that nothing in this article shall affect the status of non-Muslims including their personal laws (Art. 198 (4)). The most striking thing about Article No. 198 is the avoidance of use of the word *shariah*, only the words *Quran* and *Sunna* being used (Iqbal, Afzal, 1986: 69).

These provisions, named the 'Islamic provisions' were never carried out. Major-General Iskander Mirza is the one most accused of their non-implementation. (He is reported to have said 'we cannot run wild on Islam' (Choudhury, G.W., 1971: 105)). No move was made to appoint a Commission or to establish the organization for Islamic research.

Part of the Objectives Resolution dealing with non-Muslim minorities was made the Preamble of the Constitution - as we have seen. Minorities were assured equal treatment in Part II of the Constitution, dealing with fundamental rights. There was no discrimination on grounds of race, colour or religion in respect to citizenship or the enforcement of fundamental rights.

The Directive Principles of State Policy provided further safeguards for the minorities. Article 28(f) even assured them of the right to consume alcoholic liquor for religious purposes, which would otherwise not be allowed. Due representation of the minorities in the federal and provincial services was assured in Article 27.

2.3.3 Conclusion

The Islamic provisions of the Constitution were not effective. Neither the Preamble nor the Directive Principles, where most of the Islamic provisions were to be found, had the force of law. Islam was, in practice, legally enforceable in two major ways only. Firstly, by Article 32(2) requiring the appointment of a Muslim president, and secondly through Articles 107 and 198, providing for the organization of Islamic research and the appointment of a Commission, etc., to bring existing laws into conformity with Islam.

Most writers have analysed the Constitution as a compromise between Traditionalists and Modernists, but in the end both sides abused it because of its attitude of hypocrisy and vagueness as to its Islamic provisions. Afzal Iqbal, a Modernist, remarks: 'The Constitution had an Islamic facade, but the hard core was missing' (Iqbal, Afzal, 1986: 65). He further says:

> The declaration of divine sovereignty in the Preamble was irrelevant to the interpretation of the Constitution because Pakistan was created as a territorial state with its citizenship regulations and nationality laws. The traditional concept of the *Ummah* has now undergone a change. In the Preamble of the Constitution of 1956, which delegates authority to the people of Pakistan, the idea of the traditional Universal *Ummah* has been abandoned because the people of Pakistan comprise Muslims and non-Muslims. No distinction is made between the two in fundamental rights on the basis of faith. The Constitution also departs from the classical theory by investing the final interpretation of the *Quran* and *Sunna* to the legislature rather than to the theologians. The framers of the Constitution do not envisage Pakistan as a mediaeval Islamic state (Iqbal, Afzal, 1986, 68).

He continues:

> The first Constitution of Pakistan seems to suggest that its framers decided to borrow the political institutions of the West and made an effort to invest them with the spirit of Islam. A liberal interpretation of Islam was incorporated into the Constitution. The institution of representative government was reconciled with the fundamental principles of Islam and the idea of restoring medieval political institutions was rejected (*ibid:* 69).

Muhammad Nazeer Kaka Khel from the Faculty of Law, University of Peshawar, attributes the failure of the Constituent Assembly to embody the principles of Islamic policy in the constitution to political pressure from non-Muslims and secularist circles. He says:

The fundamentals of the Constitution were the result of the compromises, whereas on principles no compromises can be made' and 'When the very foundation of the state was laid down on wrong principles, the Constitution had to collapse and it did collapse' (Khel, 1982: 71).

In making a general evaluation of the Islamic provisions of the Constitution, G.W. Choudhury's remarks are realistic. He says:

Despite the many divergent concepts of the character of an Islamic Constitution, in the end the framers of the Constitution were successful in introducing one which was a commendable synthesis of modern needs and Islamic principles (Choudhury, G.W., 1971: 103).

The precise nature of the Islamic state was never defined. It was a compromise between Traditionalists and Modernists.

The Constitution of 1956 reflected the long years of debate and the differences between traditionalists and modernists. Its final form underscored the lack of any clear idea or consensus regarding an Islamic ideology and how to translate it into programs and policies. The document represented an eclectic compromise which embodied many of those aspects associated with a secular state while injecting several Islamic provisions (Esposito, 1980b: 143).

This Constitution was called a compromise between Modernists and Traditionalists as far as the Islamic provisions are concerned, because the Modernists were satisfied that Islam was woven into the fabric of the state as a matter of policy and not of law. This is why they also avoided the word *shariah* - while the Traditionalists hoped that the provision saying that all laws should be made in conformity with the *Quran* would mean adoption of the legal aspects of Islam. Mahfuzul Haq explains the two tendencies and their eventual compromise as follows:

The debate reflected two contrary currents; one represented by the Western-educated League leaders and the other represented by the orthodox *Ulama*. It was a difficult task for both the groups to come to an agreed formula. One leaned more to secular democracy than to religious foundation of the state, the other towards the golden days of the caliphs. The conflict resulted in a great confusion in the attempt to define the basic principles of an Islamic State. The problem to frame a constitution which would be as much Islamic as to please the *Ulama* and the religious-minded illiterate masses and also as much modern and democratic as to satisfy the Western-educated and the non-Muslim (Huq, 1966: 209-10).

The Constitution of 1956 was basically modern in its character. Islamic provisions were only symbolic in nature. Their practical influence on law was not visible. The Islamic provisions were mostly a compromise and therefore vague.

2.4 THE CONSTITUTION OF 1962 AND ITS ISLAMIC PROVISIONS

The second Constitution of Pakistan was directly affected by the thinking of President Ayub Khan (who seized power with the help of the army in 1958). As far as the religious provisions of the Constitution are concerned, he stressed a progressive interpretation of Islam. In a convocation address at the Darul Uloom Islamia, Tando Allahyar, on 3 March 1959, he said that there was a danger that with the passage of time Muslims would stress only the dogmatic aspects of Islam, which would result in a widening gap between life and religion, and those who looked forward would be regarded as disbelievers:

> This I consider a great disservice to Islam, that such a noble religion should be represented as inimical to progress. Besides, this is most unfair to our youth who do wish to be faithful Muslims in a modern world. In fact, it is a great injustice to both life and religion to impose on twentieth century man the condition that he must go back several centuries in order to prove his bona fides as a true Muslim (Khan, Mohammad Ayub, 1958-9: 111).

But his progressive Islam stood for meeting the challenge of communism as well as Western democracy:

> The world today is divided sharply into two camps. This conflict is based on differences of ideology. Communism is determined to impose its own ideology on the entire world, and an effective and complete answer to communism has not yet been found in the West because Western ideology is based primarily on materialism. Values arising from materialism no doubt have a

place in the scheme of things, but they are not so important that mankind should sacrifice everything for their sake. In these circumstances, there is only one answer to communism and that answer is to be found in Islam. Between the ideological doctrine of communism and the materialistic values of the West, Islam alone provides a natural ideology that can save the soul of humanity from destruction (*ibid:* 113).

He stressed that being true to both Islamic ideology and his progressive Islam meant a blending of religious and secular instruction (*op.cit.*, 1960-1: 53). He said:

I feel that during the early period of Islam the Nationalists and the Religious Divines were not so wide apart as they are today. Science has made tremendous progress - man has not only orbited the earth but is reaching for the moon. On the other hand, religious thought has lost its original dynamism and is bogged down in the quagmire of stagnation. Actually there is no conflict between science and religion (*op.cit.*, 1962-3: 25-6).

On 15 January 1959, President Ayub, while specifying matters to be insisted upon in the future constitution, had 'insisted on the rule of law' and 'independence of judiciary', but made no mention of Islamic provisions (*op.cit.*, 1958-9: 41-2). Herbert Feldman has, though, traced in the speeches of Ayub a declaration that the new constitution would reflect Islamic principles. This trend, however, was only apparant from the end of 1959 to the beginning of 1960 (Feldman, 1967: 196). It is relevant to remember here that the much-opposed MFLO, introducing extensive prospects of traditional Islamic law, was passed in 1961, just one year before the constitution was enacted.

The Constitution of 1962 was amended in important respects in 1964. These amendments will be referred to later.

2.4.1 The Constitution of 1962 and the Objectives Resolution

The Objectives Resolution with modifications was retained as the Preamble of the 1962 Constitution. The most important modifications made were: from the first statement of the Resolution that sovereignty over the entire universe belongs to *Allah* and authority exercisable by the people is a sacred trust, the qualifying phrase 'within the limits prescribed by Him' was eliminated in 1962. But after severe public criticism Ayub Khan had to restore the expression in January 1964. G.W. Choudhury rightly thinks that the initial exclusion was to avoid difficulties in determining the limits prescribed by God. The question could arise as to what were those limits, who would decide those limits and so forth. He further thinks that the justification for deleting the expression 'delegate' in the Preamble to the 1956 Constitution, provided by the Law Minister of that time, could have been used for the deletion of the words 'limits prescribed by God'. We think that wording was simpler than any of the earlier two drafts. But the reintroduction of this expression, he says:

> ... has not strengthened anything, but reintroduced the older confusion (Choudhury, G.W., 1971: 180).

Faruki on the other hand does not think that the 'interjection of God's sovereignty' is a confusion. He comments:

> By acknowledging the sovereignty of God we are saying that His commands must be the paramount law of the land to which all man-made rules and regulations must conform or be cast aside. This stands in sharp contrast to the constitutional position in many other countries. In England for example, it is asserted that Parliament can make or unmake any law whatsoever. In the United States, laws have to be in conformity with the written constitution but as this constitution was framed and can be amended by the people of the United States there is ultimately no check upon the American people making or unmaking any law whatsoever. But in Pakistan situation at no time does the Constitution countenance a law which contravenes the law of God (Faruki, 1966: 28).

A second important change was to the second clause of the Resolution which says that the founders of Pakistan declared Pakistan to be a democratic state based on Islamic principles of social justice; the phrase 'expressing the will of the people' was added. The rest of the Islamic provision of the Resolution was retained. The third important change made to the Objectives Resolution was in the statement that the Muslims of Pakistan should be enabled, individually and collectively, to order their lives in accordance with the teachings and requirements of Islam: the preamble in the 1956 Constitution had said 'as set out in the *Holy Quran* and *Sunna*'. This was replaced with 'Islam'. But the Amendment Act again restored the bases of all laws as being the *Quran* and *Sunna*.

2.4.2 Islamic Provisions in the Constitution of 1962

In Part I, the name of the state of Pakistan was held to be the 'Republic of Pakistan' (Art. 1(1)). The expression 'Islamic Republic of Pakistan' was eliminated. But this expression was again added in 1964. This change was brought about through the Constitution First Amendment Act of 1963 (taking effect in 1964) passed by the National Assembly. Fazlur Rahman remarked that President Ayub soon realised the importance of taking Islam seriously at the state level.

> As time went on Ayyub Khan became more and more convinced of the importance of Islam as the basis of the Pakistani nationhood (Rahman, Fazlur, 1976: 284-5).

Part II, entitled 'Fundamental Rights' in 1956, was given a new heading, i.e., 'Principles of Law-making and of Policy'. In the first principle of law-making it was declared that 'no law should be repugnant to Islam' (Art. 1). The main responsibility for deciding rested upon the legislature, although National and Provincial Assemblies, the President or the Governor of a province might refer to the Advisory Council of Islamic Ideology for advice whether a proposed law was not in accordance with the Principles (Art. 6(1)).

In the Constitution of 1956, Article 198 had referred to *Quran* and *Sunna* for enactment of laws, while in 1962 it was only referred to as 'Islam'. Moreover, this provision is not enforceable in a court of law, while Article 198 was enforceable in a law court.

In fact, there was no article to ensure the bringing of all laws into conformity with the laws of Islam. But both elements were added in the first amendment (Part II 1). In the Constitution of 1956, the phrase *'Holy Quran and Sunna'* had been used as the source of Islamic doctrine and practice. In the Constitution of 1962 it was replaced by the word 'Islam' F. Rahman says that:

> It led to the general suspicion that this has been done in order to eliminate the *Sunna* of the prophet as the second binding Islamic source besides the *Quran* (Rahman, Fazul, 1976: 286).

J.N.D. Anderson has raised another important question in this regard. He says that what does 'conformity with the *Holy Quran* and *Sunna*' really mean? He rightly asks why are only the *Holy Quran* and *Sunna* mentioned when there are four major sources of Islamic law. Even if just the *Quran* and *Sunna* are mentioned these two also need further explanation because of difference of opinion about these two as well (Anderson, J.N.D., 1967: 129-30).

The footnote to Article 198 of the Constitution of 1956, saying that '*Quran and Sunna* would mean the *Quran* and *Sunna* as interpreted by the sect concerned', was also restored in 1964. In all other fundamental rights, non-Muslims were assured of equal treatment. It was further held that no law would prevent a religious community from professing, practising or propagating their religion (Art. 7 (a)). No law would compel a person to any religious practice other than his own (Art. 7 (b)). No tax would be imposed for the purpose of supporting any religion other than his own (Art. 7 (c)). There would be no discrimination for grants or exemption of tax between different religious institutions (Art. 7 (d)). Nor would there be any authorization of the expenditure of public moneys for the benefit of a particular religious community or denomination except out of moneys raised for that purpose (Art. 7 (e)).

The Directive Principles of State Policy of the 1956 Constitution are repeated with some modifications in the Principles of Policy in 1962. The modifications were changes of expression; for example, instead of 'prevention of alcohol', the words 'consumption of alcohol would be discouraged' were used in the 1962 constitution. Another minor change in the Directive Principles was the promise to make the teaching of the *Quran* Islamiat compulsory for the Muslims of Pakistan. The word 'Islamiat' was not used in the relevant Article of the 1956 constitution. The Constitution of 1956 it had provided that the Muslims of Pakistan should be enabled, individually and collectively, to order their lives in accordance with the *Holy Quran* and *Sunna,* while the Constitution of 1962 has substituted 'lives in accordance with the fundamental principles and basic concepts of Islam'.

Further it was laid down in the Principles of Policy that unity and the observance of Islamic moral standards should be promoted amongst the Muslims of Pakistan, and that the proper organization of zakat, waqfs and mosques should be ensured (Art. 1(4)). Article 21 provided for strengthening the bonds of unity amongst Muslim countries.

In Part III, one of the qualifications for the office of the President was that he had to be a Muslim (Art.10). G.W. Choudhury finds this the only discriminatory clause against religious minorities, but he says that due to the existence of this Article in the Principles of Policy:

... members of the minorities should be given due opportunity to enter the services of Pakistan. Hence there is no basis for apprehension that the Islamic provisions in the Constitution will relegate non-Muslim citizens to an inferior status (Choudhury, G. W., 1971: 181-2).

Part X, Islamic Institutions, showed marked changes in comparison to 1956. It provided for the establishment of two institutions, the 'Advisory Council of Islamic Ideology' and the 'Islamic Research Institute' (Art. 199, Art. 207(1)). The Constitution laid down for the Council the method of appointment of its members (Art. 201), their term of office, etc. (Art. 202). Article 204 described the function of the Council as: 'To make recommendations, to the Central and Provincial government, on the means for enabling Muslims to order their lives in accordance with the principles of Islam'. The Council was also to advise whether a law referred to it disregarded, violated, or otherwise was not in accord with the 'principles of law making' (Art. 204). But no authority was obliged to follow the advice of the Council and a reference to the Advisory Council was not mandatory.

The function of the Islamic Research Institute was 'to undertake Islamic research and instruction in Islam for the purpose of assisting in the reconstruction of Muslim society on a truly Islamic basis' (Art. 207(2)). It is important to note here that the Constitution of 1962 contained no provision to bring existing laws into conformity with the *Quran* and *Sunna*, which had been provided in the Islamic provisions of 1956. But this was inserted again through an amendment in 1963. The act of creating the Advisory Council of Islamic Ideology was held to be a positive step forward in doing something practical. But it should be noted that the advice of the Council was in no way binding on the Government. This was also made clear by Ayub Khan when he said:

> This body is an advisory body. It is not an elected body. It cannot have super powers over the elected body. It is the legislature and the President who will be elected by the people. It is therefore they who finally accept the responsibility for making laws and giving decisions. The function of the Council, backed by the Islamic Research Institute, is to procure considered, well thought out and scientific advice. But they cannot be put in a position of veto. That will be fatal (Khel, 1982: 73).

Afzal Iqbal has discussed the performance of the Council, which he criticizes (Iqbal, Afzal, 82). The members of the Council were 'repeated targets' for the Traditionalists. They called the Council 'a laboratory of the government to create a new Islam not preached by the Holy Prophet' (Weekes, 1964: 131). The Council continued to exist even after the imposition of martial law. A new council was appointed in 1974.

The Islamic Research Institute was established in 1959. It continued under the Constitution of 1962.

The Constitution of 1962 differed in its Islamic provisions from that of 1956 to the extent that it established the Advisory Council of Islamic Ideology and Research Institute. This step was hailed (Iqbal, Sardar Muhammad, 1975).[14] Fazlur Rahman, making a comparison of the religious provisions of the constitution of 1956 and the constitution of 1962, says:

> Of the two constitutions, it must be said in fairness that the 1956 Constitution is far less consistent with its Islamic vocation than the 1962 (1964) Constitution. Having declared that the Muslims of Pakistan shall be enabled to lead their lives individually and collectively in accordance with Islam, it proposes to do nothing concrete about it. In Part XII, Chapter I, two 'Islamic Institutions' were envisaged - a research institute and a law commission. Neither of these is charged with making actual recommendations for the Islamization of life, for the task of the research institution is to carry out research while the purpose of the law commission is to make recommendations concerning law only. The 1962 (1964) constitution, on the other hand, not only charged the Advisory Council of Islamic ideology with the Islamization of law but also called upon it to make recommendations for the Islamization of life and also to examine and evaluate legislation in progress from the Islamic point of view (some thing which the 1956 Constitution completely neglected) (Rahman, Fazlur, 1970: 286).

The Preamble assured that '... the legitimate interests of the minorities in Pakistan (including their religions and cultural interests) should be safeguarded'. Under the title 'Principles of lawmaking', fundamental rights were guaranteed to all citizens, including non-Muslim minorities.

Then special provisions were also included to safeguard the rights of non-Muslim minorities. Concerning the effect of the provisions, Sharan remarked:

Because of the Islamic provisions in the Constitution of Pakistan, the minorities may have a legitimate ground for grievance, even though fundamental rights have been granted to them (Sharan, 1968: 118).

The non-Muslims were in theory guaranteed the right to profess, practice and even propagate their religions. But this in turn caused resentment among the Traditionalists.

Ayub Khan's period was not a swing towards secularism. It was marked only by an effort for a more liberal interpretation of Islam while framing the Constitution. He said:

Being an ideological state, our first objective must be to adhere unflinchingly to our ideology - the ideology of Islam. It is for this that we demanded and obtained Pakistan. In this world of growing scepticism, penetrating enquiry and exacting reason, we shall be proving that Islam is timeless; that it is dynamic and can move with times; that it is a practical code of life here and an effective passport for life hereafter (Iqbal, Afzal, 1986: 81).

2.4.3 Conclusion

Did the Constitution of 1962 make Pakistan a theocratic state? Parmatma Sharan simply says that Pakistan became neither a theocratic nor a secular state. It was not secular because of all the religious provisions in the constitution, but it was not theocratic either because government, was not to be carried on by religious parties - *ulema* (Sharan, 1968, 196).

In the Constitution of 1962, no particular effort was made to include Islamic provisions (Feldman, 1967: 195-6). But after pressure from the Traditionalists a compromise was made. The purpose of rephrasing the Objectives Resolution and other Islamic provisions had obviously been to make room for a more liberal interpretation of Islam (Ahmed, Manzooruddin, 1963: 252; 1965). However, such vagueness in the Islamic provisions was not tolerated by the Traditionalists. It was a courageous act of Ayub to exclude or rephrase the Islamic provisions in the 1962 constitution and, of course, he was unable to sustain this approach.

This also shows that the Modernists had to compromise with the Traditionalists on one level or another. For a state founded in the name of Islam, it was important for the reason for its existence to be included in the Constitution. Ayub knew this, especially with reference to East Pakistan: the only uniting factor between West and East Pakistan was Islam. Afzal Iqbal says:

> The Constitution of 1962 did not sharply deviate from the basic philosophy of the 1956 Constitution. It, however, adopted a more liberal attitude... The 1962 Constitution not only preserved the Islamic content of the old Constitution, but also enlarged the scope of the earlier Islamic provisions by introducing the institution of Advisory Council of Islamic Ideology (Iqbal, Afzal, 1986: 81).

I quote a concluding paragraph from Richard Weekes:

> Twenty years after the adoption of the Objectives Resolution, the political and constitutional questions then dealt with so generally were still unanswered. The tension between the universalism of Islam, which had created a Pakistani nation from the diverse raw material of Indian Muslims of many linguistic and racial backgrounds, and the particularisms of geography and culture, continued unabated. Logically, the one offered the ideal of a unitary state, based on an ideology of religious commitment and indifferent to cultural distinctions, the other the ideal of a league of linguistically defined, mutually exclusive nations indifferent to religious belief" (Weekes, 1964: 120).

2.5 ISLAMIC PROVISIONS IN THE CONSTITUTION OF 1973

The Constitution of 1973 is the only Pakistani constitution to be drawn up by an elected body. The first Constitution of 1956 was made by the Constituent Assembly and the Constitution of 1962 was framed by an army general. As with the previous constitutions, it was a tedious task to frame the 1973 Constitution (Williams, 1975).

Z.A Bhutto's period could be marked by the arrangement of such events as the Islamic Summit Conference of February 1974 in which thirty-five member states of the Islamic Conference plus Palestine, (represented by the PLO) participated, and the International Seerat Congress, held of March 1976, which was attended by the *Imam* of the *Ka'aba* and 100 prominent scholars and *ulema.*

Another aspect of this period which should be noted, with reference to the Islamic provisions of the constitution, was the nationalization of major industries and agrarian reforms. We are not concerned here with the failure or success of these reforms.

Their importance is as evidence of the political ideology of the government. Bhutto was a Modernist like Ayub Khan, but was different in that he talked more about the possibility of establishing a socialist economic system in the Islamic state of Pakistan, while Ayub had considered Communism to be the main enemy of Islam. One of the reasons for Bhutto's success in the election was his promise to introduce Islamic socialism. Bhutto's promises of Islamic socialism are reflected in the Constitution of 1973 (in the economic provisions and other social provisions), although these did not satisfy Modernists like Fazlur Rahman who expected to have the explicit use of the term 'Islamic Socialism' in the Constitution (Rahman, Fazlur, 1974: 31). Modernists expected a more secular Constitution and a clear relationship between religion and politics, to the extent of demanding that Pakistan be named the Socialist Republic of Pakistan. On one hand, the Modernists demanded a more secular Constitution and no dragging of religion into the Constitution; on the other hand, the Traditionalists were satisfied that the Constitution contained Islamic provisions - or that, at least, lip-service was paid to Islamic provisions (Hakim, 1974). The Chief Justice of the Lahore High Court remarked that

> Our nation can survive only if it remains true to its ideological foundations (Iqbal, Sardar Muhammad, 1975).

Justice Nasim Hasan Shah said:

> Thus in its aims and objects it represents a combination of Islamic and socialistic thoughts but it is named as the Constitution of the 'Islamic Republic of Pakistan' (Shah, 1979: 81).

The Constitution of 1973 was again a compromise between Modernists and Traditionalists. Modern democratic demands like social, economic and political justice and elected institutions exist side by side with professed Islamic theological content in the constitution (Shah: 1976: 106-14).[15] The effect of this compromise was that most of the provisions of the Constitution are only paper rules, enacted without any intent of implementing them; but in extreme situations they could be interpreted to satisfy the dominant section of the government. As we have seen, in the last days of Bhutto's rule, Islamization was used in an attempt to satisfy the Rightist Traditionalists who organized themselves in order to overthrow Bhutto. Let us see in detail how Islamic provisions were intermixed with modern social democratic principles.

2.5.1 The Constitution of 1973 and the Objectives Resolution

The Preamble of the Constitution was the same as that of the previous Constitution. The sovereignty of God still existed along with the sovereignty of the people - an ambigious combination to satisfy both Modernists and Traditionalists.

> However, by this compromise the Modernist managed to avoid a headlong conflict with the Traditionalist and, to his own satisfaction, obtained a sanction for working democracy. The Traditionalist, for his part, thought that he had gained what he wanted, viz., a restriction on the will of the people through God's sovereignty. That is where the crux lies in all the three Constitutions, (Rahman, Fazlur, 1974: 39).

This is an old story. G.W. Choudhury rightly calls it a replica of the earlier versions of 1956 and 1962 (Choudhury, G.W., 1974: 11) i.e., the artificial adjunct of Islam attached to modern democratic principles. The Constitution of 1973 goes one step further in its Premble by giving it a socialist flavour. It says:

> ... we the people of Pakistan, conscious of our responsibility before Almighty *Allah* and men; are dedicated to the preservation of democracy achieved by the unremitting struggle of the people against oppression and tyranny; inspired by the resolve to protect our national and political unity and solidarity by creating an egalitarian society through a new order.

Fazlur Rahman and Afzal Iqbal, two Modernists, are satisfied that this clearly implies that the present order is undesirable, which is a good sign, though Fazlur Rahman would very much like to add to 'new order' the phrase 'based on Islamic socialism' (Iqbal, Afzal, 1986: 85; Rahman, Fazlur, 1974: 33).

2.5.2 Islamic Provisions in the 1973 Constitution

'Pakistan shall be a Federal Republic to be known as the Islamic Republic of Pakistan' (Art. 1), was for the present purpose the same as the Constitution of 1956 and the amended Constitution of 1962. A new Article was added to say that Islam shall be the state religion of Pakistan (Art. 2). Neither of the two previous Constitutions provided this. Like the two previous Constitutions, it provides that the President of Pakistan must be 'a Muslim' (Art.

41(2)). Choudhury found this unnecessary, because after the secession of East Pakistan the great bulk of the population of Pakistan is Muslim, but 'its retention has been found necessary to satisfy public demand for an Islamic state' (Choudhury, G.W., 1974: 12). An Indian journal, *The Organiser*, (6 January 1973) said

> It retains the old insistence that the Head of State must be a Muslim and that makes nonsense of the freedom of religion, mentioned in the fundamental rights.

Contrary to the previous constitutions, the Constitution of 1973 also laid down that the Prime Minister should be a Muslim (Art. 91(2)). A Modernist like Afzal Iqbal also found it unnecessary to add this, as 'it certainly offends against the theoretical liberty of a sovereign parliament to elect anyone they like as their leader' (Iqbal, Afzal, 1986: 89), while another writer appreciated the addition on grounds that the ideological nature of the state should not be compromised in the 'name of toleration or liberalism' (Khel, 1984: 52).

Not only did the Constitution lay down that the President and the Prime Minister should be Muslims, it also requires a special oath to be taken by the President and the Prime Minister. The Third Schedule required a statement of their faith in Islam. This was the biggest compromise which Bhutto's government made with the Traditionalists. This special oath was inserted to harass the *Ahmadi* sect. It was an old demand by Rightist parties in Pakistan to have them declared a non-Muslim minority. This originated in the positions held by the members of this sect in the army and the administration. Later on, Articles 106 and 260 of the Constitution were amended to declare the *Ahmadis* a non-Muslim minority. This was a great injustice to this Muslim sect.

Fundamental rights as laid down in the Constitution of 1973 are not very different from those in the two previous Constitutions. Perhaps they are briefer and simpler in the 1973 Constitution. These provisions are no different from provisions that would have appeared in a secular Constitution. Such rights deal with the freedom to profess and propagate religion and the right to establish, maintain and manage religious institutions (Art. 20). The Constitution also safeguards against taxation to support of any particular religion other than one's own (Art. 21). It also safeguards educational institutions in respect of religion (Art. 22). There is non-discrimination in access to public places (Art. 26). The state also safeguards against discrimination in the services (Art. 27). The freedom of the press is subject to overall considerations of the 'glory of Islam' and 'the security of the state'. This rhetorical expression, 'the glory of Islam', is a new addition in the 1973 Constitution.

Under the Principles of Policy it is stated that steps shall be taken to enable the Muslims of Pakistan '... to order their lives in accordance with the fundamental principles of Islam ...'. This is similar to the relevant provision in 1962, with the only addition being to encourage and facilitate the learning of the Arabic language and to secure correct and exact printing and publishing of the *Holy Quran* (Art. 31). This was a provision appreciated both by Traditionalists and Modernists. It also provided, like previous Constitutions, for the strengthening of bonds with the Muslim world and the promotion of international peace, etc. It added a socialistic type of phrase, namely that of supporting the common interests of the peoples of Asia, Africa and Latin America (Art.40). It also provides, like the 1962 Constitution, for the elimination of prostitution, gambling, drug taking and consumption of alcohol (Art. 46, 47, 48).

Article 29 is similar to that of previous constitutions. It requires that 'no law shall be repugnant to the teachings and requirements of Islam as set out in the *Holy Quran* and Sunna'. The explanation to this article, which is an addition in the Constitution of 1973, provides that '*Quran* and Sunna shall mean the *Quran* and Sunna as interpreted by the school of law to which the individual belongs'. Fazlur Rahman, welcoming the change, says:

> One highly welcome change in the Constitution is that it has dropped a paragraph contained in the two earlier constitutions (1964 Principles of Policy I, Explanation): In the application of this principle (i.e., that no law shall be enacted which is repugnant to the *Quran* and the Sunna) to the personal law of any Muslim sect, the expression '*Quran* and Sunna as interpreted by that sect' This principle was obviously in contradiction with that Constitution's expressly limiting the authoritative sources of Islam to the *Quran* and Sunna only and would perpetuate the authority of different schools of law of classical Islam. It would thus prevent an achievement of uniformity of the law (and morality) of Islam in Pakistan (Rahman, Fazlur, 1974: 40).

He says that he had also pointed this out to President Ayub Khan in a letter in 1964.

Article 277 further provides that all existing laws shall be brought in to conformity with the injunctions of Islam and requires that no law repugnant to such injunctions shall be enacted. In order to achieve this objective, it provides for the setting up of a Council of Islamic Ideology (Art. 228).

G.W. Choudhury is not optimistic about the Islamic provisions. 'High sounding constitutional phrases' with 'no practical meaning', as he calls them. He says that it is the same path adopted by Ayub and followed by Bhutto to satisfy the orthodox. As far as an Islamic Council is concerned he is again very bitter. He says:

> There is again provision for an Islamic Council, borrowed from Ayub's Constitution; the Council is another showpiece for public consumption, with no real power except an advisory role vis-a-vis the legislatures, which may or may not accept its advice; the legislatures, both central and provincial, can act in the public interest without waiting for the advice of the Council - exactly similar were the provisions in Ayub's Constitution and nobody during the Ayub era even bothered to examine the role or the functions of 'The Islamic Council'. The fate of Mr. Bhutto's 'Islamic Council' is bound to be similar, but it will satisfy the public demand for an 'Islamic state' just as Ayub's satisfied the same demand (Choudhury, G.W., 1974: 12).

The 1973 Constitution does not provide for the reconstruction of the Islamic Research Institute, which was provided for by the two previous Constitutions. G.W. Choudhury resents this, because he thinks that the Islamic Research Institute was at least engaged in a large-scale programme of study and research (*ibid:* 12). Fazlur Rahman says that during his tenure as Director of the Institute (1962-8) and membership of the Council (1964-9), there was continuous tension in the Institute and Council and frequent conflicts between the two. While the Institute espoused a definitely Modernist stance, the general climate within the Council was conservative and often reactionary. The Institute was also involved in certain public controversies with the very conservative Right. Because of this history, the Institute was dropped entirely from the new Constitution. But the question was: how would the Council discharge the heavy duties of Islamization? (Rahman, Fazlur, 1974: 41). The functions of the Council, apart from the duty to compile, in a suitable form for the guidance of Parliament and Provincial Assemblies, such injunctions of Islam as can be given legislative effect, are merely recommendatory or advisory (Art.227). Justice Gul Muhammad Khan resents the idea that the Council has only recommendatory powers and that, in spite of the fact that the Council revised various laws, few of its recommendations obtained legislative sanction. (Khan, Muhammad G., 1986a: 260-1). Afzal Iqbal, also criticizing the constitutional provisions in this respect, says:

> The Constitution is silent about the conflict of views between the Council and the House. Whose view finally prevails is left to the imagination. The Council is a body appointed by the President and has an advisory function; the House is elected by the people on the basis of universal franchise; and although its 'sovereign' character is nowhere delineated in the Constitution, it is reasonable to expect that the will of the people will prevail. The Ulama will not accept this view for in Muslim history consensus on such matters is the consensus among the Ulama and not the people who are not equipped with the knowledge necessary to make such decisions (Iqbal, Afzal, 1986: 92).

Social provisions dealing with women had important implications for Islamization, referred to in a later chapter. Art.34 provides for the full participation of women in national life. It says 'steps shall be taken to ensure full participation of women in all spheres of national life'. Maternity benefits for women in employment were assured for the first time. Art.37 (e) says that 'The state shall make provision for securing just and humane conditions of work ensuring that children and women are not employed in vocations unsuited to their age or sex and for maternity benefits for women in employment'. It also provided protection for the MFLO (Art. 203 B).

There were seven amendments to the Constitution up to 1988. The second Amendment declared *Ahmadis* as non-Muslims. A new clause was inserted in Article 260, which says 'A person who does not believe in the absolute and unqualified finality of the Prophethood of Muhammad (peace be upon him) the last of the Prophets, or claims to be a Prophet, in any sense of the word, or of any description whatsoever, after Muhammad (peace be upon him) or recognizes such a claimant as a Prophet or a religious reformer, is not a Muslim for the purposes of the Constitution or law'. However, because of the slogan of Islamic socialism some of the clauses of the constitution of 1973 are different from the previous constitutions.

The socialist flavour in the Constitution is found in the provisions directly or indirectly concerned with the economic system of the country. They are not mentioned in any one place in the Constitution, but are scattered throughout it. For example, as mentioned before, the Preamble mentions an egalitarian society through a new order. Socialist tendencies are also discernible, i.e., the state shall ensure the elimination of all forms of exploitation and the gradual fulfilment of the fundamental principle 'from each according to his ability to each according to his work', which is clearly a modification of the principle of classical Communism, 'from each according to his capacity to each according to his need'. The phrasing of the principle is vague and misleading.

The Constitution also envisages nationalisation without compensation, i.e., private property can be acquired for some public purposes without the payment of compensation (Art. 24). Maximum limits of property owned can be laid down (Art. 253(a)). The state must prevent the concentration of wealth and the means of production and distribution in the hands of the few (Art. 38(a)). It must provide work and an adequate livelihood for all citizens within the available resources (Art. 30,40,42). It must endeavour to provide the basic necessities of life such as food, clothing, housing, education and medical care for all citizens, including those who are permanently or temporarily unable to earn their livelihood because of infirmity, illness or unemployment.[16] It is interesting to note that with these socialist concepts of social and economic justice, the classical concepts of Islamic economic justice such as *zakat* and *riba* are also present in the Constitution. Perhaps as a result, the Constitution omits to explain the meaning of riba (which could be interpreted to mean 'usury', not interest in the banking system), which concept the 1962 Constitution had dared to explain (Rahman, Fazlur, 1974: 35-6), (Art. 18 of the 1962 Constitution). The appendix of Islamic concepts such as *zakat* and *riba* together with socialist economic concepts is vague and ambiguous (Iqbal, Afzal, 1986: 88).

2.5.3 Conclusion

As in the previous constitutions the Islamic provisions are again a compromise between Modernists and Traditionalists. Nevertheless the interesting thing about the Constitution of 1973, was, as Bhutto himself said, 'Nobody can deny that it is an Islamic Constitution. It contains more Islamic provisions than any of the past constitutions of Pakistan as well as any of the other Constitutions of Muslim countries' (Wolf-Philips, 1989). Wolf-Philips' own research into over thirty countries bears out the same observation.

2.6   REVIVAL OF THE CONSTITUTION ORDER, 1985 AND ISLAMIC PROVISIONS

With the wave of Islamization beginning in 1977 under General Zia, the Constitution of Pakistan went through the biggest amendment ever made in the constitutional history of Pakistan, by means of a document called the Revival of the Constitution Order, 1985. This amendment was made by General Zia-ul-Haq, who came into power on 5 July 1977, through a martial law. His usurpation of power was justified by the judiciary in the famous case of *Begum Nusrat Bhutto v. the Chief of Army Staff and Federation of Pakistan* [17] (Hussain, Faqir, 1985).

In favour of the martial law regime, the court invoked various Western theories (from Hans Kelsen to the doctrine of necessity) and of course also Islam.[18] It is notable that Kelsen and other Western theories and Islam were used side by side to explain State necessity, in order to prove the maxim that 'necessity makes prohibited things permissible'. The maxim was further extended to State necessity. The court held:

> ... that the Chief Martial Law Administrator, having validly assumed power by means of an extra-constitutional step in the interest of the State and for the welfare of the people, is entitled to perform all such acts and promulgate all legislative measures which have been consistently recognized by judicial authorities as falling within the scope of the law of necessity, namely: (a) all acts or legislative measures which are in accordance with, or could have been made under the 1973 Constitution, including the power to amend it.

However, the court affirmed the supervisory jurisdiction of the courts and limited the application of the 'doctrine of necessity' in duration and in substance.

In 1981, the Provisional Constitutional Order 1981 was promulgated as the CMLA (Chief Martial Law Administer) Order. In this Order, the court's power and supervisory jurisdiction over the martial law authorities, sanctioned by the Nusrat Bhutto case, was rejected.[19] Article 16 of the PCO (Provisional Constitutional Order) says: 'The President as well as the Chief Martial Law Administrator shall have, and shall be deemed to always have had, the power to amend the Constitution'.

This period was followed by continuous, unfulfilled promises of elections. In December 1984, a referendum was held in the country. People were required to answer a simple question.

'Do you endorse the process initiated by General Zia-ul Haq for bringing the laws of Pakistan in conformity with the injunctions of Islam as laid down in the *Holy Quran* and the *Sunna* of the Holy Prophet and for the preservation of the ideology of Pakistan, the continuation and consolidation of that process, and for the smooth and orderly transfer of power to elected representatives of the people?' Through this referendum, Zia's power was safeguarded for five more years. Moreover, an election was arranged by him in 1985 which the opposition boycotted.

After this whole process of purported legitimization through judicial and political means, the Revival of the Constitution Order 1985 was promulgated to Islamize the Constitution of Pakistan (Ahmad-ud-din, Bashir, 1985). It would not be wrong to say that this is the most Islamized version of Pakistan's Constitutions. One day before the promulgation of the Order, in a nationwide radio and television broadcast, Zia said that there were two fairly plausible grounds for making amendments in the Constitution. First, to bring it closer to Islam and second, to shield it against future national instability.[20] The amendments were widely criticized throughout Pakistan. They were criticized not only for being illegal and for distorting the Constitution of 1973,[21] but also for their Islamic provisions. Modernists interpreted the amendments as 'modified martial law' (Mir, 1985; Hassan, 1985; Changez, 1985b), while Traditionalists felt that total Islamization of the Constitution had not been carried out and had been left to the Parliament to accomplish (Changez, 1985a).

Let us look at the Islamic provisions of this Order. By Article I, the word 'Parliament' was to be substituted by the word *Majlis-e-Shura*. However, the word 'Parliament' would stay in brackets. This is only the changing of an Islamic word that does not affect the constitution of the Parliament, which consists of President, National Assembly and Senate. The second main amendment is insertion of Article 2-A. It says: 'The Objectives Resolution is to form part of substantive provisions. The principles and provisions set out in the Objectives Resolution reproduced in the annex are hereby made substantive part of the Constitution and shall have effect accordingly'. In an interview, General Zia himself approved the provision.

> My own firm belief is that Pakistan should be run off the basis of an authentic *Shoora* system. What we have now, as I admitted in my speech yesterday, is not an Islamic or a *Shoorai* form of government. We have taken a step forward in this direction by

incorporating the Objectives Resolution in the Constitution. This is an achievement, although only partial of the goal set by the *Quaid* and by our first Prime Minister to make Pakistan a citadel of Islam.

He further said about the Objectives Resolution:

> Now that the Objectives Resolution has been made a part of the Constitution, rights flowing from the Resolution shall also be justiciable [sic]. You have secular human rights given in the first part together with Islamic rights defined in the Objectives Resolution. Thus liberties and privileges given by religion will be enjoyed by citizens as much as their other human rights of a secular nature.[22]

Making the Objectives Resolution part of the Constitution is very vague and the question arises: what is the difference between human rights in Islam and secular human rights? If human rights in Islam mean inequality of the sexes and for non-Muslim minorities, as is reflected in other Islamic laws, such as the *Hudood* Ordinance, then the question arises as to how can secular human rights and Islamic human rights can be enjoyed at the same time? All writers dealing with this provision have considered it a major Islamic amendment which has put the Constitution into a new key. But it is very difficult to see the real effects of the Objectives Resolution as part of the Constitution, unless it is put into practice. As we have seen before, the Objectives Resolution has been the Preamble of all the constitutions of Pakistan since 1956. It was never an operative part of the Constitution, but existed only as a preamble. The only change which can be foreseen by this provision is that it will sanction theocracy in Pakistan. In the light of this provision, courts would interpret human rights as Islamic human rights, and thus Pakistan would stand opposed to fundamental human rights. The secular human rights assured in the Constitution could be struck down on grounds of inconsistency (Lodi, 1985; Mostafa, 1985; Ahmad ud-din, Bashir, 1985). Justice (retd.) A.R. Changez said that:

> this change will undoubtedly build pressure to widen the juris-diction of Shariat courts, either through juristic interpretations or through further amendments in the Constitution (Changez, 1985b).

Due to the symbolic and vague nature of the Objectives Resolution, it could be interpreted and stretched in many ways.

Aqil Ahmad did not find that the insertion of the Objectives Resolution as Article 2A in the Constitution would have any special effect and said:

> It seems the intention of those who initiated the insertion of Article 2A in the Constitution was rooted more in emotions and sentiments than in its practical implications. The Constitution is the basic document on which the legal, social, and economic structure of a country rests, and therefore, should be free of duplication and contain only that which is essential. Article 2A must be reconsidered very closely and unemotionally to determine its constitutional utility and essentiality (Ahmad, Aquil, 1989: 6-7).

Furthermore, Article 31 of the Constitution relates to the Islamic way of life. In this Article, the word *ushr* was added along with *zakat, auqaf* and mosques whose proper organization the state shall endeavour to secure.

The amended Article 51 provides ten seats for minority religious groups, also specifying the distribution among the various groups i.e Christians, Hindus, Sikh, Buddhist, Parsi and *Ahmadis*. (The last group consider itself Muslim but, as already noted, was declared non-Muslim because of pressure from the Traditionalists).

Article 62 prescribes the qualifications required for membership of Parliament. Besides other qualifications it is also required that a member should be one who: is not commonly known as one who violates Islamic injunctions (62(e)); has adequate knowledge of Islamic teachings and practices the obligatory duties prescribed by Islam, just as he abstains from major sins (62(f)); is sagacious, righteous and non-profligate, honest and *ameen* (62(h)); has not been convicted of a crime involving moral turpitude or for giving false evidence (62(i)); has not, after the establishment of Pakistan, worked against the integrity of the country or opposed the ideology of Pakistan (62(j)). The above-mentioned are the wide range of personal qualities emphasized by the amending clause. These requirements of virtue are not to be found in any other constitutions in the world. Aqil remarks about these qualifications:

> Some of the qualifications added are unworkable and unenforceable. For instance, the Amendment says that a person has to be

'sagacious, righteous, nonprofligate, honest and *Ameen'*. These virtues are unexceptionable but difficult, and highly improbable to be enforced (Ahmad, Aquil, 1989: 28).

By Article 113 the same type of qualifications were inserted for the membership of a Provincial Assembly. To Article 203C, dealing with the Federal *Shariat* Court and appointment of judges to it, was added Clause (4) which says:

> The President may, at any time, by order in writing:
> a)   modify the term of appointment of a judge;
> b)   assign to the judge any other office; and
> c)   require a judge to perform such other function as the president may deem fit; and pass such other order as he may consider appropriate.

Another small change of the Constitution is found in Article 51 (1) which deals with Assembly members. The word 'Muslims' is inserted instead of 'members'.

Further changes were made by General Zia in Order No 14 of 1985, which came to be known as the Eighth Amendment, in which vast powers were given to the President. It raised controversial issues such as how much power Islam should give to the head of the state and how great a scope public representation should have in Islam. According to one opinion the enhancement of the powers of the president is fully consistent with Islamic constitutionalism. The Eighth Amendment gave not only wide powers to the President, but it also gave protection to all the martial law Orders and Regulations which were promulgated by the martial law regime.

2.7 CONCLUSION

This chapter attempts to show that there is inconsistency and instability in the Islamic provisions of the constitutions of Pakistan. Inconsistency has existed in the sense that most of the Islamic provisions were just written into the constitutions and there was no intention of implementing them, at least not until 1977. They were provided only as compromise clauses and Modernist and Traditionalists saw different meanings or interpretations of them. Instability existed in the sense that, on the one hand, constitutions could be abrogated without legal authority and, on the other hand, Islamic provisions could be replaced or reinterpreted, depending on which faction of Muslims were ruling. Equality for non-Muslims and women did not mean much in practice as we will see in Chapter 3 on criminal law, in which women and non-Muslims are widely discriminated against. This also depends on how different Muslims interpret the Islamic concept of 'social justice'.

Another important point to note is that, in spite of all efforts to Islamize the Constitution of Pakistan (the last of which was made in 1985), the Constitution was set out in a modern fashion no different from the one introduced by the British.

CHAPTER 3

Criminal Law

3.1 INTRODUCTION

Since 1947, the PPC (Pakistan Penal Code of 1860), together with the Criminal Procedure Code of 1989 and the Evidence Act of 1872 (inherited pieces of legislation from the British colonial rule), have formed the statutory basis of the criminal law of Pakistan. In 1979, the military regime felt the need to make changes and to Islamize the whole of the previously established criminal law of Pakistan. Orthodox or Traditionalist scholars had often criticized the three pieces of legislation for being un-Islamic (Majid, 1970: 22-4; Rahman, Tanzil-ur, 1978).

On 9 February 1979, through different ordinances, penalties such as the amputation of limbs, flogging, stoning to death and other forms of capital punishment were imposed for the crimes of theft, highway robbery, adultery, fornication, intoxication and particular kinds of defamation, etc. It should be noted here that, by Western criminological standards, these punishments seem cruel and outdated. Such punishments are justified in classical Islamic *shariah*, but are not popular in the modern Islamic world with the exception of a few countries like Iran and Saudi Arabia. The four ordinances promulgated in 1979, i.e., the *Offences Against Property (Enforcement of Hudood) Ordinance, Prohibition (Enforcement of Hadd) Order*, the *Offence of Qazf (Enforcement of Hadd) Ordinance* and *Offence of Zina (Enforcement of Hudood) Ordinance*, are seen as the beginning of the implementation of classical Islamic criminal law. In accordance with classical Islamic criminal law, the above-mentioned four ordinances divide each of the crimes of *zina*, *qazf*, the drinking of alcohol and theft into two types, i.e., *hadd* and *tazir* (Lippman & Mordechai, 1988; Bassiouni (ed), 1982).

Hadd punishments are harsh, including the amputation of limbs and stoning to death, but if they are to be applicable a strict standard of proof is set which is practically impossible to meet; therefore, most cases come under the category of *tazir*.

According to traditional *shariah*, *tazir* punishments should be left to the discretion of the judge trying the case, but these ordinances have prescribed *tazir* punishments.

The *Offence of Zina (Enforcement of Hudood) Ordinance*, 1979, provides severe punishments for fornication and adultery. This has in turn affected the offence of rape, which will be discussed in detail in Part 3.3.2. below. As adultery and fornication are regarded as as serious crimes, the making of a false allegation of these acts is also a crime called *qazf*. Thus *qazf* is related to the crimes of fornication and adultery. Before 1979, it could have been covered by the general law of defamation as laid down in Section 499 of the PPC The definition of *qazf* adopted in the Ordinance is the same as in the PPC, with the exception that Section 499 deals with defamation in general. As far as the law of theft is concerned, the Ordinance allows punishment by the amputation of limbs if the theft comes under the category of *hadd*. Section 14 of the Ordinance provides that, if a theft does not come under the category of *hadd* but under *tazir*, it shall be awarded the punishment provided in the Pakistan Penal Code (Act XLV of 1860). For practical purposes, all cases concerning theft are dealt with under the PPC The drinking of alcohol was outlawed in 1977 under Bhutto, when it became politically expedient for him to do so.

Another 1979 ordinance is the Whipping Ordinance. After 1979, whipping has become a common mode of punishment. The said ordinance provides for the mode and form to be observed while administering the punishment. The Law of Evidence was also changed in order to make it more Islamic. The utterance of derogatory remarks about the prophet of Islam was also made a crime by making changes in the relevant sections of the PPC The Law of Murder, an important area of criminal law, was in the process of change in Pakistan at the time this book was written. The draft ordinance concerning the law of murder is discussed later this chapter. The text of the *qisas* and *diyat* Ordinance, passed in 1990, is found at Appendix III.

All the changes in the criminal law of Pakistan reflect the inconsistencies discussed in the Introduction that I argued to be characteristic of laws in peripheral capitalist states. For example, in the field of criminal law, there is excessive litigation on different issues. Ordinances discriminate against women and non-Muslims, disregarding international human rights. The legal instability, from which peripheral capitalist states suffer, becomes obvious when we go through details of the ordinances and their implementation.

3.2 OFFENCES AGAINST PROPERTY (Enforcement of Hudood) ORDINANCE, VI, OF 1979

3.2.1 Theft Liable to Hadd and Tazir

This ordinance was promulgated to introduce Islamic punishments for theft and robbery in Pakistan.

Section 4 of the Ordinance divides theft into two kinds for the purpose of punishment: theft liable to *hadd* and theft liable to *tazir*. Section 5 defines theft liable to *hadd*. It provides that if an adult *surreptitiously* steals from a *hirz* property to the value of one *nisab*, he commits theft liable to *hadd* punishment.

The terms needing explanation here are *surreptitiously*, *hirz* and *nisab*. Briefly, for the accused to act *surreptitiously*, he must believe that the victim of the theft is unaware of the crime occuring. Hence, if it is daytime, the whole offence must be carried out surreptitiously; at night, it is not necessary to continue acting surreptitiously after the commencement of the offence (*ibid.*, Explanation 2, Section 5)). A *hirz* is a device intended for the custody of property (*ibid.*, Section 2 (d)). One *nisab* equals 4.457 grams or more of gold, about one hundred US dollars (*ibid.*, 3. Section 6)).

In order to more fully understand these three expressions, *The State v. Ghulam Ali*[1] is the best case to look at. In that case for the first time a person was convicted of theft liable to *hadd* punishment (i.e., amputation of the right hand) for having stolen a wall clock from a mosque. The conviction was confirmed by the *Shariat* Court. On further appeal to the Supreme Court, counsel for the accused, discussing the word *surreptitiously*, contended that, in order to be punishable by *hadd*, the theft had to be committed in such a way that the criminal believed 'that the victim of theft does not know of his action' at the time of the theft. He continued that, if something was stolen from a mosque, there would be no victim of the theft and if there was no victim, then the theft would not be liable to *hadd*. It was further argued that, even if the *khadim* (mosque guard) had been considered a victim, the theft would not have been committed surreptitiously qua him because in that case it was committed right in his presence and with his knowledge. On this basis the accused was acquitted.[2]

The expression *hirz* was well explained when the case was in the *Shariat* Court where the appeal was dismissed. It was questioned whether a mosque was a *hirz* for the protection of its property. Among the controversial views of the Muslim jurists on this aspect, the Court preferred to adopt the opinion of Imam Malik who considered the mosque to be a corporate body with the right to own property. The court rejected the *Hanafi* view according to which a mosque is not a *hirz* because it is open at all times for prayers. It was held that there was a *khadim* in the mosque and no person who came to pray was allowed to take away anything from the mosque. Moreover, the definition of *hirz* in the Ordinance did not make any exception in favour of property which was accessible to anybody. Thus the place where the wall clock was hanging was its *hirz* and its removal from that place by the appellant was enough to render him liable to punishment by the amputation of his hand.[3] The Supreme Court's *Shariat* Appellate Bench did not consider the question whether the mosque was a *hirz* since it upheld the appeal on other grounds. The point whether the accused knew or was likely to have known at the time of commission of the offence that the wall clock had a value of one *nisab* or more, was however dealt with by the Supreme Court. It held that nobody thought that the price of the wall clock could be more than 500 rupees, so 'how could the accused be burdened with the required knowledge, he is entitled to the benefit of reasonable doubt in this respect'.[4]

Proof of theft liable to *hadd* according to Section 7 of the Ordinance may be in two forms: Firstly, if the accused confesses to having committed the offence and, secondly, if at least two Muslim adult male witnesses (other than the victim of the theft), whom the court is satisfied fulfil the requirements of *tazkiyah-al-shuhood* (i.e., are truthful persons abstaining from major sins) give evidence as eye-witnesses of the occurrence. If, however, the accused is not a Muslim the eye-witnesses may be non-Muslims.

The condition that there should be two Muslim adult male witnesses other than victims of the theft was also discussed in the case of Ghulam Ali.[5] It was argued that at least three persons must be involved as prosecution witnesses in a case of theft liable to *hadd* - one must be the victim and the other two eye-witnesses. In this case, a wall clock having been stolen from a mosque, if one of the two eye-witnesses was considered the victim (the guard of the mosque), then the court was left with only one eye-witness; and if both were treated as eye-witnesses then the victim would be missing. An important requirement of law was thus found to be lacking and the appellant was entitled to acquittal on this ground as well. He was sentenced to three years under *tazir* but, at the time of conviction, he had already been in prison for six years while under trial.

Again, in the cases of *Janat Gul v. Mulki Zama* and *Sheral v. The State,* the requirement of two Muslim adult male witnesses was found to be missing, so *hadd* was not applied.[6]

In Ghulam Ali's case, the mode adopted by the trial court to examine the truthfulness and piety of the witnesses was criticized by the Supreme Court of Pakistan. It was held that a statement by a witness about his own character is not enough to ascertain his piety. There should have been a secret enquiry about the witness made by a referee.[7] However, in another case, an interesting point was raised by the Sessions Judge: he said that in view of the standard of morality in Pakistani society, a liberal interpretation should be placed in the requirement to judge the piety of witnesses.[8] This contradicts the Ghulam Ali case, in which a strict standard had been set for examining the character of witnesses. In this light, it is difficult to see which course will be adopted by future courts.

The third thing to be noticed in Section 7 is that the witnesses must have seen the actual occurrence of the theft, i.e., the thief taking the stolen object completely out of the *hirz.*

Section 9 of the Ordinance provides the punishment for theft liable to *hadd.* If the theft is for the first time, the right hand below the joint of the wrist is to be amputated. In the case of a second theft the left foot below the ankle is to be amputated and for a third theft the offender is to be imprisoned for the rest of his natural life. Amputation of hand and foot is to be carried out by an authorized medical officer and amputation can be postponed if the medical officer has reason to believe that this would cause the death of the convict. A doctors' organisation, *Voice Against Torture,* considers it against medical ethics for doctors to carry out such operations (Mehdi, Mahboob, 1990).

Sections 10 and 11 of the Ordinance provide exceptional situations where *hadd* punishment is inapplicable. These exceptions include the relationship between offender and victim and the type of property stolen. If a theft is committed under 'pressure' or 'necessity', *hadd* punishment would not be inflicted. In cases where confession of the commission of an offence is retracted or in cases of retraction of statements by witnesses, *hadd* will not be imposed.

The conditions in which a thief is liable for *hadd* punishment are so strict and so are the principles applied:

> ... that not only the maximum benefit of every reasonable doubt will be extended to the accused, but an effort, too, will be made not to inflict a *hadd* as long as it may be avoided by all legitimate and established means.[9]

Thus it is difficult to convict anybody of theft liable to *hadd*. This is why no amputation have yet been carried out.

Section 13 of the Ordinance says that when theft is not liable to *hadd* it is liable to *tazir*. Section 14 further provides that in cases of *tazir*, the punishment laid down in the P.P.C for the offence of theft is to be awarded. According to the PPC, Sections 379 and 380, punishment is in the form of imprisonment and fines.

Hara' abah (Robbery)

The Ordinance also provides Islamic punishment for the offence of *hara' abah*. Section 15 of the Ordinance defines *hara' abah*; it says that:

> ... when any one or more persons whether equipped with arms or not, make show of force for the purpose of taking away the property of another person and attack him or cause wrongful restraint or put him in fear of death or hurt, such person or persons are said to commit *hara' abah*.

The offence resembles the offence of robbery, dacoity and extortion as defined in the PPC Modes of proving *hara' abah* punishable under section 16 of the Ordinance are the same as those of theft liable to *hadd*. Section 17 (1) provides the punishment for *hara' abah* as follows:

1. Neither murder committed nor any property taken away. Punishment: 30 stripes and imprisonment (not less than three years) until the court is satisfied that the offender is sincerely penitent.

2. No property taken away but hurt caused. Punishment: 30 stripes, imprisonment and punishment for causing hurt in accordance with any law in force at the time being.

3. No murder committed but property valuing or exceeding *nisab* taken away. Punishment: Amputation of right hand from wrist and left foot from ankle.

4. Murder committed in course of offence. Punishment: Death sentence imposed as *hadd*.

imposed if the case falls under the exceptions provided for theft in sections 10 and 11. Like theft, *hara'abah* is liable to *tazir* if it is not liable to *hadd*. As we have seen, for an offence liable to *tazir* the offender is to be punished under the already existing PPC It should again be noted that the PPC provides punishment in the form of imprisonment and fines.

In a recent case, *Umar Badshah v. The State*,[10] three petitioners guilty of the offence of *haarabah* were all sentenced to death by the Session and Federal *Shariat* Court and were granted leave to appeal under the Ordinance to enable the evidence to be re-examined to see whether the petitioners had been rightly convicted of the said offences.

In other cases of *hara'abah* punishable by amputation, convictions have been set aside for lack of proof,[11] or bail has been granted on grounds of delay of trial in accordance with the PPC,[12] subject, of course, to the condition that the delay was not attributable to the accused themselves.

3.2.3 Conclusion

This ordinance has not really brought any notable change in the law of theft. The same punishments which were alleged to be un-Islamic are implemented for practical purposes. Punishment by amputation was introduced in 1979, but no hand has been amputated so far although hundreds of thefts and robberies are committed in Pakistan. *Tazir* punishment is imposed in all cases. This shows that Islamizing the law of theft has not really affected the law already prevailing in the country. The trial of cases under *hadd* has been nothing but an intellectual exercise, while the PPC still applies for practical purposes.

Asma Jahangir and Hina Jilani have critised *hadd* punishments for being ludicrous and out of proportion to the crimes committed. They say that, if a man is seen by male witnesses stealing an object worth Rs 2,000 (i.e., US $100) from an enclosed place, he shall be punished by having his hand amputated. On the other hand millions of dollars can be stolen by an adult Muslim in the sight of several women and/or non-Muslims, yet the offender escape *hadd* and be given *tazir* punishment. Similarly, a Rolls Royce can be stolen without fear of *hadd*, since the robbers did not take it from an enclosed space (Jahangir and Jilani, 1990).

If we look upon the rate of crimes against property and robberies in Pakistan since 1979, there has been no notable change. The contention that the Islamic punishment of limb amputation would help to bring down the rate of theft does not seem to have had any effect, according to figures provided by the Bureau of Police Research and Development of the Ministry of the Interior (Auolakh, 1986: 50-1; 220).

3.3 OFFENCE OF ZINA (Enforcement of Hudood) ORDINANCE, 1979

3.3.1 Fornication and Adultery

Islam recommends a strong patriarchal family and in Pakistan no need is felt to break this principle. For the preservation of such family units great stress is laid on the chastity of man and woman. This type of family unit has been functioning with the help of social values. The *Offence of Zina (Enforcement of Hudood) Ordinance*, 1979, incorporated existing values into criminal law. Before this ordinance, the PPC did not declare fornication (sexual intercourse without a marriage contract) a crime. However, adultery was an offence under Section 497 of the PPC, though it was an offence only committed by a man who had intercourse with the wife of another without his permission. In such cases, the woman was not even punished as an abettor. This section has been disputed since 1947 as failing to embody the full scope of the prohibition in Islamic law.

It may be interesting to look at a criticism of this section made by a member of the Constituent Assembly in 1951. While moving a Bill to amend Section 497, he commented on the English committee which was responsible for making this law:

> Sir, most of the members of this committee were Europeans. They introduced the notion of adultery into this penal code, but they thought that the circumstances, as they stood in India, would do great injustice to women if punishment is provided for the woman abettor. Sir, at that time in England adultery was no criminal offence. They were, therefore, guided by it. But the Islamic state has a different notion where the purity of breed is very essential and therefore the chastity of women should be honoured. There is absolute necessity for stopping adultery and to punish women as well. If men can be punished why should women escape. Sir, after the introduction of this bill I have received many letters from many ladies. They have strongly protested against this measure. They have pointed out the

injustice which is being done to women as a class by their male fellows. But there is a great force in this as adultery should be stopped in Pakistan and if it is to be stopped then it is necessary that both men and women should be made punishable as abettors of this heinous crime.[13]

Tanzil-ul-Rahman, who has played a prominent role in Islamizing Pakistani law, resents the section as it provides safeguards to the offender inasmuch as, if adultery takes place with the consent or connivance of the husband, no offence is deemed to have been committed (Rahman, Tanzil-ur, 1978: 22). Interestingly, a woman lawyer critical towards the new Islamic laws, expresses appreciation for Section 497. She says:

> The framers of the Penal Code of 1860 sagaciously excluded women from being punishable for adultery in view of their inability to protect themselves practically and legally (Patel, 1986: 42).

Conditions have totally changed since 1979. The *zina* Ordinance provides severe punishments for fornication and adultery. Fornication and adultery, known as *zina*, is defined as 'wilful sexual intercourse between a man and a woman without being validly married to each other'.

In Section 4, sexual intercourse is further explained to mean 'penetration'. For the purpose of punishment a distinction is made in Section 5 (2)(a)(b) between a married (*muhsan*) and unmarried (not *muhsan*) person convicted. The punishment for a married person convicted under *hadd* is stoning to death in a public place and for an unmarried person convicted one hundred lashes in a public place. The justification for this distinction is that married Muslims have the opportunity to satisfy their sexual urge lawfully; if they still choose to indulge in excesses they should be severely punished.

The Ordinance makes another distinction between *zina* liable to *hadd* and *zina* liable to *tazir* punishment. *Hadd* punishments are strict and require a high standard of proof (Section 8). *Hadd* occurs where the accused makes a confession of the commission of the offence, or where there is the other widely criticized form of proof: the presence of four Muslim, adult, pious, male eye-witnesses to the act of penetration. However, if the accused is a non-Muslim, non-Muslim eye-witnesses are acceptable. This section has been criticized for providing too strict standards of proof, as it is very unlikely that two people would commit *zina* in the presence of four male Muslims. Secondly, it discriminates against women and non-Muslims as women are absolutely excluded from being witnesses and non-Muslims cannot be witnesses in the case of a Muslim accused.

The exclusion of female evidence as a basis for imposing *hadd* punishment was challenged through a petition in the Federal *Shariat* Court, but it still exists in the Ordinance (Patel, 1983: 45).[14] Both forms of proof, i.e., confession or the presence of required witnesses, are subject to retraction. If the convict retracts his confession before the *hadd* punishment is imposed, the Court may order a retrial, while if any of the four eye-witnesses retracts his testimony the court may award *tazir* punishment on the basis of the evidence on record (Sections 9(1) 9(2) 9(4)).

In a case where two accused developed intimacy which resulted in the pregnancy of the girl, the accused pleaded that they were married to each other. But the Additional Sessions Judge found that the marriage had taken place after the pregnancy and sentenced both of them to *hadd* punishment, the man to stoning to death (as he was already married) and the girl to one hundred lashes. On appeal to the High Court, the *hadd* sentence was set aside on the basis that the convicts had retracted their confessions.[15] As seen in this case, it is difficult to have *hadd* implemented; after confessing, most accused would become frightened at the idea of being stoned to death and so retract their confessions.

Stoning to death as a punishment has never been inflicted in Pakistan. In a case in 1981, it was declared that *rajm* (stoning to death) had no basis in the *Quran* and therefore should be taken out of the Ordinance. This drew a strong protest from the orthodox. The case was reviewed in 1983.[16] Though the previous declaration was set aside, the judgment did not settle the controversy. The basis of the controversy is that, while punishment by *rajm* is not found in the *Quran*, it can be deduced from the *Sunna* and *Hadith* of Muhammad.

Hadd punishments, as we have seen, exist in law, but are difficult for a judge to implement, firstly because of the strict standard of proof and secondly because of the possibility of retracted confessions. But their very presence in law means that severe Islamic punishments exist and could be implemented. On the other hand, *tazir* punishments have proved to be more practical for implementation and have been widely applied. Section 7 of the Ordinance states that where proof for *hadd* punishments is not available, *tazir* punishments are to be applied. *Tazir* punishments are rigorous imprisonment for a term of up to ten years, flogging numbering thirty lashes and a fine (section 10(2)). *Tazir* punishments were again found to be unsatisfactory and were challenged in a petition as un-Islamic on the contention that a testimony which is insufficient to allow *hadd* punishment to be implemented cannot be a reliable testimony for implementing *tazir* punishments (Patel, 1986: 46). It is interesting to note that the higher court in a case where the four required witnesses were present, criticized the lower court for not sentencing the accused for *zina* liable to *hadd*. For technical reasons the court did not reverse the sentence and the accused were sentenced to *tazir* punishment.[17]

Great discrepancies are found whenever this law is implemented in Pakistan. Women have resented and protested against it because it is mostly women who are the victims of this inconsistency. In some cases of fornication and adultery the males accused were released on the benefit of the doubt while the female accused were sentenced to *tazir* punishment because of their pregnancy which was considered sufficient proof of their involvement in a criminal act. One such case which was formed the subject of widespread protests and was published in the national and international press was that of a blind girl, who was sentenced to three years imprisonment and fifteen lashes in public, plus a fine of 1,000 Rupees, while the two men who had committed the sexual act with her were acquitted due to lack of evidence. Safia Bibi was sentenced while she was pregnant and gave birth to a child. The judges did not follow the logic of an accusation of two parties of *zina* with consent: that if one gets the benefit of the doubt, so should the other. The sentence was, however, reversed in the higher court.[18] In another case the civil court sentenced a young woman to fifteen lashes, seven years R.I. (rigorous imprisonment) and a fine of 2,000 Rs; she was additionally sentenced to death for the murder of her new-born child (an act most probably done because of fear and shame at having an illegitimate child). For lack of the requisite evidence, the father of the child was released.[19]

This part of the Ordinance has also created drastic effects in the case of non-compliance with the *Muslim Family Laws Ordinance* (MFLO) of 1961. Because of ignorance of the law, the MFLO is not strictly observed anyway. Consequently a man and woman living together as a couple may be accused of adultery and become liable to punishment. An example of this is *Shera v. The State*.[20] The accused appellants claimed to be husband and wife and were stated to have been married after the female accused had been divorced by her previous husband, but it was held that non-compliance with Section 7 of the MFLO made the divorce ineffective. It was further held that even if the divorce deed was taken to be effective, the accused had been committing *zina* for some time at least. Both were sentenced to two years R.I. and thirty lashes in a public place. In the earlier similar case of *Ali Nawaz Gardezi v. Muhammad Yuosuf*,[21] it was held that the absence of notice of divorce to the chairman or the Union Committee amounted to retraction of the divorce. Consequently it was held that, the divorce of the female accused by her previous husband not having being notified, it had not put an end to their relationship, so the appellants were committing *zina* and the conviction was upheld. In the case of *Muhammad Siddique v. The State*,[22] a couple was again accused of committing *zina*. The ground here was again the invalidity of the dissolution of the first marriage of the accused woman. In the case of *Shahida Parveen & Muhammad Sarwar*,[23] Shahida claimed that she had married Muhammad Sarwar after her divorce from Khushi Muhammad. As her divorce deed was not found to be registered as required by the MFLO, her marriage with Sarwar was held to be illegal and she and Sarwar were sentenced to be stoned to death. Both were acquitted on a re-trial.

Many innocent people have been involved in cases of fornication and adultery. By no standard of morality can one appreciate that a husband and wife should be sentenced to imprisonment, flogging and a fine because a child is born to them only seven and a half months after their marriage, the implication being that they had illicit sexual relations before the date of their *nikah*. Among cases of the victimization of innocent people there is also have an example of a woman who, suffering from pressure from her parents, went to live with a man only for protection and help. Both of them were convicted because they were seen to be living in the same house. However, on appeal, they were released.[24] Rashida Patel in her recent publication says that the *zina* Ordinance has become a tool of blackmail in the hands of the unscrupulous (Patel, 1991). A practicing lawyer from Bahawarpur said in a seminar that, after the promulgation of the Ordinance, even a wife who is annoyed with her husband could be incriminated under *zina*. Also, if a girl, whose marriage was arranged in childhood, has not been sent to the husband's house due to some differences between the families, her whole family could be involved under the Ordinance. What happens sometimes is that not only is the woman in question arrested but other women of the family are taken to the police station and insulted (Mubshar, Afzal Tanweer, 1990).

Zina offences are non-bailable and not compoundable offences which means that the complainant cannot drop the charge. Bail in cases of *zina* is usually set at Rs 20,000-30,000 (US$ 1,000-1,500). As most of the female women accused come from a low income group, this sum is beyond their reach, as it is usually their husbands or other family members who are the complainants. Consequently, without the economic support of either the husband or father, the women sit helplessly in jail. If bail has been furnished by the husband, it becomes a powerful weapon to threaten the wife into submission. Kumar and Nadvi mention an incident where an 18-year-old girl's 'husband left her with her in-laws and took up a job in the Middle East. Her in-laws, in debt to a creditor, agreed to give her in exchange in order to clear the loan. He husband, on returning, filed a complaint of *zina*. She was arrested. Her husband then furnished her bail, but at the time of returning to his job in the Middle East cancelled her bail, thereby sending her back to jail' (Kumar & Nadvi, 1987: 4).

They mention another case, involving Ghulam Sakina (aged 55) where bail was used as a weapon by her husband. 'Ghulam Sakina and her husband had been falsely arrested as acccomplices in a *zina* case. Her husband obtained bail and, eventually, bailed Sakina out. In the time that lapsed between arranging for the bail and getting Sakina out, her husband had found himself a mistress. Sakina says "this was nothing new for my husband, he is always bringing women home, this time the difference was that he could avoid arguments with me by cancelling my bail". He did exactly that and Sakina was back in jail. Since Sakina doesn't have a lawyer it is unlikely that her case (in which as it is she has been falsely implicated) is going to come up for trial in the near future. As her husband is unlikely to bail her out (unless he bores of his new lover) Sakina is doomed to remain in jail' (Kumar & Nadvi, 1987: 4).

Generally, the effect of the Ordinance is repressive. It is arguable that it is unnecessary in urban areas because, due to a strong patriarchal family unit, segregation of the sexes and the dominance of religious morality, fornication and adultery are not common phenomena in the cities of Pakistan. On the other hand, Richard Kurin researched the effect of Islamization upon a village in Pakistan. He found that it was difficult for the villagers to understand the severity of *hadd* punishments, considering the uncontrollable human nature of such urges and desires. He found dozens of adulterous affairs in progress in the village of Chakpur (Kurin, 1986: 121). About one of the affairs in Chakpur he says:

This last case has provided a focus for many in discussing the *hudud* ordinances. There are perhaps as many as a dozen fairly well-known long-term adulterous affairs in progress in Chakpur. Villagers generally regard themselves as very excitable people with strong sexual urges and desires. To many, the ordinances concerning adultery and fornication are overly harsh considering human nature and the prevailing temperaments of Chakpuris. Given the "uncontrollable" nature of such urges and desires, it is difficult for many to understand the severity of *hudud* punishments. Besides, many say, sexual affairs are enjoyable, and, at least for many village men, provide a focus for much storytelling and joke-making (Kurin, 1985: 120-1).

3.3.2 Rape

In Pakistan, the common conception of rape is a situation in which the victim and the offender do not know each other at all in advance. Situations where women are acquainted with the offender beforehand are not considered rape situations. The predominance of this concept is due to the segregation of the sexes in the middle class and the non-existence of free sexual morality in this class. In most cases, rape is not reported to the police because of fear of shame and injury to the honour of the family. The victim herself is blamed for not guarding herself well enough and for exposing herself to risky situations. Among the poorer class, the segregation of the sexes is not as rigid as in the middle class because poor class women have to work to earn their living. They are thus more likely to become victims of rape. In villages, landlords raping women working in the field is a common event. In the cities, girls working as domestic servants are exposed to such risks. Village women also become victims of rape when rival parties want to revenge themselves and to damage the honour of each other's family. Usually, the only cases of rape reported to the police are those involving little girls or incest offences.

The concept of rape within marriage is non-existent in Pakistan. It is the right of a husband to have sex with his wife anytime he wants - obedience to her husband is the duty of a wife. The husband is justified in using force and violence against his disobedient wife.

There is a strong prevailing feeling among women in Pakistan that the Ordinance does not protect women against rape. The rapist is more protected by the law. In this way, the law supports full male domination in Pakistani society (Mehdi, Rubya, 1990).

Before the *zina* Ordinance of 1979, the law of rape was governed by the PPC Section 375 of the Code provided the definition of rape. This is repeated in the *zina* Ordinance of 1979. However, the PPC protected girls under fourteen years by providing that sexual intercourse, even with their consent, would constitute rape. This immunity for girls under fourteen years is not incorporated in the *zina* Ordinance.

Rape is defined in Section 6 of the Ordinance as different from wilful sexual intercourse with a woman. It says that a person commits rape:

> if he or she has sexual intercourse with a woman or man, as the case may be, to whom he or she is not validly married, in any of the following circumstances namely:
>
> (a)   against the will of the victim
>
> (b)   without the consent of the victim
>
> (c)   with the consent of the victim, when the consent has been obtained by putting the victim in fear of death or of hurt; or
>
> d)   with the consent of the victim, when the offender knows that the offender is not validly married to the victim and that the consent is given because the victim believes that the offender is another person to whom the victim is or believes herself or himself to be validly married.

According to this definition, a female could be legally punished for committing rape, i.e., the victim of rape could be a male. What it really means is not clear, since there has been no case where a woman has been accused of committing rape.

Like adultery/fornication, rape is also divided by the Ordinance into rape liable to *hadd* and rape liable to *tazir* punishment. Again, a distinction for the purpose of punishment is made between a married (muhsan) rapist and an unmarried (non-muhsan) rapist. The punishment for a married rapist under *hadd* is stoning to death, while the punishment for an unmarried rapist is one hundred lashes in a public place and may include other punishments which can include the sentence of death.

Proofs required for rape liable to *hadd* are the same as those required for fornication/adultery, i.e., confession of the rapist or evidence of four Muslim, pious, male eye-witnesses to the act of penetration. Lucy Carroll calls '*hadd* punishment' academic, because it hardly seems probable that anyone except a lunatic would commit fornication, adultery, or rape in public, i.e., in the presence of at least four male adult Muslims of unimpeachable reputation (Carroll, 1983: 68).

She further questions that:

> ... if rape were committed publicly in the presence of at least four witnesses, would not these witnesses be more appropriately described as accessories to the crime? It is hard to imagine four adult men, each fulfilling the personal requirements of respectability and probity that Islam demands of a witness, standing by and quietly watching a rape take place. And surely, if they did quietly stand by and watch the spectacle, this would amount to 'abetment' of the offence under section 19 of the ordinance (*ibid:* 68-9).

Another notable Muslim lawyer from India says that the Pakistani Ordinance recognizes rape as rape in public (Mahmood Tahir, 1982: 287).

The Ordinance excludes the evidence of a woman in a case of rape. One Pakistani author comments as follows:

> This crime is never committed in the presence of four witnesses - instead it is usually committed in a situation where no witnesses are available. In such a case, if the evidence of the raped woman is not accepted it will encourage the rapist to commit this crime again (Shehab, 1984a: 82-4).

Let us now look into rape liable to *tazir* which involves more practical questions. Section 10 of the Ordinance provides that if proof as required in Section 8 is not available, the case is to be tried under *tazir*. Punishment for rape under *tazir* is a maximum of 10 years imprisonment, thirty lashes and a fine.

The Ordinance does not provide the standard of proof required for liability to *tazir* punishment. Usually both the offender and the victim are medically examined, the man for sexual potency and the woman for the presence of semen. The main consideration before the court is whether the woman has offered 'real resistance'; lacking this element, a case of rape is not established. In the case of *Bahadur Shah v. The State*,[25] the conviction under Section 10(3) (rape) of the Ordinance was amended to one under Section 10(2) (consensual illegal sex). It was held that as Kalsoom Bibi, the victim in that case, had offered no 'real resistance' (the female doctor found no injury to the thighs, legs, elbows, arms, knees, face, back and buttocks of the victim); it therefore appeared that the act was done with her consent. As we can see in this case, the thin demarcating line between consensual sex and rape is 'real resistance'. In two other cases of rape the offenders were not convicted, because both victims were found to be women of 'easy virtue', loose character and to have habitually enjoyed sexual intercourse.[26]

One of the criticisms of the Ordinance is that it makes no distinction between adultery/fornication on one hand and rape on the other. Generally, one would think that the penalty for rape in comparison to consensual sex should be much more severe; rape should be regarded as a graver crime since it entails violation of the victim's mental and physical integrity. For comparison, we may look at the table below.

Table 1: Comparison of *Zina* and Rape

Division of offender into *muhsan* & non-*muhsan*	Proof for *zina* & rape liable to *hadd*	Punishment for *zina* & rape liable to *hadd*	Proof for *zina* & rape liable to *tazir*	Punishment for *zina* & rape liable to *tazir*
Zina (consensual sex)				
Married offender (adultery)	a). Confession to the crime b). four truthful adult male Muslim eye-witnesses	Stoned to death in a public place	No standard of proof is provided; at the discretion of the judge	Imprisonment for a maximum of 10 years, 30 lashes and a fine
Unmarried offender (fornication)	As above	One hundred lashes in a public place	As above	As above
Rape				
Married rapist	a). Confession to the crime b). four truthful adult male Muslim eye-witnesses	Stoned to death in a public place	No standard of proof is provided; at the discretion of the judge	Imprisonment for 25 years and 30 lashes
Unmarried rapist	As above	One hundred lashes in a public place & such other punishments as the death sentence	As above	As above

Lucy Carroll, an American scholar, provided some defence for the Ordinance saying that the two offences, i.e., rape and fornication/adultery, are sufficiently differentiated from each other. She may be right to the extent that a 'much more severe maximum penalty is imposed on the person guilty of rape (i.e., twenty-five years' imprisonment as opposed to ten years' imprisonment)'. Furthermore if an unmarried (non-muhsan) offender confesses in order to attract *hadd*, punishment in the case of rape is not confined to one hundred lashes (as for a non-muhsan in consensual sex), but he is also liable to 'such other punishment, including the sentence of death' (Carroll, 1983: 66-71). But my contention still is that the Ordinance fails to make enough distinction between the heinous crime of rape and consensual sex; firstly because, as we can see from the table, the standard of proof provided in both offences is the same, at least for 'rape in public' and 'consensual sex in public', secondly because as we saw the demarcating line between the two offences is so thin that if a woman comes to court with a case of rape and fails to convince the court, she can be convicted of consensual sex. The famous case of the blind girl is also before us. The father and son who raped the unfortunate girl were at least in the first instance acquitted on the benefit of the doubt, while the girl was convicted of consensual sex on the evidence of pregnancy.

There is no doubt that, after the Ordinance of 1979, women have become more reluctant than before to bring a case of rape into court. The exact number of rape cases is not known. It is astonishing to see that statistics provided by the Bureau of Police Research and Development, the Ministry of the Interior and the Government of Pakistan classify rape and consensual sex under the same category (i.e., *zina* cases). According to this the total number of *zina* cases in 1983 was 1,682, increasing in 1984 to 1,843 (Avolakh, 1986). So there are loopholes in the Ordinance through which a rapist can escape, while the women of Pakistan are more vulnerable to attacks by rapists while this Ordinance in in force. Moreover, there are no crisis centres to help the victim deal with the social and psychological problems that she faces after the event. The only solace is her own family and help from that quarter may itself not be forthcoming, as the honour of the family is damaged. In reaction to the injustice done in the case of rape, educated women in Pakistan have formed an organistion called *War Against Rape* to assist women in rape cases. A crisis centre for such women, called *Roshni*, has been established by *Voice Against Torture*.

3.3.3 Homosexuality

> We also sent Lot: he said to his people: 'Do you commit adultery
> as no people in creation (ever) committed before you? For you
> practise your lusts on men in preference to women: you are
> indeed a people transgressing beyond limit' (*Quran*, ch. 7:84).

Unlike the law of most Western countries, Islam regards homosexuality as a great crime.[27] To have anal sex with women is also
forbidden. Among Muslim jurists, there is no dispute that homosexuality is a sexual offence. However, there is a number of
disagreements regarding punishment for this offence. Some jurists
prescribe *tazir* punishment for homosexuality, while others recommend strict punishments like *hadd* to be inflicted on the offender
and equate homosexuals with adulterers. Muslim jurists also
differentiate the active from the passive partner for purposes of
punishment (Doi, 1984: 242-3; Safwat, 1982: 158). Again, this is one
of the areas in Pakistan in which almost no research has been done.

Homosexuality is a clandestine sexual practice in Pakistan.
It is something which exists in society but is not talked about. In
spite of the fact that it is forbidden by law it is not only practised
but also, in villages where it is not unusual to have 'one's boy'
simultaneously with one's wife, it can be something to be proud
of. In the cities the practice of homosexuality is usually hidden,
an unwanted but necessary alternative to the dominant hetero-
sexual milieu, not a right. Consequently, homosexual relationships
suffer from extreme forms of secrecy, guilt, hopelessness and
oppression.

Section 12 of the *Offence of Zina (Enforcement of Hudood)
Ordinance*, 1979, did not make any radical change in the law
regarding homosexuality in Pakistan. The law on homosexuality
is still governed by Section 377 of the PPC, which provides that
voluntary carnal intercourse, 'against the order of nature' with a
man, woman or animal is an offence punishable with imprisonment for life, or with imprisonment of not less than two years nor
more than ten years and shall also be liable to fine. The *zina*
Ordinance does not provide for the punishment of persons committing the offence of sodomy or homosexuality. In one case it
was held that since Section 12 of the Ordinance did not provide
for the punishment of persons actually committing sodomy, this
section seemed to punish only those who kidnap or abduct a
person for the purpose of subjecting such person to unnatural
lust.[28] Kidnapping or abduction are necessary parts of the offence
of subjecting a person to unnatural lust, according to Section 12.[29]

3.3.4 *Attempt to Commit an Offence Punishable Under the Ordinance*

Section 18 of the Ordinance provides a definition of 'attempt' and specifies the punishment for attempting to commit an offence punishable under the Ordinance. 'Attempt' has been defined in the same words as in Section 511 of the PPC as 'any act towards the commission of the offence'. The explanation provided is that a crime consists of four stages: 1) intention to commit it, 2) preparation, 3) attempt and 4) the crime itself.

A distinction is made between attempt and preparation. Preparation 'consists in devising or arranging the means or measures necessary for the commission of the offence', while attempt is 'the direct movement towards the commission'. Furthermore, an attempt is considered an act which is immediately and not merely remotely connected with the commission of the offence. It is an act which fails through circumstances independent of the will of the person who seeks its accomplishment (Zahur-ud-din, 1987: 77-8; Angam, 1983: 367-8).

The punishment provided for an attempt to commit an offence under the Ordinance is imprisonment for up to one half of the longest term provided for that offence, and/or thirty lashes and/or the fine stipulated for the offence. This means that the offence of attempt can be constituted in respect of adultery, fornication, rape, kidnapping, etc. This has again created hardship in cases of fornication and adultery. It can be seen more clearly through the case law. In the case of *Mohammad Zahoor v. Mst. Shahnaz*,[30] both the man and the woman had been found guilty of an attempt by the Sub-Divisional Magistrate in Abbottabad. The court had sentenced them to five years' imprisonment and Mohammad Zahoor had been further sentenced to ten lashes. This judgment had been made in view of the fact that the girl had visited the man's shop at 10 p.m. and after she entered the shop the door was closed and chained from inside. It was thus held that she went there with no other purpose than to commit *zina*. However, on appeal, a higher court found that the five essentials to establish an offence of attempt were missing. The five essentials to establish 'attempt', the court said, were:

i)   The existence of an intention.
ii) Some step taken towards the act after the completion of preparation.
iii) The step must be apparently, though not necessarily, adapted to the purpose designed.

iv)   It must come dangerously near to success.

v)   It must fall short of completion of the ultimate design.

At the time the police entered the shop (a tailor's), the girl was occupying the cot meant for customers and both of them were properly dressed. It was not found to be 'an attempt' to commit *zina* and the appeal was upheld.

However, in the case of *Pak Muhammad v. The State*,[31] an attempt to commit *zina* was held to be established. The facts of this case were that neighbours saw a young man and woman enter a house 'in suspicious circumstances' and when the door was opened they found them undressed, the woman lying naked on the cot and the man standing naked. On these facts, the court held that, both being beyond the stage of preparation, there had been an attempt to commit *zina*, but because of outside intervention they had been unable to proceed. Both of them were sentenced to three years' imprisonment and five lashes.

The same criterion is applied to alleged attempts to commit rape and to attempts to commit fornication or adultery. In a case of rape, *Anwarul Haq v. The State*,[32] it was said with reference to another case[33] that if the accused takes off his own *shalwar* (traditional trousers) and is also successful in removing the *shalwar* of the victim, this would amount to an attempt to commit rape. In another case, *Fahimuddin v. The State*,[34] the petitioner removed his own *shalwar* with the intention of raping a minor, but before proceeding to the actual act he was interrupted by the girl's brother. The High Court held that the petitioner was still at the stage of preparing to commit the offence of *zina*, a stage which appeared to be short of an attempt to commit *zina*. In the case of *Muhammad Shafique v The State*,[35] a woman failed to establish an attempt to commit rape, when she alleged that the petitioner had removed her *shalwar*, but had been unable to proceed because of her hue and cry. The court also mentioned the medical report in which the doctor had opined that the prosecutrix had long habitually engaged in sexual intercourse.

In the light of the above-mentioned cases, it is clearly seen that in attempts of fornication and adultery things get difficult for the parties involved, while in the case of attempted rape - which is a more heinous act - it becomes difficult to establish that an attempt was even made. Every case is decided on the facts whether there is an 'attempt' or a mere 'preparation' to commit the offence.

3.3.5 Kidnapping/Abducting or Enticing Women

Kidnapping or enticing a woman is a common act in Pakistan, especially in the villages. This can also be seen in the *dar-ul-uman* (centres which provide shelter to homeless women and are conventionally accepted in Pakistan), where a substantial number of inmates are women having been abandoned after abduction. Before the independence of Bangladesh, Bengali women were kidnapped and brought to West Pakistan. Some are still living in these centres, either thinking of going back to Bangladesh one day or being too frightened to go back after having spent such a long time away from home.

There are different reasons for kidnapping women. Sometimes a woman is kidnapped when a man wants to marry her and her parents' consent is difficult to obtain. As a woman is considered an honour to a family, kidnapping can also occur when the purpose is to disgrace a family because of some old family enmity or revenge. Women are also kidnapped from one part of Pakistan and sold in another.

In the situation where the woman herself elopes with a man, the man is usually falsely accused of abduction. I was informed by a villager in Makkawal that, in their village even if a girl leaves her home of her own free will, the case is considered one of abduction.

> The legal authorities which are invariably involved in such cases show little consideration and mercy to the girl who leaves home with her consent which is normally the case. To them she is the real culprit.
>
> Under the previous law, when an adult girl left home with someone out of her own free will, no charge could be labelled against her but now according to the Islamic law she is tried for adultery and becomes an equal participant in the crime (Abbas, Pervez, M, Shamim, Pervez, S, Seema: 1985).

A practicing lawyer explained that when girls are married in their childhood and the marriage do not work, some of the girls run away from home. This brings dishonour to the family and the family react by fabricating a case of *zina* (Mubshar, 1990).

Section 11 of the *Offence of Zina (Enforcement of Hudood) Ordinance* deals with the offence of kidnapping. According to the Section, kidnapping is an offence under the Ordinance when the purpose is to compel a female to marry against her will, or to force or seduce her to engage in illicit intercourse. The punishment for such an offence is imprisonment for life, whipping not exceeding thirty lashes and a fine. The same punishment also applies to the person who, by means of criminal intimidation, abuse of authority or any other method of compulsion, induces any woman to go from any place intending, or knowing that it is likely, that she will be seduced to illicit intercourse with another. Section 11 is almost the same as Section 366 of the PPC, which was in force before the Ordinance. The only difference between the two is that Section 11 has increased the period of imprisonment from ten years to life and added the punishment of flogging for the offence of kidnapping.

The Ordinance does not provide a definition of kidnapping, but Section 2 of the Ordinance provides that all other terms and expressions not defined in the Ordinance shall have the same meaning as in, *inter alia*, the PPC. Therefore, courts refer to the definition of kidnapping provided in Sections 359 and 361 of the PPC Kidnapping under Section 359 is either kidnapping from Pakistan or kidnapping from lawful guardianship. Section 361 defines kidnapping from lawful guardianship as the taking away or enticing of any minor female under sixteen years of age out of the keeping of her lawful guardian without the consent of such guardian. In the case of *Zafar Ali v. The State*,[36] it was found that the victim was proved to be less than sixteen years of age. Even if she was consenting party to the kidnapping as well as to the commission of *zina*, since she was less than sixteen years of age and had been taken away from the keeping of her lawful guardians without their consent, it was held that the offence of kidnapping was established under Section 11.

Section 16 of the *zina* Ordinance deals with enticing, taking away or detaining a woman with criminal intent. The Section states:

> Whoever takes or entices away any woman with intent that she may have illicit intercourse with any person, or conceals or detains with that intent any woman, shall be punished with imprisonment of either description for a term which may extend to seven years and with whipping not exceeding thirty stripes and shall be liable to fine.

Section 16 of the Ordinance resembles Section 498 of the PPC in its wording. The difference is that Section 498 confines the 'offence of enticing or taking away' only to a married woman, while Section 16 of the *zina* Ordinance makes it an offence against all women; it is not necessary for the woman to be married in order to make the act a criminal offence.

Under both Section 11 and Section 16 of the *zina* Ordinance, an accused female cannot be held guilty of the offence of abduction of a male person. In the case of *Saifur Rehman and another v. The State*,[37] it was said that in an abduction case:

> ...a woman can only be held guilty of the offence if she entices or takes away another of her own sex. The enticing or taking away or forcible removal of a male person by a female, although ethically much deplorable [sic], it would not be a culpable offence under either of the above-mentioned sections of the ordinance.

3.3.6 Prostitution and Deceitful Inducing a Belief of Lawful Marriage

Sections 13 and 14 of the Ordinance deal with the selling and buying of persons for purposes of prostitution. The punishment for both types of act is imprisonment for life and whipping not exceeding thirty lashes and a fine. Section 15 deals with the situation where a man deceitfully causes any woman to believe that she is married to him and cohabits with her. Such a person shall be punished with rigorous imprisonment of up to twenty-five years, flogging not exceeding thirty lashes and a fine.

Very little research has been done on the condition of prostitutes in Pakistan though prostitution is common. Therefore little is known about the effect of Islamization on prostitution. However research sponsored by the Women Division shows that it is seldom that prostitutes are convicted. '... though arrested several times. Even if they are challenged they get away with influence after a brief interrogation' (Abbas, Pervez. S, Shamim, & Pervez M. 1985: 7).

3.4 OFFENCE OF QAZF (Enforcement of Hadd) ORDINANCE, VIII, OF 1979

3.4.1 Definition of qazf.

Section 3 of the Ordinance provides the definition of *qazf*. According to this section, *qazf* is committed when a person by spoken word, writing, signs, or by visible representation makes or publishes a false allegation of fornication, adultery or rape, (i.e., *zina*). The intention to harm and the knowledge or reason to believe that such imputation will harm the reputation or hurt the feelings of the person to whom the crime has imputed is necessary to form the crime of *qazf*. *Qazf* can be committed against a deceased person. An imputation in the form of an alternative or expressed ironically would also amount to *qazf*.

However, it is not *qazf* if the imputation is true or is made for the public good. Neither is it *qazf* if the imputation is made in good faith against any person by any of those who have lawful authority over that person.

Three further situations would amount to *qazf*: (i) where the accusation is made in court, but the accuser fails to produce four witnesses, (ii) where the court finds that a witness has given false evidence of fornication, adultery or rape (i.e., *zina* or *zina-bil-jabr*), (iii) where the court finds that a complainant has made a false accusation of rape (i.e., *zina-bil-jabr*).

In 1982, a petition was filed challenging Section 3 of the Offence of *qazf* Ordinance.[38] Counsel's argument was that Section 3 is bad because it makes imputation against a male as well as a deceased person punishable, whereas according to the Quranic verses (24: 4) only those should be punished who accuse honourable women. The Chief Justice at that time, Aftab Hussain, while arguing against counsel, referred to other verses of the *Quran* (19) which refer to slandered males and females alike and argued that the verses which refer to women only do so because of a particular incident (when one of the beloved wives of the Prophet was alleged to have committed adultery); this does not mean that those who slander males are excluded from punishment. He mentioned the principle of *taqhlib* (applying the rule of one type of thing to another) and drew the conclusion that punishment should be the same if the person slandered is a male or deceased. Therefore, the petition was dismissed and Section 3 was held to be good and in full accordance with the *Quran*.

The expression 'intention to harm' has been considered, in different cases, the basis of the offence of *qazf*. In the case of *Muhammad Abdullah v. The State*,[39] it was held that mere failure of prosecution in *zina* cases under *Offence of Zina (Enforcement of Hudood) Ordinance*, 1979 does not automatically establish a charge of *qazf* against the complainant or witnesses appearing in such cases. In order to constitute *qazf* it must be further proved that the complainant/witnesses made an imputation of *zina* with the intention to harm the reputation or hurt the feelings of a person. There would be no offence of *qazf* in a case where such imputation is absent. The same was established in *Bashir Ahmed v. The State*,[40] where Bashir Ahmed's sentence of 80 lashes was set aside on the grounds that the allegation of *qazf* was not sufficiently supported with the intention to harm the reputation or hurt the feelings of the complainant. This entitled the accused to acquittal.

While it is important for the complainant to establish the intention to harm the reputation or hurt the feelings of a person, the accused could, however, put forward the defence that he made the accusation in good faith or had lawful authority over the person against whom the accusation was made. In the case of *Abdul Rashid v. Safia Bibi*,[41] the husband, in a written statement in reply to his wife's suit for maintenance for an infant female child and recovery of dower, disowned the female child, accusing his wife of adultery. It was held that an allegation of *zina* and disowning one's child is a serious imputation which affects the reputation of the person concerned. The appellant knowingly made this allegation of *zina* and his defence of good faith was not held to be good on the grounds that good faith implies good care and attention. It was held that the appellant did not exercise due care in the circumstances and did not act in good faith while making the allegation against his wife.

The expression 'lawful' authority was also well explained in the above-mentioned case.[42] It was said that lawful authority means legal authority where a relationship of guardian and ward is established, i.e., a husband can legitimately claim lawful authority over his wife and his children. Similarly, parents can have lawful authority over their children. But the suggestion that a Judge of the Family Court could have the lawful authority over a minor or her mother when dealing with a suit for maintenance of that minor child was rejected in the above case.

From one of the cases decided under Section 3 of the *qazf* Ordinance, it is clear that the allegation of *zina* should be made in clear words in order to form the offence of *qazf*. In the case of *Mian Abdul Qadus v. Sahib Ali and others*,[43] a written document was alleged to be *qazf* within the meaning of Section 3 of the Ordinance. The allegation levelled in the document by the respondent against the petitioner was that he had first abducted the wife of a blacksmith and then kept her as a *zoga*. The wording could be interpreted in two ways: one that she was kept by the petitioner his wife and second that she was a mistress or kept woman. It was said that, if two interpretations could be made, then the one favourable to the accused should be preferred. So the petition was dismissed as there was no mention of any adultery having been committed by the petitioner.

Section 8 of the Ordinance provides that a complaint of *qazf* can only be filed by the person who was imputed of having committed *zina*. It is interesting to note that the offence only exists when the allegation is adultery, fornication, or rape. If the allegation consists of aiding and abetting of these offences, a case of *qazf* under the Ordinance cannot be brought. In *Muhammad Abdullah v. The State*,[44] it was held that the slander only referred to assisting a rapist and this was considered something other than imputation of *zina*.

3.4.2 *Qazf Liable to Hadd*

The Ordinance classifies *qazf* as either: *qazf* liable to *hadd* and *qazf* liable to *tazir* (Section 4).

Section 5 says that any adult who intentionally and without ambiguity commits *qazf* of *zina* liable to *hadd* against a particular person who is a *muhsan* and capable of performing sexual intercourse is, subject to the provisions of this Ordinance, said to commit *qazf* liable to *hadd*. The meaning of the word *muhsan* is different from the word *muhsan* used in the *zina* Ordinance. Here, *muhsan* means a sane adult Muslim who is either a virgin or has only had sexual intercourse with his/her lawfully wedded spouse. This section further says that in cases where the allegation is that of illegitimacy, the *qazf/hadd* would be deemed as being committed against the mother of that person. Something very odd about this section is that it adds the capability of performing sexual intercourse to the definition of *muhsan*.[45]

Section 6 states what may be accepted as proof of *qazf* liable to *hadd*. Such proof may take three forms, a) if the accused confesses to having committed the offence, b) if the accused commits *qazf* in court and c) if at least two Muslim adult male witnesses give direct evidence of the commission of *qazf*. The first and the third form of proof are traditional Islamic forms but the second form is unusual. It was objected by counsel in a petition that as the position of a *qadi* (Muslim judge) is that of a witness, he cannot render judgment in the matter if the *qazf* is committed before him. Moreover, no *qazf* proceedings can be taken unless there is a complaint before the court on behalf of the person aggrieved. The objection was left unanswered.[46]

Punishment of *qazf* liable to *hadd* is eighty lashes and deprivation of the right to act as a witness in future (Section 7).

3.4.3. Qazf Liable to Tazir

Sections 10 and 11 of the Ordinance deal with *qazf* liable to *tazir*. Section 10 lays down that where *qazf* is not liable to *hadd* (if the required proofs are not available, or where *hadd* may not be imposed because of the exception in Section 9), there shall be a conviction under *tazir*. The punishment for *qazf* liable to *tazir* is imprisonment for up to two years, flogging not exceeding forty lashes and a fine.

In a case which was tried under *tazir,* it was held that where an allegation of *zina* is made and there exists some element of doubt regarding the genuineness/correctness of the nikahnama (contract of marriage), it is a well settled principle of Islamic jurisprudence that the benefit of the doubt should go to the accused. *Qazf* liable to *tazir* could not stand because the benefit of the doubt was to go to the appellant.[47]

3.4.4 Lian

Where a husband makes an allegation of adultery against his wife, both parties are offered the opportunity of going through a procedure known as *lian*. In *Haji Bakhtiar Said Muhammad v. Dure-e-Shahwar*,[48] the question before the court was whether Section 7 which deals with punishment for *qazf* liable to *hadd* also applies when an accusation of *zina* is levelled by a husband against his wife. It was held that Section 7 of the *qazf* Ordinance was not applicable to the case of a husband accusing his wife of *zina* during the existence of the marital tie. If the husband has four witnesses to prove the allegation, the question of *qazf* shall not arise. If he has no witnesses except himself and wants to avoid prosecution for *qazf*, Section 14, which lays down the procedure for *lian*, would apply. In the case mentioned above it was stressed that, before *lian* is applied, two conditions must be satisfied: firstly, that the allegation is made during the existence of the marriage; secondly, that the husband has no witness except himself to prove the allegation. It was, however, suggested that, as the second condition is not specifically mentioned, steps should be taken to amend Section 14.[49] If a husband divorces his wife for alleged unchastity, the question of the applicability of Section 14 will depend upon the fact whether the utterance or act constituting *qazf* preceded or followed the *talaq*.

Section 14 says that if a husband accuses his *muhsan* wife of *zina* before the court and the wife does not accept the accusation as true, the procedure of *lian* should apply. This consists of oath taking, the husband accusing his wife of adultery and the wife denying the allegation. Then the court passes an order dissolving the marriage. If either of them refuse to go through this procedure they are imprisoned until both agree to go through the it, or until the wife accepts her husband's accusations as true. If she confesses, she will be stoned to death in a public place in compliance with the *Offence of Zina (Enforcement of Hudood) Ordinance*, 1979. The condition laid down in Section 14 that the husband accuse his wife 'before the court' was again challenged in *Haji Bakhtiar's* case. In answer to the objection it was held that *lian* proceedings are always held before a qadi; unless the accusation is made before a court - even if it is made outside the court and brought before the court - *lian* proceedings cannot be commenced. Therefore, it follows that the words 'before a court' are good enough.[50]

According to Section 14, the *lian* procedure will always lead to a divorce. *Lian* could be taken as a form of divorce. This might be hard for couples who still want to be husband and wife after the procedure of *lian*, but the reason provided is that it is against human nature for the parties to live together happily after such an incident.[51] In the case of *Nek Bakhat v. The State*,[52] it was discussed whether, after the procedure of *lian*, the allegation of adultery should be considered dropped and the wife absolved from the charge of and punishment for adultery. The possibility of convicting her under *tazir* (which would have meant a sentence of rigorous imprisonment for up to ten years and thirty lashes) instead of *hadd* was suggested, if no material brought against her by her husband was such that she could be convicted under *hadd*.[53] But it was held that once the wife refutes the allegation of *zina* against her in the *lian* proceedings, she is completely absolved from guilt and, therefore, cannot be punished under *tazir*, notwithstanding the subsequent availability and production of evidence. However, Chief Justice Aftab Hussain supported the view that *tazir* cannot be averted in spite of *lian*.[54]

Finally, it should be noted that *lian* proceedings are only possible when a husband accuses his wife of adultery. If a wife accuses her husband of adultery, the procedure of *lian* is not applicable.

3.4.5 Conclusion

This Ordinance does not seem to serve the purpose for which it was made (Patel, 1991; Jahangir, 1990: 60, 79-83; Tanweer,

1990). The purpose of the Ordinance, as we have seen, was to stop misuse of the Offence of Zina (Enforcement of Haudood) Ordinance, 1979, so that people would think twice before bringing a charge of *zina*. But because of the inefficiency of the law-enforcing machinery and long delays, people involved in *zina* cases get such a bad reputation and bad name during the proceedings that it is too late to find protection in the *qazf* Ordinance.

Maybe it is because of the inefficiency of the Ordinance that, in the years 1983 and 1984, the total number of *zina* cases in all of Pakistan was 1,638 and 1,843, respectively, while there were only 18 registered *qazf* cases in 1983 and 17 in 1984 (Auolakh, 1986: 54). Even in notorious cases of misuse of the *zina* Ordinance that were much publicized in the national and international press, one never hears if the complainants/ witnesses were ever punished for bringing false accusation of *zina*.

3.5 THE PROHIBITION (Enforcement of Hadd) ORDER, 1979

3.5.1 Introduction

Before 1979, some steps were taken to prohibit the consumption of alcoholic liquor by Muslims. Such steps were first taken in 1949,[55] but one of the more effective in this regard was taken by Z.A Bhutto in 1977 under opposition pressure. An Act known as the Prohibition Act XXIV of 1977 was passed, extending prohibition to the whole of Pakistan and making the consumption of intoxicating liquor by a Muslim citizen an offence punishable by imprisonment.[56]

In 1979, a new prohibition (enforcement of *hadd*) order was enforced in pursuance of further Islamization (Husain, M, 1984).

According to this Ordinance, drinking is defined as the intentional taking of intoxicants without *ikrah* (fear of injury to the person's property or honour) and *iztirar* (fear of death due to extreme hunger or thirst or serious illness (Section 6)) .

A petition in 1983 objected to the allowance under the Ordinance for medicinal use of intoxicating liquor; reliance was placed on two traditions of Prophet Muhammad according to which he prohibited even the medicinal use of intoxicating liquors. Justice Salaluddim Ahmed, however, quoted from a few verses of the *Quran* in order to show that God has permitted the use of 'strictly prohibited things under conditions of necessity'; for example, he said that though it is prohibited for a man to see any portion of a woman's body, when a female patient is suffering from acute pain and is likely to die and no female doctor is available, it is permissible for a male doctor to examine the concealed portions of the body. The petition was dismissed, upholding the use of liquor under *iztirar*.[57]

Under this Ordinance, the import, export, transportation, manufacture, processing, sale and serving of intoxicants is forbidden and is punishable with a flogging not exceeding thirty lashes, imprisonment for up to five years and a fine (Section 3).

The possession of intoxicants is dealt with separately. It is punishable by imprisonment not exceeding two years, a flogging of no more than thirty lashes and a fine. Non-Muslim foreigners and non-Muslim citizens are exempted from this provision. They are allowed to possess a reasonable quantity of intoxicating liquor for the purpose of using it as part of their religious ceremonies at or about the time of such ceremony prescribed by their religion (Section 4).

These restrictions on the rights of non-Muslims were challenged in the famous case of *Nosher Rustam Sidhwa v. the Federation of Pakistan*.[58] It was argued that the use of liquor by non-Muslims should be permitted without being restricted to use in a religious ceremony.

Justice Agha Ali Hyder went further than this and argued that drinking wine and liquor was not totally unlawful even to believers, so non-Muslims should be no worse off. His judgment was interesting. He quoted verses from the *Quran* in which a list of forbidden things is provided and there is no mention of wine and liquor. He further mentioned verses from the *Quran* where for wine and liquor the words *eschew*, *avoid* or *shun* are used. The word *unlawful* is never used. Therefore he argued, also in the light of other Muslim authorities, that only some types of liquor are prohibited in Islam so Muslims are still left with strong liquors to enjoy. As God himself has promised wines in heaven, 'it will thus appear that wine, which is not heady and tempestuous, does have a place in Heaven. If used in moderation, it does not defile a believer in this world as well'.[59]

3.5.2 Offence of Drinking Liable to Hadd

The offence of drinking is divided into drinking liable to *hadd* and drinking liable to *tazir*. Drinking liable to *hadd* applies to an 'adult Muslim' taking intoxicating liquor intentionally by mouth. The *hadd* punishment is eighty lashes. Non-Muslims are exempted from *hadd* punishment (Section 8). It should be noted that in this section stress is laid on 'taking liquor by mouth'. In 1982, a case came before the court where the appellant was convicted of smoking a hashish cigarette and sentenced to 80 lashes. It was pleaded on behalf of the appellant that the offence would not fall under *hadd* punishment as there was no drinking of liquor by mouth and on the basis of this argument the sentence of flogging was revoked.[60]

For an offence of drinking to fall under *hadd*, strict proof is required. It could be in two forms. The offence could be proved either by the evidence of two pious Muslim adult male witnesses (of course fulfilling the requirement of *tazkiyah al-shuhood*) or if the accused himself confesses to the crime - in court (Section 9). It the case against the accused is not proved according to the requirements mentioned above, the Ordinance provides for sentencing under *tazir*. *Hadd* punishment shall also not be enforced if the convict retracts his confession, or if any witness retracts his testimony (Section 10).

3.5.3 *Offence of Drinking Liable to Tazir*

Tazir punishment is imposed where the standard of proof is not sufficient to allow punishment under *hadd*, but the offence stands proved by the evidence on record. *Tazir* punishment is imprisonment for up to three years or a flogging not exceeding thirty lashes, or both. *Tazir* punishment can also be imposed on non-Muslims. If a non-Muslim citizen of Pakistan is found guilty of drinking otherwise than as part of a religious ceremony, *tazir* punishment is to be imposed. A non-Muslim foreigner would also be liable to *tazir* punishment but only if found drinking in a public place. Thus non-Muslim Pakistanis are allowed to drink alcohol only in connection with religious ceremonies, while non-Muslim foreigners can consume alcohol at all times, but only in private. Describing this restriction on non-Muslims, Justice (retd.) Salahuddin Ahmed said:

> In any event the evil of drinking, etc., cannot be allowed to exist or flourish in any Islamic state. Exemptions and concessions allowed to non-Muslims to the extent mentioned above must, however, be applied strictly so as not to permit the taking of or dealing in intoxicants in public. The non-Muslims will not be allowed to violate any public law, including the law of prohibition, openly or publicly.[61]

In regard to the method of arrest, the Ordinance provides that no person shall be detained or arrested by the police on suspicion of having taken an intoxicant, unless he is referred to a medical officer.

The prohibition order under the schedule provides a list of intoxicants. They are Indian hemp including all forms known as *bhang, siddhi* or *ganja*; *charas* or mixtures thereof; opium or its derivatives; coca leaf and its derivatives, and hashish. However, it was felt that this Ordinance was not sufficient to control narcotic problems, which are felt not only on a national but also on an international level. The government increased the penalities under the Dangerous Drugs Act and the Prohibition Order by an amendment, President's Order No. 12 of 1983. Under this amendment, the transportation, import, export, manufacturing, or traffic in opium or coca leaf or their derivatives is punishable by a maximum of life imprisonment, or by a minimum of two years imprisonment, a flogging not exceeding thirty lashes and a fine (Patel, 1986: 39-40).

3.5.4 Sociological Aspect of the Prohibition Ordinance

Kurin observed in his survey that the ban hit village addicts particularly hard, as previously licensed opium shops were closed. Addicts may have access to drugs in urban areas and along the frontier but the lifelong users of opium and hashish in the villages now have none. During an interim period, village addicts were able to receive a medicinal substitute from an authorized hospital or clinic, but Kurin contends that the distance they had to travel and the lack of satisfaction they received from the substitute mitigated the possible effectiveness of the program. Though the opium addicts did not consider their addiction an object of pride it did not, on the other hand, invite the scorn or moral umbrage of their neighbours. After the ban, villagers were aware of their sufferings and sympathized with their plight. Kurin also reports the death of a former addict. I also learned that many addicts were afraid of contacting hospitals or clinics for fear of punishments under the Prohibition Ordinance. They were very distrustful of the authorities. Some survived and conquered their addiction; about one of those Kurin says: 'He doesn't feel redeemed, however. By no means does he feel it makes him more moral, a better Muslim, or anything of the sort. He did it because he had to' (Kurin, 1986: 122).

Some of the addicts continue to use less powerful but locally available drugs. In the cities people have also resorted to *dasi sharab* which, because of its bad quality, could also be dangerous to life. Kurin concludes: 'In short, forcing abstinence was painful and did not have any moral implication for village addicts *(ibid:* 123).

About the effects of the Ordinance, Rashida Patel says:

The use of and addiction to, dangerous narcotics in Pakistan has greatly increased since 1979. The production and smuggling of narcotics has also escalated tremendously (Patel, 1986: 39).

She reports one viewpoint which claims that this happened because of the Prohibition Order. A second view is that the Ordinance has simply not been enforced. The government supported the latter view and made the law more stringent and increased the punishment *(ibid:* 40).

These measures have had little effect. Even today the drug problem continues. According to a survey by journalists, Sohrab Goth (a locality in Karachi) alone receives on every fourth day 10 to 20 tons of opium and its by-products for internal consumption and for transhipment.[62]

3.6   THE EXECUTION OF THE PUNISHMENT OF WHIPPING ORDINANCE, 1979

Flogging as a method of inflicting judicial punishment has a long history (Scott, 1954). In Islamic history, during the time of the Prophet Muhammad and early Muslim rule, corporal punishment meant beating with hands, shoes and clothes. The practice later took the form of lashing.[63] In India corporal punishment including whipping was widespread under Muslim rule and during the British period (Scott, 1938: 111). The Whipping Act, 1909, made by the British was still in force in Pakistan (with perodic amendments) until the promulgation of the Execution of the Punishment of Whipping Ordinance, 1979.

George Ryley Scott distinguishes between flagellation as judicial punishment and flagellation as a species of torture. In other words, there is a possibility that flogging as judicial punishment may develop into a species of torture, for instance through the remarkable severity of the blows, the nature of the instrument used, the prolonged period of punishment, or if the condition of the culprit at the time the flogging is administered is such that permanent injury or death may be caused (Scott, 1954: 188).

The Execution of the Punishment of Whipping Ordinance (IX of 1979) provides a specification of the whip, the conditions and modes under which punishment is to be carried out and finally how it is administered. According to the Ordinance, the whip (excluding the grip) should consist of one single piece without any knob or joint in it (maybe a knot or a joint would add to the severity of the whipping). The length and thickness of the whip may not exceed 1.22 metres and 1.25 centimetres (Section 4). A medical officer must examine the convict before execution of the punishment to make sure that the convict is medically fit to undergo the punishment. A medical officer is to be present during the flogging and if he fears the convict might die, the flogging is to be halted and the remainder of the punishment postponed until the convict is physically fit to undergo it (Section 5(a),(f),(m). If the convict is too old or too weak, the flogging should be carried out in such a manner and at such intervals that it does not cause the death of the convict. In the case of *Nazir Ahmad & others v. The State*,[64] the court included 'minor' in the expression 'weak'; the question was whether punishment by flogging included juvenile offenders. It was held that the Ordinance did not exempt a minor from such punishment. It merely provided that, in case the convict was too weak (a term including juvenile offenders, according to the court), the manner and intervals of flogging should be such as not to cause the death of the convict. In case of illness, flogging was to be postponed. It was also to be postponed if the convict was pregnant, until two months after she had given birth or suffered a miscarriage (Section 5(c),(d)). The Ordinance also lays down that flogging should be carried out in moderate weather (neither too hot, nor too cold) (Section 5(e)). Moreover, the Ordinance requires the impartiality and mature understanding of the person executing the punishment; while applying the whip, the executioner should not raise his hand above his head allowing the whip to be applied with moderate force, so as not to lacerate the skin of the convict. He should not apply the whip to the head, face, stomach, chest, or other delicate parts of the body; on the other hand, lashes shall be spread over the body. The lashes shall be applied, in the case of a male, while he is standing and, in the case of a female, while she is sitting. The Ordinance does not give a description of the clothes to be worn by the convict at the time of flogging, but merely says that they should be 'as required by the injunctions of Islam' (Section 5 (g), (h), (i), (j), (k), (l). A person sentenced to punishment by flogging alone is put into simple imprisonment until the execution of the punishment (Section 6).

Section 7 of the Ordinance empowers the provincial government to make rules for the execution of whipping. Two of the rules made by the Punjab Government are worth noting.[65] As it is held by Muslim jurists that flogging in Islam is for deterrent purposes, a widespread practice in Islamic countries is to flog in public. According to one of the rules, the place should be fixed by the court, and, in cases where the court does not do so, places approved by the provincial government are to be used for such purpose.[66] It would be right to mention here that stadiums, public parks and public places of similar type have been used for floggings. The other rule dealing with the persons carrying out the punishment is interesting because it gives the convict the right to object if he/she thinks that the person appointed to execute the punishment is not impartial. If the authorities find the objection reasonable, another impartial person is to be appointed. So far there is no information as to where if at all this rule has been applied.

This Ordinance has been praised by different persons working in the administration of justice, on the grounds that it shows an improvement upon the one introduced during the British raj and which was prevalent before this Ordinance was passed (Iqbal, Javid: 1984). However, a different view is presented in a booklet published by the Government under the names of two different authors, Justice Aftab Hussain and Justice Gul Muhammad Khan. It is worth quoting the authors:

> While the emphasis of the old law was on physical torture as a punishment, the present law modelled according to *Sharia* lays stress on the humiliation of the convict rather than on causing to him physical injuries. According to the mode of execution laid down by the provincial governments under the old law, the lashes are required to be given on the bare buttocks only (with a fine disinfectant piece of cloth on it), by a well built person who runs to the victim from some distance and strikes him with as much force as he can command.[67]

The authors go on to compare the present Ordinance. They further say:

> Thus, it will be seen that the sentence of lashes in *Shariah* is not severe. It is more to awaken in the convict a realisation of his

wrong. The *Shariah* considers it necessary to expose the convict to humiliation so that he may repent his misdeeds. The *Shariah* also sees to it that humiliation does not remain a permanent scar on him since the execution of sentence followed by repentance guarantees the purification of the convict. It is in this light that the sentence, which is obligatory in Islam in some cases, has to be seen. It is worth noticing that the Whipping Act of 1909 was mainly introduced to eliminate offences against property and sex including abduction, kidnapping, theft, robbery and dacoity for which, inter alia, some of our Hudood Laws have been enforced. But the severity of sentence according to the Act of 1909 and executed according to the rules framed by the provincial governments bear no analogy to or comparison with the lightness of sentence of whipping in *Shariah* (Hussain, Aftab & Khan, Gul Muhammad, without dateline).

But it should be noted that the provisions of the British Whipping Act of 1909 rather than the Ordinance of 1979 are still sometimes observed by prison officials (Faruki 1987).

Moreover, there is conflicting information and reports about the manner in which flogging is administered. There have been anomalies and contradictions regarding the question whether the Ordinance had been complied with. And there are strange, inequitable discrepancies in the number of lashes awarded in relation to the value of the offence.

The punishment of flogging under the *zina* Ordinance has been freely implemented on male convicts freely in public places. In the case of female convicts it has always been questionable whether it was acceptable to whip them in public places, because of the common feeling that the 'weaker sex' should not be treated so harshly. So in some cases women were flogged inside jail. I would like to mention some cases where women have been flogged, which I have taken from newspapers:

Pakistan Times, 30 December 1982.
A mother of two children was given 20 lashes in Central Jail, Saidu Sharif Swat.

View Point Weekly, 28 April 1983.
Two women convicted under the *zina* Ordinance were lashed in Multan Jail. During the lashing, one of them became unconscious; on the advice of the medical officer, the remaining lashes were postponed.

Mashriq Weekly, 24 October 1984.
A woman was lashed under the *zina* Ordinance in Lahore Jail. Her name was not made known.

Jang, 8 August 1984.
A 30-year-old woman was sentenced to 10 strokes. The flogging was to take place in a public place. A big crowd gathered to watch. But the flogging was postponed.

Jang, 22 July 1987.
A 30-year-old woman was sentenced to five years imprisonment and fifteen lashes. She was flogged in the jail, which aroused anger among the other inmates. Her crime was that she could not prove that she was married to the man she was living with.

The flogging of male convicts, on the other hand, takes place in public and also attracts large crowds. In some cases, a loudspeaker has been used so that people can hear the screams of the convict from a long distance. People are attracted to see a flogging for different reasons. Part of the crowd belongs to the right-wing religious school of thinking, enjoying the punishment of the offender. They feel vengeful towards him, especially in cases of sexual crime and feel contented when punishment commences. A big part of the crowd is there out of sheer curiosity and many of them feel sympathy and pity for the offender. People opposed to whipping as a judicial mode of punishment never go to watch floggings, holding the view that to watch them means to participate in the process of torture and brutality. Of course friends and relatives of the convict and sympathizers are also on the spot to take care of him after the flogging.

One of the general effects of public floggings is to produce a state of terror among people. This state of terror has served the purpose of the authorities in Pakistan to pacify people politically, a purpose which is also considered to be one of the reasons for introducing cruel Islamic punishments.

According to one report, hundreds of political prisoners are believed to have been flogged in the years 1977-81. The Pakistan Medical Association has protested against the involvement of the medical profession in the process of flogging on the grounds that it is not only inhuman and against the dignity of man but may also cause serious physical damage and irreversible psychological traumas, especially in young people. Moreover, this punishment may activate latent diseases like TB and precipitate cardio-vascular accidents, besides permanently damaging the personality of the victim.[68]

It should also be noted that flogging is prohibited under international law as well (Comments of the Human Rights Committee, adopted on 27 July 1982, affirming that corporal punishment is prohibited under Article 7 of the International Covenant on Civil and Political Rights).

3.7 LAW OF EVIDENCE

Until 1984, the Law of Evidence Act, 1872, applied in Pakistan. Under the claim of bringing it into conformity with the injunctions of Islam, the government enforced the *Qanune-e-Shahadat* (law of evidence) Order, 1984.

A great many legal experts agreed that very few amendments were required to bring the Evidence Act of 1872 into conformity with Islam (Changez, 1984a). But according to others, the whole Evidence Act was out of tune with - and in several places in opposition to - the words and spirit of the *Quran* and *Sunna* (Rahman, Tanzil-ur, 1983).

The new Evidence Act is a lengthy document consisting of 166 sections. Very few changes have been made and they are generally of a formal nature. The number and sequence of the sections have, however, been greatly changed. This has really disturbed practising lawyers who were very much used to the old sequence (Akbar, 1986). One writer calls it the Pakistani edition of the English law, on the ground that there are no substantial changes and the law is basically the same as under the old Act of 1872 (Changez, A.R, 1984a).

However, some major changes are discernible in the Law of Evidence Order, 1984.

3.7.1 Competence of Witnesses

According to the *Qanune-e-Shahadat* Order, 1984, the court shall determine whether a person is a competent witness in accordance with the qualifications prescribed by the *Quran* and *Sunna* and, where no such competent witness is forthcoming, the court may take the evidence of any witness available.

Now the *Quran* and *Sunna* are differently interpreted by Muslims. Rashida Patel comments:

There is serious danger to the rights of witnesses by keeping the door wide open for the hundreds of courts in Pakistan to determine the competence of a witness. And, by allowing the several courts to decide what is or is not in accordance with the injunctions of Islam (Patel, 1986: 80).

Justice (retd.) A.R. Changez remarked:

I would like to add that the qualifications as required by the third proviso of Article 3, to determine the competence of a witness, should have been prescribed and should not have been left for decision by each judicial officer. I am afraid it would open a Pandora's box (Changez, 1984a).

Under classical Islamic law, the evidence of a male is considered equal to that of two females. Section 3 does not specifically discuss this point. But since it gives the court the power to determine the competence of a witness in accordance with the *Quran* and *Sunna*, it depends on the judge whether he wants to consider two female witnesses equal to one male witness. Thus the new law of evidence not only reduces women to the position of legal destitutes, but also opens the floodgates to unending controversies about the interpretation of Quranic injunctions because of its vagueness and ambiguity.

3.7.2 Legitimacy

Presumption of legitimacy is another aspect in which the *Qanune-e-Shahadat* Order, 1984, has made important changes. Section 112 of the Evidence Act of 1872 has been replaced by Section 128. According to Section 112 of the Evidence Act, there was no minimum period of gestation and the maximum period was 280 days. Under the Evidence Act, 1984, the minimum period is fixed at six months and the maximum period at two years. Muslim classical law is controversial concerning the maximum period of gestation (Rahman, Tanzil-ur, 1978: 35-7). The 1984 Act has adopted the view of the *Hanafi* school. Firstly, this is in conflict with modern science and, secondly, it could start endless controversies among different Muslim sects in Pakistan.

3.7.3 Evidence of Women

Section 17 of the 1984 Act provides:

> The competence of a person to testify and the number of witnesses required in any case shall be determined in accordance with the injunctions of Islam as laid down in the Holy *Quran* and *Sunna*. Unless otherwise provided in any law relating to the Enforcement of *Hudood* or any other special law - (a) in matters pertaining to financial or future obligations, if reduced to writing, the instrument shall be attested by two men, or one man and two women, so that one may remind the other, if necessary and evidence shall be led accordingly; and (b) in all other matters the court may accept, or act on, the testimony of one man or one woman, or such other evidence as the circumstances of the case may warrant.

Since a single woman is not considered a reliable witness on financial matters, her capacity as a principal party in financial transactions has been put in doubt by this section. This may make it increasingly impossible for women to enter into such contracts independently.

This section is claimed to be based on a Quranic verse (verse 282:2) which may be interpreted in different ways.

Rashida Patel points out that the section 'has belittled the status of several women working as administrators, bankers, lawyers and judges, for they often have to request their male clerks and peons to attest documents drawn up by them' (Patel, 1986: 81).[69]

3.8 AMENDMENT TO THE PAKISTAN PENAL CODE (XLV of 1860) FOR DEROGATORY REMARKS AGAINST THE PROPHET OF ISLAM, HIS FAMILY AND QURAN

People in Pakistan feel very concerned if anywhere in the world bad words or negative expressions are used about the prophet of Muslims. The importation of such material in the form of books and films can lead to such events as the burning of cinemas and bookstalls. This has occurred a number of times since the foundation of Pakistan. An interesting example is that of a book named *Angelique and the Sultan* which was imported into Pakistan and in which 'derogatory remarks' were made about the prophet Muhammad. This led to a long discussion of two hours in the National Assembly of Pakistan, in which all types of suggestions were made as to what the government of Pakistan could do, although the book was published in the UK where the press is free.[70] The reaction against the book of Salman Rushdie a few years later is another example.

During the process of Islamization in the late seventies and eighties, three Ordinances were implemented in Pakistan, as an addition to the Pakistan Penal Code (XLV of 1860), for the purpose of providing punishments for the criminal offence of making derogatory remarks about the prophet Muhammad, his family and the *Quran*. The first addition, made in 1980, says:

> Whoever by words, either spoken or written, or by visible representation, or by any imputation, innuendo or insinuation, directly or indirectly defiles the sacred name of any wife, or members of the family of the Holy Prophet, shall be punished with imprisonment of either description for a term which may extend to three years, or with fine, or with both.[71]

The second Ordinance made in 1982 says:

> Whoever wilfully defiles, damages or desecrates a copy of the Holy *Quran* or an extract therefrom or uses it in any derogatory manner or for any unlawful purpose shall be punishable with imprisonment for life.[72]

The third Ordinance deals with derogatory remarks against the prophet Muhammad. It says:

> Whoever by words, either spoken or written, or by visible representation, or by any imputation, innuendo, or insinuation, directly or indirectly, defiles the sacred name of the Holy Prophet Muhammad (peace be upon him) shall be punished with death, or imprisonment for life and shall also be liable to fine.[73]

Thus the three ordinances provide punishments of three years' imprisonment, a fine, imprisonment for life and death. Capital punishment for using derogatory remarks against the Prophet caused a lot of discussion in Pakistani media. The discussion dealt with the point whether the death penalty is justified for the aforementioned offence in the light of the *Quran* and *Sunna* (Shafi, 1986: Razvi, 1986a,b,c). The issue was also discussed in the Federal Shariat Court, where it was argued that there was no direct authority in the *Quran* and *Sunna* to support the death penalty for using derogatory remarks against the Prophet.[74]

3.9 DRAFT ORDINANCE RELATING TO THE LAW OF QISAS AND DIYAT

The law of murder, called the law of *qisas* (life for life) and *diyat* (ransom in lieu of murder) in Muslim terminology, has been one of the most controversial laws during the process of Islamizing the law in Pakistan.

Since the creation of Pakistan, the PPC and criminal code procedure created by the British in 1860 and 1898 have been applied to deal with the law of murder.[75] The punishments for murder laid down in the PPC are death, imprisonment and a fine according to the circumstances of the case. During Islamization, efforts were made to replace the codes by the Islamic law of murder, which implies that murder should not be considered an offence against the state, but an offence against the individual and should be compoundable. The PPC does not recognize the option of blood money and clemency for the next of kin or heirs of deceased victims and is therefore considered not to be in accordance with the Islamic law of murder (Hanif, 1985; Majid, 1980; Rahman Tanzil-ur-, 1978).

The *qisas* and *diyat* Ordinance became law in 1990. It is discussed in some detail here because the draft ordinance generated a lot of public discussion, in which there was pressure - especially from women - against its implementation.

The draft ordinance relating to the law of *qisas* and *diyat* was prepared in June 1981 by the Council of Islamic Ideology. It was debated by committees in the *Majlis-i-Shura* and the Ministry of Religious Affairs. They were reported to be divided on different issues in the draft ordinance. It was later recommended to make the Shariat Benches or the Federal *Shariah* Court responsible for determining the issue. The draft ordinance drew a massive public response when it was published in order to elicit public opinion about it.[76]

It should also be noted here that, besides arising in the draft ordinance, the issue has also been raised in the courts. A case came up before the Shariat Bench in 1980, in which Gul Hassan, who had been convicted and sentenced to death for murder under Section 302 of the PPC, moved a *Shariat* petition and sought a declaration that the above mentioned provision was repugnant to the injunctions of Islam. The court established that *qisas*, *diyat* and a pardon are the only three options available for dealing with a murder case in Islam. As the PPC contained no such provisions, therefore, the court held that not only Section 302, but all the law relating to murder needed amendment.[77]

The court also specified a period of two months for bringing about the desired changes to the law of murder. In the same year, eight applications were filed to initiate contempt proceedings against the Government of Pakistan for not having complied with the order of the Bench in Gul Hassan's case to make the stipulated changes in the relevant codes. The appeal was, however, dismissed on the grounds that, as the constitution did not provide any time limit for the executive or the legislature to create the necessary legislation to implement their decisions, the violation of any such period stipulated by the *Shariat* Bench could not, in a strictly technical sense, entail contempt of court. It is interesting to note that only a year before this, Prime Minister Bhutto had been convicted and hanged under sections of the PPC and the court had refused to apply the *Shariah* Law of Murder in his case (Patel, 1986: 135-46).

While these developments for the implementation of the Islamic law of murder were taking place in the courts, the draft ordinance on *qisas* and *diyat* was an organized attempt to change the law of murder. The draft ordinance divided murder into four forms: *qatal-i-amad* (premeditated murder), *qatal-i-shibha* (suspected premeditated murder), *qatal-i-khata* (accidental murder) and *qatal-bi-sabab* (consequential murder). Injuries or bodily harm were divided into five forms. They were *itlaf-i-udu* (cutting off a limb or limbs), *itlaf-i-salahyat-i-udu* (permanently impairing the functioning of parts of the body), *shajjah* (injury to head or face), *jurh* (iunjury other than to the head or face, leaving a mark) and all kinds of other injuries. The ordinance made the above-mentioned offences compoundable. The most important points about the draft ordinance was the following:

1. In cases of *qatal-i-amad* the evidence of women was not entertained at all.[78] For proof of *qatal-i-amad* at least two pious Muslim adult male witnesses were accepted.

2. If the victim was a female, her *diyat* shall be one half of that of a man.[79]

This was resented by the women of Pakistan. They argue that both sexes enjoy equal status in Islam and this distinction in the rate of *diyat* discriminates against women (Shehab, 1984b; 84-6: 1984c; 86-8: Changez, 1984b).

The issue was also debated between Traditionalists and Modernists. About this distinction between the *diyat* of a man and that of a woman, Rafi Ullah Shehab observed that as to punishment of *qisas* no distinction was made between a man and a woman, while a distinction was made in the case of punishment of *diyat* only. He argued:

> If the same principle is applied, as in the case of *diyat*, to the case of *qisas* it will imply that it should also be reduced to one half of the actual punishment of *qisas*. The idea of one half of *qisas* will be impracticable as a half person cannot be killed. Its implementation would only be possible in the killing of two women by the same murderer. Killing of the half person is practically impossible, it will require killing of two women.

Shehab concluded that the draft ordinance had created a very awkward situation for women in Pakistan (Shehab, 1984d: 90-2; Patel, 1983: 148).

Another contradiction was found concerning the *ursh* of a finger of a man and a woman. The *ursh* for damage to one finger was fixed at one tenth of the full *diyat* of a man. According to this rate, the *ursh* for damaging all ten fingers of a woman would be equal to the full *diyat* of a man.[80] This was contradictory to the rule that, when a woman loses her life, her *diyat* was reduced to one half of that of a man.[81]

The third important point about the draft ordinance was that it also provided a law concerning abortion.[82] This was considered to be vague and contradictory. A distinction was made between *isqat-i-janin* (miscarriage caused where the limbs or organs were formed) and *isqat-i-haml* (miscarriage caused where the limbs or organs were not formed). Punishments were provided in both cases. According to one Islamic viewpoint, abortion is allowed up to one hundred and twenty days of pregnancy, but this ordinance did not seem to recognize that verdict, although it was accepted by almost all renowned Muslim jurists (Shehab, 1984e: 88-90).

Note: The text of the *Qisas* and *Diyat* Ordinance is found at Appendix II.

3.10 CONCLUSION

Pakistani legal experts fully agree that Islamic criminal law thoroughly suited tribal Arab society. This is especially so if we look at the Islamic law of murder. Murder is considered a private vengeance and in tribal Arabian society the avenging of a murder fell on the victim's next-of-kin; so it was the right of the family to demand satisfaction. Punishment was effected on the principle of retaliation, commuted to a payment of blood money or compensation for the injury. Cutting off limbs, stoning to death and flogging were also prevalent as punishments.

The position of women in tribal society was also secondary to that of men (Hanif, 1985). In the light of modern developments in criminology where the insistence is on reform and rehabilitation of criminals, the claim of the Muslim traditionalist, however, is that Islamic concepts are not contrary to the modern spirit of criminology (Shibli, 1961; Sandeela, 1983; Mohajir, 1974; Masoodi, 1982; Hussain, Hidiyat, 1970; Grilani, 1982; Iqbal, Javid, 1984).

Pakistan is one of those Muslim countries (the first being Saudi Arabia) where Islamic criminal law has partly been put into practice. Generally speaking, there has been a significant increase of crime in Pakistan since the implementation of Islamic punishments in 1979 (Auolakh, 1986: 50-1, 53-4). This is notably in crimes against property, which include highway robbery, theft from petrol pumps, housebreaking and bank robbery, cattle rustling, motor vehicle theft, etc. An increase of crime has also been noted in *zina*, *qazf* and prohibition of alcohol cases. According to the above-mentioned statistics the crime rate reached its climax in 1985, being the highest in the 39 year history of Pakistan.

It is difficult to determine the real causes of increase of these crimes. To show an increase of crime in official statistics could also mean that there is a need to increase police powers but on the other hand this contradicts the State's claim that Islamic punishments are a deterrent. As such, it is worthwhile looking at some of the reasons provided by Pakistani experts. Before 1979, the PPC was blamed for the increase of crime (Hussain, Hidiyat, 1974). But, as we have seen from the above data, crime has also increased since 1979. Justice Javid Iqbal, Chief Justice of the High Court of Pakistan, has suggested the migration of the population from rural to urban areas and the smuggling into Pakistan of US and Indian movies which are obscene, full of bloodshed, violence and sadism, as reasons for the increase of crime (Iqbal, Javid, 1984). In this respect, it was argued from many quarters that the slow results of these laws were due to the unfamiliarity of Pakistani society with Hudood punishment. Consequently suggestions were made to make up for this deficiency.[83] Another writer has suggested a marked increase of population as the basic cause of the increase in crime (Auolakh, 1986: 56-7).

Besides all the reasons provided by the above-mentioned writers, Modernists question whether the criminal policy adopted in Pakistan is compatible with the requirements of a modern society. The Modernist demand in this respect is that the codification of Islamic criminal law should be done in the light of modern circumstances. There can be no return to the past. Islamic law has to face the challenges of the modern world. Otherwise, Islamic law is just a mockery, as we now know from the experience of Pakistan.

Cases has been mentioned where there was a reluctance to implement punishments like amputation and stoning to death. This reluctance might be due to the possibility that people would react strongly against this type of punishment. This clearly shows that the policy of Pakistan has up to now been not to implement certain *hadd* punishments, i.e., stoning to death and the amputation of hands or feet (Iqbal, Javid, 1984; Jahangir, Asma and Hina Jilani, 1990). If offenders have been sentenced, the sentences have been converted on appeal into *tazir* punishment, although, on the other hand, punishment by flogging has been widely used.

Islamic criminal law is certainly not compatible with the status that women already have in Pakistani society. It was a shock to the women of Pakistan to have to accept that they are not accepted in law as full human beings, that in *hudood* cases they are not considered capable of appearing as witnesses and that in financial matters two women are considered equal to one man. So, after the Islamization of criminal law in 1979, women have organized themselves better than ever before.

The effect of Islamization had been very limited. As is shown in Richard Kurin's study of the effect of Islamization in a village. Islamization has increased the gap between rich and poor. Moreover Islamic laws as administered in Pakistan are highly flexible. *Hadd* sentences are merely symbolic, but their very existence has a negative effect. *Tazir* punishments for theft, *qazf* and the drinking of alcohol have not made a substantial difference. *Tazir* punishments for *zina* have been the most operative part of the Islamic system of punishment and reflect inconsistency.

Islamization in the field of criminal law is very instable as there is lot of pressure to amend the *hudood* Ordinances (Weiss, Anita M., 1990). The Islamization of criminal law has caused instability in the sense that there is a difference of opinion concerning the interpretation of the *shariah*. A group of Modernists are constantly demanding its amendment.

CHAPTER 4

Family Law

4.1 INTRODUCTION

The first reform in the family laws of Pakistan was the Muslim Family Laws Ordinance (MFLO) of 1961, the principal subject of this chapter.

Previously, in the first fourteen years of Pakistan's history, no reforms had been made to family law. In May 1954, the Punjab Legislative Assembly made the first attempt and presented a Marriage Reform Bill. In August 1955, the government set up a Marriage and Family Law Commission headed by Justice Abdur Rashid, including three women representatives and a Pakistani philosopher, Khalifa Abdul Hakim. In June 1956, the Commission submitted its report. A dissenting note by Maulana Ihteshamul Haq was submitted in August, 1956.[1] The note of dissent presents an orthodox viewpoint on family affairs.

Many of the recommendations presented by the Commission, especially concerning the maintenance of wives and the custody and guardianship of children, were not incorporated in the MFLO. The Commission's report and the dissenting report showed that two viewpoints existed in Pakistan - those of Modernists and those of Traditionalists. The MFLO reflects the compromise between Traditionalists and Modernists. This compromise weakened the effect of the reforms (Esposito, 1977: 299; Pearl, 1969).

A Pakistani scholar, Rafi Ullah Shehab, interprets the opposition to the MFLO not as ideological opposition based on religious tenets but as opposition based on political exigencies. He says that Maulana Maudoodi, one of the opponents of the MFLO, appreciated the family law reforms of 1929 in Egypt and presented them in his book *Haqooq-uz-zojain*. But when similar reforms were made in Pakistan in 1961 he opposed them (Shehab, 1986b, 1987; Rosenthal, 1965: 332-7; Feroze, 1962: 129).[2]

The MFLO did not abolish the statute law concerning family affairs in force before 1961 and which had been made as early as 1929 and 1939.[3] Thus, the Ordinance of 1961 reaffirmed the reforms made during British rule in India and made further reforms. However, it should be noted here that Muslim family law was the field which was least touched by British Indian legislature, while other branches of law like criminal law, the law of evidence, the law of transfer of property and the law of contract were replaced by modern laws of British origin. In the field of family law, the case law system of legally binding precedents was adopted, continued after 1947, after the MFLO in 1961 and even after the Islamization of the law in the seventies. John Esposito interprets the reforms in Pakistan as a shift in emphasis from the extended to the nuclear family (Esposito, 1982: 91).

4.2 REGISTRATION OF MARRIAGE

According to classical Islamic law, marriage is contracted by offer and acceptance in the presence of witnesses. Two Muslim males or one male and two females are required to witness the contract. There is no need for a contract of marriage to be registered. In recent years, Muslim countries have felt a need for marriages to be registered in order to keep records. Therefore, laws have been made for compulsory registration. Failure to obey the law makes the parties concerned liable to imprisonment or a fine. But the marriage contract itself is not invalid. The orthodox consider this type of arrangement made by the state as an interference with sacred law. Thus it becomes a subject of conflict between the orthodox and modern law reformers in the field of Islamic family law (Anderson, Norman, 1983).

In Pakistan, compulsory registration of marriages was recommended by the Family Law Commission with reference to a verse from the *Quran* recommending that important transactions should be reduced to writing.[4] The need for compulsory registration was felt because, in both civil and criminal cases, questions often arose concerning the existence of marriage contracts. In the absence of a written contract, uncertainty and confusion are created; for example, in cases of criminal abduction, inheritance, legitimacy, maintenance and dowry (Patel, 1979: 53; Choudhury, G.W., 1986).

The orthodox *ulema* of Pakistan agree on the importance of registration, but are opposed to criminal sanctions to enforce its implementation. According to them, Islamic law is sacred and immutable, and even a small administrative reform is taken as a threat to classical Islamic law (Aslam, 1986; Tonki, 1985) The minority report stated:

> As for the registration of marriage, we don't deny its advantage. If arrangements for the registration of marriages are made at various places in the length and breadth of the country and the people are made cognizant of its advantages, we are sure that the people will in their own interest get the marriages registered. But to make the non-registration thereof an offence punishable with imprisonment or fine or both, is a wrong step.[5]

In spite of all the resistance from the orthodox *ulema* in Pakistan, compulsory registration of marriages was made law in Pakistan in Section 5 of the MFLO. Nevertheless, though this law remains in force, hundreds and hundreds of marriages in Pakistan are still not registered (Ram, 1990).

Section 5 of the MFLO legislates the compulsory registration of marriages and sets up procedures for registration. It requires the registration of marriages before *nikah* registrars appointed by the Union Council under the Basic Democracies. If a marriage is performed outside Pakistan, one copy of the marriage contract should be sent to the *nikah* registrar of the ward in which the bride is a permanent resident. Non-registration of a marriage is punishable with imprisonment of three months and/or a fine of one thousand rupees. A loophole left in the law of registration to satisfy the orthodox is that non-registration does not make a marriage invalid or unlawful. But, in some cases, the court has considered registration an important factor in proving that a marriage has taken place (Carroll, 1979: 119-21; Patel, 1979).

In two cases, one of murder and the other a suit for the restitution of conjugal rights, non-registration was considered a crucial factor in determining the non-existence of marriage. In the murder case, the woman was released as she pleaded self-defence. Her marriage to the person who was murdered, and who purported to be her husband, was not registered. In the second case, the woman was held to be free to marry and the man's suit for restitution of conjugal rights was dismissed.[6]

However, in another case, *Bagh Ali alias Bagh Din v. Almna*,[7] the court did not consider the fact that the alleged marriage was not registered a basic factor but dismissed the appeal on the grounds that the evidence was not sufficient to prove valid marriage. It should be noted here that judicial relief is not denied to unregistered marriages in Pakistan, if they can be proved by other means. Thus suits involving marriage, divorce, inheritance and maintenance are admissable in respect of unregistered marriages (Esposito, 1977; Khan, M. Aslam, 1986; Mahmood, Shaukat, 1986: 15) though strong proof would be required in such cases. In a recent case it was held:

> I may straightaway observe that under Islamic law, *nikah* can be performed orally and such a *nikah* is not invalidated merely because it is not registered according to the provisions of the Muslim Family Laws Ordinance, 1961. However, that Ordinance provides a punishment if one contravenes the provisions regarding the registration of *nikah*.[8]

Afzal Tanveer, a practicing lawyer, drew attention to the fact that there is lot of corruption in the registration of marriages He says that everyone knows that *nikah* registrars will, for a very small sum, enter a forged *nikah* of any previous date in the records to oblige a customer. He said that this trend of procuring a pre-dated *nikah* has increased since the promulgation of the *Hudood* Ordinance in 1979. Whenever an unmarried or widowed daughter ventures to marry a man of her own choice, she is prosecuted on the evidence of a pre-dated forged *nikah* (Tanveer, 1990). Ram also drew attention to the fact that marriages are not generally registered or, if registered, the registers and files are not properly kept and no supervision is maintained of the staff charged with that function (Ram, 1990).

I must conclude by saying that 'compulsory' registration of marriages in Pakistan has not been successful; firstly, failure to register a marriage does not affect the validity of the marriage; secondly, the maximum sentence for non-registration is only three months (which is not high, compared to other maximum sentences); thirdly, judicial relief is not denied in unregistered marriages; and, lastly, because of the abolition of Basic Democracy and consequently of the Union Council, the functioning of the system of registration has suffered a lot. In many instances it is difficult to find the required copies of a *nikahnama* (Patel, 1979: 55). Illiteracy and ignorance of the law on the one hand and deliberate non-compliance on the other are further reasons for the ineffectiveness of Section 5. Marriages are conducted simply in people's own customary ways.

4.3 *POLYGAMY*

Polygamy is a very controversial issue in Islamic law. There could be several reasons for this: firstly, the Prophet Muhammad was married to a number of women; secondly, there is a system of concubinage in Islam according to which, in addition to four wives (the number of wives generally permissible among Muslims), a Muslim man can have sexual relations with his female slaves - although this practice has become a thing of the past thanks to the abolition of slavery (Anderson, J.N.D. 1968: 222-4; Daura, 1969); thirdly, Quranic verses on the subject are so vague that they can be interpreted either in favour of or against polygamy.[9] The vagueness is so great that the *Zahiri* school considers the possibility of a fifth lawful wife, in the light of the *Quran*. Moreover, it should be noted that the *Ithna 'Ashari'* sect of *Shia* also allows a man to have, in addition to four permanent wives, any number of temporary wives. With such wide scope given to men in matters of sexual cohabitation, controversies around the subject are natural.

There is general agreement among Muslim jurists that a man may have four wives at the same time, though sisters, and mother and daughters by blood or fosterage, should not be co-wives simultaneously. The duty of a husband regarding the maintenance of co-wives is again not without controversy, but the general formula is that he should not only give them equal treatment in granting them material comforts but also give them equal amounts of his time. Disputes also exist as to whether a woman may add to the marriage contract a stipulation to the effect that she is to be the only wife and whether such a contract would be valid and binding or void because divine law cannot be varied by the unilateral decisions of the involved parties.

I do not have the space to deal with the controversies on polygamy in Islam, which are mostly academic anyway, but it is relevant to state some modern arguments between the Modernists and the Traditionalists on the issue of polygamy.

According to Muslim Modernists, polygamy is tolerated on grounds of necessity, for example for the protection of widows and orphans after a war. The *Quran* also discourages polygamy by insisting that all wives of a man should be treated equally, at the same time declaring man's inability to do this. Muhammad's own marriages are described as 'no act of enjoyment or pleasure seeking', but as an example of 'self-sacrifice and self-denial', i.e., necessity (Mahmudunnasir, 1968: 60; Khan, Raja Said Akbar, 1972: 1; Hussain, Syed Jaffer, 1965: 384; Daura, 1969). So the

Modernists justify legal restrictions on polygamy so that men do not abuse the option of polygamy.

The Traditionalist view, on the other hand, is that polygamy is a husband's absolute right and that he is legally free to exercise it at will, provided that he does not exceed the maximum number of wives at any one time. According to the Traditionalists, it is not limited to cases of utter necessity. The Prophet Muhammad, four Caliphs and a majority of eminent personages in Islamic history had more than one wife. They compare the situation with the West where men have mistresses and girlfriends, and hold that polygamy is better than this practice. Thus any restriction on polygamy would in fact be an apology to the West, which severely criticises polygamy in Islamic *shariat* without looking at the problems in its own society (*ulema*'s critical views about the 1961 MFLO, 13 March 1961). It would be an interference with revealed religion if the plurality of marriages were declared unlawful, or any restriction imposed upon polygamy.

Many Muslim countries, such as Syria, Iraq and Morocco, have placed various restrictions upon the practice of polygamy. Tunisia is, however, the only Muslim country in which polygamy is completely prohibited. In the Indian subcontinent, Muslim Modernists like Sayed Ahmad Khan, Mumtaz Ali and Chiragh Ali have argued that monogamy is the marriage ideal in Islam, and that there is therefore a need for reform in family law (Esposito, 1982b: 73-5). Before the partition of India and Pakistan, polygamy was a common practice among Muslims. In the State of Pakistan, polygamy has started to decrease. This decline has not only been due to the restrictions placed upon its practice by the MFLO but also due mainly to economic conditions and furthermore to the relative improvement in the position and education of women. The APWA (All Pakistan Women Association) promoted the viewpoint that polygamy is morally undesirable by showing women the problems inherent in its practice and mobilizing them against it (Anderson, Norman, 1983: 63; Hinchcliffe, 1970: 19). Men also realized that they could not afford to maintain polygamous families due to limited means; furthermore, they realized that it would be difficult to handle quarrelling and dissatisfaction within such a family so that, instead of a pleasure, it would be a double burden on a man.

Conditions in Pakistan have driven even Traditionalists not to recommend polygamy to men. Tanzil-ur Rahman says that polygamy is beyond the reach of the Muslims of Pakistan because, firstly, the daily conduct of Muslims has so deteriorated that the idea of mutual obligation has almost become extinct; thus 'they are expected to neglect criminally one wife in preference to the other'. Secondly, 'economic and other complicated matters of life would make the family prey to famine and misery'. Thus he says that the state should interfere and put a stop to polygamy (Rahman, Tanzil-ur, 1967: 38-9).

It is interesting to note that, while polygamy is so fiercely condemned by local scholars, some English experts on Islamic law feel that polygamy is advantageous in Muslim countries where security for women still lies in marriage. They claim that restrictions on polygamy would make a Muslim man use his right of unilateral repudiation to marry a second wife. This would certainly not help the first wife, who would be left without protection. Thus a restriction on polygamy would only fully be effective if the man's right of unilateral repudiation were also taken away. The problem is not 'simultaneous polygamy', but 'successive polygamy'. There are then, argue some writers, some grounds for continuing polygamy in societies where means by which women can help themselves are absent (Hinchcliffe, 1970: 35; Anderson, J.N.D. 1968; Ali, Ameer 1965, 230).

In Pakistan, the remnants of polygamy are mostly found in the village landlord class, where a male child is married at an early age in order to keep the property within the family; when he grows up he usually marries a second wife of his own choice. Cases are also found in the cities when a man becomes attracted to another woman and, although having a wife and children already, marries her (Patel, 1979). In magazines and newspapers one comes across requests by women for legal advice if the husband marries a second wife.[10]

Even though the practice of polygamy is not common in Pakistan, the very fact that polygamy is lawful has a negative effect on women's position within the family because it enables emotional pressure to be used as a constant threat to women. Even if there were any advantage in polygamy to women, it is so slight that one cannot favour polygamy when it comes to the dignity of womenhood (Khan, Mazhar ul Haq, 1972). By way of background regarding the law of polygamy in Pakistan, it may be noted that, before the enactment of the 1961 Ordinance, the report presented by the Commission on Marriage and Family Laws recommended that a man could be permitted to take a second wife. However, this was to be only on condition that court approval be obtained and that, in matters of maintenance and other treatment, no injustice was done to the first wife or her children. The Ordinance did not adopt these recommendations.[11]

Polygamy is restricted by Section 6 of the MFLO. Section 6(1) of the Ordinance makes it mandatory to refer the case to the Arbitration Council if any person wishes to contract a polygamous marriage. A marriage contracted without such permission is not invalid, but it is denied official registration, which means that any grievance arising from such a marriage would be denied judicial relief.

An application for approval to contract a polygamous marriage should contain the reasons for contracting the second marriage, along with the consent of the existing wife or wives (Section 6(2)). The chairman is required to organize an Arbitration Council consisting of representatives of the applicant and his existing wife or wives. If the Arbitration Council is convinced that the proposed marriage is 'necessary and just', permission is granted (Section 6(3)). In deciding whether a marriage is 'necessary and just', the Arbitration Council shall consider circumstances such as sterility, physical infirmity, physical unfitness for conjugal relations, wilful avoidance of a decree for restitution of conjugal rights, or insanity on the part of an existing wife (West Pakistan Rules under the MFLO, 1961, Section 14). Any person not satisfied with the decision of the Arbitration Council may appeal to the *collector* (Section 6(4)).

The penalty for contracting another marriage without permission from the Arbitration Council is immediate repayment by the man of the entire dowry to his existing wife or wives; he can also be imprisoned for up to one year and/or fined, which fine may extend to five thousand rupees (Section 5(a) (b)). Moreover, a wife can seek judicial dissolution of her marriage on the ground that her husband has taken an additional wife in contravention of the provisions of the Ordinance concerning polygamy (Section 13(9)). This goes further than the *Dissolution of Muslim Marriages Act, 1939*, according to which a wife had to prove that her husband had failed to treat all his wives equally in order to obtain judicial termination of her marriage. Finally, though the Ordinance provides penalties and the right of a wife to have her marriage dissolved if a second marriage is contracted in violation of the Ordinance and such a marriage is not allowed registration, the Ordinance does not declare such marriages illegal and void.[12] This makes the Ordinance less effective against arbitrary and unjustified polygamy. Besides, says Rashida Patel:

> ... if restrictions on polygamy are to be effective, the law should go further and lay down, that if another marriage is contracted during the subsistence of a marriage, without the prior

permission from the relevant judicial authority, such polygamous marriage shall be illegal and void *ab initio* (Patel, 1979: 95).

There are other reasons for the ineffectiveness of the section on polygamy. Firstly, the Arbitration Council, the basic institution created by the Ordinance, has 'neither the experience and detachment, nor the authority and sanctions possessed by a court' (Carroll, 1979: 132). Secondly, the important part of the Arbitration Council, i.e., the chairman of the Union Council, does not exist at all because of the abolition of the Basic Democratic system. Moreover, an appeal against the decision of the Arbitration Council has to be filed with the Union Council, which was dissolved in 1971 under martial law.

> Though the powers of the Chairman of the Union Council to perform functions under the Muslim Family Laws Ordinance 1961 have been assigned, no person has been appointed to perform the functions of the dissolved Union Councils, thus creating a vacuum (Patel, 1979: 94).

Furthermore, Union Councils are also required for enforcement of penal action against violation of the Ordinance, as 'no court shall take cognizance of any offence under the Ordinance or these rules save on a complaint in writing by the Union Council, stating the fact constituting the offence' (West Pakistan Rules under the MFLO, 1961, Rule 21).[13] Because of these factors, the restrictions on polygamy are ineffective in practical terms. David Pearl in his conclusion to the work done in Quetta noted:

> Many men risk the penalties inherent in section 6(5) (a) and (b) of the Ordinance, and marry a second wife without bothering to apply to the Arbitration Council for its approval. However, of the 32 men who did abide by the law, only one man had his application refused. This remarkable fact illustrates the importance of the Arbitration Council even when the formalities are to be complied with (Pearl, 1971: 564).

A practising lawyer from Bahawalpur drew attention in a recent conference on family law in Pakistan to the fact that the Punjab government has amended the law according to which a wife can lodge a complaint while, in the provinces of Pakistan, complaints are registered by the Union Council. He says that husbands frequently marry another women without securing regular permission and the Union Council seldom prosecutes such husbands (Tanveer, 1990).

All this shows that, though Pakistan has put academically impressive restrictions on man's unrestricted and arbitrary right to polygamy, in practice the requirement that prior permission for a polygamous marriage be obtained from an Arbitration Council appears to be a formality rather than an effective deterrent.

4.4 DIVORCE

In Islam, divorce is not considered a good thing. It is considered the most detestable of all permitted things. However, the important question in family law is: if a divorce should take place who should have the power to make the decision? If a woman wants to exercise this power, she has to rely on the intervention of the court; she may also be granted this power in the marriage contract as a concession given to her by her husband. (A wife's power of divorce is discussed in Part 4.5 below).

On the other hand, in Islamic law, a husband's right of divorce is absolute and need not be exercised through a court. The husband can exercise this absolute right without citing a cause. If the formula of repudiation is pronounced in jest, in drunkenness or even under compulsion, it is still considered to be valid and effective. The wife has no part in the procedure to the extent that she does not have to be present, nor need she be informed about it. Whatever justification might be provided for this one-sided power of a husband, it is highly discriminatory in modern society. Not entrusting this power to women on equal terms with men can be attributed to nothing but the secondary position in society given to women by Islam (Hodkinson, 1984: 246). It is important to understand traditional Islamic law on a man's right of divorce in order to appreciate the change of position represented by the Muslim Family Law Ordinance of 1961; because the traditional Islamic practice of divorce still exists side by side with the restrictions of 1961.

Traditional Islamic law provides a husband with three different forms of divorce. The more approved forms of divorce are *talaq-al-ahsan* and *talaq-al-hasan*, also called *talaq-al-sunnah*, and these forms of *talaq* are revocable. If a husband chooses to divorce in the *al-ahsan* form he makes a single pronouncement during the period of *tuhr* (when his wife is not menstruating) and abstains from sexual intercourse during one *iddah* (a period of three menstrual cycles). Divorce is revocable during *iddah*. In *talaq-al-hasan* there are three pronouncements of divorce in three separate *tuhrs*. The third pronouncement is final and irrevocable. The third form of divorce is *talaq al-bidah*, which is not much approved but is widely practised among the Muslims of Pakistan. It consists of three declarations of divorce occurring at one time and the marriage is then irrevocably dissolved. The main difference between *talaq-al-sunnah* and *talaq-al-bidah* is that the former two forms are revocable within a prescribed period, while the latter form is irrevocable (Ahmad, K.N, 1984). The revocable nature of *talaq-al-sunnah* is compared in Morocco to the situation of a man who holds a small bird in his hand; to repudiate a woman for the first time would be like releasing the bird with a string attached to one of its legs, provided that the bird does not get three months distant, the captor can reel it back whenever he chooses to. In a second repudiation, however, the bird has been released completely unfettered and will return to its master if properly enticed. And after a third repudiation the bird will fly away altogether to seek a new and more congenial source of subsistence (Rosen, 1970: 35).

Another aspect important to look at are the rules applicable to a husband wanting to marry his divorced wife again. The procedure or form provided by traditional Islamic law is that if divorce has become irrevocable - whether it be *al-bidah, ahsan* or *hasan* - he is not permitted to marry her again until she has taken another husband and lived with him as a wife; after she has parted from her new husband, the first husband may then remarry her.

The Muslim claim for such divorce laws is that they are fully in accordance with human nature and made for the protection of morals and cultural considerations (Maududi, 1981: 18).

Before we go into details of the 1961 Family Law, let us look at the social effects of divorce in Pakistani society. Firstly, it should be noted that the divorce rate is very low in Pakistan compared with Western countries (Patel, 1979: 97). It is notable that this is so in spite of the fact that the procedure of divorce is very simple. Though divorce procedure is getting easier in the West, it is still far easier in Pakistan. This clearly shows that an 'easier procedure of divorce' provided for the man does not increase the divorce rate in a society like Pakistan.

There is a host of social and economic factors which influence the man's unilateral and seemingly unlimited legal power of divorce. The legal code does not provide a full view of the husband/wife relationship in a patriarchal joint family system.

In a system where marriages are arranged by the families, and a big dowry is provided by the bride's family while the husband offers a large dower, the relationship is not simply one of two individuals, but one of families. There is much family politics and manipulation involved with dower and dowry. The dowry consists of a huge collection of household effects which the bride brings with her and the dower is a large sum of money which the husband has to pay for a wife. A divorce means loss of the dowry and of the dower paid for a wife. Under such financial pressure, a husband hesitates to make use of his right of instant repudiation. In addition to these economic pressures, there are many social pressures. In Pakistan, husband and wife are usually first paternal cousins or are otherwise related or, as very commonly happens, two brothers are married to two sisters. In such situations, family ties constitute a pressure on the husband not to use his power of divorce freely (Rosen, 1970). (Rosen discusses the dynamic interplay of family law and social structure in Moroccan society, but his observations also apply to Pakistan.)

Other reasons for a limited divorce rate in Pakistan include the economic dependence of a wife on her husband. This results in her adopting a subservient status: she is more likely to give way and submit to the will of her husband. Furthermore, conflicts between husband and wife are suppressed under traditions, customs and social norms. People live in unhappy marriages all their lives, but do not dare to split up because of the pressures. The existence of children is another factor which is a strong consideration for a husband not to divorce his wife (Patel, 1979: 97-8).

Now let us look at the reasons for divorce in Pakistan. Firstly, the divorce rate is higher among working and educated women. The reason for this could be attributed to the independent status of these women. Secondly, in a system where child marriages and arranged marriages are popular, some situations will arise where there is a great disparity in the education of the two spouses. This can lead to divorce. Thirdly, in a joint family system, conflicts between mothers-in-law and daughters-in-law are common. They sometimes take such a form that the man is torn between the two loyalties and, under extreme pressure from his mother or family, divorces his wife. Fourthly, in arranged marriages, false impressions of the girls are sometimes given in order to get them married off, for example by hiding physical defects. In a few cases this is also grounds for divorce. Finally, barrenness in women is grounds for divorce (Hussain, Syed Jaffer, 1983).

In the event of divorce, it is usually the woman who suffers most. Parents, relatives and friends are more sympathetic to the male than to the female divorcee, although the social reaction may differ with class. Divorced women with no economic support have a miserable life indeed. In some situations the parents themselves are so poor that they cannot support their divorced daughter and in other situations they refuse to help or protect their daughters because they were against the divorce. Such helpless women sometimes end up in women's crisis centres (*dar-ul-uman*).

In a situation like that, the unilateral power of the husband to divorce his wife is a constant threat to her and produces inequality and an inevitable instability in the Muslim marriage (Hodkinson, 1984: 247). This attracted the attention of the makers of the 1961 family law reforms, especially because in Pakistan, where *Hanafi* law prevailed, a husband could pronounce the three declarations of *talaq-al-bidah*. Simply by saying the words *talaq, talaq, talaq,* an irrevocable *talaq* was affected and remarriage between the same parties was not possible without an intervening marriage with a third person. This form of divorce creates hardship for both men and women who have no chance to reconsider the decision of divorce. The ordinance of 1961 attempted to abolish this form of divorce in Pakistan. Nothing compared to the 1961 ordinance exists in India. *Talaq-al-bidah* is still recognized in India, where it is the dominant mode of divorce among Muslims. (Hussain, Syed Jaffer, 1983; Hodkinson, 1984: 222; Shabbir, 1988).

In Pakistan, the MFLO provides a procedure according to which, in whatever form divorce is pronounced, notice should be given to the chairman of the relevant Union Council and a copy supplied to the wife (7(1)). The divorce does not become effective until ninety days after notice has been given to the president (7(3)); if the wife happens to be pregnant, this period is extended (7(5)). Anderson suggests that this interval of ninety days was chosen because of its similarity to the *iddah* period (Anderson, J.N.D., 1968: 227-8; Hussain, Syed Jaffer, 1965: 384). The chairman of the Council is to provide an opportunity for an arbitration committee to attempt conciliation within thirty days of receiving the notice; if the attempt at conciliation succeeds the divorce becomes null and void. Section 7(2) of the Ordinance provides punishment for non-observance. This is imprisonment for up to one year, or a fine of up to 5,000 Rs. Section 7(6) of the Ordinance lays down that remarriage between a divorced couple can be validly contracted without an intervening marriage to a third person if the marriage has been terminated under the provisions of the Ordinance, unless such termination is made for the third time.

It is clear from Section 7(1) that the Ordinance does not nullify the traditional forms of divorce. The expression used in the Section is 'after the pronouncement of *talaq* in any form whatsoever'. In the case of *Mst. Maqbool Jan v. Arshad Hassan*,[14] it was held that, if *talaq* was valid under the personal law of the parties, it would become effective under that law; but the only brake upon it was that its effectiveness would be postponed for ninety days (Ahmed, Saber, 1971). This interpretation of the Ordinance has reduced its effect. *Talaq-al-bidah* is still practised, the Ordinance being taken as a legal formality which is followed side by side with the traditional forms of *talaq*. However, non-service of notice to the Council could have drastic effects and could result in there being no legal divorce.[15]

Whether giving notice to the wife is a necessary condition is not very clear. In *Zikria Khan v. Aftals Ali Khan*,[16] the court held that the non-supply of a copy of the divorce notice to the wife did not prevent the divorce from becoming effective after ninety days. The whole emphasis is on the date of receipt of the notice by the chairman, said the court. However, in *Inamul Islam*,[17] it was held that service of the copy on the wife was as important as service of the notice on the chairman. Lucy Carroll suggests that the interpretation of Section 7 is preferable in the latter case (Carroll, 1985a: 272). As we have seen, according to traditional Islamic law, it is not necessary to communicate a divorce to the wife. It is not clear which precedent the courts will follow in the future.

If the parties fail or refuse to participate in the reconciliation procedure, a function which is now performed by a judge, this in no way invalidates the divorce. If the authorities fail to form an Arbitration Council again this has no effect upon the validity of the divorce. The function of an Arbitration Council is to attempt to reach reconciliation. It has no authority either to nullify a divorce or to declare a divorce valid.[18] It is noteworthy that non-observance of the procedure prescribed by the Ordinance does not render a divorce ineffective. Omission to give notice is an offence only punishable under the Ordinance. This was clearly held in a recent case, *Chuhar v. Ghulam Fatima*.[19]

The law on divorce is very much opposed by the Traditionalists. They feel that Section 7 has made an absolute right of divorce, granted to a husband by God, subject to and dependent on the actions of a third agency, i.e., an Arbitration

Council. Their argument is that the Ordinance creates a conflict between the law and the conscience of the people, because the majority of the people in Pakistan belong to the *Hanafi* School of thought (Tonki, 1985).

The main conflicting points between classical law as practised in Pakistan and the Ordinance are:

1. By *talaq-al-bidah*, which is commonly practised in Pakistan, divorce is irrevocable as soon as pronounced. There is no room for reconciliation, while the Ordinance provides for reconciliation.

2. Classical law does not require notice of divorce to any agency, not even the wife, while the Ordinance requires notice to the chairman of the Council and a copy of the notice to the wife.

3. In classical law, if after a third divorce a man wants to marry the same woman, an intervening marriage is required. The Ordinance has abolished this restriction (Mahmood, Tahir, 1972: 251; Ahmed, Saber, 1971).

Shortcomings of Section 7 and Problems of its Implementation

Although the Ordinance appears to deviate drastically from the classical Islamic law of divorce, it fails in practice to restrict the man's right of divorce. The divorce procedure provided in the Ordinance has become a mere formality instead of an obstacle (Anderson, J.N.D. 1968: 227-8; Carroll, 1979: 125). Here, David Pearl's words are noteworthy:

> The Quetta figures illustrate how futile the Ordinance has been in approaching its objective. In the last three years (that is 1966, 1967, and 1968), just under 3% of the registered *talaqs* have been compromised. An Arbitration Board of the type created by the Ordinance has not been able to slow down the increasing number of divorces by *talaq*. Once again, we are unable to ascertain how many unregistered *talaqs* take place every year, but one can presume that they must be substantial in number, since they are valid although illegal (Pearl, 1971: 565).

A major loophole in the restriction on divorce is that failure to comply with the Ordinance, though it incurs penalties, does not affect the validity of the divorce. John L. Esposito furthermore feels that the penalties provided for non-compliance (imprisonment of one year and/or a fine of 5,000 Rs) are relatively light (Esposito, 1977: 303, 1982b: 85; Carroll, 1979: 124).

Rashida Patel has drawn attention to other shortcomings. She says that at times a husband pronounces divorce without giving notice to the chairman; this puts the wife in a state of anguish, because she is uncertain of her status. In other situations, the husband provides notice to the chairman, but withdraws it without informing his wife. This also amounts to harassing her. Remedies should be provided for this type of problem. Rashida Patel further suggests that, before a divorce becomes effective, the liabilities of the husband (e.g., the maintenance of his children and the return of property in his possession) should be settled (Patel, 1979: 112). Rochi Ram says that though the law provides for efforts to be made by the trial judge to bring about compromise and reconciliation, no opportunity is taken to do this and it is generally considered a mere formality (Ram, 1990).

Finally, I would like to repeat that, in spite of the 1961 Ordinance, the classical form of divorce is still predominant in Pakistan. In the legal advice given by the lawyers of Pakistan in reply to readers' questions in newspapers and magazines, they suggest that people should practise the classical form of divorce and say that it is un-Islamic and a sin to remarry a divorced wife without an intervening marriage; however, they also suggest that people follow the Ordinance, but only as a procedural formality. This contributes to the ineffectiveness of the Ordinance in practice.[20] I was told by a villager who works as an arbitrator in a local *panchayat* that, firstly, there are not very many cases of this type but, in their village, if any person wants to remarry his divorced wife, she is expected to go through an intervening marriage and a subsequent divorce before marrying her first husband again.

After Islamization in 1977, courts in Pakistan have taken a different (i.e., more Traditionalist) approach towards Section 7 (Pearl, 1989). In *Chuhar v. Ghulam Fatima* and *Noor Khan v. Haq Nawaz*,[21] the court took the stand that the strict application of Section 7 would produce harsh results and therefore undue emphasis on the mandatory obligation to inform the chairman was not important. On the other hand it was held in *Aziz Khan v. Muhammad Zarif* that it was not within the jurisdiction of the court to declare Section 7 to be repugnant to the Holy *Quran* keeping in view Article 203 (b) of the Constitution.[22]

David Pearl has drawn attention to the case of *Qamar Raqa v. Tahira Begum*,[23] where Tanzil-ur-Rahman relied on Article 2A in the Constitution, according to which the Objectives Resolution was declared to be part of the Constitution. He said that Section 7 was contrary to Article 2A i.e contrary to the Holy *Quran*. Tanzil-ur-Rahman's approach was upheld in *Muhammad Sarwar v. the State*.[24] David Pearl concludes:

> The conclusion must be therefore that the Ordinance is, at the time of writing, no longer sustainable as the governing law even though it has not been repealed or abrogated by any enactment (Pearl, 1989).

4.5 WOMEN'S RIGHTS OF DIVORCE IN PAKISTAN

The only form of divorce in Islam in which marriage is dissolved by mutual agreement and with a mutual release from any outstanding financial commitments is known as *mubara'a*.

Womens' rights of divorce in Pakistan can be considered under the following headings:

1. Womens' rights of divorce under the Dissolution of Muslim Marriages Act, 1939.

2. Grounds for divorce provided by the Muslim Family Laws Ordinance, 1961.

3. *Khula* and judicial *khula*.

4. *Li'an*, Section 14 of the *Offence of qazf (Enforcement of Hadd) Ordinance* (VII of 1979).

Let us look at Pakistani women's rights of divorce under these headings and see if the right available to women in so many different ways provides a counterbalance to the husband's unilateral right of divorce.

It should be noted that the right to dissolve a marriage available to a Pakistani woman - even if not equal to that of a man - is against traditional Islamic law. Therefore, the movement towards Islamizing the law in Pakistan has threatened some of these rights.

4.5.1 Dissolution of Muslim Marriages Act, 1939

As I have already mentioned, the majority of Muslims living in the subcontinent belong to the *Hanafi* school of Islam. According to *Hanafi* jurists, the right to dissolve a marriage rests almost entirely with the husband. *Hanafi* law provides very limited grounds for a wife to dissolve an unwanted marriage, thus providing the man with a position superior to that of the woman (Pearl, 1981: 226-31). The position taken by the *Quran* in this respect is open to a variety of interpretations concerning a woman's right to a divorce (Hinchcliffe, 1968). We are here concerned with prevalent practices in Pakistan. Other Muslim schools of law, i.e., *Shafi*, *Hanbali* and *Malaki*, are more liberal in providing Muslim women with this right. Using the views of these other schools as a justification, the British enacted the *Dissolution of Muslim Marriages Act, 1939*. This Act has been criticized by Traditionalists for disregarding *Hanafi* law. It has also been criticized as a mere paper reform. (This aspect was discussed in Chapter 3).

Section 2 of the Act provides Muslim women with eight grounds for obtaining divorce from their husbands. Moreover, the residuary provision of the section provides that a wife can dissolve her marriage 'on any other ground which is recognized as valid for the dissolution of marriages under Muslim law' (Section 21(ix)). The Act of 1939 with additions and amendments continued to be the law in Pakistan after 1947. Under this Act a Pakistani woman may dissolve her marriage in the following circumstances:[25]

(i)   the whereabouts of the husband have not been known for a period of four years;

(ii)   the husband has neglected or has failed to provide for her maintenance for a period of two years;

(iii)   the husband has been sentenced to imprisonment for a period of seven years or upwards;

(iv)   the husband has failed to perform, without reasonable cause, his marital obligations for a period of three years;

(v)   the husband was impotent at the time of the marriage and continues to be so;

(vi)   the husband has been insane for a period of two years or is suffering from leprosy or a virulent venereal disease;

(vii)   she, having been given in marriage by her father or guardian before she attained the age of fifteen years (changed to sixteen years by the MFLO, 1961), repudiated the marriage before attaining the age of eighteen years; provided that the marriage has not been consummated;

(viii)   the husband treats her with cruelty, that is to say:
  (a)   habitually assaults her or makes her life miserable by cruelty of conduct, even if such conduct does not amount to physical ill- treatment, or
  (b)   associates with women of evil repute or leads an infamous life, or
  (c)   attempts to force her to lead an immoral life, or
  (d)   disposes of her property or prevents her from exercising her legal rights over it, or
  (e)   obstructs her in the observance of her religious profession or practice, or
  (f)   if he has more wives than one, does not treat her equitably in accordance with the injunctions of the *Quran.*

The *Dissolution of Muslim Marriages Act, 1939*, was a major step in granting women rights denied by *Hanafi* believers. These rights are of course not equivalent to the rights available to a Muslim husband. Lucy Carroll rightly says:

> Obviously, in order to take advantage of this statute the wife not only has to be able to prove one of the recognized grounds but also has to institute litigation which might not be concluded for several years (Carroll, 1982a: 278).

However, an important aspect of the Act is that divorce under it does not affect the financial claims of the wife against her husband. Section 5 says: 'Nothing contained in this Act shall affect any right which a married woman may have under Muslim law to her dower or any part thereof on the dissolution of her marriage.' This is important, because women do not have this right in *khula* and judicial *khula*. In a society where women are dependent on men, dower money provides financial support to a divorced woman who might otherwise be left with no means. The second important aspect of the Act is that the 'husband's consent' to the dissolution of the marriage is not required. This is again important considering the prevalent concept, which is that dissolution of marriage, even if initiated by the wife, should have the husband's consent (Carroll, 1985b: 234-5).

4.5.2 Grounds for Divorce Provided by the MFLO

The MFLO firstly made an addition to the *Dissolution of Muslim Marriages Act* of 1939. It provides a further ground for divorce for Pakistani women, i.e., that the husband has taken an additional wife in contravention of the provisions of the MFLO (which means in practice, without the consent of the first wife). Secondly, as already indicated, the provision in the 1939 Act allowing a woman given in marriage under the age of fifteen to dissolve her marriage before she is eighteen, is amended by extending the right to women married under the age of sixteen.[26]

The third important aspect covered by the MFLO, is the approval of a form of divorce available to the wife in traditional Islamic law, called *talaq-i-tafwid*. Section 8 says: 'Where the right to divorce has been delegated to the wife and she wishes to exercise that right, or where any of the parties to a marriage wishes to dissolve the marriage otherwise than by *talaq*, the provisions of section 7 shall, *mutatis mutandi* and so far as applicable, apply'. *Talaq-i-tafwid* is a right of divorce which the wife gets from her husband by express agreement in the marriage contract. It is the only way in which the equation of matrimonial power can be rebalanced, says Lucy Carroll (Carroll, 1982a). A wife can use the right to divorce her husband in the same way as he can divorce her. In this form of dissolution she retains her claim to the full amount of dower. *Talaq-i-tafwid* can be conditional or unconditional. The usual practice is that of conditional *talaq-i-tafwid*, the normal condition being that the husband shall not marry an additional wife, and conditions concerning maintenance, etc.

However, although there is a place in the marriage contract where a woman's right to divorce can be entered, very few people know about this and few women avail themselves of it. Not only is there ignorance of the availability of such a right but also, at the time of marriage, not much thought is usually given to the possibility that the marriage might end in divorce and especially not to the fact that situations might arise in which the woman would need to exercise that right. Usually she is expected to be submissive. Nowadays almost all women's organisations provide information about the possibility of the wife being able to stipulate her right of divorce in the marriage contract.

Section 8 requires that all forms of divorce should be notified to the chairman of the Union Council in writing with a copy to the husband, the divorce then becoming effective after ninety days.

4.5.3 Khula and Judicial Khula

The traditional *Hanafi* concept of *khula* is that if the wife wants to dissolve the marriage she must obtain the consent of her husband and she should then pay compensation to him, normally by giving up her dower. This was the concept prevalent in Pakistan until judicial *khula* was introduced, not by legislation but by judicial decision.

Until 1959 it was impossible for a woman to dissolve her marriage unless she had grounds under the Dissolution of Muslim Marriages Act or managed to convince her husband that he should give her a *khula*. Incompability of temperament was no ground under the 1939 Act; and it could be difficult to obtain the consent of her husband to exercise *khula*. In 1952, the courts of Pakistan reaffirmed the traditional *Hanafi* concept of *khula* and refused to give a woman the right to divorce without her husband's consent. The court said:

> ... if the wives were allowed to dissolve their marriage without consent of their husbands by merely giving up their dowers, paid or promised to be paid, the institution of marriage would be meaningless as there would be no stability attached to it.[27]

That case established that arbitrators could only dissolve the marriage if authorized to do so by the husband.

However, in 1959, in the case of *Balquis, Fatima*,[28] the court departed from traditional *Hanafi* law and allowed judicial dissolution without the consent of the husband. But the court attached two conditions for a wife seeking such a divorce: (a) she must show that incompability prevented a harmonious marriage, and (b) she must return her dower (Anderson, J.N.D., 1970: 47). It should be noted here that her right would, however, remain subject to her obtaining a court order. While on the one hand the case of *Balquis, Fatima* brought a great change in the position of women, on the other hand the law concerning women's right of divorce became uncertain because of conflicting decisions in this regard. In some cases, the court distinguished *mubara'a* from *khula*, holding that a divorce effected by mutual agreement should be known as *mubara'a* and, if effected without the consent of the husband, should be known as *khula*.[29] In other cases the court held that in both *mubara'a* and *khula* the consent of the husband was necessary.[30] Let us look briefly at the attitude of the courts in different cases.

Khurshid Bibi v. Muhammad Amin [31]

The Supreme Court of Pakistan decided that *khula* is the right of a wife if she can show that she is unable to live with her husband 'within the limits prescribed by Allah'; it is not necessary to obtain the approval of her husband for the divorce, though she must be prepared to renounce her right to a dower.

In regard to this case, some remarks by Doreen Hinchcliffe are of considerable weight. She says that the court misunderstood the traditional law, according to which both *khula* and *mubara'a* involve mutual agreement, i.e., entail the husband's consent. Maybe it was not important that the court should make a distinction between *khula* and *mubara'a*, saying that the former is without the consent of the husband and the latter with the consent of the husband. Hinchcliffe further observes that the expression that wife's right is dependent on the fact that 'the limits of God will be transgressed' is:

> ...vague, and might allow a more traditionally minded judge to distinguish a future case from *Khurshid Bibi v. Muhammad Amin* by deciding that on the facts he was not satisfied that 'the limits of God' would necessarily be transgressed if he failed to order a dissolution, despite the existence of discord between the spouses (Hinchcliffe, 1968: 19-24).

Other writers have approved the development in *Khurshid Bibi's* case.

> Thus, while the right of the man to repudiate his wife has remained unfettered, the granting of a unilateral *khula* divorce to a woman in case of incompability represents significant headway in achieving a balance of human rights (Esposito, 1977: 298).

A Pakistani professor of law approves the case in a review article in the following words:

The ruling in the case ... has also served as a reminder that Islam has definitely raised the status of women, and it is our sacred duty to our religion not to let misconceptions and narrow interpretation of the *Quran* and *Hadith* concerning them cloud the horizons of Islamic law by making it appear as if it were a religion merely of men, for men, and by men (Ali, Shaheen Sardar, 1985: 60).

Of course, her appreciation is in an Islamic perspective.

Nishat Ahmad Khan v. Ramlach [32]
In this case, a decree of dissolution of marriage was granted on the ground that the wife strongly disliked her husband and would not be able to love him and would certainly be transgressing the limits of God, if she stayed married to him.

Muhammad Yasin v. Rafia Bibi [33]
Here it was said:

It must be clearly understood that just as a husband is given the right to pronounce *talaq* on his wife, in the same way a wife has a right to get the marriage dissolved on the basis of *khula* if she could satisfy the conscience of the court that she did not want to live with her husband, and that she was prepared to return the benefits.

Rashidan Bibi v. Bashir Ahmad [34]
In this case, women's rights of divorce were clearly expanded further. The woman in the case had left her husband and had stated that she was not going back to live with him even if he shot her.[35] In the first instance, the judge of the family court, who rejected her application for a divorce, said:

She would have to justify her conduct, and then she could claim divorce. If it would be made a general principle that every woman who becomes corrupt not due to any fault of her husband, but due to present day life, then any woman can adopt that way and seek divorce. This would hit the very basis of the society and be against public policy. Islam does not accept corrupt men and women and prescribes severe punishments for them.

However, in the appeal court where her appeal for *khula* was accepted, it was held:

> ... when a woman has stated categorically that she would prefer to be shot dead rather than to go and live with the husband, and that she was ready and willing to forego all her claims in case her marriage was dissolved, then what more facts and circumstances did he want so that it could be established that there existed extreme hatred in the mind of the petitioner as against her husband.

It was further said that:

> ... it is not necessary on the part of the woman to produce evidence of facts and circumstances to show the extent of hatred to satisfy the conscience of the court.[36]

Muhammad Akram v. Majeed Begum [37]

This was also the case in Azad Jammu and Kashmir, where *khula* was granted on the simple ground that Majeed Begum disclosed that she had developed so much disrespect and hatred for her husband that under no circumstances could she become reconciled with him in order to restore a harmonious and happy life.

Abdul Rahim v. Shahida Khan [38]

Khula to the wife was granted on the simple grounds that 'it was quite evident that the husband and wife cannot live a life of sukoon and harmony in conformity with their obligation.' The judge in the High Court said:

> The emotions of love and hatred may not invariably have a rational basis, and I think that all that the courts have to see is whether there is any possibiity of the parties ever living together in order to perform their marital oligations. If after examining all the circumstances the court comes to the conclusion that the marriage has irretrievably broken down, and there is no hope of the parties ever living together to perform their marital obligations, a case for the invocation of the doctrine of *khula* is made out.[39]

In this case the court's attitude to *khula* was, of course, very liberal.

Ghulam Mustafa v. Ghulam Sakina [40]

The court granted *khula* on the grounds that the facts of the case were such that the court was satisfied:

...that the relations between the parties had deteriorated beyond repair; and also that the malady was such as was likely in all probability to give rise to further moral and social wrongs and indiscreet acts by the spouses towards each other, so as to lead to disrespect of the limits of God; it would become a case for grant of decree of *khula*.[41]

Bashiran Bibi v. Bashir Ahmed [42]

Khula was granted in this case and the court said:

> There is no such requirement of law that a wife seeking *khula* must give objective reasons and prove the circumstances justifying her aversion for the husband.[43]

The above-mentioned are all cases in which *khula* was granted by the court without the consent of the husband, on the grounds that to live within the limits of God was not possible for the parties. But the court required in all the cases that the wife repaid/relinquished her *mahr* (dower). Let us look at some other cases which have created uncertainty regarding the principle on which *khula* is granted.

Siddiq v. Sharfan [44]

In this case, *khula* was not granted. It was held that:

> The judge has to consider the circumstances of each case before he may dissolve the marriage. The fact that the rift exists, and the *qazi* comes to the conclusion that the parties will not observe the limits of God, by itself is not sufficient for the dissolution of marriage on the principle of *khula*. The judge will have to consider as to what is the cause for such a rift. If the cause is attributable to the husband, and the judge arrives at the finding that the parties will not live a harmonious life, he may dissolve the marriage. On the other hand, if the husband is not responsible for it, and the wife has also not created any such situations herself for bringing about the rift, but there are circumstances in existence which render it difficult for the spouses to observe the limits of God, the judge may proceed to dissolve the marriage.[45]

It was further said:

> The judge will not dissolve the marriage for a reason for which the wife is exclusively responsible. If it is established before him

that the wife was seeking the divorce to have a sexual enjoyment, the judge will not dissolve the marriage because it will amount to placing a premium on an immoral life.[46]

In the above case the district judge had approved the dissolution of the marriage on the basis of *khula*; an appeal by the husband was upheld.

Lal Muhammad v. Gul Bibi [47]

Khula was again refused in this case. I quote:

> But right to claim dissolution of marriage on the basis of *khula* is not absolute, and no blanket is given to wife for automatically denouncing marital bounds. In fact, this right is reasonably controlled and is dependent on scrutiny of 'court' competent to decide in the matter after properly satisfying itself about existence of reasonable circumstances whereby separation is being claimed, so as to terminate sacrosanct relationship of the spouse.[48]

It was further held:

> For the consideration of this right, in our opinion it would not be mere choice, discretion, or mere desire or wish of the wife, to come forward and make loose allegations of hatred, disharmony, or disliking, and expect that court by acting mechanically should allow this right. We feel that Islamic principle of law enjoins upon the court a solemn duty to reasonably scrutinize plausibility and desirability of facts and circumstances brought before it, and on the basis thereof to arrive at a judicious satisfaction to ascertain entitlement of wife. If such care and caution is not taken, in that case right to claim dissolution by way of *khula* as ordained by Holy *Quran* and interpreted by the jurists would be completely flouted.[49]

The facts in the case were that the relationship was strained because the husband wanted to take his wife back home for the celebration of a Muslim festival (*Id*), while the parents of the wife wanted her to stay with them. This had resulted in an unpleasant situation and Gul Bibi, the wife, pleaded that their relations had become so strained that it was not possible for her to live with the petitioner as his wife. The court, on the basis of the aforementioned reasoning, found that it was not impossible for the parties to live as husband and wife.

Let us now sum up the various forms by which a woman can dissolve her marriage. If divorce is obtained under the *Dissolution of Muslim Marriages Act, 1939*, or on the basis of judicial *khula*, the husband's consent is not necessary. The difference between the two forms is that, under the 1939 Act, she retains her dower and no financial consideration is due to her husband but in judicial *khula* she has to give up her dower, i.e., the wife gives some financial consideration. So, if grounds for dissolution are not found under the eight grounds provided by the Act, the residuary provision of the Act (Section 3(IX)) should be tried. However, it is a question whether 'incompability of temperament' could be extended to this clause. If dissolution is possible under the 1939 Act, this would save the wife from financial hardship. The difference between classical and judicial *khula* in Pakistan is that, in the former, dissolution of the marriage takes place with mutual consent, while, in the latter, the husband's consent is not required. But both forms involve some financial consideration to the husband.[50] The parties have to go to court in both cases (Carroll, 1987).

When evaluating the woman's right of divorce in Pakistan, as I have said before it is important to look at it in the light of the man's right of divorce. Before we make a general evaluation of the situation, let us look at the points of difference. It appears that judicial *khula* is not a right of the woman equal to the man's unilateral right of divorce (Hinchcliffe, 1968: 25). David Pearl observes:

> A man has the unrestricted right to repudiate his wife, whereas the woman has to satisfy the court that the marriage has irretrievably broken down. Furthermore, one case has stated that she will not be entitled to the *khula* divorce if the reason for the breakdown is due to her own impeachable behaviour (Siddiq v. Sharfan, 1968, 20. PLD Lahore, p.411). The financial implications, of course, are very severe indeed (Pearl, 1976: 73).

Another problem arising from judicial *khula* to which Lucy Carroll has drawn attention is that in cases where the dower is high and a restraint on the husband, he may pressurize his wife 'to buy her way out of an unhappy marriage', i.e., apply for *khula* or judicial *khula* (Caroll, 1982a: 277; Hinchcliffe, 1968: 25). Moreover,

> ... it is considered reprehensible for a husband to ask for more by way of compensation than the amount paid as dower. Nevertheless in law any amount can be fixed as compensation

and thus this type of divorce is open to abuse by husbands who may demand very large sums in return for divorcing wives who have no other means of obtaining their freedom (Hinchcliffe, 1968: 15).

In spite of these disadvantages for women in judicial *khula*, it is nevertheless appreciated in Pakistan that this development takes the law beyond the classical *Hanafi* concept. (Hinchcliffe, 1968: 24). J.N.D. Anderson found it a 'novel reasoning' in the case of *Balquis Fatima v. Najm al-Ikram Qureshi*, when the court in granting judicial *khula* said that, as a husband has full power to repudiate his wife at his discretion, it would be 'unreasonable if such power were granted to one spouse and denied to the other' (Anderson J.N.D., 1970: 46). Pakistani writers have, however, approved judicial *khula*, justifying it in the light of Islam (Hussain, Mohd Ahsanuddin, 1978; Saqib, 1986). To them, judical *khula* is a landmark reform made by the judicary (Anderson, Norman, 1976: 80-1).

4.5.4 Li'an

This is a right of divorce which women have in Pakistan. If a husband falsely accuses his wife of adultery, they go through a ritual known as *li'an* and the marriage is dissolved after that. This has been described already in Chapter 3 in the discussion on the *Offence of Qazf (Enforcement of Hadd) Ordinance, VIII of 1979*.

Considering the position of women in Pakistan and the social stigma attached to divorce, the right of women to dissolve their unhappy marriages does not, in comparison to that of men, present a satisfying picture. Women are already so oppressed that it requires great energy to petition for a divorce. Moreover, if a woman is economically dependent on her husband, his dower could be the only immediate support for her, yet she would have to repay/relinquish this if divorce is not available to her under the *Dissolution of Muslim Marriages Act* of 1939. David Pearl found in 1968, over three years, fourteen cases of divorce within ten Union Committees in Quetta. Only three of these cases were initiated by the wife (Pearl, 1971: 565-6). This clearly indicates that in spite of judicial reform it is hard for a wife to initiate divorce.

With the wave of Islamization in Pakistan, instead of further reforms to this law, it is possible that even the limited rights that women have acquired will be eroded.

4.6 MAINTENANCE

In Pakistan it is usually the man who is the income-earning member of the family. Pakistani law lays down the husband's obligation to maintain his wife, although her right to maintenance is limited. Firstly, the *Dissolution of Muslim Marriages Act, 1939*, gives the woman the right to dissolve her marriage if her husband fails to maintain her for a period of two years (Section 2(ii)). Secondly, according to Section 9 of the 1961 Ordinance, a Muslim husband is obliged to maintain his wife during marriage. The Ordinance entitles the wife to seek a certificate from the Arbitration Council, specifying the amount. Thirdly, in the event of divorce, a man is obliged to maintain his wife during the period of *iddat*. This is normally three menstrual periods, but, in the event of pregnancy, it extends to the time of delivery or miscarriage, as the case may be. Fourthly, in the event of divorce, the woman is entitled to her unpaid dower (*mahr*).

These are all the provisions for financial security that Pakistani women have, according to family law. Before the promulgation of the MFLO in 1961, a woman could make an application under Section 488 of the Criminal Procedure Code for maintenance payments but that procedure was replaced by those laid down in the Ordinance.

A survey conducted by David Pearl (Pearl, 1971: 566-7) showed that this provision in the MFLO is practically the only one which has been effective. The ten Union Committees, to which 105 applications for recovery of maintenance were made between 1966 and 1968, granted certificates in 104 of them. Many cases could be quoted to show that certificates of maintenance are granted to neglected wives.[51] The procedure for recovery of maintenance under the Ordinance sounds simple and expeditious.

But there are, however, some shortcomings in the remedies available to women. These have been pinpointed by different writers and practising lawyers. Firstly, the Ordinance provides remedy only for the wife and no mention is made in it of the maintenance of children (Carroll, 1979). Secondly, though the procedure for obtaining maintenance under the Ordinance is cheaper and quicker than that under the code of criminal procedure, still the 'time factor' in the present procedure is problematic, especially in cases where the husband is unwilling to pay. Where there is immediate need, remedies should be provided for at least basic needs, perhaps in the form of a provisional order (Patel, 1979: 67-8; Tanveer, 1990; Zareen,

Samina, 1990). Thirdly, there are the problems concerning past maintenance. Under the criminal procedure code, past maintenance was non-recoverable. The court could only order maintenance from the date of order or from the date of application. The suggestion by the Marriage Commission in 1956, which was not adopted by the 1961 Ordinance, was that a wife should have a right to at least three years' past maintenance. Section 9 of the Ordinance, though, does not mention past maintenance, although courts in Pakistan have held that past maintenance due to a neglected wife is recoverable.[52] It should be noted, however, that the courts have been able to make this interpretation only because the Ordinance does not prohibit past maintenance as the criminal procedure code does. A clear, positive provision in law could save women from uncertainty and litigation in claiming past maintenance.

Fourthly, there is the problem of future maintenance. As I have mentioned under 'womens' right to divorce', a woman's right to future maintenance could be secured by entering a proviso to this effect in the marriage contract. But very few husbands agree to a term making them liable to support their wives even after divorce and many people are unaware that such a possibility of providing security for women exists. In the Pakistani social set-up, where women are economically dependent on men and there are many situations where they could be left without a roof over their head, it is important that there should be some form of future security for them. It was one of the recommendations of the commission that the court should have the authority to order maintenance to a divorced woman for life or until she remarries.[53] This suggestion was not adopted by the MFLO. As it is now, women in Pakistan have no future economic security when they get divorced. They have a right to support only in the *iddat* period. 'The Ordinance thus falls short of the recommendation of the Marriage Commission' (Carroll, 1979: 138; 1986).

Fifthly, the present law provides no scale or standard. Lawyers from Multan, in the conference on family law held in 1990, mentioned a case where children were receiving a college education but were given the small sum of 100 Rs per month as maintenance.

In Pakistan, there are controversies between Traditionalists and Modernists regarding the providing of future maintenance (Shehab, 1986a; Ibrahim, 1986). In neighbouring India, the problem of maintenance to divorced Muslim women has also been a point of controversy (Krishnaiyer, 1987; Malik, 1988).

4.7 DOWER (MAHR)

Dower is an amount of money or property in Muslim marriages settled by the husband on his wife. The man is under an obligation to settle dower upon his wife. In other words, he is under debt to his wife.

There are various explanations of the origin of this custom in Muslim marriages. Some writers relate it to the custom of bride price, others consider it a mark of respect for the wife. None of the theories provide a sufficient explanation of the origin of the custom and its continuation.

Here we are primarily concerned with what this practice means in Pakistani society today. Socially, the practice serves different purposes. Dower may constitute a status symbol in Pakistan, such that the larger the amount, the higher the status of the parties. It should be mentioned here that there is no fixed maximum dower. However, the fixed minimum is thirty-two rupees. In cases where dower is a status symbol it can be a burden on the man. In some families an excessive amount of mahr is stipulated in the marriage contract in order to maintain the reputation of the family. It then sometimes becomes a paper transaction, never meant to be paid. This can be problematic if a husband wants to divorce his wife because he may be unable to pay the exorbitant dower. In order to escape from such problems men can make life very unhappy for their wives and drive them to the point where the wives initiate divorce; as we have observed, a wife has to forego her dower if she initiates the divorce.

In some strata of Pakistani society, a high dower is fixed specifically for the purpose of creating an obstacle to the dissolution of marriage. Among *Hanafi* sects, dower is divided into prompt and deferred dower. The former is payable at any time on the wife's demand; if the husband does not pay on demand she can refuse to cohabit with him. Deferred dower, however, is paid if the marriage is dissolved or on the husband's death. If the deferred dower is high, the husband has to think before planning to divorce his wife, because he will be obliged to pay the whole amount. In order to serve this purpose the dower is fixed large enough to deter the husband. In the arranged marriage system where the size of the dower is fixed with this in mind, it can create bitterness between the families. Sometimes marriage arrangements founder when the bride's family tries to fix a high amount and the bridegroom's family does not agree to it. In some families the purpose of dower is considered to be security for the wife. This is especially so where she is economically dependent on her husband, which is mostly the case. A sufficiently large amount of deferred dower may be of real benefit to the wife if she is divorced or widowed. This should be seen in the light of the limitation of Pakistani womens' right of maintenance in the post-marriage period to a mere ninety days. If a woman is suddenly left with no financial support, the dower money can provide at least some security.

It is difficult to accept that dower is meant to be a bride-price in some parts of Pakistan, because it is an established practice that the wife is the only recipient of dower. But the idea that it is a mark of respect for the wife is commonly found behind the practice, and this seems plausible. There are also many families who consider the practice to have symbolic value and fix the amount according to the means of the husband. It should be noted that the practice of dower is flexible enough and the amount can be reduced or increased after marriage by mutual consent. If a husband is unable to pay the whole amount he can pay instalments with the consent of his wife. A wife can also forego her dower. However, it should be established that she has not been under pressure to do so. Considering it their religious duty to pay dower, men have a bad conscience if they have not paid it. Sometimes, if the dower is unpaid and the man is on his deathbed, wives remit their right to dower in order to remove the burden from his man's conscience. Dower is like a debt, so that if the husband dies it is payable out of the property and assets of the deceased.

A great number of families in Pakistan fix a nominal dower. The lowest amount fixed is thirty-two rupees which is established after the saying of the Prophet of Islam. In such cases, dower is neither a security for the woman nor a deterrence against divorce, but only a symbolic practice. Rashida Patel estimates that in 20% of marriages solemnized the dower consists of the customary thirty-two rupees. In cases where no dower is specified in the marriage contract the marriage itself is valid, but the dower is nevertheless required by Islamic law to be paid to the wife. In such situations she is entitled to a 'proper dower' (*mahr-mithl*). When fixing a proper dower, the court takes into consideration the status of husband and wife and especially the circumstances of the woman.

The Ordinance of 1961 has not made any remarkable change to the practice of this custom. The Ordinance has merely clarified the problem concerning the forms of specified dower. As I have mentioned already, the part called prompt dower (*mahr-i-*

muajjal), is payable on the wife's demand any time after the marriage contract. The other part called deferred dower (*mahr-i-muwajjal*) is payable on the death of the husband or dissolution of the marriage.

When the form is not expressed in the marriage contract, the question arises as to whether the dower is to be treated as prompt or deferred. There is a conflict of opinion among the various Muslim schools of law on this point (Russell & Suhrawardy, 1979). Section 10 of the 1961 Ordinance says: 'Where no details about the mode of payment of the dower are specified in the *nikahnama* or the marriage contract, the entire amount of the dower shall be presumed to be payable on demand'. In so providing the Ordinance has adopted the *Shia* stand on this point. According to the *Sunni* viewpoint, which is dominant in Pakistan, it is a matter for the court in cases of dispute to determine what portion may be treated as prompt and what portion as deferred. When deciding this the court should take into consideration the amount of dower, the position of the wife and her family, the custom of the locality, etc. Thus one portion may be prompt and another deferred. Erwin I.J. Rosenthal holds that the purpose of Section 10 is 'to safeguard the wife in respect to the dower paid for her on marriage and due to her' (Rosenthal, 1965: 334). This section has not been opposed by the majority of *Sunni* residents in Pakistan, though it is opposed to the *Hanafi* school's stand on the matter.

A further problem as to dower is summarized by a lawyer practising in Pakistan. She says that:

> ... a large number of family suits are filed by the estranged or divorced wife against her husband for recovery of mahr. Litigation is usually long and distressing for the wife, and execution of decree becomes difficult where the husband owns no property (Patel, 1979: 82).

The Ordinance does not provide any remedy to this problem.

4.8 INHERITANCE

Section 4 of the MFLO deals with the problem of a grandchild inheriting from a deceased grandfather. All schools of *fiqh* agree that an orphaned grandchild does not inherit from a deceased grandfather (paternal or maternal) if there are other children. This has created problems for Muslims; Lucy Carroll explains:

> In a tribal society where the surviving son took over responsibility for the children of his deceased brother in the extended family group, the traditional rules of succession may not have occasioned much hardship. But in a society where nuclear families are more common, the total exclusion of one line of the deceased's descendants appears both unjust and unjustified (Carroll, 1979: 139).

A famous Oriental expert recognizes the problems in the following words:

> The family has also been increasingly affected by the changing nature of society produced by the growth of impersonal cities, an industrial civilization, and a constant movement of population, which changes have adversely affected the protection afforded to orphaned children by their deceased parents, brothers and sisters as was normal in the larger family groups of the past (Faruki, 1965: 271-2).

As for the appropriate solution of this modern problem, there is a difference of opinion among Muslims. Two contrasting solutions have been adopted: obligatory bequests and a system of inheritance by right. The former has been adopted in Middle East countries and the latter in Pakistan. Both solutions try to find justification in Islamic sources and legal principles; both solutions have their advantages and disadvantages as discussed by different writers (Khan, Hamid: 1980).[54] It is agreed by all that the Pakistani solution, i.e., inheritance by right, is the more radical. Traditionalists in Pakistan oppose 'inheritance by right' on the grounds that it violates the spirit and the structure of the Islamic law of inheritance. Everybody agrees that orphaned grandchildren should be protected and that there is no third acceptable solution; therefore Traditionalists in Pakistan prefer the solution of obligatory bequest.

4.8.1 History of orphaned grandchild's right of inheritance in Pakistan

Before the promulgation of the MFLO in 1961, the traditional *shariah* law that an orphaned grandchild is totally excluded by the other surviving sons was applied. A Bill for the Entitlement of

Orphaned Grandchildren to Inheritance was moved for the first time in the Punjab Assembly on 3 December 1953. In 1955 the Family Law Commission recommended that the children of a predeceased son be entitled to inherit a share of the property of the grandfather. In spite of all the opposition to the Commission's suggestions, the MFLO was passed in 1961. Section 4 of the Ordinance says that the children 'in the event of the death of any son or daughter, if any, living at the time the succession opens, shall *per stirpes* receive a share equivalent to the share which such son or daughter, as the case may be, would have received if alive.'

Section 4 was strongly opposed by the *ulema* of Pakistan and since its promulgation there has been a continuing demand from the Traditionalists to amend it.[55] On 7 July 1966, a bill for this purpose was moved in the National Assembly of Pakistan, but it did not become law. With the Islamization movement in the seventies, the demand of the Traditionalists to change the MFLO became stronger. Before we look at developments in the seventies, let us look briefly at Section 4.

It has been said that the solution to the problem of orphaned grandchildren's right of inheritance, as provided in Section 4, 'brings about radical changes in the structure of inheritance, affecting not only the heirs' quantum of entitlement but also their priorities' (Coulson, 1971: 152). N.J. Coulson also finds that the Pakistani reform is more extreme than the Middle Eastern one 'in regard to the extent to which one system or the other is more or less disruptive of the traditional law!' Another American expert on Oriental law, Lucy Carroll, says that the major blow which these reforms have given to the traditional law is:

> ... in granting to the children of the predeceased daughter the share which their mother would have received if alive, for although a daughter is a primary heir in the traditional law, her children are 'distant kinsmen' who have virtually no right of inheritance to their maternal grandparents (Carroll, 1979: 140).

These and other Western writers have argued that the Pakistani reforms have no basis in traditional law. Another remarks:

> This action was rationalized on the grounds of social desirability and a lack of any prohibition in the primary soures of Islamic law (*Quran* and *Sunna*) (Esposito, 1977: 307, 1982: 88).

In contrast, an Oriental expert finds Section 4 of the Ordinance more in spirit with Islam. He says:

> The system of obligatory bequests seeks to justify itself by an interpretation of *Quranic* verse II:180, which interpretation is by no means consistent, while the system of inheritance by right seeks to justify itself by exposing a lacuna, even contradiction, in classical rules of interpreting the *Quranic* and *Hadith* references as they find expression in the exclusion rule (Faruki, 1965: 272).

He further says:

> If the strengthening of the agnatic family in its direct lineal order from generation to generation is an enduring Islamic ideal, then the 1961 law is fully in harmony with this (Faruki, 1965: 273).

This type of approval of Section 4 is found among other progressive Pakistani writers (Husain, S.M., 1962).

4.8.2 *Islamization and Section 4*

Tanzil-ur-Rahman, former chairman of the Council of Islamic Ideology, who has played an important role in Islamizing the law in Pakistan, feels that only a small group of modern individuals holds Section 4 to be in accordance with Islamic law. He says:

> I hold that Quranic injunctions, Prophet's traditions, and the verdicts of the Companions and practice of the *Ummah* easily establish the conclusion that Section 4 the Family Laws of Ordinance VIII of 1961 is contrary to the collective viewpoint of the *Ummah* (Rahman, Tanzil-ur, 1982: 101).

He proposes the adoption in Pakistan of a law of obligatory bequest (Rahman, Tanzil-ur, 1982). He strongly condemns the system of inheritance by right and calls the reformists' interpretations fallacious, 'a mental obfuscation unworthy of any serious discussion'. He further says that Section 4 is inspired by not Islamic law, but by Roman law, English law and Hindu law, being an adaptation of the repealed customary law of the undivided Punjab.

In 1980 a petition, *Mst. Farishta v. the Federation of Pakistan*,[56] came before the *Shariah* Bench of Peshwar High

Court. The Bench referred to the *Quran, Sunna* and also to the works of Tanzil-ur-Rahman, and came to the conclusion that Section 4 of the law was repugnant to the injunctions of Islam and should, therefore, be repealed. However, the case came up before the *Shariah* Bench of the Supreme Court in 1981.[57] The Supreme Court set aside the judgment of the High Court on the ground that the High Court had no jurisdiction in the matter, because it was a matter of Muslim personal law which, according to Article 203 B of the Constitution of Pakistan, 1973, is outside the jurisdiction of the courts. That decision might not be followed today after the passing of the Ninth Amendment and the *Shariat* Bill in 1988, as the jurisdiction of the Federal *Shariat* Court seems to have been enlarged. But since the death of General Zia, the process of Islamization is not proceeding with the same intensity. Nevertheless, if the process continues, there is a possibility that the issue will come up again, and the judgment of Peshawar High Court could then become relevant.

In 1983, the court decided a case in accordance with Section 4 of the Ordinance of 1961.[58] A more liberal writer, while commenting on the case of Mst. Farishta, said:

> It is humbly submitted that when the object of both the solutions is the welfare of the orphan grandchildren, then why not retain the one which is more in harmony with the rules of succession that succession is a matter of right and not need. The Pakistani reformers have hit the nail on the head, as the rule of representation under Section 4 of the Muslim Family Laws Ordinance gives the orphan grandchildren the right of inheritance irrespective of the fact whether they are needy or not. The credit goes to the reformers who have boldly cut the Gordian knot (Ali, Ahmad, 1986: 82).

David Pearl rightly says that, after Islamization in Pakistan, the MFLO will inevitably be interpreted in such a way as to reflect the fundamentals of *Hanafi* distribution in cases involving *Hanafis* (Kamal Khan v. Zainab; Mai v. Falak Sher; Muhammad Fikree v. Fikree Development Corporation.[59]

4.9 ARRANGED MARRIAGE /CHILD MARRIAGE

The institution of arranged marriage is still common in Pakistan (Donnan, 1988). A marriage may be arranged between two people who have never seen each other, or in some situations never heard each other's name. Another type of arranged marriage which is also common in Pakistan is called 'exchange marriage' (*watta-satta*). In this type of marriage, arrangements are made between two families to arrange the marriage of two couples, who are usually brothers and sisters. The evil attached to this type of arrangement is that if one marriage is not working well it affects the relationship of the other couple as well. In this way extra pressure is put upon the marriage which is not working well (Ahmed, Jamil, 1983). The arrangement is made exclusively by the two families. However, in more liberal arranged marriages, the arrangement may be made by the families, but the consent of the bride and groom are obtained. Sometimes photographs are exchanged, or the young people are given a chance to see each other.

A still more liberal form of arrangement is where two people want to marry each other and obtain the consent of their parents, in which case the parents arrange the marriage ceremony. It is not unusual for parents to refuse their consent, in which case the parties either submit, which means life long misery - or marry in spite of opposition. In such love matches the parties may face a lot of social pressure after marriage and this may affect their married life, but in other cases the parents consent after the marriage. The institution of arranged marriage has its roots in the segregation of the sexes. As a result of segregation, young people become dependent on their families to find their future partners. In large joint families, the institution is also used to control the lives of young people and make them submit to family interests. The institution of arranged marriage is strongest among the lower classes of Pakistan. Ideologically, it is supported by the orthodox traditionalist Muslim who finds the justification for the segregation of the sexes in Islam, in which stress is laid on *purdah* (the veil) and the modesty of women. The concept has been strengthened in Pakistan during the last decade of Islamization. With the segregation of the sexes, young people do not develop free love relationships. It also gives rise to criminal acts like men abducting women.

As far as the legal position of two people who want to get married of their own free will is concerned, there is no bar to such a marriage.

Arranged marriages against the will of the parties, or with insufficient consideration of their compatability, creates one type of social problem. Another problem arises from marriages arranged in childhood. Child marriage is common practice in the villages. Restrictions on child marriage were strengthened in the *Child-Marriage Restraint Act, 1929*, which prescribed penal sanctions where the bridegroom had not reached the age of eighteen and the bride fourteen.[60] This Act continued to be law in Pakistan after 1947. However, in 1961 Section 12 of the MFLO raised the minimum marriageable age of girls from fourteen to sixteen and that of boys from eighteen to twenty-one. Where a child marriage takes place, Section 2 (vii) of the *Dissolution of Muslim Marriages Act, 1939*, amended by Section 13 of the MFLO allows the woman to repudiate the marriage (if it has not been consummated) when she reaches the age of eighteen.[61] If Section 12 is not obeyed, the marriage becomes illegal but not invalid, i.e., penalties are provided for the guardian, bridegroom and the marriage registrar. Under Section 5 of the *Child Marriage Restraint-Act, 1929* the penalties are imprisonment (of up to one month) and a fine (up to 1,000 Rs).[62]

The remedies available to a girl who is married in childhood are complicated. The Dissolution of Muslim Marriages Act, 1939, laid down three conditions for exercising the option of puberty:

1. Performance of marriage during minority with the consent of the guardian.

2. Consummation of marriage, i.e., cohabitation with consent, does not take away the wife's right to exercise option of puberty. However, consummation must be proved.

3. The woman must be between the ages of sixteen and eighteen.

Although the option of puberty grants a theoretical right to the girl, it is obviously a right that would be difficult if not impossible for a young girl to exercise without the support and backing of her family (Carroll, 1979: 135-6). A practising lawyer from Bahawarpur in Pakistan said that, though this remedy is available in law, it is not easy for a girl to express her like or dislike, because of social conditions it is almost impossible for her to file a case (Mubshar, 1990).

J.A. Kroson found in his research that three areas of Karachi did, in general, abide by the minimum age requirements (Kroson, 1959), but David Pearl's results from Quetta showed that a great number of parents were marrying off their daughters at an extremely early age (Pearl, 1971: 61-3; Alam, 1968: 489-98). Other available statistics show that there is a rise in the age of marriage in Pakistan (Patel, 1979: 489-98).

It is really difficult to know what the precise figures of child marriage is Pakistan are. One of the basic reasons for this is the element of corruption. It is not uncommon for a *nikah* registrar to accept a bribe and register the marriage of girls and boys under the legal marriage age. According to a practising lawyer in Bahawarpur, this is widespread in Pakistan (Mubshar, 1990). In January 1991 when I was visiting the small village of Makawal in the Punjab, I was told by a boy of ten married to a girl of twelve that he was in his fifth year at school and that there were four other married boys in his class. As well, people in villages often do not know their ages, also making it difficult to find out the precise number of child marriages in Pakistan.

4.10 DOWRY

Dowry is not a concept derived from the *Quran* and *Sunna* of the Prophet of Islam. It is a custom which the Muslims of Pakistan have adopted from Hindu traditions. The basic idea of dowry is that some necessary household items are provided by the bride's family for the married couple to begin married life with. But with the passage of time it has become a social evil.[63]

The evils of dowry are not as great in Pakistan as in India. It is well-known that brides in India have been murdered by in-laws in dowry-related offences. These murders are often made to look like kitchen accidents. In India dowry is completely prohibited by law, while Pakistan does not prohibit dowry absolutely but puts a restriction on its amount instead (Arora, 1982: 70-8; Awasti, 1986).[64] In recent years, since women's movements have become strong in Pakistan, women have claimed dowry related violance also common in Pakistan (women's organizations published pamphlets on this issue in 1989/1990).

In Pakistan it is nevertheless a big problem in the lower and middle classes. It is the responsibility of parents to marry off their daughters and provide them with the traditional dowry. This is often a big task in relation to their limited economic resources. Consequently, instead of spending money on the education and training of their daughters, they devote all their resources to providing them with a dowry. This preparation starts when the girl is born. Girls are taught embroidery and sewing in order to prepare for their dowry. The idea is not only to provide a household for the bride; dowry has also become a status symbol. The dowry is displayed to family and friends, and this leads to competition and becomes a question of prestige (Chishti, 1964). Sometimes the parents of the bride incur heavy debts which they are still paying off a long time after the girl has been married. Moreover, the bride's parents are expected to provide meals and entertainment at the marriage ceremony, which again can be too much for people of the lower and middle classes (Patel, 1979: 27; Esposito, 1982b; Shehab, 1987a). Dowry provided by the bride's family becomes the property of the husband's family.

Various attempts have been made at different times to eradicate the evils of dowry. A bill was presented as early as 1952.[65] A commission reported in 1965.[66] In 1967 an Act was passed. This Act attempted to make the display of dowry an offence punishable by imprisonment and a fine, and also to ensure that the woman would be the absolute owner of her dowry (Patel, 1979: 27; Esposito, 1982b: 87).[67] The Act was repealed in 1976 and a new attempt made. The Dowry and Bridal Gifts (Restriction) Act, 1976 provides limitations not only on the total value of the dowry but also on gifts given by the bridegroom's family and by friends and relatives. The limit to dowry and gifts provided by the bridegroom's family is 5,000 Rs (Section 3:1), while the value of presents provided by friends and relatives should not exceed 100 Rs (Section 4). The 1976 Act, contrary to that of 1967, makes the display of dowry compulsory (Section 7). A list of dowry and bridal gifts, presents and wedding expenses is to be submitted to the Registrar of Marriages (Sections 7 and 8). The amount of money spent on the wedding ceremony must not exceed 2.500 rupees (Section 6). The Act provides a penalty of imprisonment and fine for infringement (Section 9). In order to curb corruption it absolutely bans the receipt of presents from state dignitaries, VIPs and high government officials (Section 4) (Shehab, 1987a). Dowry, gifts or presents given or accepted in contravention of the provisions of the Act are to be forfeited to the federal government and utilised in the marriage of poor girls (Section 9:1). Lawful dowry is to be vested absolutely in the bride (Section 5). An amendment to the Act of 1976 was made in 1980. The most notable aspect of this is that it repeals Section 7.[68]

These attempts to eradicate the evils of dowry are not realistic, as the restriction on the aggregate value, i.e., 5.000 rupees or £500, has been said to be 'too high for the lower income group and too low for the higher income group'. It has been argued that 'the amount should be commensurate with the status and income of the parties' (Patel, 1979: 34). The practice of dowry is still widely followed in Pakistan.

4.11 FAILURE OF THE MUSLIM FAMILY LAWS ORDINANCE, 1961

There are various reasons for the failure of the MFLO, pin-pointed by different writers. By some its failure is attributed to the fact that it was linked with the system of 'Basic Democracy' which in the end failed in Pakistan. It is said that because the Ordinance was linked with this system, the reforms also became part of politics (Pearl, 1971: 567, 1976: 72; Patel, 1979: 92). Moreover, people lost confidence in the 'Basic Democracy' system.

Secondly, there is a weakness in the Ordinance, in that the restrictions contained therein, if contravened, result in acts becoming illegal but not invalid; for example, a second marriage contrary to Section 6 is illegal but nevertheless still valid. The same is true of other restrictions concerning divorce and registration, etc (Pearl, 1971: 567-8; Patel, 1979: 95).

Thirdly, John L. Esposito suggests that the lack of a systematic Islamic rationale creates serious problems and 'the apparent discontinuity of many reforms with traditional *fiqh* subjects them under heavy fire at times from Traditionalist leaders and their followers, the masses of the population, who tend to be more conservative in outlook' (Esposito, 1977: 309). There is no doubt that a small number of people do not observe the MFLO because they consider it to be un-Islamic. Non-observance also occurs because of ignorance of the law. Non-observance of the Ordinance is found more often in rural than in urban areas.

> A large number of marriages in these areas are not registered, and there is still a proportion of marriages where the bride is under 16. Many divorces are not communicated to the chairman, thus at least in strict legal theory that marriage would still be in existence where the matter is communicated to the chairman and he establishes an Arbitration Council, the council more often than not will follow prevailing social norms in making decisions regarding polygamy and divorce. Contrariwise amongst the upper middle-class in large towns such as Karachi, Lahore and perhaps Dacca, the Ordinance has done no more than continue a trend already apparent (Pearl, 1976: 73).

This was the observation of David Pearl in 1976, i.e., fifteen years after the promulgation of the Ordinance and we have seen that the situation is not very much different now.

Rashida Patel has drawn attention to the problem that, according to Rule 21 of the Ordinance, no court can take cognizance of any offence under the Ordinance or its rules, except on a complaint in writing by the Union Councils. After the dissolution of Union Councils, no institution has been introduced to replace them. Thus there is a vacuum (Patel, 1979: 94-5).[69] Of course, such obscurities create distrust of the Ordinance.

4.12 CHALLENGES TO THE MUSLIM FAMILY LAWS ORDINANCE, 1961

Despite the fact that the MFLO has been a partial failure in practice, it has at different times - both before its promulgation and after its enactment - been challenged, the intention being to abolish it. One such attempt was made in July 1963, when the West Pakistan Provincial Assembly passed a resolution recommending the repeal of the Ordinance. But the Bill was defeated in the National Assembly on November 26, 1963. There was also pressure to defeat the Bill from the All Pakistan Women Association, the President and the Law Minister of Pakistan (Esposito, 1977). The Constitution of 1973 provided a safeguard for the MFLO with Article 203B, which excludes from the purview of the courts the examination of Muslim Personal Law.

During the period of Islamization in the seventies, family law again became a point of opposition for Traditionalists. General propaganda was made against the MFLO. Textbooks in the educational institutions were Islamized. In the *Civics Textbook for Intermediate Classes* the following was inserted:

> One of the causes of the failure of the Ayub Constitution was the adoption of laws repugnant to the shariah, like the Muslim Family Laws Ordinance, and steps that subverted morality, like family planning.[70]

In order to Islamize of the legal system, *Shariat* Benches and later the *Shariah* Court were given powers to pass judgements on petitions received from various individuals, challenging laws as being repugnant to the *shariah*. Family law was excluded from the jurisdiction of *Shariah* Benches and Courts. As we have already noted in a petition in 1981, *Mst. Farishta* applied for a declaration that Section 4 of the MFLO (inheritance) was against the injunctions of Islam.[71] The Supreme Court set aside the order of the High Court as being without jurisdiction.

However, a Bill known as the *Shariah* Bill (also called the ninth amendment) removing the prohibition on the *Shariah* Courts to review family law, was a great point of discussion between Traditionalists and Modernists. Since the court also supported the Bill, it was passed in June 1988, leaving the MFLO unprotected. Because of the death of General Zia it did not became law however. The Bill was delayed, as it did not fulfill procedural requirements, until 1991 when it became law (This is attached as Appendix III to this book).

The MFLO has been challenged from different directions. Tanzir-ur-Rahman, who was the chairman of the Council of Islamic Ideology for 1980-84, suggested amendments to the MFLO. He said that the MFLO had protection under the Constitutions of 1962 and 1973, and that this protection continues even after the revival of the Constitution by Presidential Order in 1985, which he deplored because of 'the secular influences working both in and outside the relevant quarters'. He further said that Government 'for fear of opposition of a section of women, felt hesitant to implement the recommendations in respect of MFLO'. He insisted that the protections extended to the MFLO had become 'nugatory' because it was in contradiction to the Objectives Resolution (Rahman, Tanzil-ur: 1989).[72]

While on the one hand the MFLO has become vulnerable during the period of Islamization by being declared un-Islamic in the *Shariat* Courts, on the other hand it has been strictly applied in cases under the *Zina (Enforcement of Hudood) Ordinance, 1979*. Let us look at a recent case, *Shahida and Sarwar v. the State*.[73]

The main question in that case was the validity of the marriage of the two accused persons. Shahida was previously married. She claimed that her marriage to her previous husband had been dissolved. She produced a 'divorce deed' purporting to be signed by her previous husband and attested by a magistrate. The co-accused Sarwar was also previously married. He claimed that his marriage to Shahida was a second marriage. The trial court decided that the marriage of Shahida and Sarwar was illegal, disbelieving the genuineness of Shahida's divorce deed and the marriage deed of Shahida and Sarwar.

Asma Jahangir, a woman lawyer, has raised the question whether the criminal courts had the jurisdiction to make a finding on the validity of a marriage, inasmuch as family courts, which are appellate courts in *Hudood* cases, have specifically been debarred from determining whether laws relating to personal law are in conformity with Islam. I quote from Asma Jahangir:

> The *Hudood* Ordinances specifically define 'marriage' as that which is not void according to the personal law of the parties. Under the Muslim Family Laws Ordinance, 1961, marriages are required to be registered, and divorce is not effected until the expiry of 90 days from the communication to the Arbitration Council at the Local Body level, of the fact of its pronouncement. However, such statutory requirements are alien to the personal law of Muslims. This would mean that if marriage is defined as that which is not void according to the personal law of the parties, the registration and intimation requirements of the Muslim Family Laws Ordinance could be ignored by the court in determining the validity of a marriage, while trying an accused under the *Offence of Zina (Enforcement of Hudood) Ordinance, 1979* (Jahangir, 1988: 28).

She further says:

> The present Muslim family law requires registration of divorces and marriages at the Local Body level. The responsibility of registration is on the husband. Quite frequently divorce is pronounced on a wife, but the husband deliberately or owing to lack of awareness does not get the divorce deed registered. In such cases the 'divorced' wife can be charged with zina on remarriage. The onus of proof of divorce is on her. This puts women in jeopardy, owing to the loopholes in the legal system.
>
> Although the definition of 'marriage' under the *Hudood* Ordinance is marriage that is not void according to personal law, the judgments of the Federal *Shariat* Courts have varied from case to case in this regard. At times they have held that when husband and wife admit the existence of marriage it is sufficient proof of marriage (PLD 1982, FSC, page 42). But this has been applied selectively and, particularly if a woman has been married previously, the courts apply very rigid standards of proof to the legality of the second marriage. This is wholly unnecessary for Muslims, since Muslim women can obtain divorce on the basis of *khula*. *Khula* is an Islamic form of divorce on the basis of physical aversion, which being a subjective state of mind has a very slight burden of proof (Jahangir, 1988: 29).

4.13 CONCLUSION

There are many controversies surrounding the interpretation of various issues in family law. Unanimity of opinion is difficult to achieve amid such mighty controversy. Though developments in the state family laws of Pakistan are considered to be most advanced in comparison to other Muslim countries, these laws are only used to a limited extent.

These reforms are basically ineffective because of the wide gap between the laws of the State and the plurality of legal practices existing in Pakistan. Other factors are found in the laws themselves, e.g., the difference between void and illegal actions. Corruption in manipulating the reforms is another reason for the ineffectiveness of the MFLO.

Another important aspect is the instability of the MFLO. It could be amended any time it is not thought to be in accordance with the injunctions of Islam. The MFLO has become a symbol of progress in Pakistan and women's organisations in the cities not only want to preserve it but also demand further improvements to it, removing the lacunae in the law in order to make it more effective.

CHAPTER 5

The Procedure Used in the Islamization of the Law

5.1 INTRODUCTION

In Chapter 1, the lack of agreement in ideas concerning the nature of Islamic law was discussed. In this chapter, I will deal with the uncertainty or instability of the mechanism through which the Islamization of the law was to be achieved. Most of this process, as has been mentioned, was carried out from 1977 until 1988 under military rule.

The biggest problem regarding the Islamization of the law was that the Traditionalist *ulema* and the Muslim Modernist have never been in agreement. Their stands have substantially always been mutually irreconcilable. The Modernist strictly believes that the best procedure for amending the country's laws is to leave this task to the parliament which has the mandate to do so. Malik Muhammad Jafar has argued that the *Shariat* courts and the Islamic council are not the proper institutions through which the objectives of Islamization can be achieved. On the other hand, he suggests that the exercise of the right of *ijtihad* (judgement), in modern times, can be entrusted only to a body of elected representatives of the people (Jafar, 1979).

Some of the important questions regarding the procedure for the Islamization of the law are the following: What are the powers of the head of state? How independent is the judiciary? Is there any executive interference in judicial affairs? Does Islamic law validate appellate review? Is the system of precedent recognised in Islam? There are disagreements on all these questions.

There are examples in Islamic history where the judiciary was fully independent from the executive and also had the power to impeach the head of state. But there are also examples where the executive impinged on the freedom of the judges (Kamali, M.H, 1990; Khan, Gul Mohammad, 1986a). As to the system of appeal there are again different views. According to some the decision of the *qadi* is binding; according to others, it is in certain conditions reversable.[1]

Usually the starting point for Muslims is that Islamic law derives its legitimacy from God so there is no legislature in that sense. The question that arises is whether Islamic law should consist of nothing but procedure. This is the current situation in Pakistan, where we already have an Anglo-Muhammadan pattern and different sects having various opinions, so the further question arises regarding *which* Islamic law is to be chosen.

> But if the 'public laws' were also to be changed according to the thinking of the orthodox *ulema*, there is bound to be a great confusion in the legal system of the country, because besides many other important features involved in this, it is well-nigh impossible to reconcile the rules of *fiqh* acceptable to the various schools. The claim of the *ulema* to the contrary is absolutely invalid. As far as we know, there are very few amongst these revered gentlemen who know much about the rules of *fiqh* acceptable to the various schools (Jafar, 1978: 9).

Malik Jafar has also pointed to the fact that *ulema* have never accepted the thinking of Muhammad Iqbal, a poet philospher who is considered to be the founder of the idea of Pakistan and who stood for complete *ijtihad* in the field of lawmaking to be exercised by a popularly elected legislative assembly.

For Pakistan, the first difficulty was to decide the nature of a body of Islamic law that could satisfy Muslims of different beliefs (Ahmad, Mumtaz, 1988). This was dealt with in the Chapter 1. The second difficulty was how to achieve it. An interesting petition came up in 1980, *B.Z. Kaikaus v. President of Pakistan*.[2] In this case questions were raised about the relationship between the judiciary and the executive and the legislature. It was held that the task of finalising the process of Islamization lies with the government. The limited powers of the judiciary were also made clear in the case of *Farishta v. Federation of Pakistan* (Hodkinson, 1981).

The procedure adopted for the Islamization of the law in Pakistan shows that it was mostly accomplished by one man, General Zia, by means of various ordinances. Other institutions participating in Islamization are mostly advisory and secondary for this purpose. The judiciary has also played a secondary but prominent role, details of which have been provided. As will be seen in this chapter, there was great confusion throughout as to who would be empowered to legislate, who would decide legal issues, how the decision-making process was to be regulated and what substantive sources of law would be deemed authoritative. One could also note the Anglo-Muhammadan pattern, especially in the functioning of the *Shariat* courts.

5.2 INSTITUTIONS FOR ISLAMIZATION

Some of the institutions for Islamizing the law were established under the first constitution of 1956, for example the Islamic Research Institute. A Council of Islamic Ideology was set up under the constitutions of 1962 and 1973. But, as we have seen, no Islamization took place until the Islamization movement of 1977. We will now look at the historical development of the institutions used for Islamization. We will also examine the role of the Islamic University, the *Shariah* Academy, the Law Commission, the Ministry of Law and the *Majlis-i-shura* in the Islamization of the law. *Shariat* Benches and *Shariat* courts have played a vital role in the Islamization of laws. These will be dealt with in detail. In so doing, different cases decided by the *Shariat* Court are discussed.

5.2.1 Islamic Research Institute

The Islamic Research Institute (IRI) was founded in 1954, i.e., two years before the first constitution was passed. In 1952 a resolution for the establishment of the institute was presented in the Constituent Assembly. The foundation of the Institute was supported even by non-Muslim members of the Assembly. One of the members of the Assembly opposed it on the grounds that 'we do not want such researches as long as we keep before us for our guidance the word of God, i.e., the Book of God and the example of His Prophet, and such an enviable treasure as Islam' (Khan, Sardar Asadullah Jan, 1952: 1304). However the resolution was supported by the majority of the members. The existence of the IRI was provided for in the constitution of 1956. From that time, the IRI remained a constitutional body, it being also provided for in the constitution of 1962. It was dropped in the constitution of 1973 and has since worked as an autonomous body.

The institute is divided into a research wing, an instruction wing and a publication wing. Its role was basically to research in order to assist the Council of Islamic Ideology, the Federal *Shariat* Court, lawyers, judges and legislators.

It is a well known fact that the Institute's reputation was damaged because of the religious views of one of its directors, Fazlur Rahman, who was a Modernist whom the orthodox lobby did not like. Fazlur Rahman was appointed director of the Institute in 1962 but had to resign later because of demonstrations against him. 'Their views evoked great controversy in Pakistan and an adverse attitude towards the Institute developed in the minds of the public' (Amin, 1989: 92). Others have been more appreciative of the contribution of the Islamic Research Institute under Fazlur Rahman, finding that it 'attempted to utilize natural science and social science learning in its work' (Braibanti, 1966: 18). Since Fazlur Rahman, the character of the Institute has changed.

5.2.2 *Council of Islamic Ideology*

The formation of the Council was provided for in the constitution of 1962 (Article No. 199) and the constitution of 1973 (Article 228). Its functions were laid down in Articles 204 and 230 respectively. The function of the Council was to act in an advisory capacity to parliament, Provincial Assemblies, President and Governors on questions regarding whether proposed laws were or were not repugnant to Islam. Before martial law in 1977, the Council made a number of recommendations for Islamizing laws, but their recommendations were never really implemented. In 1964 the Council recommended the prohibition of alcoholic drinks, which was recommended again in 1969. In 1964 and 1965 the Council also recommended checking obscenity which meant among other things, 'films which exhibit moral degradation and are pornographic'. It was further explained that:

> obscene and sexy literature which was spoiling the character of our young generation was widely in circulation in the country. Radio and television programmes, exciting films and erotic advertisements were also making their unhealthy contribution towards moral degradation. Indecent sculptures, statues and paintings were frequently exhibited in the public meetings.[3]

This was repeated again in 1978. In 1974 the Council suggested that Friday be declared a public holiday and that there be prayers in public offices, special dress to be worn, *azan* five times a day on TV and radio, a prohibition on dancing, etc.

These suggestions were never implemented in President Ayub's period. However, General Zia showed a special interest in the work of the Council. He increased the number of members from fifteen to twenty (through a constitutional amendment, P.O. No. 16, of 1980) and approved the appointment of five full-time members. General Zia reconstituted the Council to include two judges from the High Court or Supreme Court (sitting or retired) one of whom serves as chairman, six *Sunni ulema*, two *Shia* and one woman. The other members come from the fields of law, economics and banking. In June 1981 the Council was reconstituted again. Its scope was extended: it became the President's Chief Advisory Council. In 1981 the Council was given the task of considering Pakistan's Islamic system of government, including the question of national elections. In June 1982 the Council prepared its report and submitted it to the President. It was sent back to the Council many times for reconsideration. In the report presented in 1983, the Council declared that a presidential form of government was 'nearest to Islam', the existence of political parties was un-Islamic and that only a male Muslim could be the President of Pakistan. The report also suggested a Council for non-Muslim citizens, which would be a legislative body based on a separate electorate comprising of non-Muslim citizens; this suggestion was however opposed by the minority members. 'Free mixing of men and women' was to be prohibited according to the report.[4]

In 1977 the Council made an interesting suggestion for a reconciliatory system of courts. They also recommended a day to be observed for 'renewing the pledge', when one would pray for forgiveness and make a pledge to abstain from social evils like corruption, smuggling and adulteration and to work for the aim for which Pakistan was created. In 1978 the Council suggested the permanent settlement of Muslim women living in India, who were detached from their families in Pakistan. It also suggested that before giving any responsible position to the *Ahmadis*, their moral character and loyalty should conform. Another suggestion was teaching the *Quran* to the police, hanging quotations from the *Quran* and *Sunna* in lawyers' chambers and setting up special courts for illiterate women in the villages. In 1979 the Council objected to photos appearing on the currency of Pakistan. In 1980 the it criticized the definition of 'family' employed for the purpose of medical assistance, in which only the wife and children are included, while the parents, brothers and sisters are excluded. In 1980 the Council made a very controversial suggestion in which it opposed the participation of women in hockey, cricket and other games in the presence of male spectators, although it recommended that such participation should be permitted in the presence of female spectators only. In 1981 the Council stressed once again the importance of a national dress and stated its opposition to smoking. It also prescribed that women should cover their heads and breasts in public and if they were found not doing so, they should be punished for it.[5]

In 1984 the Council published a report on family planning and declared contraception to be against the *Quran* and *Sunna*. The report rejected the argument that an increase in population was a burden on the economy of Pakistan.[6]

On the recommendation of the Council, a *Shariat* benches order and an order establishing a permanent law commission were promulgated. The promulgation of *Hudood* laws (comprising five ordinances) and a *zakat* and *ushr* ordinance were also the recommendations of the council. The council prepared a detailed report on the elimination of interest from the country's economy and on the law of *qisas* and *diyat* (law of murder), etc.

A number of regulations for the implementation of *shariah* were implemented on the recommendation of the council. Some of these regulations were: facilities for performing Islamic prayers in government and quasi-government offices, educational institutions, airports, railway stations and bus stations; observance of the month of *Ramadan* (fasting) including the closure of cinemas for a few hours; and orders for all public functionaries to wear the Pakistani/national official dress.

On the recommendation of the Council, the government amended the constitution and the PPC (Pakistan Penal Code) in order to provide definitions of Muslim and non-Muslim, the purpose being to demarcate *Ahmadis* as non-Muslim and to make derogatory remarks about and disrespect to the Prophet Muhammad punishable with imprisonment or fine or with both.[7]

Beginning in December 1981, the Council of Islamic Ideology submitted a series of reports containing comments and recommendations on the large body of statutory laws to see if they were in accordance with the *Quran* and *Sunna*. Its first report covered laws enacted during the period from 1836 to 1871; the second, laws enacted from 1872 to 1881; the third, from 1882 to 1897; and the fourth, from 1898 to 1906. By the fourth report, 197 Acts had been covered. Out of 137 Acts, 97 Acts had been found by the council not to be in conflict with the *Quran* and the *Sunna*.

Among the laws considered un-Islamic by the council, were the provisions of *The Land Improvement Loans Act of 1883 (XIX of 1883)*, dealing with loans grant for agricultural improvements. Similar provisions for charging interest on loans were held to be un-Islamic in the *Agriculturists Loans Act, 1884 (VII of 1884)*. In the *Charitable Endowments Act, 1890 (VI of 1890)*, a charitable purpose was to be redefined to include 'religious teaching and worship'. As for the *Guardians and Wards Act of 1890 (VIII of 1890)*, the council recommended that the husband should not be entitled to guardianship of his minor wife instead of her mother, until she had attained puberty. Exclusion of a parent or guardian from guardianship in case of apostasy was also recommended for this Act. Regarding the *Railways Act, 1890 (IX of 1980)*, the Council recommended that one compartment in all trains should be restricted to women, in order to facilitate the observance of *purdah*. Railway servants found in a state of intoxication while on duty were to be punished with 80 lashes. Recommendations for the establishment of separate reformatory schools for girls to be managed by women were made by the council in respect of the *Reformatory Schools Act, 1897 (VII of 1897)*. The Council recommended amending the *Church of Scotland Kirk Sessions Act, 1899 (XXIII of 1899)*. According to the recommendation, the power conferred by the kirk session to acquire and hold any property for the purpose of congregation or of any trust, should no longer be enjoyed. The council also recommended that the practice of nominating the bishop as an *ex officio* Fellow and Member of the Senate of the Punjab University in the *Universities Act, 1904 (VIII of 1904)*, should also cease. In the *Prisoners Act, 1900 (III of 1900)*, the Council recommended that a proviso be added to Section 18, so as to refrain from executing the death sentence, if the person to be executed is a pregnant woman, until her child attains two years of age, or if there is no other suitable person to bring up the child.[8] Most of these recommendations were initiated by Tanzil-ur-Rahman.

5.2.3 Islamic University

On 8 October 1979, a *Shariat* law faculty was established at Islamabad's Quaid-e-Azam University. In 1980, an Islamic University was established, to which the *Shariah* Faculty was transferred. This university was made a separate institution through the promulgation of the Islamic University, Islamabad Ordinance. It was reconstituted and reorganised in 1985 as the International Islamic University. It is situated in Faisal *masjid*, Islamabad. King Abdul Aziz University of Saudi Arabia has extended its full support and co-operation in the establishment of the *Shariah* Faculty. Al-Azhar University of Egypt also helped the University in several respects and it is now headed by an Egyptian scholar as its vice-chancellor. About fifty-six teachers from Egyptian and Saudi Arabian universities have been employed in the International Islamic University.

The aims of the University were described as being to produce scholars 'who are imbued with Islamic learning and character and capable of meeting economic, social, political, technological, physical, intellectual and aesthetic needs of the society'.⁹ Carroll (1982b: 74) contends that the government's objective was the creation of an integrated system of education bridging the bifurcation between the traditional/religious and the modern/ scientific streams (Weiss, 1986b: 15). Different writers stress the aforementioned role of the University:

> The purpose and goal of the university is to fuse Pakistan's dual or parallel systems of secular and religious learning 'so as to provide an Islamic vision for those engaged in education and to enable them to reconstruct human thought in all its forms on the foundations of Islam' (Esposito, 1982a: 215).

The University has five major and several smaller institutes:

1. Institute of *dawah* and *usul-al-din* (to train teachers and mullahs for the mosques).
2. Institute of *Shariah* Training.
3. Islamic Research Institute.
4. Institute of Islamic Education.
5. Institute of Islamic History, Culture and Civilization.
6. International Institute of Islamic Economics.
7. Institute of Linguistics and Languages.
8. Institute of Applied Sciences.
9. Institute of Social Sciences.
10. *Shariah* Academy
11. Institute of Medicine and Health.
12. Institute of Engineering and Technology.

The Pakistan Bar Council has raised an objection to the LL.B (*Shariah*) degree of the University where students are admitted after the intermediate stage and undergo a four-year course leading to the LL.B. The Bar Council claimed that the possession of a B.A degree is a must for holders of an LL.B *Shariah* degree in Pakistan.

The University has been the target of criticism for its financial irregularities and for inviting political leaders instead of scholars to address the students. These charges have been denied.[10]

5.2.4 Shariah Academy

This is a constituent part of the International Islamic University, Islamabad. It was originally established in 1981 as the Institute of Training in *Shariah* & Legal Profession and was raised to the status of an Academy when international status was conferred upon the Islamic University in 1985.

The Academy describes its objectives as being to promote Islamic legal philosophy and the Islamic concept of justice through training the judges, attorneys and prosecutors who collectively operate the judicial system. In its aims and objectives it further holds:

> The efforts of the Academy are based on the assumption that the process of Islamization of the laws and the society, which is a constitutional imperative for Pakistan, will be facilitated if our intellectuals who hold responsible positions in the governance of the country, especially the administration of justice, develop a clear understanding of the *Shariah* and acquire professional competence in its application.[11]

A series of *Shariah* (Islamic Law) courses for judges, attorneys and prosecutors has been held regularly since 1981. The *Shariah* course is usually of sixteen weeks' duration and is held at least twice a year. Participants are District and Sessions judges, Civil judges, District Attorneys, Public Prosecutors, Assistant Commissioners etc. They are nominated by their respective provincial governments and the government of Azad Kashmir. A total number of 557 judicial and executive officers of various classifications had taken the fifteen *Shariah* courses held up to the end of 1986.

5.2.5 Law Commission

On the recommendation of the Council of Islamic Ideology, General Zia promulgated an order establishing a permanent Law Commission, headed by the Chief Justice of Pakistan, for reviewing the laws of Pakistan, with a view to bringing them into line with Islamic social justice and particularly to suggest ways and means of simplifying the procedure for obtaining speedy and fair justice by all citizens. The Commission thus gives priority to such enactments which have a direct bearing on the social life of the community, particularly Muslims.

5.2.6 Ministry of Law

According to the *Rules of Business, 1973*, the function of the Ministry of Law is to provide information on the law to all the other ministries and the provincial governments. It also gives opinions to the federal government in respect of criminal or civil cases. The opinion given by the Law Ministry to other ministries is binding. However, if there is a difference of opinion, it is to be resolved by the Attorney General of Pakistan, Law Minister and Cabinet. The Ministry works in cooperation with the Ministry of Religious Affairs and the Council of Islamic Ideology. It has also direct connections with the Supreme Court, the High Court and the Federal *Shariat* Court. The Ministry is also closely associated with the organisation of the Islamic Conference. It is difficult to see how great a part the Ministry has played directly in the Islamization of the law in Pakistan.[12]

5.2.7 Federal Shariat Court and Shariat Benches

In 1979, General Zia-ul-Haq promulgated the *Constitution (Amendment) Order, 1979*, whereby five *Shariat* Benches were established in the various High courts of the country and a *Shariat* Appellate Bench was set up in the Supreme Court. On 27 May 1986 the four *Shariat* Benches in the High Courts were replaced by a Federal *Shariat* Court (FSC) consisting of five judges and three *ulema*. All were to be appointed by Zia. There have been at least sixteen amendments concerning the FSC. Rashida Patel says 'the numerous amendments make it evident that not sufficient thought and consideration was given to introducing the judicial process for the Islamization of laws'. She further says:

> It was amended as and when required and when ever considered politically expedient. It was introduced by the chief martial law Administrator and President of Pakistan and changed by him from time to time as considered necessary (Patel, Rashida, 1986: 88).

Esposito explains that these courts should not be confused with the traditional Islamic legal system where *qadis* applied *shariah* law. 'Pakistan's *shariat* courts are essentially courts which determine whether or not a specific law is contrary to the *sharia*' (Esposito, 1982a: 207). The power to declare laws inconsistent with the *shariah* was given to the courts for the first time in the history of Pakistan by General Zia. This was the suggestion of the Council of Islamic Ideology. For this purpose special courts were set up in Pakistan. Also for the first time in the history of Pakistan, in 1981 *ulema* were given the function of judges in the FSC.

Besides having two full-time research advisers, the FSC maintains a panel of judicial advisers comprising *ulema* of different schools of thought and having an extensive and intensive knowledge of *shariah*. The five judges of the FSC including the chairman are not independent as they are appointed by the President and the terms of their appointment are also controlled by the President (Section 203-C (2), President's Order 1 of the *Constitution (Amendment) Order, 1980*). Section 203-C (5) says that a High Court judge who does not accept appointment shall be deemed to have retired from his office.

Federal *Shariat* Court (Procedure) Rules, 1981, also prescribe dress for counsel appearing in the court i.e., black *sherwani*, white *shalwar* or a *pajama*, with black socks and shoes or Court Dress (S. 64). The language of the court shall be English or Urdu.

The FSC has acquired a very good collection of valuable and some rare books for its library from local sources and from the Muslim countries on *shariah* as well as other laws, case law of superior courts, Islamic history, etc.

Shariat Benches and the *Shariat* Courts may take cognisance of a matter in three ways, namely, upon petition by a citizen of Pakistan or the Federal Government or a Provincial Government or on its own (*suo moto*). *Shariat* bench decisions may be appealed to the Appellate *Shariat* Bench of the Supreme Court and laws or provisions found to be un-Islamic are to be amended through legislative action. Under its *suo moto* power the FSC started this work of examining the consistency of laws with Islam in 1982 and completed it in 1984. The court also published public notices in newspapers and magazines asking the general public and experts on Islamic law to appear before the court if they felt any law under consideration was repugnant to Islam, but the response was very poor. Some people suggest that the reason is that people are against the Islamization of laws, others that it is the people are incapable of understanding Islamic law.

Shariat Benches and the *Shariat* Courts were given the jurisdiction to examine and decide whether or not any provision of law is repugnant to the injunctions of Islam as laid down in the Holy *Quran* and *Sunna* of the Prophet. By the definition of the word 'law' the following branches of law are excluded from the jurisdiction of the Federal *Shariat* Court: the constitution, any fiscal law, Muslim personal law, any law relating to the procedure of any court or tribunal, and any law relating to the levy and collection of taxes and fees or banking or insurance practice and procedure section (203 B). The famous case of *Farishta v. Federation of Pakistan*[13] has been discussed in detail in the chapter on family law.

> Farishta reduces the potential role of the judiciary in Islamicisation by excluding from its scrutiny almost all the controversial legislation in matters of family and succession law, which is probably what the President, General Zia wanted. Within this narrow field, however, the judiciary has considerable power. By Article 203 when a law can be rendered ineffective without leaving a vacuum, it ceases to have any effect, as soon as declared unIslamic. Where such a vacuum would result, the court may order the legislature to make a suitable amendment to the impugned law. We do not yet know what will happen if (when) the legislature feels unable to enact legislation in compliance with such an order. Will the judiciary do battle with organs of the Constitution less enthusiastically Islamic than itself? (Hodkinson, 1981: 251).

Ulemas and some other writers have demanded that restrictions should not be imposed on the powers of the FSC.

Over a period of three years from June 1982 to June 1985, a total of 512 federal laws and 999 provincial laws were examined and judgements delivered. Out of the 1,511 laws so examined, some provisions were found repugnant in 261 laws. During the first five years, 291 *Shariat* petitions were filed challenging provisions of various laws and 268 were dealt with leaving twenty-three petitions pending. The laws found to be repugnant to Islam were either modified or appeals were lodged against them.

The following are examples of cases brought by petitions of the citizens of Pakistan. It is interesting to note that a good number of petitions challenge customary Muslim law.

Federation of Pakistan v. Hazoor Bukhsh and others [14]

In March 1981 the Federal *Shariah* Court had held that the punishment of *rajm* was 'repugnant to the injunction of Islam'. The government subsequently lodged an appeal with the *Shariah* Bench of the Supreme Court. Before the appeal was heard, an amendment was made to the constitution allowing the Federal *Shariah* Court to review its own decision. The Bench of the Federal *Shariah* Court was reconstituted, the chairman was removed, a new Chief Justice was appointed and two *ulema* added to the bench. On reviewing the government's appeal against this judgment, on 20 June 1982 the reconstituted Federal *Shariah* Court overturned its earlier decision and declared the punishment to be lawful.

Qasim Shah v. Government of Pakistan [15]

The petitioner sought a declaration to the effect that the sharing of the *malikana* (rent) in *biar, diar, pludar* and *sum* types of trees grown on the land of the petitioner by the entire proprietary body of the village was repugnant to the injunctions of Islam. This usufruct had been enjoyed by the property-owners of the whole village since time immemorial. It was held by the court that the custom or practice of sharing the sale proceeds of the trees by the whole property-owning body of the village had long ago acquired the sanctity of agreement and the consensus of the community and did not, therefore, violate any injunctions of Islam as laid down in the *Quran* and *Sunna* because of the absence of any element of *batil* and *ghasab* in it.

Saeedullah Kazmi v. Government of Pakistan [16]

The petitioner sought that the following acts should be declared against the *Quran* and *Sunna:* (a) permission for the womenfolk of *Fiqa-e-Ja'afria* to perform *haj* without a *mahram* (near relation; (b) permission to make religious processions; (c) performance and practice of I; (d) women walking without *purdah* was against the injunctions of Islam and that government actions which aid such customs should be stopped. All the appeals were dismissed.

Most of the petitions which came before the FSC were thrown out on the grounds that these fell within the jurisdiction of the lower court.

Al-Haj H.I. Sheikh v. Mahmood A. Haroon, Federal Minister, Religious Affairs [17]

The petioner sought a declaration for the removal of certain lacunae in the *haj* policy of the Government of Pakistan allegedly not in conformity with the injunctions of Islam. It was held by the court that this matter pertained to a branch of law known as Muslim personal law, i.e law applied to the community of Muslims alone as distinct from general law applied to all citizens of Pakistan. The scrutiny of such law was thus beyond the jurisdiction of *Shariat* Benches.

Mansoor Ali v. Federation of Pakistan [18]

A petitioner belonging to the Muslim sect of *Bohars* sought a declaration as to whether institutions and practices of their sect known as *imam, dai, amil, barrat* and *raza* were contrary to injunctions of Islam. It was held that the jurisdiction of the court was limited to such law usage and custom which had force of law and was enforceable by a court of law. The matters mentioned in the petition pertained to the faith and beliefs of the sect of Muslims *Bohars* and the Federal *Shariat* Court could not entertain the controversy.

Bilal Hussain v. Government of Pakistan [19]

The Bench found itself lacking in jurisdiction to declare Article 147 and 148 of the Limitation Act repugnant to the injunctions of Islam.

Saeedullah Kazmi v. Government of Pakistan [20]

The petitioner claimed that the giving of *Azan* or declaring or announcing of *Sehri,* by any person or institution like Radio Pakistan, exactly at the time of twilight given in a chart issued by the Pakistan Meteorological Department was not compulsory. The court held that the said matter was not custom or law of custom and hence was not cognizable under Art 203-B and the petition to challenge the same in the High Court was totally misconceived and not maintainable.

Essa E. H. Jafar v. Federation of Pakistan [21]

It was held by the court that the Pakistan Refugee Rehabilitation Finance Corporation Ordinance (II of 1960) is law concerning 'interest' and falls under 'Fiscal Law'. It was held that the matter was excluded from the jurisdiction of the court.

Some of the petitions especially concerned the position of women. The following two were decided in favour of women, i.e., taking a more liberal stand towards women.

Ansar Burney v. Federation of Pakistan [22]

This petition was filed to challenge the appointment of women as judges or magistrates. The petition said that the reason that the function of a *qadi* is discharged without observing *purdah* was that during the Prophet's time this function was never entrusted to a female. According to Muslim law the evidence of a woman is half that of a man and her share in inheritance is equal to half of that of her brother which means that the judgement of two ladies can only be equivalent to that of one male and these 'ladies' do not fulfil the qualifications of a *qadi*. The court answered the questions one by one. It said that the logic according to which the number of *qadi* should correspond to the number of witnesses is not correct; it is not a ground for excluding women from acting as *qadi* that the prophet did not appoint any women as such; the deficiency of women in relation to intelligence is not correct; and, lastly, *purdah* is no problem as Islam does not distinguish between man and women on account of *purdah*.

Mussarat Uzma Usmani and another v. Government of the Punjab [23]

The petitioner claimed that girl candidates obtaining very high marks had been told by the authorities that they would not be admitted to medical colleges because they were girls. It was held that the action of the authorities in denying the petitioners equality before the law was contrary to the constitution.

The following are examples of petitions dismissed by the FSC on the grounds that the relevant laws were in accordance with Islam.

Abu Dawood Muhammad Sadiq v. The State [24]

The petitioner belonging to the *Sunnat-wal-Jamaat (Hanafi*, Baralvi) challenged the National Registration Act, under which every citizen should be registered with the government of Pakistan and an identity card be issued to him with his photograph affixed. His contention was that photography, painting and other works of fine art are *haram* for a Muslim. The court held that 'it can be easily appreciated that before the advent of Islam, a vast majority of Arabs were idolators and despite their conversion to Islam trends of partial or total reversion to their ancestral practices remained intact for some time and the Holy

Prophet had to initiate all such steps by which these trends could be eliminated for good - so much so that even the use of the printed cloth was prohibited. But this prohibition was later relaxed because with the passage of time it was not important as people started forgetting their ancestral beliefs'. The court further said that an Identity Card and passport requiring photographs 'do lend a helping hand in beneficial administration of the country'. Therefore the petition was dismissed.

Khushbakht-ur-Rehman v. Province of Punjab [25]

The petitioners challenged the *Punjab Prevention of Gambling Ordinance No. VII* of 1978, issued by Bhutto for the purpose of Islamizing the laws of Pakistan. The case of the petitioners was that the way betting at horse-races was organized and conducted was in conformity with the injunctions of Islam and therefore, the ban was unjustified. The court found no fault with the law and the petition was dismissed.

One of the biggest problems for these Islamic courts was the lack of experts on Islamic law as all the judges were trained in common law. Amin has blamed the lack of expertise on the part of the judges as the reason that stoning to death was declared un-Islamic in the Hazor Bakhsh case (Amin, 1989: 74). Others cite this incident to show the power of the state to manipulate the courts for the purpose of achieving the desired results.

5.2.8 Federal Council (Majlis-i-Shura)

General Zia introduced a Federal Council or *majlis-i-shura* in 1981, comprising 350 members. All its members were selected and appointed by the government. Its function was strictly advisory, as the power to initiate new legislation or amend the Constitution rested solely with the President of the military government. Four main functions of the Council were stated to be:

1) To help the government accelerate the process of Islamization;

2) To create conditions congenial for the establishment of Islamic democracy;

3) To apprise the government of its views on important international issues;

4)   To assist the government in overcoming social and economic difficulties faced by the people.

Some people declined to accept seats in the Federal Council, refusing to co-operate with the government and considering it unconstitutional (Esposito, 1982a). But a great number of members of the Pakistan Peoples Party and other political parties still accepted appointment to the *shura*. This was also seen as a move on the part of Zia to weaken the parties' structure. 'President Zia viewed the role of his appointed *shura* as an intermediate step to the eventual development of what he calls an Islamic democracy' (Korson, J. Henry & Maskiell, Michelle, 1985).

5.3   CONCLUSION

The process of Islamization has been inconsistent and instable as most of it was carried out by one man. Little or no reference was made to the sources of Islamic laws.

The judiciary was not independent as the judges were appointed by the President and it was also held in most of the cases that the powers of the judiciary were curtailed by the President. Its construction could also be easily changed if the desired decisions were not reached.

The FSC did not have much power anyway, not being allowed to touch any important aspect of the law. The FSC spent most of the time examining what was within its jurisdiction and what was not.

CHAPTER 6

Conclusion

The legal structure the post-colonial state of Pakistan is complicated by a number of different factors. This is the reason that analyses of the Islamization of the law in Pakistan require social-political and legal-anthropological analyses of these factors.

The legal system was complicated by colonial interference with the legal pluralist structure of the sub-continent. The effect on the legal system of the sub-continent was that local units maintained their independence but developed a special attitude towards the courts set up by the colonial state to cope with the new situation. Anglo-Muhammadan law evolved with the aim of ruling the vast land of India and its policy was one of centralisation. Anglo-Muhammadan law was developed by the British and inherited by Pakistan in 1947. The ambition of the rulers of the new state of Pakistan was to create an Islamic state but it was unclear what was meant by 'Islamic'. Things were complicated by of the special nature of the post-colonial state structure, which was peripheral to the capitalist countries. Various theories were mentioned in an attempt to understand the special nature of the peripheral capitalist state and the role of ideology.

The lack of unaminity about the Islamic clauses of the constitution have been discussed in detail in Chapter 2. In the discussion of different aspects of ideology, differences of opinion regarding the Islamic state have been generally classified as Traditionalist and Modernist. The tension between the two factions has been also shown throughout the book. It has been seen in Chapter 4 that even the minor issue of marriage registration was a bone of contention between Traditionalists and Modernists. Other points of controversy were restrictions on polygamy, restrictions on a man's right of divorce and inheritance by a grandchild whose father was dead.

The lack of unanimity further gives rise to compromise clauses which consequently produce ineffectiveness, the problem taken up in the Chapter 2. It is especially in family law that many reforms have become ineffective because of this type of clause. The most interesting example of this involves the difference between invalid and unlawful acts dealt with in family law. In criminal law there are controversies between Modernists and Traditionalists on such issues as the evidence of women, cruel and torturous punishments and controversies concerning *qasas* and *diyat*.

The wave of Islamization in the law which started in 1977 is the special focus of this study. Women became the special victims of Islamization and its inconsistencies. A Traditionalist interpretation of Islam and the customary practice of segregating the sexes hinders women's participation in some economic activities. On the other hand, women's participation in economic activity in general is underestimated, since women are in fact 'invisible workers'. It was easy to make them the victims of Islamization although they did, in fact, show strong resistance to it. The hypotheses of Weiss and Alavi regarding the connections between class formation, women, and certain kinds of Islamic precept are important here. In Chapters 3 and 4 it was demonstrated how, because of inconsistency in the law, women are suffering.

In this peculiar situation, Islamic law in Pakistan is inconsistent and unstable. The nature of the state and the role of ideology are basic factors causing instability and inconsistency in the Islamic legal system. Instability means that the law is frequently changing or is under threat of change because of differences of opinion among the ruling factions. Inconsistency implies various contradictions which can be found in all societies but my question is whether such inconsistency and instability is peculiar to Pakistan.

The theoretical concept of inconsistency and instability mentioned in Chapter 1 is the subject of the entire book, and is shown in relation to the constitution, criminal law, family law and the procedure adopted for Islamization.

The ineffectivness of state laws is one aspect, resulting from many factors. These were discussed theoretically in Chapter 1 and examples were provided in Chapter 2, where it was demonstrated that the Islamic clauses in the constitutions were dead letters. In Chapter 3 it was shown that family law reforms only affected a small group of educated women while, in the villages, non-registration of marriages, unrestricted polygamy and disregard for other family law reforms are common. In the same way criminal law is also widely disregarded in the villages of Pakistan. Again this is documented at least with the help of some empirical research. A great deal of research on the above-mentioned aspect still needs to be done. In criminal law, *hadd* punishments are ineffective as they are not really implementable but their very existence in the statute book, and the fact that lower courts at least have sentenced people to these punishments, make the law appear to be a sword of Damocles. In the same way, the MFLO, though not widely observed, has neverthless become a symbol of the women's movement because it brought about some reforms for women.

Three of the most obvious inconsistencies in Islamic law are (a) those between legal norms and socially observed norms; (b) those between statutory legal norms and the norms applied in practice in the courts (e.g., *hadd* is difficult to implement as confession, retraction of confession and strict standards of proof make it difficult to execute); (c) those between different formal legal norms (e.g., non-compliance with the MFLO is compromised by the courts but is strictly punished under the *zina* Ordinance). This was explained in Chapters 3 and 4 with reference to the case of Shaidha Parveen and other cases. Another example of this contradiction is that the Constitution assures women equal status on the one hand but, on the other hand, they are greatly discriminated against in criminal law.

Of course myths of consistency, legal centralism, legal omnipotence and legal uniformity are not desirable. But the types of problem resulting from inconsistency and instability are such that they are not desirable either. Instability is a constant threat, which also produces insecurity for the public. This is especially true of family law which has reached the stage of being amended many times. Controversies about the issue of Islamic punishment are also so severe that there is constant pressure to change the law. So many constitutions and constitutional changes in the short history of Pakistan are a threat to democratic forces.

Other important features which really need more detailed research are the discriminatory nature of various secular and Islamic laws and highly manipulable procedures (e.g., bail in *zina* cases has been used by husbands to coerce their wives, excessive litigation, the dualistic and anarchic nature of the legal system and corruption). In family problems, the registrar of marriages would enter a forged *nikah* for a small sum. Due to this type of corruption, it is difficult to obtain precise figures for child marriages in Pakistan. The ideas about the above mentioned pecularities of Islamic law in a peripheral capitalist state have mostly been based on material collected regarding the opinions of lawyers, and need, of course, detailed analysis.

Besides this, Islam, which is the religion of the great majority of people in the country, cannot be perceived as a unitary phenomenon. Even if we ignore the different Muslim sects and cultural postulates, Islam in practice is pluralistic. This is also reflected in people's way of resolving their conflicts. During Islamization this was not respected, which also created problems with different sects and different sections of society. The perspective of a legal pluralist could be helpful in enabling progress to be made in Pakistan.

It has been held that legal pluralism is only a viewpoint which, if used in Islamic law, would give more room to different sects and Muslim practices, which have been influenced by local customs and are in fact part of the culture of Muslims in Pakistan. Customary law has not been presented here as an alternative to the state legal system as it has its own power politics which have not been studied in this book. However it does mean that these practices are more real for people, and that legal phenomenona do require all-round understanding.

In Chapter 1, it was held that, in spite of all the Islamization, the Anglo-Muhammadan framework was never broken in Pakistan. This is clearly seen in Chapter 2. Constitutions are framed in the modern way and, in spite of Islamization, lip service is paid to fundamental human rights not peculiar to classical Islam. Chapter 3 shows that, in spite of the introduction of classical Islamic punishments, the Anglo-Muhammadan framework is still there (for example, the law of theft which, in spite of all the Islamization, is the same in practice as that introduced by the British). The same findings can be seen in Chapters 4 and 5.

The role of lawyers is very important and has been discussed in detail. Furthermore, the results of an interview survey of lawyers is provided to air some opinions on different legal phenomenona. The purpose of the survey was absolutely not to provide statistics but to provoke dicussion and to collect some opinions on some of the propositions, which provided the confidence and a ground to proceed with the analysis.

One of the important theoretical aspects of Chapter 1 concerns the sources of Islamic law. This shows the flexible nature of Islamic law. It is demonstrated in later chapters that different governments were at different times successful in promoting some reforms, the best example being the 1955

Commission Report on Marriage and Family Laws and the MFLO of 1961. In Chapter 4 it has been shown in detail how Pakistan made progress in family law through the MFLO and the prominent role played by the judiciary in this, an example being judical *khula*. In criminal law the injustice caused by the *zina* ordinance to women and other inhuman and tortures punishments could be avoided by a modernist and flexible interpretation of *shariah*. Chapter 4 provides a detailed analysis of each aspect of family law with the sociological background of the conditions around the problem. The effect of custom on Islam has been given a special place in the sources of Islamic law. The place of a pluralistic legal structure is also noted because of the recognition of custom in Islam as a source of law.

The future of Islamic law in Pakistan depends, on the one hand, on the development of the military, which is related to Pakistan's peripheral role *vis-a-vis* the capitalist countries. On the other hand, there are questions regarding the extent to which Islamic ideology should be modernised in keeping with the needs of the age. Thirdly, the recognition that a plurality of practices in resolving disputes is more natural to people would strengthen these practices but this, of course, would require the distribution of power to units at a local level.

CHAPTER 7

Postscript

Inconsistency and instability in the law in Pakistan have continued since the death of General Zia in 1989. What follows is a brief sketch of legal developments in the past two years, especially the consequences of the passing of the *Qisas and Diyat Ordinance* in 1990 and of the *Shariah Act* in 1991. (The full text of these two significant laws is found at Appendices II and III). What is clear from these events and others not discussed is that recent events confirm the analysis of the legal situation in Pakistan as stated in the body of this book.

With the passing of the *Qisas and Diyat Ordinance* in 1990, the victim (or heirs of the victim) of a crime now have the right to inflict injuries on the offender identical to the ones sustained by the victim. The law also allows offenders to absolve themselves of the crime by paying compensation to the victim or the heirs. In the already existing system of bribery and corruption, it gives free hand to the people with money. The Director of the Human Rights Commission, Aziz Siddiqui, is reported to have said, 'That means, in effect, that rich people can get away even with wilful murder'.[1] The controversy surrounding the ordinance when first drafted (described in Chapter 3) has continued since its promulgation. For instance, in 1992 Senator Yahya Bakhtiar stated:

> The performance of this gruesome operation in public may please the prime minister, Mian Nawaz Sharif, who always speaks of public hangings, and will also satisfy the sadistic tendencies of some others but it is nothing except brutalising and dehumanising our society.[2]

Just how the *qisas* is to be executed remains unclear. Section 337–P of the ordinance reads:

> *Qisas* shall be executed in public by an authorised medical officer who shall before such execution examine the offender

and take due care so that the execution of qisas does not cause the death of the offender or exceed the hurt caused by him to the victim.³

As such, this ordinance requires the active participation of doctors for its execution. But it should be noted that one of the main reasons why no amputation of limbs has yet been performed under the (much older) *Offences Against Property (Enforcement of Hudood) Ordinance* VI of 1979 is that doctors have refused to perform such operations. A doctors' human rights organisation, Voice Against Torture, is struggling to pressurise the Pakistan Medical Council to adopt the position that, keeping in mind medical ethics and international codes of practice, doctors should not be involved in such inhuman operations.

The *Shariah Act* was passed in June 1991. This was a significant event in the Islamization of laws in Pakistan. The meaning of this Act in fact depends on Muslims in Pakistan agreeing on their interpretation of the Ordinance. The interpretation of the *Shariah* Ordinance has also been challenged by the FSC (Federal *Shariat* Court). Sections 3(2) and 19 of the Act, which safeguard the existing political system and the country's financial obligations (including interest payments), have been declared un-Islamic by the FSC because of the *riba* (interest) involved. In its ruling of January 1992, the court held that rules and regulations relating to interest were repugnant to the *Quran* and *Sunnah* and should be brought into accordance with Islam. This ruling was embarrassing to the government because, while on the one hand they wanted to satisfy the Traditionalists, on the other hand the ruling was not in accordance with the government's international obligations. A private appeal was thus lodged with the Supreme Court and there (at this time of writing) the matter lies.

The *zina* ordinances, which have been particularly discriminatory against women, continued to be law despite all the demands from women's organisations for its annulment. These women's organisations have organised themselves better than in earlier years. Among the quite potent pressure groups are the Women's Action Forum, *Badari* and *Roshni*. Despite the fact that women are better organised, there has been an increase in the number of crimes (for instance, rape and torture) perpetrated by police against women while they were in police custody.

Another *hudood* ordinance, for the *Offence of Qazf (Enforcement of the Hadd)*, was challenged in the FSC during 1992 in the case *Capt. Abdul Gafoor v. Federation of Pakistan*.⁴

The petitioner contended that recourse to the provision of *lian* could only be taken if the husband did not have the evidence available with him in the form of medical, circumstantial or some ocular evidence less than the testimony of four witnesses. The FSC rejected this contention and ruled that the course of the procedure of *lian* could not be obviated unless the husband proved the adultery by producing four witnesses. This requirement could not be relaxed by producing medical or circumstantial evidence as proof of adultery. However, the court recommended that Section 14(1) of the ordinance be amended with the addition of the words 'In the absence of evidence of four witnesses'.[5]

As always, the Muslim Family Laws Ordinance, 1961 (MFLO) is continuously under challenge. In 1992 there was an interesting case in the Supreme Court where the court declared Section 7 of the MFLO to be against Islam. The court stated that any divorce pronounced or written by the husband cannot be ineffective or invalid in *shariah* merely because its notice was not given to the chairman of the Union Council. This was a case where a husband challenged the divorce of his wife and her subsequent marriage to another man, accusing her of living in *zina*. The basic question was whether or not the petitioner had divorced his wife and if therefore her *nikah* with the other man was valid. The court did not adopt the stand it has taken in some previous cases. Making the decision in favour of the woman, the court stated that a notice of *talaq* to the chairman is not mandatory under the injunctions of Islam (*Allah Dad v. Mukhtar and Mst. Rashida Akhtar*).[6] Though in this particular case the court decided in favour of the woman, this is not usually so in cases of non-registered marriages. The disadvantages facing women here are discussed in detail in Chapter 4.

Other rulings of the FSC in 1992 included one stating the the country's system of employment quotas was un-Islamic, as was the charging of court fees. The court stated:

> Islam ordains administration of justice as one of the foremost obligations of man (after the belief in Allah and his messenger). It is thus obligatory for an Islamic state to set up an easy, speedy and effective, and free of charge judicial system.[7]

Another example of inconsistency was a ruling in October 1992 that has alarmed many human rights activists. This backs a government decision that the identification cards of all citizens should state their religion. This action human rights activists have compared to apartheid. It is also in contradiction of the fundamental rights guaranteed in Pakistan's constitution.

Nor is this the only issue to alarm many human rights activists. Big changes have also taken place in the law of blasphemy. The process of these changes began in October 1990 when an advocate pleaded that contempt of the Prophet Muhammad could only be punishable with death. In due course, Section 295C of the PPC was amended, withdrawing its earlier options of a fine and imprisonment for life, so that today an offence under this Section is only punishable by death.

Cases like that of blasphemy charges against Akhter Hameed Khan (a renowned development worker whose work has demonstrated a credible alternative of self-help for the poor to escape the clutches of the *mullah* and the moneyed elite) have caused grave concern among human rights activists and in Amnesty International that Sections 295 and 295C are open to misuse by vested interest groups and individuals. That apart, this law exposes people to manipulation.

The struggle between Traditionalists and Modernists continues in Pakistan. Moreover, the progressive Islamization is creating and widening other rifts. Sectarianism is increasing, as is the dissatisfaction of those groups believing in a different interpretation of Islam than that laid down in the new Islamic laws.

Notes

CHAPTER 1: Theoretical Framework

1) Mufassal Regulation of Warren Hastings, 1772, re-enacted formally as Section 27 of the Regulation of 1780. Regulation I of 1872 provided that these subjects of the Crown were to be governed by their own laws in 'Suits regarding inheritance, marriage and caste and other religious usages and institutions'.

2) Lord Hobhouse in *Waghela v. Shekh Masludin*. (1887, 14 Indian IA, 89).

3) Report of the court of inquiry constituted under Punjab Act 11 of 1954, to enquire into the Punjab disturbances of 1953. (Printed by the Superintendent, Government Printing, Punjab 1954).

4) Reference to Bhutto's Islamic reforms.

5) Seminar on Family Laws from 19-20 December, 1990. Held at Karachi Hall, Lahore High Courts Bar Association, Lahore.

6) *Federation of Pakistan v. Hazoor Bukhsh* PLD 1983, FSC 255.

7) **Pakistan Times**, 19 April 1987.

8) **Pakistan Times**, 18 October 1987.

9) **Pakistan Times**, 5 July 1989. From M.Farani, 'Judicial Review of Martial Law Actions'.

10) Nusrat Bhutto PLD 1977, SC 657.

11) Seminar organized by the Young Lawyers' Forum at Lahore High Court Bar. **View Point**, 19 July 1984.

12) **View Point**, 11 February 1982.

12) **View Point**, 11 February 1982.

13) Warren Hastings acted upon the grant of the Diwani by ordaining Regulation II of 1772, (Section 27)

14) SIMORGH Paper presented at Asian conference on Women, Religion & Personal Laws. 16-20 December 1987, Women Centre Bombay.

15) J.N.D. Anderson provides a detailed account of the devices used for modernising Islamic family law (Anderson, J.N.D., 1960 pp 187-98).

16) 'Legal verses of the *Quran* do not, on the whole, furnish the comprehensive code of law in Islam', says Tahir Mahmood. In his article "Law in the *Quran* - a draft code", Tahir Mahmood has collected the verses of *Quran* which directly and clearly relate to what in modern times is termed as 'law' (Mahmood Tahir, 1987).

17) *Balquis Fatima v. Najm-ul-Ikram Qureshi.* PLD 1959, 566.

18) *Rashida Begum v. Shahab Din.* PLD 1960, Lahore 1142.

19) *Khurshid Jan v. Fazal Dad.* PLD 1964 (W.P) Lahore 58.

20) See also Rankin, George, 1940, pp.16-17.

CHAPTER 2: Islamic Provisions in the Constitutions

1) Full text of the Objectives Resolution is found in Constituent Assembly of Pakistan Debates, vol. V, No.1 (7 March 1949), p.1.

2) *ibid.*, vol. V, No.1, pp.2-3.

3) *ibid.*, vol. V, No. 2, (8 March 8 1949) p.13; and No.5, Vol.V, (12 March 12 1949) p.89.

4) *ibid.*, vol. V, No.4, (10 March 1949) p.51.

5) For this interpretation of the Traditionalists, see also Sayed, Riaz Ahmad: **Maulana Maududi and the Islamic State**, 1976, chapter entitled: 'The Problems of Constitution Making in Pakistan and Islam'.

6) Constituent Assembly of Pakistan Debates, Vol V, No.2 (8 March 1949) p.13.

7) 4 March 1949, from **Public Opinion and Political Development, p.8.**

8) Constituent Assembly of Pakistan Debates, vol V, No.2 (8 March 1949) p.14.

9) *ibid.*, vol. V, No.2, p.13, and No.5, p.89.

10) *ibid.*, vol. V, No.1, p.3.

11) Report of the court of inquiry constituted under Punjab Act II of 1954 to enquire into the Punjab disturbances of 1953. The Superintendent, Government Printing, Punjab. Lahore. 1954, p.203.

12) Mian Iftikhar-ud-din, one of the Muslim members of the Constituent Assembly, called it sectarian, making the state constitution more narrow-minded, more parochial (**Selected Speeches and Statements, Mian Iftikhar-ud-din.** Edited by Abdullah Malik, Lahore, West Pakistan. p.483).

13) **The Three Constitutions of Pakistan,** by Y.V. Gankovsky and V.N. Moskalenko. U.S.S.R Academy of Sciences, Institute of Oriental Studies. People's Publishing House, Lahore, 1978, p.32.

14) Justice A.R. Cornelius, Chief Justice, Supreme Court of Pakistan said: 'These institutions are standing proof of the fact that the will of the people as expressed in the noble words of the preamble is being duly implemented'. PLD 1967, Vol. XIX - **Spirit of Pakistan Constitution: An Act of Faith.**

15) "Pakistan's New Constitution", **Link,** 27 May 1973, p.29. Link calls the Constitution 'a mixed porridge'. 'The *Mullahs* and *Jamaat-e-Islami* get what they want and President Bhutto also satisfies the modernists and democrats in his party who have made high claims of ushering in a new era of democratic institutions in Pakistan' p.29. See for general description: Shah Nasim Hasan (1976).

16) For socialistic provisions in the Constitution, see: "Constitution of Pakistan", a speech delivered by Justice Dr. Nasim Hasan

Shah, Judge, the Supreme Court of Pakistan, to students at the National Defence College, Rawalpindi (30 September 1979). PLD, vol. XXX, 1979.

17) PLD, 1977, SC 657.

18) Two articles are interesting in this respect: Jafar, Malik Mohammad (1979); and Hussain, Faqir (1985).

19) Under the new dispensation, judges in higher courts were required to take a new oath of office. The Chief Justice of Pakistan and other judges refused to take the oath.

20) **Pakistan Times**, Lahore, 4 March 1985.

21) Anwarul Haq, a former Chief Justice of Pakistan, describes the amendments as having knocked the 1973 constitution out of shape.

22) General Zia's interview in **Pakistan Times**, 5 March 1985.

CHAPTER 3: Criminal Law

1) PLD 1982 FSC 259.

2) *ibid.*, p.23.

3) *The State v. Ghulam Ali*, PLD 1982 FSC, 259.

4) *Ghulam Ali v. The State*, PLD 1986. SC, 741.

5) *Ghulam Ali v. The State*, PLD 1986. SC 741.

6) NLR 1984 SD 260, and NLR 1984 SD 219.

7) *Ghulam Ali v. The State*, PLD 1986. SC 741.

8) **View Point**, 1979, p.25.

9) *Ghulam Ali v. The State*, PLD 1986. SC 741, see remarks of justice Muhammad Afzal Zullah.

10) NLR 1987 SD 377.

11) *Shahid Ahmad v. The State*, NLR 1984 SD 296. *Suleman v. The State*, NLR 1984 SD 241. *Ali Ahmad v. The State*, NLR 1985 SD 12.

12) *Qadir Bux v. The State*, NLR 1987 SD 274. *Muhammad Ayoub Alias Lakhpati v. The State*, NLR 1987 SD 170.

13) Bill moved by Nur Ahmed. The Pakistan Penal Code (amendment), Bill Constituent Assembly (legislature), 21 November 1951.

14) **Dawn**, 22 December 1983.

15) *Allah Bux v. The State*, PLD 1982 FSC 101.

16) *Federation of Pakistan v. Hazoor Bukhsh*. The judgment is spread over 236 pages. PLD 1983 FSC 2550.

17) *Nazir Ahmad v. The State*, PLD 1986 SC 132.

18) *Safia Bibi v. The State*, PLD 1985 FSC, 120. See also **Pakistan Times**, 5 August 1983, and **Pakistan Times**, 28 July 1983. Another case of the same nature was reported in the Danish newspaper **Information** in March 1985 by Bo Gunnarsson.

19) **View Point**, 17 February 1983. See also *Shabbir Ahmad v. the State*, PLD 1983 FSC, 110.

20) PLD 1982 FSC 229.

21) PLD 1963 SC 51.

22) PLD 1983 FSC 173.

23) NLR 1988 SC 188. However, the FSC acquitted the couple upon appeal. **Dawn**, 4 November 1985; see also reference in Weiss 1986, p.101.

24) *Muhammad Nawaz v. The State*, PLD 1983 FSC, 522.

25) PLD 1987 FSC, 11, see p.15.

26) *Falak Sher v. The State*, PLD 1982 FSC, 240. *Abid Hussain v. The State*, PLD 1983 FSC, 200.

27) For example, homosexuality is recognised in Denmark to such an extent that homosexual partners have a legal right to register themselves as married couples; see **Politiken**, Wednesday, 24 February 1988.

28) *Muhammad Saleem v. The State*, NLR 1984 - SD. 262(1).

29) *Amjad Tubrez v. The State*, PLD 1982. FSC 174.

30) PLD 1982 Peshwar 104.

31) PLD 1983 FSC 165.

32) PLD 1983 FSC 234.

33) *Yaseen v. The State*, PLD 1983 FSC 53.

34) NLR 1984 SD 45.

35) NLR 1984 SD 77.

36) PLD 1982 FSC 248. See also: *Niamat v. The State*, PLD 1982, FSC 220.

37) PLD 1982 FSC 29.

38) *Zaheer Ahmed v. the Federation of Pakistan*, PLD 1982. FSC 244.

39) NLR 1987 SD 551, see pages 553 and 554.

40) NLR 1986, SD.

41) PLD 1986 FSC 10.

42) *ibid.*, see p.21-23.

43) NLR 1984 SD 20.

44) NLR 1987 SD 551.

45) This objection was also raised in *Zaheer Ahmed v. the Federation of Pakistan*, PLD 1982 FSC 244, but went unanswered.

46) *Zaheer Ahmed v. the Federation of Pakistan*, PLD 1982 FSC 244.

47) *M. Mumtaz v. The State*, NLR 1984, SD 202.

48) PLD 1986 FSC 187.

49) *Haji Bakhtiar Said Muhammad v. Dure-e-Shahwar*, PLD 1986 FSC 187, see p.195.

50) *Haji Bakhtiar Said Muhammad v. Dure-e-Shawar*, see p.195.

51) *Nek Bakhat v. The State*, PLD 1986 FSC 174.

52) *ibid.*

53) *ibid.*

54) *ibid.*, see p.178.

55) In the Punjab, a substitution of Section (4) of Section 24 of the West Pakistan Act XX of 1949. Notifications No. 1407 - Excise and Taxation Repentment was in force. Similar law enforced in NWFP.

56) Provincial ordinances known as Baluchistan Prohibition Ordinance XI of 1978, NWFP Prohibition Ordinance VI of 1978, Punjab Prohibition Ordinance VI of 1978, and Sind Prohibition Ordinance VI of 1978 were enforced in all the provinces.

57) *Ghulam Nabi Awan v. the Federation of Pakistan*, PLD 1983, FSC 55, see p.57 and 59.

58) PLD 1981, FSC 245.

59) *ibid.*, see p.261.

60) *Shah Muhammad v. The State*, PLD 1982 FSC 239.

61) *Nosher Rustam Sidhwa v. the Federation of Pakistan*, PLD 1981, FSC 245, see p.252; see also *The State v. Majid*, NLR 1984, SD 274.

62) **Morning News**, 3 July 1985.

63) *Federation of Pakistan v. Hazoor Bukhsh*, PLD 1983, FSC 255, see p.289.

64) PLD 1982, FSC 252, see p.256.

65) The Punjab Execution of the Punishment of Whipping Rules, 1979. Rules 4 and 5.

66) In the case of *Nazir Ahmad and others v. The State*, PLD 1982, FSC, 252, it was held that the provincial government has been so empowered because of the provision for whipping convicts in public places, which requires extra administrative arrangements, see p.258.

67) Federal Shariat Court in Pakistan, Justice Gul Muhammad Khan, Chief Justice - in the other place Justice Aftabs Hussain, Chief Justice - Federal Shariat Court, Islamabad, see p.15, and p.13.

68) **Report on Human Rights: Violations in Pakistan.** Published by Political Prisoner's Release and Relief Committee, London. 20 June 1985.

69) See also *The State v. Nazir*, 1986 SC (AJ & K) 143.

70) National Assembly of Pakistan, 8 June 1967. Adjournment motion, see pp.1131-48.

71) Section 298 A, Ordinance XLV of 1980. The Pakistan Penal Code (second amendment) Ordinance, 1980.

72) Section 295 B, inst. by the Pakistan Penal Code (amendment) Ordinance I of 1982.

73) Section 295 C, 1986. Criminal Law (Amendment) Act, 1986. (An Act further to amend the Pakistan Penal Code & the Code of Criminal Procedure, 1898).

74) **Jang**, London, 22, 1988.

75) Provisions relating to murder are contained in Sections 299, 300, 301, 302, 303, 304, and 304 A of the Pakistan Penal Code. Implementation of the punishments are regulated by Criminal Procedure Code, for example Section 367 (5).

76) For details, see Nawa-i-waqt, 25 October 1984, **Pakistan Times,** 22 July 1984, Jang, 10 August 1984, and Dawn, 21 February 1984. See also **View Point,** 2 August 1984.

77) *Gul Hassan Khan v. the Government of Pakistan,* PLD 1980 Peshawar I.

78) *Mumtaz Khan v. the Government of Pakistan,* PLD 1980 Peshawar 154.

79) Section 10 (b).

80) Section 28 (2).

81) Section 88.

82) Sections 100 and 102.

83) **Pakistan Times,** 27 May 1983.

CHAPTER 4: Family Law

1) The **Gazette of Pakistan** (extraordinary), 20 June 1956 (Majority report), 30 August 1956 (note of dissent).

2) Feroze (1962) refers to Ayub Khan's reply to a letter opposing the Ordinance in which he called upon the *ulema* to move with the times and describing polygamy as a 'barbaric torture of highest order'.

3) Child Marriage Restraint Act, 1929. Dissolution of Muslim Marriages Act, 1939.

4) Minority Report in reply to the Commission on Marriage & Family Laws. For minority Report also see 'The Maulana's Note of Dissent' 75-79. In **Religion, Politics, & Social Change in the Third World.** (A Sourcebook) edited with introductory notes by Donald Eugene Smith. The Free Press, New York 1977.

5) *ibid.*

6) *Nasim Akhtar v. the State,* PLD 1968 Lahore 841. *A.L.M. Abdulla v. Rokeya Khatoon,* PLD 1969 Dacca 47.

7)   *Bagh Ali alias Bagh din v. Almna*, PLD 1968 Lahore 1216.

8)   Habib v. the State, PLD 1980 Lahore. (Muhd-Sarwar J.) in Keith Hodkinson: Muslim Family Law. A Source Book, p.117.

9)   The *Quran*, chapter 33, verse 50. Chapter 4, verse 3. Chapter 4, verse 129.

10) **Jang**, Karachi, 16 May 1986 (example of such a letter).

11) Commission on Marriage and Family Laws 1956, report. In **The Gazette of Pakistan** (extraordinary), 20 June 1956 (majority report).

12) *Syed Ali Gardezi v. Lt. Col. Muhammad Yusuf*, PLD 1963, SC 51. *Zulaikhan v. Noor Muhammad*, PLD 1986, Quetta, 290.

13) **Gazette of West Pakistan**, extraordinary, 21 July 1961.

14) *Mst. Maqbool Jan v. Arshad Hassan*, PLD 1975 Lahore 147.

15) *Mst. Basra v. Abdul Hakim*, PLD 1986 Quetta 298. *Ali Nawaz v. Mohd Yosuf*, PLD 1963, SC 51.

16) *Zikria Khan v. Aftals Ali Khan*, PLD 1985 Lahore 319. See also *Parveen Chaudhry v. VIth Senior Civil Judge*, 1976 PLD Karachi 416.

17) *Inamuel Islam v. Hussain Bano*, PLD 1976 Lahore 1466.

18) *Mst. Fahmida Bibi v. Mukhtar Ahmad.* PLD 1972, Lahore 694. *Akhtar Hussain v. Collector*, PLD 1977 Lahore 1173.

19) *Chuhar v. Ghulam Fatima.* PLD 1984 Lahore 234.

20) A good example is the legal suggestions in **Jang** (daily Urdu newspaper), 27 June 1986.

21) PLD 1984 Lahore 235; PLD 1982 FSC 265.

22) PLD 1982 FSC 156.

23) PLD 1988 Karachi 169.

24) PLD 1988 FSC 42.

25) Dissolution of Muslim Marriages Act, 1939, Section 2(IX).

26) Also discussed under the heading of Child Marriage.

27) *Sayeeda Khanam v. Muhammad Sami*, PLD 1952 (W.P.), Lahore, 113 (F.B.).

28) *Balquis Fatima v. Najm. Ullkram Qureshi*, PLD 1959 Lahore 566. J.N.D. Anderson remarks that the court even fell into the error of asserting that a divorce by mutual agreement of the parties is called *mubara'a*, while a divorce claimed by a wife and to which her husband does not consent is called *khula*.

29) *Khurshid Bibi v. Muhammad Amin*, PLD 1967, SC 97.

30) *Ghulam Sakina v. Omar Baksh*, PLD 1964 SC 456.

31) *Khurshid Bibi v. Muhammad Amin*, PLD 1967 SC 97.

32) 1969, SCMR 118.

33) PLD 1983 Lahore 377, see p.382.

34) PLD 1983 Lahore 549.

35) *ibid.*, see p.550.

36) *ibid.*, see p.551.

37) PLD 1984 Azad J. & K., 36.

38) PLD 1984 SC 329.

39) *ibid.*, p.332.

40) PLD 1986 Lahore 32.

41) *ibid.*, see p.326.

42) PLD 1987 Lahore 376.

43) *ibid.*, see p.380.

44)   PLD 1968 Lahore 411.

45)   *ibid.*, see p.414.

46)   *ibid.*, see p.414.

47)   PLD 1986 Quetta 185.

48)   *ibid.*, see p.190.

49)   *ibid.*, see p.191.

50)   *Parveen Begum v. Muhammad Ali*, PLD 1981 Lahore 116.
      Shamshad Begum v. Abdul Haque, PLD 1977 Karachi 855.

51)   *Muhammad Nawaz v. Mst. Khurshid Begum*, PLD 1972, SC.
      Sardar Muhammad v. Mst. Nasima Bibi, PLD 1966 Lahore.
      Rashid Ahmad Khan v. Mst. Nasim Ara, PLD 1968 Lahore 93.
      Gul Bibi v. Muhammad Saleem, PLD 1978 Quetta 117.

52)   *Gul Bibi v. Mohammad Saleem*, PLD 1978, Quetta 117.

53)   Report of the Commission on Marriage and Family Laws - **The
      Gazette of Pakistan**, (extraordinary) June 20, 1956.

54)   Hamid Khan (1980) has discussed in detail the defects in both
      solutions.

55)   See Ulams Report. **The Gazette of Pakistan** 30 August 1956
      (note of dissent).

56)   PLD 1980 Peshawar 47.

57)   PLD 1981 SC 120.

58)   *Kamal Khan alias Kamla v. Mst. Zainab*, PLD 1983 Lahore 546.

59)   PLD 1983 Lahore 546; PLD 1986 SC 228; PLD 1988 Karachi
      446.

60)   Section 2(a).

61)   Section 2(vii) amended by Section 13(b) of the Muslim Family
      Laws Ordinance.

62) Section 5, Child Marriage Restraint Act, 1929.

63) Evils of Dowry, **Pakistan Times**, 10 March 1987.

64) In India, 9,000 wives died in dowry feuds during 1981, 7,324 were assaulted. **Pakistan Times**, 27 March 1988. For comparison of India and Pakistan, see **Legislation** by Arora Pradyumua (1982) and Awasti & Lal (1986).

65) The Pakistan Marriage (Expenditure) Bill was presented in 1952 by Nur Ahmed. The purpose was to regulate expenditure in respect of marriage. The Constituent Assembly (legislature), 2 April 1952, pp.969-71.

66) Report of the Commission for the Eradication of Social Evils, Government of Pakistan, Ministry of Health, Labour and Social Welfare, 1965.

67) West Pakistan Dowry (Prohibition on Display) Act. **Gazette of West Pakistan** Extraordinary, 23 November 1967.

68) Dowry and Bridal Gifts (Restriction) Amendment Ordinance, 1980.

69) Ministry of Law and Parliamentary Affairs. Government of Pakistan. Law Division. Report of the Pakistan Women's Rights Committee. 1976.

70) **View Point**, 27 March 1986, p.13.

71) NLR 1988 SC 188.

72) Also see *Qamar Raza v. Tahira Begum*, PLD 1988 Karachi 169.

73) *The Federation of Pakistan v. Mst. Farishta*, PLD 1981, SC 120.

CHAPTER 5: Procedure Used in the Islamization of the Law

1) Lawrence Rosen has shown that there is flexibility in *qadi*'s way of judgement in Morocco. See Rosen (1989).

2) PLD 1980 SC 160.

3)   'Islamic Social Order Report of the Council of Islamic Ideology 1962-1982'. June 1982 Council of Islamic Ideology Government of Pakistan, Islamabad, p.20.

4)   'Constitutional Recommendations for the Islamic System of Government'. Council of Islamic Ideology, Government of Pakistan, Islamabad. June 1983.

5)   'Islamic Social Order Report of the Council of Islamic Ideology 1962-82'. Council of Islamic Ideology, Government of Pakistan, Islamabad. June 1982.

6)   Report on family planning. Council of Islamic Ideology, Islamabad, Pakistan. April 1984.

7)   See for details: 'Implementation of Shari'ah in Pakistan', by Justice Tanzil-ul-Rahman (chairman), Council of Islamic Ideology, Islamabad.

8)   All the above examples are taken from the Third and Fourth Reports of the Council of Islamic Ideology.

9)   'Faisal Masjid: A symbol of Islamic unity', **Pakistan Times**, 24 June 1988.

10)   **Pakistan Times** 5 July 1989.

11)   Shari'ah Academy. Inservice Training Programmme for Judges, Attorneys and Prosecutors. International Islamic University Islamabad.

12)   **Pakistan, an Official Handbook: 1978-81.**

13)   PLD 1981 SC 120.

14)   PLD 1983 FSC 255.

15)   PLD 1980 Peshwar 239.

16)   PLD 1981 SC 627.

17)   PLD 1981 SC 334.

18)   PLD 1981 SC 331.

19) PLD 1981 Peshwar 46.

20) PLD 1981 SC 42.

21) PLD 1982 FSC 212.

22) PLD 1983 FSC 73.

23) PLD 1987 Lahore 178.

24) Shariat Petition No.6 1980.

25) PLD 1986 FSC 49.

CHAPTER 7: Postscript

1) Najam Sethi, 'Pakistan Installs Islam's Slippery Slope', **The Asian Wall Street Journal**, 3 November 1992.

2) Yahya Bakhtiar, **The Frontier Post**, 16 April 1992.

3) See Appendix II for full text.

4) NLR 1992, SD: 747.

5) *ibid.*, see p.762.

6) NLR 1992, SD.

7) *Dr Mahmood Rahman Faisal v Secretary M/O L.J. & P.A. Pak. and others*, NLR 1992 SD.

Works Cited

Abbas, S., Pervez M., Shamim, T., Pervez, S. (1985) **A Study of Abducted Women in Pakistan**, Women Division, Islamabad. (An introductory booklet).

- (1985) **A Study of Prostitutes in Pakistan**, Women Division, Islamabad. (An introductory booklet).

Abbott, Freeland (1966) 'Pakistan and the Secular State', in Donald Eugene Smith (ed.): **South Asian Politics and Religion**, pp.352-70, Princeton University Press, Princeton.

- (1968) **Islam and Pakistan**, Cornell University Press, Ithaca.

Abel, Richard L. (1979) 'Western Courts in Non-Western Settings: Patterns of court use in colonial and neo-colonial Africa', in Sandra B. Burman & Barbara E. Harrell-Bond (ed.): **The Imposition of Law**, pp.167-98. Academic Press, New York.

Abercrombie, N., Hill, S., and Turner B.S. (1980) **The Dominant Ideology Thesis**, George Allen & Unwin, London.

Ahmad, Aquil (1989) **The Eighth Amendment: A Commentary**, Royal Book Company, Karachi.

Ahmad, K.N. (1984) **Muslim Law of Divorce**, Kitab Bhavan, New Delhi.

Ahmad, M.B. (1951) **The Administration of Justice in Medieval India**, The Manager of Publications, Karachi.

Ahmad, Mumtaz: (1988) Pakistan, in Shireen T. Hunter (ed.): **The Politics of Islamic Revivalism. Diversity & Unity**, Indiana University Press, Bloomington & Indianapolis.

Ahmad-ud-din-, Bashir: (1985) 'Constitutional Amendments', in **Pakistan Times**, 17 March.

Ahmad, Sayed Riaz: (1976) **Maulana Maududi and the Islamic State**, People's Publishing House, Lahore.

Ahmed, Ali Khan: (1985) **Islamization of Laws in Pakistan, Past and Present**, School of Oriental & African Studies, Law Department. University of London (unpublished L.L.M thesis).

Ahmed, Ishtiaq: (1987) **The Concept of an Islamic State: An analysis of the ideological controversy in Pakistan**, Frances Pinter, London.

Ahmed, Jamil: (1983) **Exchange Marriage System: An Ethnographic study a Saraiki Village**, Unpublished Master's research report in the Department of Anthropology, Quaid-i-Azam University, Islamabad.

Ahmed, Manzooruddin: (1963) 'Islamic aspects of the New Constitution of Pakistan', **Islamic Studies**, Vol. II, pp.249-77.

- (1965) 'Sovereignty of God in the Constitution of Pakistan: A Study in the Conflict of Traditionalism and Modernism', **Islamic Studies**, Vol IV, No.2, pp.201-12.

Ahmed, Saber: (1971) 'Dissolution of Marriage Under Muslim Family Laws Ordinance', **PLD**, Vol. XXIII, pp.35-8.

Ahsan, Bushra: (1987) 'Fundamentalism & its Impact upon Women', Asia Conference on Women, Religion and Personal Laws, Organised by the Women's Centre, Bombay.

Akbar, Raja Amir: (1986) 'The Law of Evidence, a Disgrace to Oath', **Daily Jang**, London, 11 March 1986.

Alavi, Hamza: (1971) 'The Crisis of Nationalities and the State in Pakistan', **The Journal for Contemporary Asia**, Vol. I, No.3-4, pp.42-66.

- (1972) 'The State in Post Colonial Societies: Pakistan and Bangladesh', **New Left Review**, No.74, pp.59-81.

- (1982) 'State and Class under Peripheral Capitalism', in Hamza Alavi and Teodor Shanin (eds.): **Introduction to Sociology of the Developing Societies**, pp.289-307, Macmillan Press, London.

- (1983) 'Class & State: The State in Crisis in Pakistan', in Hassan Gardezi and Jamil Rashid (eds.): **Pakistan: The Roots of Dictatorship**, pp.40-93. Zed Press, London.

- (1985) 'Background to the Women's Struggle in Pakistan', **Pakistan Commentary**, Vol. 8, No.4, pp.4-6.

- (1986) 'Ethnicity, Muslim Society, and the Pakistan Ideology', in Anita M. Weiss (ed.): **Islamic Reassertion in Pakistan**, Syracuse University Press, Syracuse.

- (1988) 'Pakistan and Islam: Ethnicity and Ideology', in Fred Halliday and Hamza Alavi (eds.): **State and Ideology in the Middle East and Pakistan**, Macmillan Education Ltd., London.

Alam, Syed Iqbal: (1968) 'Age at Marriage in Pakistan', **The Pakistan Development Review**, Vol. VIII. pp.489-98.

Ali, Ahmad: (1986) 'Case Book: Mst. Farishta vs The Federation of Pakistan', **Journal of Law and Society**, Vol. V, No.6, pp.73-85.

Ali, Ameer: (1965) **The Spirit of Islam**, Pakistan Publishing House, Karachi.

Ali, Shaheen Sardar: (1985) 'Case Book - Supreme Court on Khula', **Journal of Law and Society**, Vol. IV, No.4, pp.51-61.

Allot, Antony & Woodman Gordon R. (1985) **Peoples Law & State Law** (The Bellogio papers) Foris Publications, Dordrecht, (Holland)/Cinnaminson (U.S.A.).

Amin, Mohammad: (1989) **Islamization of Laws in Pakistan**, Sang-e-Meel Publications, Lahore.

Anderson, J.N.D. (1960) 'The Significance of Islamic Law in the World Today', **American Journal of Comparative Law**, Vol. 9, pp.187-98.

- (1966) 'Codification in the Muslim World', **Rabels Zeitschrift**, No.30, pp.241-53.

- (1967) 'Pakistan: An Islamic State?' in R.H. Code Holland and G. Schwarzenberger (eds.): **Law, Justice and Equity**, pp.127-36, Sir Isaac Pitman & Sons Ltd., London.

- (1968) 'The Eclipse of the Patriarchal Family in Contemporary Islamic Law', in J.N.D. Anderson (ed.): **Family Law in Asia and Africa**, pp.221-34. Frederick A. Praeger, New York.

- (1970) 'Reforms in the Law of Divorce in the Muslim World', **Studia Islamica**, Vol. XXXI, pp.41-52.

- (1971) 'Modern Trends in Islam: Legal Reforms and Modernisation in the Middle East', **The International and Comparative Law Quarterly**, Vol. 20, pp.1-21.

Anderson, Michael R. (1989) 'Islamic Law and the Colonial Encounter in British India', paper, SOAS Conference on Islamic Family Law, London, 18-19 May 1989.

Anderson, Norman: (1976) **Law Reform in the Muslim World**, The Athlone Press, London.

- (1983) 'Islamic Family Law', **International Encyclopedia of Comparative Law**, chapter II, pp.55-79, Mohr et al., Tübingen.

Angam, Ahsan Sohail: (1983) **The Pakistan Penal Code**, Mansoor Book House, Lahore.

Arora, Pradyumua: (1982) 'Legislation', **Islamic and Comparative Law Quarterly**, Vol. 2:1. pp.

Aslam, Choudhry Muhammed: (1986) 'Family Laws in the Light of Islam', **Daily Jang**, London. 28 April 1986.

Aubert, Vilhelm (1966) 'Some social functions of legislation', **Acta Sociologia**, No 99, pp.98-120.

Auolakh, Ch. Abdul Majeed A. (1986) **Criminal Justice, Crime, Punishment, and Treatment in the Islamic Republic of Pakistan**, Pakistan Muslim Academy, Lahore.

Awasti, S.K. & U.S. Lal: (1986) **Dowry Prohibition**, National Law Agency, Allahabad.

Bassiouni, M. Cherif (ed) (1982): **The Islamic Criminal Justice System**, Oceana Publications, London.

Baxi. U. (1986) 'Discipline, Repression & Legal Pluralism', in Peter Sack & Elizabeth Minchin (ed.): **Legal Pluralism, Proceedings of the Canberra law workshop VII**, Law Department, Research School of Social Sciences, Australian National University, Canberra.

Bentzon, Agnete Weiss: (1982) 'The Struggle over Law', paper at a conference on 'Forms of Government and Political Systems in Scandinavian Countries', Perugia, March 1982.

Bentzon, Agnete Weiss and Henning Brøndsted: (1983) 'Recognition, Repression and Transformation of Customary Law in Greenland during the Last Forty Years of Transition to Capitalism', Paper at The XIth International Congress of Anthopological and Ethnological Sciences, Canada.

Binder, Leonard: (1963) **Religion and Politics in Pakistan**, University of California Press, Berkeley.

Braibanti, Ralph: (1966) **Research on the Bureaucracy of Pakistan**, Duke University Press, Durham.

Burki, Shahid Javed: (1980) **Pakistan under Bhutto, 1971-1977**, Macmillan Press Ltd., London.

Calder, Grace J. (1956) 'Constitutional Debates in Pakistan', **The Muslim World**, Vol. XLVI, pp.40-60.

Calkins, Philip B. (1968/69) 'A Note on Lawyers in Muslim India', **Law and Society Review**, Vol. III, No.2, pp.403-6.

Callard, Keith: (1957) **Pakistan, A Political Study**, Allen & Unwin Ltd., London.

Carroll, Lucy: (1979) 'The Muslim Family Laws Ordinance, 1961: Provisions and Procedures - a reference paper for current research', **Contribution to Indian Sociology (NS)**, Vol. 13, No.I. pp.117-43.

-      (1982a) 'Talaq-i-Tafwid and Stipulations in a Muslim Marriage Contract: Important Means of Protecting the Position of the South Asian Muslim Wife', in Gordon Johnson (ed.): **Modern Asian Studies**, Vol. 16, pp.277-309, Cambridge University Press, Cambridge.

\- (1982b) 'Nizam-i-Islam: Process and Conflict in Pakistan's Programme of Islamization, with Special Reference to the Position of Women', **Journal of Commonwealth and Comparative Politics**, pp.57-95.

\- (1983) 'Rejoinder' to the proceedings of the seminar on 'Adultery & Fornication in Islamic Jurisprudence: Dimensions & Perspectives', **Islamic and Comparative Law Quarterly**, Vol. III: I.

\- (1985a) 'Wife's Right to Notification of Talaq under Muslim Law Ordinance, 1961', **PLD**, Vol. XXXVII, pp.272-6.

\- (1985b) 'Muslim Women and Judicial Divorce; an apparently misunderstood aspect of Muslim law', **Islamic and Comparative Law Quarterly**, Vol. V, No.3-4, pp.226-45.

\- (1986) 'Divorced Muslim Women and Maintenance', **PLD**, Vol. XXXVIII, pp.1-6.

\- (1987) 'The Muslim Woman's Right to Divorce', **Manushi**, No.38. pp.37-8.

Changez, A.R. (1984a) 'The Qanune-Shahadat, 1984', **Pakistan Times**, 8 November 1984.

\- (1984b) 'The Law of Quisas and Diyat', **Pakistan Times**, 23 August 1984.

\- (1985a) 'The Revival of the Constitution of 1973 Order', **Pakistan Times**, 9 March 1985.

\- (1985b) 'Constitutional Change: An Appraisal', **Pakistan Times**, 17 March 1985.

Chishti, Muhammad Aslam: (1964) **Dowry as a Social Problem faced by Lower Middle Class**, unpublished term report in the Department of Sociology, University of Punjab, Lahore.

Choudhury, G.W. (1956) 'Religious Minorities in Pakistan', **The Muslim World**, Vol. XLVI. pp.313-23.

\- (1971) **Constitutional Development in Pakistan**, Lowe & Brydone, London.

-     (1974) '"New" Pakistan's Constitution, 1973', **The Middle East Journal**, Vol. 28, No.1. pp.10-18.

Choudhry, Khalil-ul-Rahman: (1986) 'Family Laws in the Light of Islam', **Daily Jang**, London, 15 April.

Cohn, Bernard S. (1959) 'Some Notes on Law and Change in North India', **Economic Development and Cultural Change**, Vol. VIII, No.1, pp.79-93.

-     (1965) 'Anthropological Notes on Disputes and Law in India', **Amercian Anthropologist**, Vol. VI. 67 No.6, pp.82-122.

Collins, Hugh: (1984) **Marxism and Law**, Oxford University Press, Oxford.

Cornelius, A.R. (1967) 'Spirit of the Pakistan Constitution, an Act of Faith', **PLD**, Vol. XIX, pp.78-90.

Coulson, N.J. (1959-1961) 'Muslim Custom and Case Law', in **The World of Islam: International Journal for the Historical Development of Comtemporary Islam**, Vol. VI, pp.13-24. E.J. Brill, Leiden.

-     (1969) **Conflicts and Tensions in Islamic Jurisprudence**, University of Chicago Press, Chigaco.

-     (1971) **Succession in the Muslim Family**, Cambridge University Press, London.

Dalberg-Larsen, Jørgen (1989) **Lovene og livet**, Akademisk Forlag, Copenhagen.

Daura, Bello: (1969) 'The Limit of Polygamy in Islam', **Journal of Islamic and Comparative Law**, Vol. 3, pp.21-6.

Doi, Abdur Rahman I. (1984) **Shariáh: The Islamic Law**, Ta Ha Publishers, London.

Donnan, Hastings (1988) **Marriage among Muslims: Preference & Choice in Northern Pakistan**, E.J.Brill, Leiden.

Dunn, W.N. (1971) 'Law and the Political Development of New States: Review and Commentary', **Social and Economic Studies**, Vol. 20, No.1, Jamaica.

Dwyer, Daisy Hilse: (1979) 'Law actual and perceived: The sexual politics of law in Morocco', **Law and Society Review**, Vol. 13, No.3, pp.739-56.

Eberhard, Wolfram: (1959-60) 'Modern Tendencies in Islam in Pakistan', **Sociologus**, No.9/10, pp.139-52.

Ehrlich, Eugen: (1936) **Fundamental Principles of the Sociology of Law** (transl. W. Moll), Harvard University Press, Cambridge.

Elson, Diane and Ruth Pearson: (1981) 'Nimble Fingers Make Cheap Workers: An Analysis of Women's Employment in Third World Export Manufacturing', **Feminist Review**, pp.87-107.

Engineer, Asghar Ali: (1980) **The Islamic State**, Vikas Publishing House, Delhi.

- (1984) 'Islam and Polity: Contradictions in the State Building of Pakistan', in Pandov Nayak (ed.): **Pakistan Society and Politics**, South Asian Studies, Series 6, pp.1-12. South Asian Publishers, New Delhi.

Esposito, John L. (1976) 'Muslim Family Law Reform: Towards an Islamic Methodology', **Islamic Studies**, Vol. XV, No.1, pp.19-51.

- (1977) 'Muslim Family Law Reform in Pakistan', Journal of Malaysian and Comparative Law, December, Vol. 4, part 2, pp.293-310.

- (1980a) 'Perspective on Islamic Law Reform: The Case of Pakistan', New York University Journal of International Law & Politics, Vol. 13, No.2, pp.217-45.

- (1980b) 'Pakistan: Quest for Islamic Identity', in John L. Esposito (ed.): **Islam & Development**, Pp.139-62. Syracuse University Press Syracuse.

- (1982a) 'Islamization: Religion and Politics in Pakistan', **The Muslim World**, Vol. LXXII, July-October, pp.197-223.

- (1982b) **Women in Muslim Family Law**, Syracuse University Press, Syracuse.

Faruki, Kemal A: (1965) 'Orphaned Grandchildren in Islamic Succession Law', **Islamic Studies**, Vol. IV, No.3, pp.253-74.

- (1966) 'The Islamic Provisions of the Pakistan Constitution', **The Karachi Law Journal**, Vol. 111, No.1, pp.25-32.

- (1983) 'The Islamic Resurgence: Prospects and Implications', in John L. Esposito (ed.): **Voices of Resurgent Islam**, pp.277-91. Oxford University Press, New York.

- (1987) 'Pakistan: Islamic Government & Society', in John L. Esposito (ed.): **Islam in Asia**, Oxford University Press, New York.

Feldman, Herbert: (1967) **Revolution in Pakistan: A Study of the Martial Law Administration**, Oxford University Press, London.

Feroze, Muhammad Rashid: (1962) 'The Reform in Family Laws in the Muslim World', **Islamic Studies**, Vol. I, No.1, pp.107-30.

Fisch, Jorg: (1983) **Cheap Lives and Dear Limbs**, Franz Steiner Verlag, Wiesbaden.

Fyzee, Asaf A.A: (1962-63) 'Muhammadan Law in India', **Comparative Studies in Society and History**, Vol. V, pp.401-15. Mouton & Co, The Hague.

Galanter, Marc: (1968) 'The Displacement of Traditional Law in Modern India', **Journal of Social Issues**, Vol. XXIV, No.4, pp.63-91.

- (1969) 'Introduction: The Study of the Indian Legal Profession', **Law and Society Review**, Vol. III, Number 2. pp.201-17.
- (1972) The Aborted Restoration of 'Indigenous' Law in India, **Comparative Studies in Society and History**, Vol. 14. pp.53-69.

- (1978) 'Indian Law as an Indigenous Conceptual System', **Items**, Vol. 32, No.3/4, pp.42-6.

Gardezi, Hassan N. (1982) 'The Resurgence of Islam, Islamic Ideology & Encounters with Imperialism', **Journal of Contemporary Asia**, Vol. 12, No.4, pp.451-63.

Ghai, Yash P. (1976) 'Notes Towards a Theory of Law and Ideology: Tanzanian Perspectives', **African Law Studies**, No.13, pp.31-84.

Griffiths, John: (1986) 'What is Legal Pluralism?', **Journal of Legal Pluralism and Unofficial Law**, No.24, pp.1-55.

Grilani, Riaz-ul-Hasan: (1982) **The Reconstruction of Legal Thought in Islam**, Idara Tarjuman al Quran, Lahore.

Gusfield, Joseph R: (1976) **Symbolic Crusade**, University of Illinois Press, Urbana.

Hakim, Maulana Abdul: (1974) 'Islamic Provisions in the New Constitution', in Malik, Zahid (ed.): **Pakistan After 1971**, Pakistan National Centre Publication, Lahore.

Halliday, Fred and Hamza Alavi: (1988) **State and Ideology in the Middle East and Pakistan**, Macmillan Education Ltd., London.

Hanif, C.M. (1985) 'Punishments in Islamic Criminal Law: an Analysis', **PLD**, Vol. XXXVII, pp.191-98.

Haque, Ahmed Shafiqul (1982) 'The Army and the State: Military Intervention in the Politics of Bangladesh and Pakistan', **Indian Political Science Reviews**, Vol 16, pp.80-93.

Haque, Ziaul: (1983) 'Pakistan and Islamic Ideology', in Hassan Gardezi and Jamil Rashid (eds.): **Pakistan: The Roots of Dictatorshi,**. Zed Press, London. pp 367-83.

Hasan, Ahmed: (1976) 'The Principle of Qiyas in Islamic Law - an Historical Perspective', **Islamic Studies**, Vol. XV, No.3, pp.200-10.

Hasan, Ibn: (1936) **The Central Structure of the Mughal Empire**, Munshiram Manoharlal, New Delhi.

Hassan, Itaiz: (1985) 'Constitutional Amendments', **Daily Jang**, London, March 27.

Hinchcliffe, Doreen: (1968) 'Divorce in Pakistan: Judicial Reform', **Journal of Islamic and Comparative Law**, Vol. 2, pp.13-25.

-     (1970) 'Polygamy in Traditional and Contemporary Islamic Law', Islam and the Modern Age', Vol. I, No.3, November, pp.13-38.

Hodkinson, Keith: (1981) 'Islamization of Law in Pakistan: Ways, Means and the Constitution', **The Cambridge Law Journal**, pp.248-51.

-     (1984) **Muslim Family Law: A Sourcebook**, Croom Helm, London.

Hoebel, E. Adamson: (1965) 'Fundamental Cultural Postulates and Judicial Law Making in Pakistan', **American Anthropologist**, Special publication: The Ethnography of Law 8, edited by Laura Nader. Vol. 67, No.6, part 2, pp.43-56.

Hooker, M.B. (1975) **Legal Pluralism: An Introduction to the Colonial and Neo-Colonial laws**, Oxford University Press, Oxford.

Huq, Mahfuzul: (1966) 'Some Reflections on Islam and Constitution-making in Pakistan 1947-56', **Islamic Studies**, Vol. V, No.2. pp.209-20.

Husain, M. (1984) 'Provisions in the laws of Pakistan to combat serious drug-related offences', **Bulletin on Narcotics**, No.3, pp.15-17.

Husain, S.M. (1962) 'Grandchildren whose Father is Dead - Share in Grandfather's Estate', **PLD**, Vol. XIV, pp.1-8.

Husain, Wahed: (1977) **Administration of Justice during the Muslim rule in India**, Idarah-i-Adabiyat-i-Delli, Delhi.

Hussain, Faqir: (1985) 'Review of the Supreme Court Judgement in Begum Nusrat Bhutto v. Chief of Army Staff etc', **Journal of Law and Society**, Vol. IV, No.5, pp.65-85.

Hussain, Hidiyat: (1970) 'Criminology, Crime and Punishment', **PLD**, Vol. XXII, pp.53-65.

-     (1974) 'Musalman Criminal Law in Indo-Pakistan Sub-Continent', **The Voice of Islam**, Vol. XXIII, No.2, pp.75-85.

Hussain, Mohd Ahsanuddin: (1978) 'Marriage and Khula in Islam', **Islam and the Modern Age**, Vol. IX, No.2. pp.86-8.

Hussain, Syed Jaffer: (1965) 'Legal Modernism in Islam: Polygamy and Repudiation', **Journal of the Indian Law Institute**, Vol. 7. pp.384-98.

- (1983) **Marriage Breakdown and Divorce Law Reform in Contemporary Society**, Concept Publishing Company, New Delhi.

Ibrahim, Ahmad: (1986) 'Provision for Divorced Women under Islamic Law', **PLD**, Vol. XXXVIII. pp.234-9.

Iftikhar-ud-din, Mian: (1971) Abdullah Malik (ed.): **Selected Speeches and Statements: 1907-1962**, Nigarishat, Lahore.

Iqbal, Afzal: (1986) **Islamization of Pakistan**, Vanguard, Lahore.

Iqbal, Javid: (1984) 'Islamization in Pakistan', **PLD**, Vol. XXXVI, pp.65-74.

Iqbal, Muhammad: (1977) **The Reconstruction of Religious Thought in Islam**, Hafeez Press, Lahore.

Iqbal, Sardar Muhammad: (1975) 'The Constitution of Pakistan', **PLD**, Vol. XXVII, pp.77-86.

Jafar, Malik Mohammad: (1978) 'The Shariat Benches' **View Point**, 10 December.

- (1979) 'The Deepening Crisis', **View Point**, 12 August 1979.

- (1980) 'Experiments in Islamization', **View Point**, 10 August 1980, pp.10-12.

Jahan, Tanveer (1990) 'The Invisible Workers', **View Point**, 15 March 1990. Pakistan. pp.21-5.

Jahangir, Asma: (1988) 'Stoning to Death in Pakistan', **The Lawyers**, February-March 1988, pp.28-33. Bombay.

Jahangir, Asma and Hina Jilani: (1990) **The Hudood Ordinances, A Divine Sanction?** Rhotas Books, Lahore.

Jain B.S. (1970) **Administration of Justice in Seventeenth Century India**, Metropolitan Book Co., Delhi.

Jalal, Ayesha: (1990) **The State of Martial Rule: The Origins of Pakistan's Political Economy of Defence**, Cambridge University Press, Cambridge.

Kamal, Sultana: (1987) 'Impact of Colonialism on the Family Laws of Bangla Desh', paper presented at Asian conference on Women, Religion, & Family Laws, 16-20 December 1987, Women's Centre, Bombay.

Kamali M.H. (1990) 'Appellate Review & Judicial Independence in Islamic Law', Conference on Islam & Public Law, SOAS, 29-30 June. London.

Keddie, Nikki: (1988) 'Ideology, Society and the State in Post-Colonial Muslim Societies', in Fred Halliday and Alavi Hamza: **State and Ideology in the Middle East and Pakistan**, Macmillan Education Ltd., London.

Kennedy, Charles H. (1990) 'Islamization & Legal Reform in Pakistan, 1979-1989', **Pacific Affairs**, Vol.63, No 1. pp 62-77.

Khan, Gul Muhammad: (1986a) 'Islamization of Laws in Pakistan', Presidential address, Chief Justice, Federal Shariat Court of Pakistan', **PLD**, Vol. XXXVIII, pp.249-68.

- (1986b) **Role of Judiciary in the Development of Islamic Law**, Federal Shariat Court Islamabad, Pakistan.

Khan Hamid: (1980) **Islamic Law of Inheritance: A comparative study with emphasis on contemporary problems**, Lahore Law Times Publications, Lahore.

Khan, Mazhar ul Haq: (1972) **Purdah and Polygamy**, Nashiran-e-ilm-o-Taraqiyet. Peshwar.

Khan, Mohammad Ayub: (1958-59) **Speeches and Statements**, Vol. I. October 1958 - June 1959.

- (1960-61) **Speeches and Statements**, Vol. III, July 1960 - June 1961.

\-   (1962-63) **Speeches and Statements**, Vol. V, June 1962 - June 1963.

Khan, Nighat Said: (1989) **Setting the Record Straight: Women Workers**, ASR, Lahore.

Khan, M. Aslam: (1986) 'Registration of Marriages Under Family Law Ordinance', **Daily Jang**, London, 6 June 1986.

Khan, Raja Said Akbar: (1972) 'Polygamy in Islam: a Humane Institution', **PLD**, Vol. XXIV, pp.1-16.

Khan, Sardar Asadullah Jan: (1952) **Constituent Assembly (Legislature) of Pakistan Debates**, 14 April 1952.

Khare, R.S. (1972) 'Indigenous Culture and Lawyer's Law in India', **Comparative Studies in Society and History**, Cambridge University Press, Vol. 14. pp.71-96.

Khel, Muhammad Nazeer Kaka: (1982) 'The Role of Ideology in Constitutional Development in Pakistan', **Journal of Law and Society**, Vol. I, No.1. pp.67-77.

\-   (1984) 'Status of non-Muslim Minorities in Pakistan', **Islamic Studies**, Vol. XXIII, No.1, pp.45-54.

Korson, J. Henry & Michelle Maskisell: (1985) 'Islamization and Social Policy in Pakistan: The Constitutional Crisis and the Status of Women', **Asian Survey**, Vol. XXV, No.6, pp.589-612.

Krishnaiyer V.R: (1987) **Muslim Women (Protection of Rights on Divorce) Act, 1986**, Eastern Book Company, Lucknow.

Kroson, J.A. (1959) 'Age and Social Status at Marriage', **Pakistan Development Review**, Vol. V, No.4.

Kulshreshtha, V.D. (1981) **Landmarks in Indian Legal and Constitutional History**, 5th ed. revised by V. Malik, Eastern Book Co, Lucknow.

Kumar, Sabiha & Khalid Nadvi: (1987) 'Zina: The Hudood Ordinance and Its Implications for Women', Asian Conference on Women Religion and Personal Laws, organized by the Women Centre, Bombay.

Kurin, Richard: (1986) 'Islamization: A View From the Countryside', in Anita M. Weiss (ed.): **Islamic Reassertion in Pakistan**, pp.115-28. Syracuse University Press.

Lando, Ole (1965): 'Om de store europæiske retssystemer og om inddelingen af retssystemerne i familier', **Juristen**, pp.37-49. København.

Leavy, Reuben: (1957) 'Usage, Custom and Secular Law under Islam', Chapter VI, in **The Social Structure of Islam**, University Press, Cambridge.

Lewis, I. M. (1966) 'Islamic law & Customary Practice', in I. M. Lewis (ed.): **Islam in Tropical Africa**, pp.45-57, Oxford University Press, London.

Leys, Colin: (1981) 'The "Overdeveloped" Post Colonial State: A Re-evaluation', **Review of African Political Economy**, No.5, pp.39-48.

Liddle, Joanna & Rama Joshi (1986) **Daughters of Independence: Gender, Caste and Class in India**, Zed Books Ltd., London.

Liebesny, Herbert J. (1953): 'Religious Law and Westernization in the Moslem Near East', **American Journal of Comperative Law**, pp.492-504.

-     (1967) 'Stability and Change in Islamic law', **The Middle East Journal**, Vol. 21, No.1, pp.16-34.

Lippman, Matthew, Sean McConville, & Mordechai Yerushalmi: (1988) **Islamic Criminal Law & Procedure: An Introduction**, Praeger, New York.

Lipstein, K. (1957) 'The Reception of Western Law in India', **International Social Science Bulletin**, Vol. IX, pp.85-95.

Lodhi, Maleeha. (1988) 'Pakistan's shia movement: an interview with Arif Hussaini', **Third World Quarterly**, Vol. 10, No 2, April 1988.

Lodi, Sirdar M.M. (1985) 'Return to the Rule of Law', **Pakistan Times**, 17 March 1985.

Mahammadi, A. (1977) 'The custom and its significance in Islamic Law', **Islam and the Modern Age**, Vol. VIII, No.2, pp.32-8. May 1977.

Mahmood, Shaukat: (1986) **Muslim Family Laws**, Legal Research Centre, Pakistan.

Mahmood Tahir: (1965) 'Custom As a Source of Law in Islam', **Journal of the Indian Law Institute**, Vol. 7, pp.102-6.

- (1972) **Family Law Reforms in the Muslim World**, N. M.Tripathi Pvt. Ltd. Bombay.

- (1982) 'Convener's Note', **Islamic and Comparative Law Quarterly**, Vol. II:4.

- (1987) 'Law in the Quran - A draft code', **Islamic and Comparative Law Quarterly**, Vol. VII, No.1, pp.1-32.

Mahmudunnasir, S. (1968) 'Polygamy in Islam', **PLD**, Vol. XX, pp.60-6.

Majid, Rana Abdul: (1970) 'Islamic Law of Retaliation', **PLD**, Vol. XXII, pp.22-4.

Malik, Vijay: (1988) **Muslim Law of Marriage, Divorce & Maintenance**, Eastern Book Company. Lucknow.

Malmström, Åke: (1969) 'The System of Legal Systems: Notes on a Problem of Classification in Comparative Law', in Folke Schmidt (ed.): **Scandinavian Studies in Law**, Vol. 13, pp.129-49, Almqvist & Wiksell, Stockholm.

Martinussen, John: (1980) **Staten i perifere og postkoloniale Samfund. Indien og Pakistan**, published in 4 vols, Politica, Århus.

Masoodi, G. Saqlain: (1982) 'Modern Criminal Law and the Quranic Penal Philosophy', **Islamic and Comparative Law Quarterly**, Vol. II, No.3, pp.161-74.

Maududi, Abu'l A'la: (1980) **The Islamic Law and Constitution**, Translated and edited by Khurshid Amed, Islamic Publications Ltd., Lahore.

-    (1981) 'Islamic & Western Laws on Divorce - A Comparative Historical Perspective', **Islamic and Comparative Law Quarterly**, Vol. I, pp.17-23.

Mayer, Ann Elizabeth: (1984) 'Islamic Law', in Marjorie Kelly (ed.): **Islam, the Religious & Political Life of a World Community**, Praeger Publishers, New York.

Mazari, Shireen: (1983) 'Islamization and the Status of Women in Pakistan: A Note', **South Asia Bulletin**, Vol. III, pp.19-82, University of California, California.

Means, Gordon, P. (1969) 'The Role of Islam in the Political Development of Malaysia', **Comparative Politics**, Vol. I, pp.264-84.

Mehdi, Mahboob: (1990) 'Death Penalty, Inhuman Punishments & Doctors in Pakistan', paper in Amnesty International meeting, (April), La Sorbonne, Paris.

Mehdi, Rubya: (1990) 'The Offence of Rape in the Islamic Law of Pakistan', **International Journal of the Sociology of Law**, No 18, pp.19-29.

Mehren, Arthur Taylor von: (1965) 'Law and legal Education in India: Some Observations', **Harvard Law Review**, Vol. 78. No 6. pp.1180-9.

Merillat, H.C.L. (1966) 'Law and Developing Countries', **American Journal of International Law**, Vol. 60, pp.70-9.

Minto, Abid Hassan: (1986) 'Human Rights in Pakistan and the Struggle of the Lawyers', in International Affairs - Christian Conference of Asia: **Pakistan Struggle for Human Rights: A Collection of Essays Relating to the Human Rights Struggle in Various Sectors of Pakistan Society**, pp.56-87. Idara-e-Aman-o-Insaf, Kowloon.

Mir, Waris: (1985) 'Constitutional Amendments in Pakistan', **Daily Watan**, London, 28 February 1985.

Mitha, Y., Anwar, M., Khan N.S., Asmaa J. Pal, (1989) **Solid Foundations Solid Contributions: Women in the Brick Kiln Industry**, ASR, Lahore.

Mohajir, M.A.R. (1974) 'Reform is the aim of Islamic Punishment', **The Voice of Islam**, pp.46-9.

Moore, Sally Falk (1973) 'Law & social change: The Semi-Autonomous Social Field as an Appropriate subject of study', **Law & Society Review**, Vol. VII, No.4, pp.719-46.

- (1978) **Law as Process. An Anthropological Approach**, Routledge & Kegal Paul, London.

Mostafa, Salahuddin (1985) 'Stride towards Islamic Constitution', **Pakistan Times**, 17 March.

Mubshar, Afzal Tanweer (1990) 'Family Laws Problems in Practice' (In Urdu), paper for Seminar on Family Laws, 19-20 December, Karachi Hall, Lahore High Bar Association, Lahore.

Muhammed, Ullah Al-Haj (1986) **The Administration of Justice in Islam**, Kitab Bhavan, New Delhi.

Mumtaz, Khawar and Farida, Shaheed (1987) **Women of Pakistan**, Zed Books Ltd., London.

Nolte, Richard H. (1958) 'The Rule of Law in the Arab Middle East', **The Muslim World**, Vol. XLVIII, pp.295-307.

Patel, Rashida: (1979) **Women and Law in Pakistan**, Faiza Publishers, Karachi. Pakistan.
- (1986) **Islamization of Laws in Pakistan?** Faiza Publishers, Karachi.

- (1991) **Socio-Economic Political Status & Women & Law in Pakistan**, Faiza Publishers, Karachi.

Pearl, David: (1969) 'Family Law in Pakistan', **Journal of Family Law**, No.9, pp.165-89.

- (1971) 'The Impact of the Muslim Family Law Ordinance (1961) in Quetta (Baluchistan) Pakistan', **Journal of the Indian Law Institute**, Vol. XIII, pp.561-9.

- (1976) 'The Legal Rights of Muslim Women in India, Pakistan, and Bangladesh', **New Community**, Vol. V. pp.68-74.

- (1979) 'Codification in Islamic Law', **The Jewish Law Annual**, Vol II. pp.162-7.

- (1981) 'The Wife's Right to Divorce in Muslim Law', **The Jewish Law Annual**, Vol. IV. pp.226-31.

- (1989) 'Executive, Legislative and Judicial Amendments to Islamic Family Law in Pakistan (1961-1989)', Paper: SOAS Conference on Islamic Family Law, London, 18-19 May.

Pedersen, Ove K. (1990) '...Og der var 10 og 11 og mange fler! Om ni grundlæggende problemer for en teori om institutionel forandring', **Grus**, Nr. 30, Ålborg, pp.97-120.

Pospisil, Leopold: (1971) **Anthropology of law: A Comparative Theory**, Harper and Row, New York.

Qadearuddin (1985) 'Islamic Law of Evidence', **Jang**, London, 12 Jan.

Qureshi, Maqbool Ahmad: (1988) 'Our Judicial System and Official Routine', **Pakistan Times**, 24 September.

Rahman, Fazlur: (1966) 'The controversy over the Muslim Family Law' in: Donald Eugene (ed.): **South Asian Politics & Religion**, Princeton University Press, Princeton, pp.414-27.

- (1970) 'Islam and the Constitutional Problem of Pakistan', **Studia Islamica**, Vol. XXXII, No.4, pp.275-87.

- (1971) 'The Ideological Experience of Pakistan', **Islam and the Modern Age**, Vol. II, No.4, pp.1-20.

- (1974) 'Islam and the New Constitution of Pakistan', in Henry J. Korson (ed.): **Contemporary Problems of Pakistan**, pp.30-44. E.J. Brill, Leiden.

- (1976) 'Some Islamic Issues in the Ayyub Khan Era', in Donald P. Little. (ed.): **Essays on Islamic Civilization**, pp.284-302. E.J. Brill, Leiden.

- (1979) 'Towards Reformulating the Methodology of Islamic Law: Sheikh Yamani on 'Public interest' in Islamic law', **New York University Journal of International Law and Politics**, Vol. XII, No.2, pp.219-24.

Rahman, Tanzil-ur-: (1967) 'Polygamy in Pakistan and other Muslim Countries', **PLD**, Vol. XIX. pp.38-40.

-    (1978) **Islamization of Pakistan Law**, Hamdard Academy. Karachi.

-    (1983) 'Some Aspects of the Islamic Law of Evidence', **PLD**, Vol. XXXV, pp.199-207.

-    (1982) 'Succession under Muslim Family Laws Ordinance, 1961', **PLD**, Vol. XXXIV, pp.99-113.

-    (1989) 'Family Laws Ordinance & the Constitution', **PLD**, Vol. XLI, pp.20-280.

Ram, Rochi: (1990) 'Family Court Practice: Experience in Courts', paper for Seminar on Family Laws. 19-20 December, Karachi Hall, Lahore High Court Bar Association, Lahore.

Rashiduzzaman, M. (1967) **Pakistan: A Study of Government and Politics**, Chapt. V: 'Dilemmas of Constitution Making', pp.76-105. Ideal Library, Dacca.

Razvi, Mahmod Ahmad: (1986a) 'Death sentence for derogatory remarks against prophet Muhammad', **Nawa-i-waqt**, 28 August 1986. (In Urdu).

Rehman, Inamur: (1982) **Public Opinion and Political Development in Pakistan, 1947-1958**, chapt. 1: 'The Debate Over an Islamic Constitution', Oxford University Press, Karachi.

Richter, William L. (1979) 'The Political Dynamics of the Islamic Resurgence in Pakistan', **Asian Survey**, Vol. XIX, No.6, pp.547-57.

-    (1986) 'The Political Meaning of Islamization in Pakistan: Prognosis, Implications and Questions', in Anita M. Weiss (ed.): **Islamic Reassertion in Pakistan**, Syracuse University Press.

Rosen, Lawrence: (1970) 'I Divorce Thee', **Transaction**, Vol. 7, No.8, pp.34-7.

-    (1989a) **The Anthropology of Justice: Law as Culture in Islamic Society**, Cambridge University Press, Cambridge.

-     (1989b) Islamic "Case law" and the logic of Consequence, in June Starr & Jane F. Collier (ed.): **History and power in the Study of Law. New Directions in Legal Anthropology**, Cornell University Press, Ithaca & London.

Rosenthal, Erwin I.J. (1964) 'Some Reflections on the Seperation of Religion and Politics in Modern Islam', **Islamic Studies** Vol. 3, pp.249-84.

-     (1965) **Islam in the Modern National State**, The University Press, Cambridge.

-     (1970) 'Religion and Politics in Islam', **Islam and the Modern Age**, Vol. I, pp.50-64, May 1970.

Rudolph, Lloyd I. & Susanne Hoeber Rudolph (1965) 'Barristers and Brahamans in India: Legal Cultures and Social Change', **Comparative Studies in Society and History**, Vol. VIII, No.1, pp.24-49. Mouton & Co., The Hague.

Russell, Alexander David & Suhrawardy, Abdullah Almamum (1979) A Manual of the Law of Marriage: from the Mukhtasar of Sidikhalil. Law Publishing Company, Lahore.

Sack, P.G. (1986) 'Legal Pluralism: Introductory Comments', in Peter Sack & Elizabeth Minchin (ed.) **Legal   Pluralism. Proceedings of the Canberra law Workshop VII**, ANU, Canberra, pp.1-16.

Safwat, Safia M. (1982) 'Offences and Penalties in Islamic Law', **The Islamic Quarterly**, Vol. XXVI, No.3, pp.149-81.

Sandeela, Eateh M. (1978) 'Sovereignty of Allah as a Political Fact', **PLD**, Vol. XXX, pp.102-8.

-     (1983) 'Ethics of Islamic Punishments', **Islamic and Comparative Law Quarterly**, Vol. III, No.4, pp.233-48.

Saqib, Mohammad Armaghan: (1986) 'Khula through Western Civil Courts', **Pakistan Times**, 16 January.

Saul, John S. (1974) 'The State in Post-Colonial Societies: Tanzania', in Ralph Milikand & John Saville (eds.): **The Socialist Register**, pp.349-72. Merlin Press, London.

Sayeed, Khalid bin: (1980) **Politics in Pakistan. The Nature and Direction of Change**, Praeger, New York.

Scott, George Ryley: (1954) **The History of Torture Throughout the Ages**, Torchstream Books, London.

- (1938) **The History of Corporal Punishment**, T. Werner Laurie Ltd., London.

Scott, James C. (1985) **Weapons of the Weak, Everyday Forms of Peasant Resistance**, Yale University Press, New Haven.

Shabbir, Mohammad (1988) **Muslim Personal Law and Judiciary**, The Law Book Company, Allahabad.

Shafi, Muhammad Ahmed: (1986) 'Death sentence for derogatory remarks against prophet Muhammad', **Nawa-i-waqt**, 28 August 1986.

Shah, Nasim Hasan: (1976) 'The Constitution of Pakistan, 1973', **PLD**, Vol. XXVIII, pp.106-14.

- (1979) 'Constitution of Pakistan', **PLD**, Vol. XXXI, pp.71-90.

Sharan, Parmatma (1968) **Political System of Pakistan**, Meenakshi Prakashan. New Delhi.

Shehab, Rafi Ullah (1984a) 'Islamic Law of Evidence', in **PLD**, Vol. XXXVI, pp.92-5.

- (1984b) 'Diyat of Women in Islamic Law', **PLD**, Vol. XXXVI, pp.84-6.

- (1984c) 'Proposed Law on Qisas and Diyat', **PLD**, Vol. XXXVI, pp.86-8.

- (1984d) 'Interrelation between Qisas and Diyat', **PLD** XXXVI, pp.90-2.

- (1984e) 'Law on Diyat and Sources of Islamic Law', **PLD** XXXVI, pp.88-90.

- (1986a) 'Islamic Shariat and Shah Bano Case', **Pakistan Times**, 9 January.

- (1986b) 'The Muslim Family Laws and Islamic Norms', **Pakistan Times**, 7 February.

- (1987a) 'Marriage and Marriage Feasts in Islam Society', **Pakistan Times**, 19 March.

- (1987) Letter to the editor **Pakistan Times**, 28 February.

- (1988) 'Status of Women', **Pakistan Times**, 1 February.

Shibli, Muhammad: (1961) 'Punishment in Islam', **The Voice of Islam**, Vol. IX, No.8, pp.318-54.

Smith, Donald Eugene: (ed. 1971) **Religion, Politics, & Social Change in the Third World**, The Free Press New York, pp.67-79.

Starr, June (1989) 'The Role of Turkish Secular law in changing the lives of Rural Muslim Women, 1950-1970', **Law & Society Review**, Vol. 23, No.3, pp.497-523.

Tanveer, Afzal (1990) 'Family Laws', paper for Seminar on Family Laws, 19-20 December 1990, Karachi Hall, Lahore High Court Bar Association, Lahore.

Taylor, David (1983) 'The Politics of Islam and Islamization in Pakistan', in James P. Piscatori (ed.): **Islam in the Political Process**, Cambridge University Press, Cambridge.

Tonki, Maulana Mufti Wali Hussan (1985) **Family Laws in the Light of Shariat** (in Urdu), Majlis-i-dawat-Tahik Islami, Karachi.

Verinder, Grover (1984) 'Enigma of an Islamic State: The Case of Pakistan', **The Indian Political Science Review**, Vol. XVIII, No I, pp.107-16.

Weaver, Mary Anne (1990) 'A Reporter at Large: Balochistan', **The New Yorker**, (Jan 1990), pp.82-101.

Weekes, Richard (1964) **Pakistan: Birth and Growth of a Muslim Nation**, D. van Nostrand Company Inc., Toronto.

Weinbaum, Marvin G. & Stephen P. Cohen: (1983) 'Pakistan in 1982: Holding on', **Asian Survey**, Vol. XXIII, No.2, pp.123-32.

Weiss, Anita M. (1985) 'Women in Pakistan: Implications of the Current Program of Islamization', Working Paper No.78. University of California, Berkeley.

- (1986a) 'The Historical debate on Islam and the State in South Asia', in Anita M. Weiss (ed.): **Islamic Reassertion in Pakistan**, Syracuse University Press.

- (1986b) 'Implications of the Islamization Programme for Women', in Anita M. Weiss (ed.): **Islamic Reassertion in Pakistan**, Syracuse University Press.

- (1990) 'Benazir Bhutto & the Future of Women in Pakistan', **Asian Survey**, Vol.XXX, No.5. May. pp.433-45.

Weiss, Bernard: (1978) 'Interpretation in Islamic Law: The theory of Ijtihad', **The American Journal of Comparative Law**, Vol. 26, pp.199-212.

Westergaard, Kirsten: (1985) **State and Rural Society in Bangladesh**, chapt.11: 'Theoretical Discussion on the Nature of the State', Scandinavian Institute of Asian Studies, Monograph Series 49, Curzon Press, London.

Williams, L.F. Rushbrook: (1975) **Pakistan Under Challenge**, chapt. 8: 'Framing a Constitution', pp.133-50. Stacey International

Wolf-Phillips, Leslie: (1989) '1973 Constitution: A heritage for the Future', **Pakistan Times**, 15 April.

Yamani, Ahmed Zaki: (1979) 'The Eternal Sharia', **New York University Journal of International Law and Politics**, Vol. 12, No.2, pp.205-12.

Zahur-ud-din, Mian: (1987) **New Islamic Laws**, Mansoor Book House, Karachi.

Zareen, Humaira: (1989) **Economic Contributions of Women in Rural Punjab**, unpublished Master of Science thesis, Department of Anthropology, Quaid-i-Azam University, Islamabad.

Zareen, Samina: (1990) 'Family Courts Practice, Experiences of Lawyers in Courts', Seminar on Family Laws. 19-20 Dec. 1990, Karachi Hall, Lahore High Court Bar Association, Lahore.

Ziemann, W. and M. Lanzendorfer: (1977) 'The State in Peripheral Societies', in Ralph Milikand & John Saville (eds.): **The Socialist Register**, pp.143-77. Merlin Press, London.

Ziring, Lawrence: (1984) 'From Islamic Republic to Islamic State in Pakistan', **Asian Survey**, Sept 1984, No.9, pp 931-46.

Zubaida, Sami: (1987) 'The Quest for the Islamic State: Islamic Fundamentalism in Egypt and Iran', in Linnel Caplan (ed.): **Studies in Religious Fundamentalism**, pp.25-49. Macmillan Press, Houndmills.

Glossary

Alim (Arabic pl. Ulema)
Learned religious authority, a scholar of Islam.

Abbasids (Arabic)
The name of a dynasty descended from al-Abbass. They ruled the Arabian Empire from A.D. 749 to 1258.

Adah (Arabic)
Tradition/Custom.

Ahmadis (Urdu pl.)
A Muslim sect of Indo-Pakistani origin, followers of Mirza Ghulam Ahmed. They are also called *Mirzai*s and *Qadiani*s in a derogatory sense.

Allah (Arabic. sing.)
God. Muslims are monotheists.

Al sunnah-al-fi'liyah (Arabic)
The right path as shown by the Prophet Muhammad through his deeds.

Al sunnah-al-qawliyah (Arabic)
The right path as shown by the Prophet Muhammad through his sayings.

Al sunnah-al-taqririyah (Arabic)
According to tradition, actions performed without the disapproval of the Prophet Muhammad.

Ameen (Arabic sing.)
Faithful. An honest person, to whom one could entrust the safe custody of one's valuables and goods.

Amil
Institutions and practices of the *Bohras* sect.

Auqaf (Arabic pl., sing. waqf)	Religiously endowed properties entrusted to the *ulema*. Dedication of property to a charitable cause. Such property cannot be sold or transferred to others. For example, if a person builds a mosque, he loses the right of ownership from the moment the first prayers are said in the mosque.
Azan	Announcement. The call to public prayers proclaimed in mosques before the stated times of prayers.
Babus (Urdu)	Clerks, typists, assistants to lawyers etc.
Barrat	Institution and practices of the *Bohras* sect.
Basra	A city in Iraq, a cultural and intellectual centre during the Arabian Empire.
Batil (Arabic)	Unvalid. Not true. That which is false in doctrine.
Bhang (Urdu)	Intoxicating drink made of the leaves of a wild plant popularly called *bhang* hemp.
Biar (Urdu)	Name of a fruit-bearing tree.
Biradri (Urdu)	A clan. Brotherhood. Patrilineal kinship group.
Bish (Hindi)	A caustic drink.
Bohars	Merchant. *Bohars* are a Muslim community of traders doing business in all parts of the world.
Charas (Urdu)	Hashish. A narcotic resin made of the leaves of a plant named *bhang* hemp, cannabis resin.

Cutchi Memons	*Memons* are divided into two groups, the *Cutchi Memons* and the *Halai Memons*. The *Cutchi Memons* are converts from a Hindu trading community; they mostly speak the Cutchi language. They follow the *Hanafi* law.
Dai	Assistant of the *Bohars' Imam*, the *Dai* has great power regarding the interpretation of religion.
Dar-ul-uman	Women's refuge.
Dasi Sharab (Urdu)	An alcoholic drink, distilled at home/indigeniously.
Diar	Type of tree.
Dawah	Institute in Islamic University.
Diyat	Blood money.
Dhimmis (Zimmis) (Arabic pl.)	Non-Muslim subjects of an Islamic state, enjoying security of person and property against the payment of a poll tax.
Fatwa (Arabic)	Opinions. A religious or judicial decree, pronounced either by a *khalifah* (ruler), *mufti* (authority on law and jurisprudence) or a *qadi* (judge).
Fiqh (Arabic)	Islamic jurisprudence. A body of rules gradually developed from interpretations of the *Shariah*.
Fiqa-e-Ja'afria (Arabic)	A school of Islamic jurisprudence based on the works of Imam Ja'afar Sadiq (a theologian). His followers are also called *Shi'its*.
Ganja (Urdu. n.)	Marijuana.
Ghasab (Arabic)	Usurpation of one's personal right or property.

Hadd (Arabic sing.)	Limit. Punishment for the offences for which limits have been defined in the *Quran* and *Hadith*.
Hadith (Arabic)	Tradition. Record of the Prophet Muhammad's sayings and deeds.
Hajj	Pilgrimage.
Hanafi (Arabic)	Followers of the Islamic school of jurisprudence expounded by *Imam* Abu Hanifa al-Nu'man, the greatest *Sunni* (Hanafi) theologian and jurist.
Hanbli (Arabic)	Followers of the Islamic school of jurisprudence expounded by Imam Abu Hanbel.
Haqooq-uz-zojain (Arabic)	Rights and duties of spouses towards each other.
Hara'abah (Arabic)	Robbery.
Haram	That which is forbidden in Islam.
Hegira (Arabic)	'Migration'. The Prophet Muhammad moved from Mecca to Medina (Yasrib) in A.D.622. This event has become the starting point of a Muslim calendar based on the lunar system, i.e every month begins with the appearence of the new moon.
Hikma (Arabic)	'Wisdom'. The term expresses knowledge of the essence or the truth.
Hirz (Arabic)	'Protection'. An enclosed place, where one's valuables and goods are safe, where admittance of outsiders is prohibited e.g. one's home, a cupboard etc.
Hudood (Arabic pl.)	See *hadd*.

Id (Arabic sing.)	An important Muslim festival, celebrated on two occasions: once at the end of the month of *Ramadan* (fasting) when it is known as *id-ul-fitr.* The other occasion is known as *id-ul-adha* when Muslims slaughter animals to commemorate the Prophet Ibrahim's offering his son Ismail as a sacrifice to Allah, which God commanded to be substituted by a lamb.
Iddah (Arabic)	A period of time corresponding to 3 consecutive menstrual periods. The standard period of time during which a women should not remarry after divorce or the death of her husband.
Iddat (Arabic)	See above.
Ijma (Arabic)	The third cardinal tenet of Islam. Literally 'collecting', as a term it means the unanimous consent on a point of law of the *mujtahidun* (learned doctors). Consensus of opinion among Muslims.
Ijtihad (Arabic)	Independent reasoning or judgement. The logical deduction on a legal or theological question by a *mujtahid* (doctor of theology). It is distinguished from *ijmah*, which is the collective opinion of a council or a body.
Ijtihad-fi'l-Masal (Arabic)	A degree of special independence, authorizing the bearer to solve cases which have not been decided by the four schools of Islamic jurisprudence.
Ijtihad-fi'l-Mazhab (Arabic)	This degree was conferred upon the immediate disciples of the *Imam*, who participated in the works of their teachers. In some cases the disciples were allowed to retain their opinion even when it went against the opinion of the master. In secondary matters their opinion carries significant weight.

Ijtihad-fi'sh-shar (Arabic)	Independence in legislation, while seeking to discover the meanings of Divine Law, by a person who is qualified to conduct *ijtihad* in matters of *Shariah*.
Ikrah (Arabic n.)	'Compulsion'. 'Cohesion'. A state of affairs where there is a fear or threat of injury to a person's property or honour. For example one may drink alcohol in this situation, although it is forbidden in Islam.
Illa (Arabic)	That which can be objectively ascertained and measured. A reason or cause.
Imam (Arabic)	Muslim religious leader. The one who leads the prayers. According to the *Boharas*, the *Imam* is the final religious head, but is hidden from human sight.
Imam of Ka'aba	The one who leads prayers in the *masjid-ul-haram* (grand mosque) in Mecca. It is a profoundly respected position, as Muslims from all over the world come to the *Ka'aba* on pilgrimage.
Ismai'li	Muslim sect. Isma'lis of varying kinds are to be found all over the world.
Isqat-i-Haml (Arabic)	Miscarriage to be caused when the limbs or organs have not been formed.
Isqat-i-Janin (Arabic)	Miscarriage (of foetus) caused after the limbs or organs have been formed.
Istihsan (Arabic)	Approval. Juristic preference especially based on contradictions of equity. A well-known principle in *Hanafi fiqh*, it rejects the use of *qiyas* and instead admits the law of expediency.
Istislah (Arabic)	Seeking the best solution for the general interest. Consideration of the public interest (*maslaha*) in the elaboration of legal rules.

Ithna 'Ashari' (Jafari)	Sect of *Shia*.
Itlaf-i-salahyat-i-udu	Dismembering the parts of the body.
Itlaf-i-udu (Arabic)	Permanently impairing the functioning of parts of the body.
Iztirar (Arabic)	'Compulsion'. An extreme situation where one is allowed to do things which otherwise are forbidden in Islam, for example if one's life is in danger.
Jizya (Arabic)	Special poll tax or capitation levied on the non-Muslim subjects (*dhimmis*) of an Islamic state. Upon payment of the tax they become entitled to personal security and the safety of their property.
Jurh (Arabic)	Injury on other than head or face, leaving a mark or wound.
Ka'aba (Arabic)	The sacred House in Mecca (Saudi Arabia) around which pilgrims walk while performing *Hajj* (pilgrimage). Muslims all over the world offer their prayers facing towards the *Ka'aba*.
Kech	A cultural and historical belt in the Baluchistan province of Pakistan.
Khadim (Urdu)	A servant. The caretaker of a mosque.
Khalji	A Muslim dynasty, which ruled India from 1290 to 1320.
Khojas	*Ismai'li Shiities*. The Aga Khan is the head of the community and the final interpreter of religion. The original faith of this group was a mixture of Hinduism and Islam but it has gradually come more under the influence of Islam.

Khula (Arabic)	Agreement entered into to allow the dissolution of a marriage, if the woman seeks the divorce by paying an amount of money in compensation or a consideration to her husband.
Khumar	Intoxicant in the form of liquid. According to some it only applies to wine made of grapes.
Koh Murad	Mountain in the province of Baluchistan in Pakistan.
Kufah	City in Iraq, once a cultural and intellectual center.
Li'an (Arabic)	Procedure to be followed when a husband accuses his wife of adultery and fails to support the allegation by producing the necessary four witnesses. He then swears on the *Quran* that God may curse him if he is telling a lie. The woman then takes an oath denying the charge. This procedure leads to an irrevocable divorce.
Lodi	A Muslim dynasty.
Lot	A prophet whose followers indulged in homosexuality.
Mahr (Arabic)	The dower, without which marriage is not legal.
Mahr-i-Mithl	Proper dower.
Mahr-i-Muajjal	Dower which is to be paid immediately upon entering into a marriage contract.
Mahr-i-Muwajjal	Deferred dower. Under this condition dower becomes payable upon the dissolution of the marriage contract.
Mahram (Arabic)	Unlawful. A near relation with whom marriage is forbidden.

Majlis-i-Shura (Arabic)	Advisory council (Parliament).
Malikana	The amount of money which is paid to the landlord by the tenant (rent).
Maliki (Arabic)	Followers of the Islamic school of jurisprudence as expounded by *Imam* Malik.
Masalih-al-Mursalah	Public interest. See *istihsan*.
Masjid	Mosque.
Maulvi (Urdu)	A term used in the past for learned men. Nowadays it means the one who leads prayers in the mosque. A Muslim religious leader.
Medina	City in Saudi Arabia, whose name literally means 'city' and previously was called Yasrib. The prophet Muhammad and other Muslims moved to Medina.
Medinese	From or pertaining to Medina.
Mohallah (Urdu)	A unit of an administrative division of a city.
Mubara'a (Arabic)	Marriage dissolved by mutual agreement.
Mufti (Arabic)	Legal consultant qualified to pronounce a *fatwa* (see *fatwa*).
Mughals (Urdu)	A Muslim dynasty that ruled India from 1526 to 1750.
Muhsan (Arabic)	A sane, adult and free (not slave) person, who is married and has consummated his marriage.
Mujtahidun (Arabic)	Those who exercise *ijtihad* or independent judgement. The highest degree conferred upon men of high position in scholarship.

Mullah (Urdu)	This term was used in the past for a man of knowledge and intellectual qualities, but nowadays it is used for a person who stands for orthodoxy and conservatism in Islam. In Pakistan it is often used in a derogatory sense.
Nikah (Urdu)	Marriage contract.
Nikah-nama (Urdu)	Marriage certificate.
Nisab (Arabic)	Estate or property liable to *zakat*.
Nisab-e-Sarqa (Arabic)	Fixed sum, used in evaluating stolen goods. If the amount stolen exceeds this amount, the thief becomes liable to *hadd* punishment i.e., amputation of the hand. Various schools of jurisprudence disagree as to the actual amount.
Nizam-i-Islam (Urdu)	'Islamic System'. Slogan coined by the religious orthodoxy in their struggle against Zulfikar Ali Bhutto's administration. They maintained that if they came to power they would implement the 'Islamic System' in the country. There has always has been controversy about the definition of this term.
Nizam-i-Mustapha	'The system of *Mustapha*' (Muhammad). Slogan of similar type to the one mentioned above.
Panchayat (Urdu)	Council of village elders where disputes are settled. It has popular roots in the civic system of Indo-Pakistan.
Pludar	Type of tree.
Purdah (Urdu)	'Veil'. It is a tradition for women to cover themselves whenever they go out of the house.

Qadi	Muslim judge.
Qanun-e-shadat (Urdu)	The law of evidence.
Qatal-bi-sabab (Arabic)	Consequential murder.
Qatal-i-amad (Arabic)	Premeditated murder.
Qatal-i-khata (Arabic)	Accidental murder.
Qatal-i-shibha (Arabic)	Suspected premeditated murder.
Qazf (Arabic)	Accusing an innocent woman or man of adultery.
Qisas (Arabic)	Punishment by causing similar hurt to the same part of the body of the offender as he has caused to the victim, or by causing his death if he has committed *qatal-i-amd*, in exercise of the right of the victim or of a *wali* (person entitled to claim *qisas*).
Qiyas (Arabic)	Analogical reasoning or deduction.
Quaid (Urdu)	Leader. The founder of Pakistan is called *quaid-i-azam* (the great leader).
Quran (Arabic)	The holy book of the Muslims.
Rajm (Arabic)	Lapidation. Stoning to death.
Ramadan	Month of fasting.
Ray	Opinion.
Raza	Institution and practice of the *Bohars* sect.
Riba (Arabic)	'Usury'. The practice of lending money at a high rate of interest.
Sehri	Time of twilight, when Muslims start fasting.

Shafi (Arabic)	The followers of Imam Muhammad Idris-ash-Shafi'i, the founder of an orthodox *Sunni* sect.
Shajjah (Arabic)	Injury to the head or face.
Shalwar (Urdu)	Loose trousers worn by both sexes in India and Pakistan.
Shariat (shariah)	'Path'. Divinely ordined law. Islamic law.
Shia (Arabic)	'Followers'. An Islamic sect that regards Ali (Muhammad's cousin and son in law) and his decendants as the rightful succeessors of Muhammad.
Siddhi	Intoxicant.
Sindhi (Urdu)	Language spoken and written in the province of Sindh and an inhabitant thereof. The province is situated in the south of Pakistan.
Sukoon (Urdu)	Peace of mind.
Sultan	The (male) sovereign of an Islamic country, like the *Sultan* of Turkey. *Sultanate* - the kingdom.
Sum	Type of tree.
Sunna (Arabic)	'Custom'. The tradition of the Prophet Muhammad, including his sayings and deeds.
Sunnat-wal-Jamaat	Muslim sect (includes *Hanafi* and *Baralvi*).
Sunni (Arabic)	One on the path. A large sect of Muslims who, unlike *Shias*, acknowledge the first 4 caliphs as the rightful sucessors of the Prophet Muhammad. They belong to the four schools of jurisprudence founded by *Imam* Abu

	Hanifa, *Imam* Ash-Shafi'i, *Imam* Malik and *Imam* Ahmad Ibn-e-Hanbal.
Talaq (Arabic)	Divorce. Dissolution of marriage contract.
Talaq-al-Ahsan (Arabic)	Single pronouncement of divorce during the period of *tuhr* and abstention from sexual intercourse during her *iddah*. This type of divorce is revocable during *iddah*.
Talaq-al-bidah (Arabic)	Divorce in a single pronouncement.
Talaq-al-Hasan (Arabic)	A procedure of divorce, stretching over three months. There are three pronouncements during three *tuhrs*. Before the third pronouncement divorce is revocable.
Talaq-al-sunnah (Arabic)	A name for *talaq-al-hasan* and *talaq-al-ahsan*.
Talaq-al-tafwid	A form of divorce where the woman exercises the right of divorce delegated to her by the man while signing the marriage contract.
Taghlib (Arabic)	'Imitation'. Strict adherence to legal precedent.
Taqlid (Arabic)	This term is used in Islamic law for following the edicts of a religious leader without due inquiry. It is the opposite of *ijtihad*.
Tazir (Arabic)	To censure or repel. That discretionary power which is administered for offences for which hadd or fixed punishment has been appointed.
Tazkiyah-al-Shuhood (Arabic)	The screening of witnesss to establish their creditability.

Tuhr (Arabic)	When a woman is not menstruating. The period of purity.
Ulema (Arabic pl.) (Alim sing.)	Those who know. Scholars of Islamic religion and law.
Ummayads (Arabic)	A dynasty of rulers who, after the defeat of Ali, occupied the throne of the Arabian Empire.
Ummah (Arabic)	'Nation'. The Universal Islamic community.
Urf	Literally 'what is known' about a thing, and so - loosely - custom (what is commonly known and accepted).
Urs	Marriage cermony or ceremonies observed on the anniversary of the death of any celebrated saint or *murshid* (spiritual guide).
Ushr (Arabic n.)	One-tenth (a tithe) of the yield given to the Islamic state as an agriculture tax.
Ursh (Arabic)	Compensation to be paid by a convict to his victim or victim's heirs for causing hurt.
Usul-al-din	The roots or fundamentals of Islam.
Watta-satta	Exchange marriage.
Waqf (Arabic)	This term signifies the appropriation or dedication of property to charitable usages. The endowment must be in perpetuity. The property can neither be sold nor transferred. A religious trust. (See *auqaf*).
Zahiri	A school of Islam that stresses an entirely literal or explicit interpretation of the *Quran* and the *Sunna*.

Zakat (Arabic)	Islamic income tax. Alms giving, one of the five 'pillars of Islam'.
Zikri	A tribe in the Baluchistan province of Pakistan.
Zina (Arabic)	The offence of illicit sexual relations, i.e., sexual intercourse between persons who are not married to each other. This term includes: adultery, fornication, prostitution, homosexuality etc.
Zina-bil-Jabr (Arabic)	Rape.
Zoga (Urdu)	A lawfully wedded wife.

Table of Abbreviations

APWA   All Pakistan Women Association.
FSC   Federal Shariat Court.
IA   Law Reports, Indian Appeals Series.
IRA   Islamic Research Institute.
MFLO   Muslim Family Laws Ordinance.
NLR   National Law Reporter.
NSLS   Non-State Legal system.
PLD   All Pakistan Legal Decisions.
PNA   Pakistan National Alliance.
PO   President's Order
PPC   Pakistan Penal Code.
RI   Rigorous Imprisonment.
RS   Rupee.
SC   Supreme Court.
SD   Shariat Decision.

Table of Cases

Muhammad Saleem v. The State, NLR 1984 SD 262.
Muhammad Abdullah v. The State, NLR 1987 SD 551.
Muhammad Ayoub Alias Lakhpati v. The State, NLR 1987 SD 170.
Muhammad Nawaz v. The State, PLD 1983 FSC 522.
Muhammad Shafique v. The State, NLR 1984 SD 77.
Muhammad Siddique v. The State, PLD 1983 FSC 173.
M. Mumtaz v. The State, NLR 1984, SD 202.
Mumtaz Khan v. The Government of Pakistan, PLD 1980 Peshawar 154

Nazir Ahmad and others v. The State, PLD 1982 FSC 252.
Nazir Ahmad v. The State, PLD 1986 SC 132 (Shariat Apellate Bench)
Nek Bakhat v. The State, PLD 1986 FSC 174.
Niamat v. The State, PLD 1982 FSC 220.
Nosher Rustam Sidhwa v. The Federation of Pakistan, PLD 1981 FSC
    245.

Pak Muhammad v. The State, PLD 1983 FSC 165.

Qadir Bux v. The State, NLR 1987 SD 274.

Safia Bibi v. The State, PLD 1985 FSC 120.
Safia Bibi v. The State, PLD 1986 SC 132.
Saifur Rehman & another v. The State, PLD 1982 FSC 29.
Shabbir Ahmad v. The State, PLD 1983, FSC 110.
Shah Muhammad v. The State, PLD 1982 FSC 239.
Shahid Ahmad v. The State, NLR 1984 SD 296.
Shahida Parveen and Muhammad Sarwar v. The State, NLR 1988 SC
    188.
Shera v. The State, PLD 1982 FSC 229.
Sheral v. The State, NLR 1984 SD 219.
Suleman v. The State, NLR 1984 SD 241.

The State v. Ghulam Ali, PLD 1982 FSC 259.
The State v. Majid, NLR 1984 SD 274.
The State v. Nazir, PLD 1986 SC (AJ & K).

Umar Badshah v. The State, NLR 1987 SD 377.

Yaseen v. The State, PLD 1983 FSC 53.

Zafar Ali v. The State, PLD 1982 FSC 248.
Zaheer Ahmed v. The Federation of Pakistan, PLD 1982 FSC 244.

Chapter 4

Abdul Rahim v. Shahida Khan, PLD 1984 SC 329.
Abdulla v. Rokeya Khatoon, PLD 1967 Dacca 47.
Akhtar Hussain v. Collector Lahore etc, PLD 1977 Lahore 1173.
Ali Nawaz v. Mohd Yosuf, PLD 1963 SC 51.
Aziz Knan v. Muhammad Zarif, PLD 1982 FSC 156.

Bagh Ali alias Bagh Din v. Almna, PLD 1968 Lahore 1216.
Balquis Fatima v. Najm. Ullkram Qureshi, PLD 1959 Lahore (W.P)
    566.
Bashiran Bibi v. Bashir Ahmed, PLD 1987 Lahore 376.
Basra v. Abdul Hakim, PLD 1986 Quetta 298.

Chuhar v. Ghulam Fatima, PLD 1984 Lahore 234.

Fahmida Bibi v. Mukhtar Ahmad, PLD 1972 Lahore 694.
Federation of Pakistan v. Farishta, PLD 1981 SC 120.

Ghulam Mustafa v. Ghulam Sakina, PLD 1986 Lahore 32.
Ghulam Sakina v. Umar Baksh, PLD 1964 SC 456.
Gul Bibi v. Mohammad Saleem, PLD 1978 Quetta 117.

Habib v. The State, PLD 1980 Lahore. 791.

Inamal Islam v. Hussain Bano, PLD 1976 Lahore 1466.

Kamal Khan v. Zainab, PLD 1983 Lahore 546.
Khurshid Bibi v. Muhammad Amin, PLD 1967 SC 97.

Lal Muhammad v. Gul Bibi, PLD 1986 Quetta 185.

Mai v. Falak Sher, PLD 1986 SC 228.
Maqbool Jan v. Arshad Hussan, PLD 1975 Lahore 147.
Muhammad Akram v. Majeed Begum, PLD 1984 Azad J. & K., 36.
Muhammad Fikree v. Fikree, PLD 1988 Karachi 466.
Muhammad Nawaz v. Khurshid Begum, PLD 1972 SC.
Muhammad Sarwar v. The State, PLD 1988 FSC 42.
Muhammad Yasin v. Rafia Sultana, PLD 1983 Lahore 377.

Nasim Akhtar v. The State, PLD 1968 Lahore 841.
Nishat Ahmad Khan v. Ramlach, 1969 SCMR 118.
Noor Khan v. Haq Nawaz, PLD 1982 FSC 265.

Parveen Begum v. Muhammad Ali, PLD 1981 Lahore 116.
Parveen Chandhry v. Senior Civil Judge, PLD 1976 Karachi 416.

Qamar Raqa v. Tahira Begum, PLD 1988 Karachi 169.

Rashid Ahmad Khan v. Nasim Ara, PLD 1968 Lahore 94.
Rashidan Bibi v. Bashir Ahmad, PLD 1983 Lahore 549.

Sardar Muhammad v. Nasima Bibi, PLD 1966 Lahore. 703.
Sayeeda Khanam v. Muhammad Sami, PLD 1952 Lahore 113.
Shahida & Sarwar v. The State, NLR 188 SC 188.
Shamshad Begum v. Abdul Haque, PLD 1977 Karachi 855.
Siddiq v. Sharfan, PLD 1968 Lahore 411.
Syed Ali Gardezi v. Lt. Col. Muhammad Yusuf, PLD 1963 SC 51.

Zikria Khan v. Aftals Ali Khan, PLD 1985 Lahore 319.
Zulai Khan v. Noor Muhammad, PLD 1986 Quetta 290.

Chapter 5

Abu Dawood Muhammad Sadiq v. The State, Shariat Petition no. 6 of
    1980.
Al-Haj H.I. Sheikh v. Mahmood A. Haroon, Federal Minister,
    Religious Affairs, PLD 1981 SC 334.
Ansar Burney v. Federation of Pakistan, PLD 1983 FSC 73.

Bilal Hussain v. Government of Pakistan, PLD 1981 Peshawar 46.

Essa E.H. Jafar v. Federation of Pakistan, PLD 1982 FSC 212.

Farishta v. Federation of Pakistan, PLD 1980 S.C 160.
Federation of Pakistan v. Hazoor Bukhsh & others, PLD 1983 FSC 255.

Khushbakht-ur-Rehman v. Province of Punjab, PLD 1986 FSC 49.

Mansoor Ali v. Federation of Pakistan, PLD 1981 SC 331.
Mussarat Uzma Usmani & another v. Government of Pakistan, PLD
    1987 Lahore 178.

Qasim Shah v. Government of Pakistan, PLD 1980 Peshwar 239.

Saeedullah Kazim V. Government of Pakistan, PLD 1981 SC 42.
Saeedullah Kazim V. Government of Pakistan, PLD 1981 SC 627.

Appendix I:
Survey Conducted Among Lawyers

A NOTE ON THE FIELD RESEARCH

This survey was carried out in two stages. Firstly, the written questionnaire was distributed in 1990 to lawyers having chambers (always known as Bar Rooms in Pakistan) in the Punjab. Fifty questionnaires were sent out, twenty-six of which were returned in a more or less completed state. In 1991, when I was in Pakistan working on a human rights report, I talked to more than eighty lawyers, sixty-five of whom filled in a questionnaire on human rights. Many of them were the same lawyers who had filled in the first questionnaire and most of the questions in the new questionnaire were the same as the ones in the first questionnaire relating to human rights issues.

The questionnaires were not set out according to strict sociological methods, as the purpose was not to provide a statistical survey but to provoke discussion.

Interviewing the lawyers was very easy as they were very happy to be consulted on various issues. They found the questions very provoking and the discussion would usually last for hours. Sometimes they would gather in groups, either inside or outside the Bar Room. It took very little time to gather them. I would go and sit with one of them and lots of them would gather round. Usually they were open in communication. Communication was in Urdu, as most of the lawyers are not particularly at ease with the English language.

The interesting point was that the lawyers would trust me, especially when they knew that I was also working with a Non-Government Organization, the Rehabilitation and Health Aid Centre for Torture Victims (RAHAT). They were open though some of them of course were careful when speaking about corruption, especially in the higher courts. But they were satisfied that, if desired, their identity could be kept confidential.

CONTENTS OF QUESTIONAIRE

This survey is the part of a research project, conducted by the University of Copenhagen on the nature of the legal system of Pakistan, laying special emphasis on the Islamisation of laws. If desired the identity of the participant will be kept confidential. Thank you very much for your cooperation.

Name
Address

What court do you practice in most/What is your occupation in the legal profession

Do you want your identity to be kept confidential. Yes/No

1. Do you think the law is different for rich and poor? Please give an example.

2. Do you think corruption prevails in the legal system of Pakistan? Give a concrete example of corruption.

3. Give an example of corruption in legal practice which you come across every day and which is not considered as corruption but everyday practice.

4. The prestige of the law in Pakistan today is very much below what it was thirty years ago. With this statement, do you

strongly agree ( ) or agree ( ) or
strongly disagree ( ) or disagree ( )
        or if you don't know, check here ( ).

5. Would you say corruption is increasing? Decreasing?

6. Do you think in general that the law is effective in Pakistan?

7. Is the system better since independence? Has the legal profession improved in quality since independence? Declined? Same? Are courts as good? Worse?

8. Do you think the present legal system works well? Poorly? Needs change? What kind of change? Make it simpler? Less expensive? More Pakistani? More democratic? More Islamic?

9. "The law of the police and courts is not the law of the people". Do you agree with this statement?

10. When people have a problem they don't contact the state legal agencies immediately, the courts are only the last resort. What do you think about this?

11. What is the mode of sorting out disputes in Pakistani villages? How popular is the '*panchayat* system'?

12. Do you feel that many disputes are settled according to local custom contrary to modern law?

13. What do you think of some of the social reform legislation? For example, the legislation concerning dowry and child marriage etc. Is it effective?

14. Most Islamisation of the law was done not for the purpose of its implementation, e.g., *hadd* punishments are impossible to implement because of the high standard of evidence required, the only purpose was to affirm the principles of traditional Islam. Do you agree?

15. Keeping in view the statement that most of the Islamization was done for the purpose of legitimizing power. What part, in your opinion, have lawyers played in it?

16. Please comment on the role of the Bar Councils in politics.

17. Do you think the Islamisation of laws is going to last long? Please give the reason for your answer.

18. Do you think that dissatisfaction with the Islamisation of the laws is due to a wrong procedure or misinterpretation of Islamic laws?

19. Would you support the statement that the judiciary is independent in Pakistan? How?

20. What do you think about the training of lawyers in Pakistan? Is there a big gap between training and practice?

21. The Pakistani legal system does not follow a consistent pattern i.e., it is frequently changed or faces threats of change. Do you agree?

22. Would you call the legal system of Pakistan a stable system?

DETAILED RESULTS OF SURVEY

These are the results of my first survey, conducted among lawyers in Pakistan by means of a written questionnaire in 1989-90. All the lawyers were from the province of the Punjab. The twenty-six respondents were picked at random.

The main object of the survey was to gather the general opinion of lawyers concerning legal pluralism, ineffectivity and corruption in the legal profession. As such, the survey should not be taken as representative but only shows a general trend of thinking among lawyers. This is important as the different issues are looked at from the viewpoint of advocates working in courts of differing levels in Pakistan.

Occupation in Legal Profession
Nine lawyers practised in the High Court. One barrister at law practised in the Supreme Court and Federal *Shariat* Court. Sixteen practised in lower courts like the District Court and Sessions Court etc. All of them took both civil and criminal cases, one specialised in family law and one in constitutional law.

Identity
Sixteen wanted their identity to be confidential. Ten said their names and addresses need not be confidential.

Laws different for rich and poor
Twenty lawyers replied that this statement was correct although some of them modified it to say that the laws were fair but their implementation was discriminatory. One lawyer working in the High Court said that it was rare for a rich person to be involved in a *hudood* case though they often indulged in this type of illegality. Another, again a High Court lawyer, said the same, commenting, 'I have never seen one case of drinking liquor or a case under the *zina* Ordinance where a rich person is involved, while the majority of rich persons commit this crime'. One who also conducted High Court cases said that the law is applied discriminatorily because of favouritism, recommendations, bribery and other modes of corruption. One practicing in the District Court said an accused person or party in a civil case may have to fight a case for more than twenty years, which a poor person could not afford. One said that rich persons had ample resources to affect the judge's opinion. One advocate from the District Court, Islamabad, said that the law enforcment authorities did not apprehend rich people while poor people were always being dragged to the police station and made to appear in court. One District and

High Court advocate stated that the rich generally purchased the law through influence. One said that this statement was partially correct, while five maintained that the law was no different for rich and poor.

Corruption
Fifteen said straight out that corruption prevailed in the legal system of Pakistan. A lawyer practising in the High Court and lower courts said that there was no more than one in a million judges who was not involved in corruption. One said that, due to corruption, persons with financial resources or high status could do as they liked and force others to do likewise. One said that notorious drug smugglers could be easily granted bail because of corruption. One gave the example that it was difficult to even get a copy of a judgement without bribing the clerks of the Copying Agency. Moreover, bail could be gained through bribery. Two said no, corruption did not exist but in answer to the next question gave an example of corruption. Two said that corruption did simply not exist. Three said that it existed to some degree. One said that corruption was prevalent at the lower level. One said that corruption was intermittent. Two said that it was mostly the police department that was corrupt.

Examples of corruption
One gave the example of bribes taken by state attorneys in the lower courts saying that this was a daily practice. Another one said that the filing of cases, getting cases fixed for hearing and obtaining copies of court orders or inspection of the files were matters which did not proceed without bribery. One said that bribery was taken as a right, and was therefore not even considered corruption. The Clerk of the Court would always take money to find a suitable date for a case and or to issue bail bonds. A fresh suit could not be filed without paying money. The daily work could not be accelerated without making special payments to the staff. One lawyer said that if a person could pay he could easily find witnesses, though he did not explain this statement. Another said that 'Gratification from the litigants as well as from the advocates of the courts to minions has been the order of the day without let and hindrance'.

Corruption increasing
Twenty-three said corruption was increasing, three said it was decreasing.

Prestige of law lower than thirty years ago
Eleven very much agreed, eight agreed to some extent, three strongly disagreed, four disagreed to some extent.

Effectiveness of the law

Fourteen said the law was not effective, but all meant it differently. One said that the reason the law was not effective was that people with resources could purchase the law and even the lawmakers. Another said, "Either 'money makes the mare go' or 'might is right'." One blamed the men in power. One said that some laws were defective such as family laws and the *Hudood* Ordinance, and this was the reason for the law's ineffectiveness. Poor people could not easily claim their rights because of procedure and corruption. One said that the law in general was effective for those who respected it. The law in general was effective but not for the law enforcment agencies. One lawyer said that the law was ineffective because most of the laws were made a hundred years ago. Two said that they were partially effective. One said that if any influential person was behind it, the law was effective, otherwise not. Nine said they were effective.

Quality of legal profession improved since 1947

Fifteen said it had declined, eleven said it had improved.

Legal system works well

Eight said that it worked poorly. All agreed that it needed change. In answer to what type of change, twenty-two said that it should be simplified, sixteen that it should be less expensive, ten that it should be more Pakistani, twelve more democratic and fourteen more Islamic. One added that socio-economic change was necessary.

The law of the police and courts is not the law of the people

Twenty-one lawyers agreed with this statement. One commented that the legal system has lost its credibility. Most of them blamed the police. One said that the law of the police was not the law of the people, the police only tortured peace-loving citizens. One said that in an underdeveloped country like Pakistan the police and courts should be strengthened, otherwise the law of the jungle would prevail. One said that the law was directed by the police and the courts as they wanted. Another opinion was that all murders, acts of corruption and thefts were committed due to the negligence of the police. Therefore he suggested that more qualified persons were required. The law was under the pressure of influential personalities. The police have unlimited powers in Pakistan. One lawyer opined that laws are not made according to the true demands of the people. Another said that ordinary people cannot get justice. One especially stressed the negative role played by the police. One said that the above statement was only partially true, five said that it was not correct.

Courts are only last resort
Twenty said yes, one explained that people do not go to court because they do not trust the state courts. Six said that people do go to court to resolve their disputes.

Panchayat system
Eighteen said the *panchayat* system was used, although two of them said that it existed but did not fulfil the requirements of justice. Two said they were popular only for small disputes. Six denied the existence of such a system.

Settlement of disputes according to local custom
Fourteen said yes, two said yes, to some extent, eight said no. Two accepted the existence of such custom in tribal areas and the interior of Sind. Four disagreed with the statement that such customs are contrary to modern law.

Social reform through legislation
Seventeen said that the statutes were not effective. Two said they were effective to some extent, two said they were effective. Two said that their effectiveness had to be improved, one said reform legislation needed to be changed, one said that social reform legislation, although not effective, was necessary. Two misunderstood the question. Four said that social reforms by means of legislation were effective.

Hudood Punishments symbolic
Fifteen agreed that *hudood* punishments were symbolic, eleven said that *hudood* punishments were not symbolic but real, three said that Islamization had not been properly carried out or had not been implemented in its true sprit, and that this was the reason that *hudood* punishments looked symbolic.

Lawyers supported Islamization
Eight lawyers said that lawyers had opposed Islamization, expressed their dissatisfaction with it and had played a positive role in combating it. Five appreciated the role of women, six said that lawyers were helpless, seven said that lawyers had not played the significant role they could have played.

Role of the Bar Councils
Twenty said that the Bar Councils played a positive role in the struggle for democracy in Pakistan, a few even said that politics could not grow without Bar Councils. Six said that the Bar councils had not played any special role and they should not indulge in politics.

Would Islamization last long

Twelve said it would not last long. Twelve said it would. One strongly supported Islamization and said Islamic laws should be implemented, one said that if the government were sincere Islamization would last long.

Why was Islamization unsuccessful?

Because of wrong procedure or misinterpretation of Islamic law? Eight said that Islamization was unsuccessful for both reasons, five maintained its failure was due to the wrong procedure. Thirteen said that Islamization had failed due to the misinterpretation of Islamic law. Two said that the persons implementing Islamic laws were not sincere, five said it was because fundamentalism had become divorced from modernity and the interpretation of the law had become non-progressive. One said that its failure was due to a mixture of European and Islamic law, three misunderstood the question, one claimed that it was due to a higher standard of evidence and one did not reply.

Independence of Judiciary

Nineteen said that the judiciary was not independent, four said it was partially independent. However, three said that the judiciary in Pakistan was independent. Four explained that the judiciary was independent only at a higher level, i.e., above magistrate court or, in other words, only High Courts are independent. One maintained that the judiciary had only been independent in the democratic period.

Legal training

Twenty-two said that the standard of legal training was low in Pakistan and there was a big gap between theory and practice, and it needed improvement. Four said that legal training was satisfactory in Pakistan. One said that there was a gap between training and practice all over the world and Pakistan was no exception.

Inconsistency

Seventeen agreed that the legal system did not follow a consistent pattern. One said that this was because there was no permanent policy-making institution. Nine disagreed.

Instability

Twelve said straight out that the legal system of Pakistan was a stable system. Two said yes to some extent. Twelve said that it was not stable, one said it would not be stable until all the laws were Islamized. One said it had a certain degree of stability and one said there was a need to stabilise it.

SUMMARY OF RESULTS OF FIRST SURVEY

Confidential: 16 of the lawyers (i.e. more than half) wanted their identity to be confidential.

Laws different for rich and poor: 21 Yes: 5 No.

Corruption: 24 Yes: 2 No.

Forms of Corruption: Bribery

Prestige of law declined: 19 Yes: 7 No.

Corruption increasing: 23 Yes: 3 No.

Ineffectivity of laws: 17 Yes: 9 No.

Quality of legal profession improved since 1947: 11 Yes; 15 No.

Legal system works well: 8 No: 18 Yes. All agreed that it needed change.

Law of the police and courts is not the law of people: 21 Yes: 5 No.

Courts only last resort: 20 Yes: 6 No.

Existence of *Panchayat* system: 20 Yes: 6 No.

Dispute settled in accordance with local customs: 18 Yes: 8 No.

Effectivity of social reforms legislations: 4 Yes: 22 No.

Hudood Punishments symbolic: 15 Yes: 11 No.

Lawyers supported Islamization: 13 Yes: 13 No.

Role of Bar Councils in struggle for democracy: 20 Yes. 6 No.

Would Islamization last long: 12 Yes: 14 No.

Failure of Islamization due to misinterpretation or wrong procedure of Islamic law: 8 both: 5 wrong procedure: 13 misinterpretation.

Is Judiciary independent? 7 Yes: 19 No.

Is legal training good? 4 Yes: 22 No.

Inconsistency: 17 Yes: 9 No.

Instability: 14 Yes: 12 No.

Appendix II:
Text of the *Qisas & Diyat* Ordinance, 1990 and the Criminal Law (2nd Amendment) Ordinance, 1990

The Criminal Law Second Amendment) Ordinance 1990

THE CRIMINAL LAW (SECOND AMENDMENT) ORDINANCE, 1990
Ordinance No VII OF 1990

Gazette of Pakistan Extraordinary dated 5-9-1990

AN ORDINANCE

further to amend the Pakistan Penal Code and the Code of Criminal Procedure, 1898.

No F, 2(2)/90-Pub.—The following Ordinance made by the President on 5th September, 1990 is hereby published for general information:—

WHEREAS it is expedient further to amend the Pakistan Penal Code (Act XLV of 1860), and the Code of Criminal Procedure 1898 (Act V of 1898), to bring them in conformity with the Injunctions of Islam as laid down in the Holy Quran and Sunnah,

AND WHEREAS the National Assembly is not in session and the President is satisfied that circumstances exist which render it necessary to take immediate action:

NOW THEREFORE in exercise of the powers conferred by clause (1) of Article 89 of the Constitution of the Islamic Republic of Pakistan, the President is pleased to make and promulgate the following Ordinance:—

1.   *Short title and commencement.*—(1) This Ordinance may be called the Criminal Law (Second Amendment) Ordinance, 1990

(2) It shall come into force on the twelfth day of *Rabi-ul-Awwal*, 1411 *Hijri*.

2.   *Substitution of section 53, Act XLV of* 1860—In the Pakistan Penal Code (Act XLV of 1860), hereinafter referred to as the said Code, for section 53 the following shall be substituted, namely:—

"53. Punishments.—The punishments to which offenders are liable under the provisions of this Code are:—

Firstly,	Qisas;
Secondly,	Tazir;
Thirdly,	Diyat;
Fourthly,	Arsh;
Fifthly,	Daman;

Sixthly,	Death;
Seventhly,	Imprisonment for life;
Eighthly,	Imprisonment which is of two descriptions, namely:—
	(i) Rigorous *i.e.* with hard labour;
	(ii) Simple;
Ninthly,	Forfeiture of property;
Tenthly,	Fine".

3.   *Amendment of section 109, Act XLV of 1860*—In the said Code, in section 109 for the full stop a the end a colon shall be substituted and thereafter the following proviso shall be added, namely:

"Provided that, except in case of *Ikrah-i-Tam* the abettor of an offence referred to in Chapter XVI shall be liable to punishment of *ta'zir* specified for such offence including death".

4   *Substitution of sections 299 to 338, Act XLV of 1860.*—(1) In the said Code, for sections 299 to 338 the following be substituted namely:—

"299. *Definitions.*—In this Chapter, unless there is anything repugnant in the subject or context—

(a)   "adult" means a person who has attained, being a male, the age of eighteen years, or being a female, the age of sixteen years or has attained puberty, whichever is earlier;

(b)   "*arsh*" means the compensation specified in this Chapter to be paid by the offender to the victim or his heirs;

(c)   "authorised medical officer" means a medical officer or a Medical Board, however designated, authorised by the Provincial Government;

(d)   "*daman*" means the compensation determined by the court to be paid by the offender to the victim for causing hurt not liable to *arsh*;

(e)   "*diyat*" means the compensation specified in section 323 payable to the heirs of the victim by the offender;

(f)   "Government" means the Provincial Government;

(g)   "*ikrah-e-tam*" means putting any person, his spouse or any of his blood relations within the prohibited degree of marriage in fear of instant death or instant permanent impairing of any organ of the body or instant fear of being subjected to sodomy or *zina-bil-jabr*;

(h)   "*ikrah-e-naqis*" means any from of duress which does not amount to *Ikrah-i-tam*;

(i)   "minor" means a person who is not an adult;

(j)   "*qatl*" means causing death of a person;

(k)   "*ta'zir*" means punishment other than *qisas*, *diyat*, *arsh* or *daman*; and

(l)   "*wali*" means a person entitled to claim *qisas*.

300.   *Qatl-i-amd.* Whoever, with the intention of causing death or with the intention of causing bodily injury to a person, by doing an act which in the ordinary course of nature is likely lo cause death, or with the knowledge that his act is so imminently dangerous that it must in all probability cause death, causes the death of such person, is said to commit *qatl-i-amd.*

301.   *Causing death of person other than the person whose death was intended.*— Where a person, by doing anything which he intends or knows to be likely to cause death, causes death of any person whose death he neither intends nor knows himself to be likely to cause, such an act committed by the offender shall be liable for *qatl-i-amd.*

302. *Punishment of qatl-i-amd.*—Whoever commits *qatl-i-amd* shall, subject to the provisions of this Chapter be—

    (a)   punished with death as *qisas*;

    (b)   punished with death or imprisonment for life as *ta'zir* having regard to the facts and circumstances of the case, if the proof in either of the forms specified in section 304 is not available; or

    (c)   punished with imprisonment of either description for a term which may extend to twenty-five years, where according to the Injunctions of Islam the punishment of *qisas* is not applicable.

303. *Qatl committed under ikrah-i-tam' or ikrah-i-naqis.*—Whoever commits *qatl.*—

    (a)   under *ikrah-i-tam* shall be punished with imprisonment for a term which may extend to twenty-five years but shall not be less than ten years and the person causing *ikrah-i-tam* shall be punished for the kind of qatl committed as a consequence of his *ikrah-i-tam*; or

    (b)   under *ikrah-i-naqi* shall be punished for the kind of *qatl* committed by him and the person causing *ikrah-i-naqis* shall be punished with imprisonment for a term which may extend to ten years.

304. *Proof of qatl-i-amd liable to qisas, etc*—(1) Proof of *qatl-i-amd* liable to *qisas* shall be in any of the following forms, namely:—

    (a)   the accused makes before a court competent to try the offence a voluntary and true confession of the commission of the offence; or

    (b)   by the evidence as provided in Article 17 of the Qanun-e-Shahadat, 1984 (P.O. No. 10 of 1984).

    (2)   The provisions of sub-section (1) shall, *mutatis mutandis*, apply to a hurt liable to *qisas*

305. *Wali*—In case of a *qatl*, the *wali* shall be—

    (a)   the heirs of the victim, according to his personal law; and
    (b)   the Government, if there is no heir.

306. *Qatl-i-amd not liable to qisas.*—*Qatl-i-amd* shall not be liable to *qisas* in the following cases, namely:—

    (a)   when an offender is a minor or insane:
        Provided that, where a person liable to *qisas* associates with himself in the commission of the offence a person not liable to *qisas* with the intention of saving himself from *qisas*, he shall not be exempted from *qisas*;

    (b)   when an offender causes death of his child or grandchild, how low-so-ever; and

    (c)   when any *wali* of the victim is a direct descendant, how low-so-ever, of the offender.

307. *Cases in which qisas for qatl-i-amd shall not be enforced.*—*Qisas* for *qatl-i-amd* shall not be enforced in the following cases, namely:-

(a) when the offender dies before the enforcement of *qisas*;

(b) when any *wali*, voluntarily and without duress, to the satisfaction of the court, waives the right of *qisas* under section 309 or compounds under section 310; and

(c) when the right of *qisas* devolves on the offender as a result of the death of the *wali* of the victim, or on the person who has no right of *qisas* against the offender.

Illustrations

(i) A kills Z the maternal uncle of his son B Z has no other *wali* except D the wife of A D has the right of *qisas* from A. But if D dies, the right of *qisas* shall devolve on her son B who is also the son of the offender A B cannot claim *qisas* against his father. Therefore the *qisas* cannot be enforced.

(ii) B kills Z, the brother of her husband A Z has no heir except A. Here A can claim *qisas* from his wife B. But if A dies, the right of *qisas* shall devolve on his son D who is also son of B, the *qisas* cannot be enforced against B.

308. *Punishment in qatl-i-amd not liable to qisas etc.*—(1) Where an offender guilty of *qatl-i-amd* is not liable to *qisas* under section 306 or the *qisas* is not enforceable under clause (c) of section 307, he shall be liable to *diyat:*

Provided that, where the offender is minor or insane, *diyat* shall be payable either from his property or, by such person as may be determined by the court.

Provided further that where at the time of committing *qatl-i-amd* the offender being a minor, had attained sufficient maturity or being insane, had a lucid interval, so as to be able to realise the consequences of his act, he may also be punished with imprisonment of either description or a term which may extend to fourteen years as *ta' zir:*

Provided further that where the *qisas* is not enforceable under clause (3) of section 307, the offender shall be liable to *diyat* only if there is any *wali* other than offender and if there is no *wali* other than the offender, he shall be punished with imprisonment of either description for a term which may extend to fourteen years as *ta' zir.*

(2) Notwithstanding anything contained in sub-section (1), the court having regard to the fact and circumstance of the case in addition to the punishment of *diyat*, may punish the offender with imprisonment of either description for a term which may extend to fourteen years, as *ta' zir.*

309. *Waiver-Afw of qisas in qatl-i-amd.*—(1) In the case of *Qatl-i-amd* an adult sane *wali* may, at any time and without any compensation, waive his right of *qisas:*

Provided that the right of *qisas* shall not be waived—

(a)   where the Government is the *wali*; or
(b)   where the right of *qisas* vests in a minor or insane.

(2)   Where a victim has more than one *wali*, any one of them may waive his right of *qisas*.
Provided that the *wali* who does not waive the right of *qisas* shall be entitled to his share of *diyat*.

(3)   Where there are more than one victim, the waiver of the right of *qisas* by the *wali* of one victim shall not affect the right of *qisas* of the *wali* of the other victim

(4)   Where there are more than one offenders, the waiver of the right of *qisas* against one offender shall not affect the right of *qisas* against the other offender.

310.   *Compounding of qisas (Sulh) in qatl-i-amd*—(1) In the case of *qatl-i-amd*, an adult sane *wali* may, at any time on accepting *badal-i-sulh*, compound his right of *qisas*:
Provided that only giving a female in marriage shall not be a valid *badal-i-sulh*.

(2)   Where a *wali* is a minor or an insane, the *wali* of such minor or insane *wali* may compound the right of *qisas* on behalf of such minor or insane *wali*:
Provided that the value of badal-i-sulh shall not be less than the value of *diyat*.

(3)   Where the Government is the *wali*, it may compound the right of *qisas*:
Provided that the value of badal-i-sulh shall not be less than the value of *diyat*.

(4)   Where the *badal-i-sulh* is not determined or is a property or a right the value of which cannot be determined in terms of money under *Shari'ah* the right of *qisas*, shall be deemed to have been compounded and the offender shall be liable to *diyat*.

(5)   *Badal-i-sulh* may be paid or given on demand or on deferred date as may be agreed upon between the offender and the *wali*.
Explanation.—In this section *Badal-i-sulh* means the mutually agreed compensation according to *Shari'ah* to be paid or given by the offender to a *wali* in cash or in kind or in the form of movable or immovable property.

311.   *Ta'zir after waiver or compounding of right of qisas in qatl-i-amd*—notwithstanding anything contained in section 309 or section 310 the court may, in its discretion having regard to the facts and circumstances of the case, punish an offender against whom the right of *qisas* has been waived or compounded with imprisonment of either description for a term which may extend to ten years as *ta'zir*.
Provided that the court may punish an offender who is a previous convict, habitual or professional criminal with imprisonment of either description for a term which may extend to fourteen years as *ta'zir*.

312. *Qatl-i-amd after waiver or compounding of qisas.*—Where a *wali* commits *qatl-i-amd* of a convict against whom the right of *qisas* has been waived under section 309 or compounded under section 310 such *wali* shall be punished with—

    (a)   *qisas*, if he had himself waived or compounded the right of *qisas* against the convict or had knowledge of such waiver or composition by another *wali*; or

    (b)   *diyat*, if he had no knowledge of such waiver or composition.

313. *Right of qisas in qatl-i-amd*—(1) Where there is only one *wali*, he alone has the right of *qisas* in *qatl-i-amd* but, if there are more than one, the right of *qisas* vests in each of them.

    (2)   If the victim—

        (a)   has no *wali* the Government shall have the right of *qisas*; or

        (b)   has no *wali* other than a minor or insane or one of the *wali* is a minor or insane, the father or if he is not alive the paternal grandfather of such *wali* shall have the right of *qisas* on his behalf:
        Provided that, if the minor or insane *wali* has no father or paternal grandfather, how high-so-ever, alive and no guardian has been appointed by the court, the Government shall have the right of *qisas* on his behalf.

314. *Execution of qisas in qatl-i-amd*—(1) *Qisas* in *qatl-i-amd* shall be executed by a functionary of the Government by causing death of the convict as the court may direct.

    (2)   *Qisas* shall not be executed until all the *wali* are present at the time of execution, either personally or through their representatives authorised by them in writing in this behalf;
    Provided that where a *wali* or his representative fails to present himself on the date, time and place execution of *qisas* after having been informed or the date, time and place as certified by the court, an officer authorised by the Court shall give permission for the execution of *qisas* and the Government shall cause execution of *qisas* in the absence of such *wali*.

    (3)   If the convict is a woman who is pregnant, the court may, in consultation with an authorised medical officer, postpone the execution of *qisas* up to a period of two years after the birth of the child and during this period she may be released on bail on furnishing of security to the satisfaction of the court or, if she is not so released she shall be dealt with as if sentenced to simple imprisonment.

315. *Qatl shibh-i-amd*—Whoever, with intent to cause harm to the body or mind of any person causes the death of that or of any other person by means of a weapon or an act which in the ordinary nurse of nature is not likely to cause death is said to commit *qatl shibh-i-amd*.

Illustration

A in order to cause hurt strikes Z with a stick or stone which in the ordinary course of nature is not likely to cause death, Z dies as a result of such hurt. A shall be guilty of *qatl shibh-i-amd*.

316.   *Punishment for qatl shibh-i-amd.*—Whoever commits *qatl shibh-i-amd* shall be liable to *diyat* and may also be punished with imprisonment of either description for a term which may extend to fourteen years as *ta'zir*

317.   *Person committing qatl debarred from succession.*—Where a person committing *qatl-i-amd* or *qatl shibh-i-amd* is an heir or a beneficiary under a will, he shall be debarred from succeeding to the estate of the victim as an heir or a beneficiary.

318.   *Qatl-i-khata*—Whoever, without any intention to cause the death of, or cause harm to, a person, causes death of such person, either by mistake of act or by mistake of fact, is said to commit *qatl-i-khata*.

Illustration

(a)   A aims at a deer but misses the target and kills Z who is standing by. A is guilty of *qatl-i-khata*.

(b)   A shoots at an object to be a boar but it turns out to be a human being. A is guilty of *qatl-i-khata*.

319.   *Punishment for qatl-i-khata.*—Whoever commits *qatl-i-khata* shall be liable to *diyat*.
       Provided that where *qatl-i-khata* is committed by any rash or negligent act, other than rash or negligent driving, the offender may, in addition to *diyat*, also be punished with imprisonment of either description for a term which may extend to five years as ta'zir.

320.   *Punishment for qatl-i-khata by rash or negligent driving.*—Whoever commits *qatl-i-khata* by rash or negligent driving shall, having regard to the facts and circumstances of the case, in addition to *diyat*, be punished with imprisonment of either description for term which may extend to ten years.

321.   *Qatl-i-sabab*—Whoever, without any intention to cause death of, or cause harm to, any person, does any unlawful act which become a cause for the death of another person, is said to commit *qatl-bis-sabab*.

Illustration

A unlawfully digs a pit in the thoroughfare, but without any intention to cause the death of, or harm to, any person. B while passing from there falls in it and is killed. A has committed *qatl-bis-sabab*.

322.   *Punishment for qatl-bis-sabab.*—Whoever commits *qatl-bis-sabab* shall be liable to *diyat*.

323.   *Value of diyat* —(1) The court shall, subject to the Injunction of Islam as laid down in the Holy *Qur'an and Sunnah* and keeping in view the financial position of the convict and the heirs of the victim fix the value of *diyat* which shall not be less than one hundred seventy thousand and six hundred and ten rupees being the value of 30,630 grams of silver.

(2)   For the purposes of sub-section (1) the Federal Government shall, by notification in the official Gazette, declare the value of silver on the first day of July each year

324. *Attempt to commit qatl-i-amd.*—Whoever does any act with such intention or knowledge, and under such circumstances that, if he by that act caused *qatl*, he would be guilty of *qatl-i-amd*, shall be punished with imprisonment or either description for a term which may extend to ten years, and shall also be liable to fine, and, if hurt is caused to any person by such act, the offender shall be liable to the punishment provided for the hurt caused:

Provided that, where the punishment for the hurt is *qisas* which is not executable, the offender shall be liable to *arsh* and may also be punished with imprisonment of either description for a term which may extend to seven years.

325. *Attempt to commit suicide.*—Whoever attempts to commit suicide and does any act towards the commission of such offence, shall be punished with simple imprisonment for a term which may extend to one year, or with fine, or with both.

326. *Thug.*—Whoever shall have been habitually associated with any other or others for the purpose of committing robbery or child-stealing by means of or accompanied with *qatl*, is a thug.

327. *Punishment.*—Whoever is a thug, shall be punished with imprisonment for life, and shall also be liable to fine.

328. *Exposure and abandonment of child under twelve years by parent or person having care of it.*— Whoever being the father or mother of a child under the age of twelve years, or having the care of such child, shall expose or leave such child in any place with the intention of wholly abandoning such child, shall be punished with imprisonment of either description for a term which may extend to seven years, or with fine, or with both.

Explanation.—This section is not intended to prevent the trial of the offender for *qatl-i-amd* or *qatl-i-shibh-i-amd* or *qatl-bis-sabab*, as the case may be, if the child dies in consequence of the exposure.

329. Concealment of birth by secret disposal of dead body.—Whoever, by secretly burying or otherwise disposing of the dead body of a child whether such child dies before or after or during its birth, intentionally conceals or endeavours to conceal the birth of such child, shall be punished with imprisonment of either description for a term which may extend to two years, or with fine, or with both.

330. Disbursement of *diyat*.—The *diyat* shall be disbursed among the heirs of the victim according to their respective shares in inheritance:

Provided that, where an heir forgoes his share, the *diyat* shall not be recovered to the extent of his share.

331. Payment of *diyat*.—(1) The *diyat* may be made payable in lump sum or in installments spread over a period of three years from the date of the final judgment.

   (2)   Where a convict fails to pay *diyat* or any part thereof within the period specified in sub-section (1) the convict may be kept in jail and dealt with in the same manner as if sentenced to simple imprisonment until the *diyat* is paid full or may be released on bail if he furnishes security equivalent to the amount of *diyat* to the satisfaction of the court.

(3)   Where a convict dies before the payment of *diyat* or any part thereof, it shall be recovered from his estate.

332.   Hurt—(1) Whoever causes pain, harm, disease, infirmity or injury to any person or impairs, disables or dismembers any organ of the body or part thereof of any person without causing his death, is said to cause hurt.

(2)   The following are the kinds of hurt :—

(a)   *Itlaf-i-udw*
(b)   *itlaf-i-salahiyyat-i-udw*
(c)   *shajjah*
(d)   *jurh*; and
(e)   all kinds of other hurts.

333.   Itlaf-i-udw.—Whoever dismembers, amputates, severs any limb or organ of the body of another person is said to cause itlaf-i-udw.

334.   *Punishment for itlaf-i-udw.*—Whoever by doing any act with the intention of thereby causing hurt to any person, or with the knowledge that he is likely thereby to cause hurt to any person causes *itlaf -i-udw* of any person, shall, in consultation with the authorised medical officer,be punished with *qisas* and if the *qisas* is not executable keeping in view the principles of equality in accordance with the Injunctions of Islam, the offender shall be liable to *arsh* and may also be punished with imprisonment of either description for a term which may extend ten years as *ta'zir.*

335.   *Itlaf-i-salahiyyat-i-udw.*—Whoever destroys or permanently impairs the functioning, power or capacity of an organ of the body of another person, or causes permanent disfigurement is said to cause *itlaf-i-salahiyyat-i-udw.*

336.   *Punishment for itlaf-i-salahiyyat-i-udw.*—Whoever, by doing any act with the intention of causing hurt to any person, or with the knowledge that he is likely to cause hurt to any person, cause *itlaf-i-salahiyyat-i-udw*, of any person, shall, in consultation with the authorised medical officer, be punished with *qisas* and if the *qisas* is not executable keeping in view the principles of equality in accordance with the Injunction of Islam, the offender shall be liable to *arsh* and may also be punished with imprisonment or either description for a term which may extend to ten years as *ta'zir*

337.   *Shajjah.*—(1) Whoever causes, on the head or face of any person, any hurt which does not amount to itlaf-i-udw or *itlaf-i-salahiyyat-i-udw*, is said to cause *shajjah*

(2)   The following are the kinds of shajjah namely
(a)   *Shajjah-i-Khafifah*
(b)   *Shajjah-i-mudihaa*
(c)   *Shajjah-i-hashimah*
(d)   *Shajjah-i-munaqqilah*
(e)   *Shajjah-i-ammab*
(f)   *Shajjah-i-damighah*

(3)   Whoever causes shajjah

(i)   without exposing bone of the victim, is said to cause *shajjah-i-khafifah*;

(ii) by exposing any bone of the victim without causing fracture, is said to cause *shajjah-i-mudihah*;

(iii) by fracturing the bone of the victim without dislocating it, is said to cause *shajjah-i-hashimah*;

(iv) by causing fracture of the bone of the victim and thereby bone is dislocated, is said to cause *shajjalh-i-munaqqilah*;

(v) by causing fracture of the skull of the victim so that the wound touches the membrane of the brain, is said to cause *shajjah-i-ammah*; and

(vi) by causing fracture of the skull of the victim and the wound ruptures the membrane of the brain is said to cause *shajjah-i-damighah*.

337-A. *Punishment of shajjah*—Whoever, by doing any act with the intention of thereby causing hurt to any person or with the knowledge that he is likely thereby to cause hurt to any person, causes—

(i) *Shajjah-i-khafifah* to any person, shall be liable to *daman* and may also be punished with imprisonment of either description for a term which may extend to two years as *ta'zir*:

(ii) *shajjah-i-mudihah* to any person, shall, in consultation with the authorised medical officer, be punished with *qisas* and if the *qisas* is not executable keeping in view the principles of equality in accordance with the Injunctions of Islam, the convict shall be liable to *arsh* which shall be five per cent of the *diyat* and may also be punished with imprisonment of either description for a term which may extend to five years as *ta'zir*.

(iii) *shajjak-i-hashimah* to any person shall be liable to *arsh* which shall be ten per cent of the *diyat* and may also be punished with imprisonment of either description for a term which may extend to seven years as *ta'zir*;

(iv) *shajjah-i-munaqqilah* to any person, shall be liable to *arsh* which shall be fifteen per cent of the *diyat* and may also be punished with imprisonment of either description for a term which may extend to ten years as *ta'zir*;

(v) *shajjah-i-ammah* to any person, shall be liable to *arsh* which shall be one-third of the *diyat* and may also be punished with imprisonment of either description for a term which may extend to ten years as *ta'zir*: and

(vi) *shajjah-i-damighah* to any person, shall be liable to *arsh* which shall be one-half of *diyat* and may also be punished with imprisonment of either description for a term which may extend to fourteen years as *ta'zir*.

337-B. *Jurh.*—(1) Whoever causes on any part of the body of a person, other than the head or face, a hurt which leaves a mark of the wound, whether temporary or permanent, is said to cause *jurh*.

(2)   *Jurh* is of two kinds, namely:—
    (a)   *Jaifah*; and
    (b)   *Ghayr-Jaifah.*

337-C. *Jaifah.*—Whoever causes jurh in which the injury extends to the body cavity of the trunk, is said to cause *jaifah*

337-D. *Punishment for jaifah.*—Whoever by doing any act with the intention of causing hurt to a person, or with the knowledge that he is likely to cause hurt to such person, causes *jaifah* to such person, shall be liable to *arsh* which shall be one-third of the *diyat* and may also be punished with imprisonment of either description for a term which may extend to ten years as *ta'zir.*

337-E. *Ghayr-jaifalh*—(1) Whoever causes *jurh* which does not amount to *jaifah* is said to cause *ghayr-jaifah.*

    (2)   The following are the kinds of *ghayr-jaifah*, namely:—
        (a)   *Damiyah*
        (b)   *badi' ah*
        (c)   *mutalahimah*
        (d)   *mudihah*
        (e)   *hashimah*
        (f)   *munaqqilah*

    (3)   Whoever causes *ghayr-jaifah*—

        (i)   in which the skin is ruptured and bleeding occurs, is said to cause *damiyah*

        (ii)   by cutting or incising the flesh without exposing the bone, is said to cause *badi' ah*;

        (iii)   by lacerating the flesh, is said to cause *mutalahimah.*

        (iv)   by exposing the bone is said to cause *mudihah*;

        (v)   by causing fractures of a bone without dislocating it, is said to cause *hashimah*; and

        (vi)   by fracturing and dislocating the bone, is said to cause *munaqqilah*

337-F. *Punishnent of ghayr-jaifah*—Whoever by doing any act with the intention of causing hurt to any person, or with the knowledge that he is likely to cause hurt to any person causes—

        (i)   *damiyah* to any person, shall be liable to *daman* and may also be punished with imprisonment of either description for a term which may extend to one year as *ta'zir*;

        (ii)   *badi' ah* to any person, shall be liable to *daman* and may also be punished with imprisonment of either description for a term which may extend to three years as *ta'zir*;

        (iii)   *mutalakimah* to any person, shall be liable to *daman* and may also be punished with imprisonment of either description for a term which may extend to three years as *ta'zir*;

(iv)   *mudihah* to any person, shall be liable to *daman* and may also be punished with imprisonment of either description for a term which may extend to five years as *ta'zir*;

(v)   *hashimah* to any person, shall be liable to *daman* and may also be punished with the imprisonment of either description for a term which may extend to five years; and

(vi)   *munaqqilah* to any person, shall be liable to *daman* and may also be punished with imprisonment of either description for a term which may extend to seven years as *ta'zir*;

337-G. *Punishment for hurt by rash or negligent driving.*—Whoever causes hurt by negligent driving shall be liable to the *arsh* or *daman* specified for the kind of hurt caused and may also be punished with imprisonment of either description for a term which may extend of five years as *ta'zir*.

337 H. *Punishment for hurt by rash or negligent act.*—Whoever causes hurt by rash or negligent act other than rash or negligent driving shall be liable to the *arsh* or *daman* specified for the kind of hurt caused and may also be punished with imprisonment of either description for a term which may extend to three years as *ta'zir*.

337-I. *Punishment for causing hurt by mistake (Khata).*—Whoever causes hurt by mistake (*Khata*) shall be liable to *arsh* or *daman* specified for the kind of hurt caused.

337-J. *Causing hurt by means of a poison.*—Whoever administers to or causes to be taken by any person, any poison or any stupefying intoxicating or unwholesome drug or such other thing with intent to cause hurt to such person or with intent to commit or to facilitate the commission of an offence or knowing it to be likely that he will thereby cause hurt may, in addition to the punishment of *arsh* or *daman* provided for the kind of hurt caused, be also punished having regard to the nature of the hurt caused, with imprisonment of either description for a term which may extend to ten years.

337-K. *Causing hurt to extort confession or to compel restoration of property.*— Whoever causes hurt for the purpose of extorting from the sufferer or any person interested in the sufferer any confession or any information which may lead to the detection of any offence or misconduct or for the purpose of constraining the suffer, or any person interested in the suffer to restore, or to cause the restoration of any property or valuable security or to satisfy any claim or demand, or to give information which my lead to the restoration of any property or valuable security shall in addition to the punishment of *qisas*, *arsh* or *daman*, as the case may be, provided for the kind of hurt caused, be also punished having regard to the nature of the hurt caused, with imprisonment of either description for a term which may extend to ten years if for such hurt the punishment of *qisas* cannot be awarded.

337-L. *Punishment for other hurt*—(1) Whoever causes hurt, not mentioned hereinbefore, which endangers life or which causes the suffer to remain in severe bodily pain for twenty days or more or renders him unable to follow his ordinary pursuits for twenty days or more, shall be liable to *daman* and also be punished with imprisonment of either description for a term which may extend to seven years.

(2)   Whoever causes hurt not covered by sub-section (1) shall be punished with imprisonment of either description for a term which may extend to two years, or with *daman* or with both.

337-M. *Hurt not liable to qisas.*—Hurt shall not be liable to *qisas* in the following cases namely:—

(a)   when the offender is a minor or insane:
Provided that he shall be liable to *arsh*: and also to *ta'zir* to be determined by the court having regard to the age of offender, circumstances of the case and the nature of hurt caused:

(b)   when an offender at the instance of the victim causes hurt to him:
Provided that the offender may be liable to *ta'zir* provided for the kind of hurt caused by him:

(c)   when the offender has caused *itlaf-i-udw* of a physically imperfect organ of the victim and the convict does not suffer from similar physical imperfection of such organ:
Provided that the offender shall be liable to *arsh* and may also be liable to *ta'zir* provided for the kind of hurt caused by him; and

(d)   when the organ of the offender liable to *qisas* is missing:
Provided that the offender shall be liable to *arsh* and may also be liable to *ta'zir* provided for the kind of hurt caused by him.

Illustrations

(i)   A amputates the right ear of Z, the half of which was already missing. If A's right ear is perfect, he shall be liable to *arsh* and not *qisas*.

(ii)   If in the above illustration Z's ear is physically perfect but without power of hearing, A shall be liable to *qisas* because the defect in Z's ear is not physical.

(iii)   If in illustration (i) Z's ear is pierced, A shall be liable to *qisas* because such minor defect is not physical imperfection.

337-N. *Cases in which qisas for hurt shall not be enforced.*—(1) The *qisas* for a hurt shall not be enforced in the following cases namely:

(a)   when the offender dies before execution of *qisas*:

(b)   when the organ of the offender liable to *qisas* is lost before the execution of *qisas*:
Provided that the offender shall be liable to *arsh* and may also be liable to *ta'zir* provided for the kind of hurt caused by him:

(c)   when the victim waives the *qisas* or compounds the offence with *budl-i-sulh*; or

(d)   when the right of *qisas* devolves on the person who cannot claim *qisas* against the offender under this Chapter:

Provided that the offender shall be liable to *arsh*, if there is any *wali* other than the offender and if there is no *wali* other than the offender he shall be liable to *ta'zir* provided for the kind of hurt caused by him:

(2)   Notwithstanding anything contained in this Chapter in all cases of hurt, the court may in addition to payment of *arsh* award *ta'zir* to an offender who is a previous convict habitual or hardened, desperate or dangerous criminal having regard to the kind of hurt caused by him.

337-O. *Wali in case of hurt.*—In the case of hurt the *wali* shall be:

(a)   the victim:
provided that, if the victim is a minor or insane his right of *qisas* shall be exercised by his father or paternal grandfather, how-high-so-ever.

(b)   the heirs of the victim, if the later dies before the execution of *qisas*; and

(c)   the Government in the absence of the victim or the heirs of the victim.

337-P. *Execution of qisas for hurt.*—(1) *Qisas* shall be executed in the public by an authorised medical officer who shall before such execution examine the offender and take due care so as to ensure that the execution of *qisas* does not cause the death of the offender or exceed the hurt caused by him of the victim.

(2)   The *wali* shall be present at the time of execution and if the *wali* or his representative is not present, after having been informed of the date, time and place by the court an officer authorised by the court in this behalf give permission for the execution of *qisas*.

(3)   If the convict is a woman who is pregnant, the court may, in consultation with an authorised medical officer, postpone the execution of *qisas* up to a period of two years after the birth of the child and during this period she may be released on bail on furnishing of security to the satisfaction of the court or if she is not so released, shall be dealt with as if sentenced to simple imprisonment.

337-Q. *Arsh for single organs.*—The *arsh* for causing *itlaf* of an organ which is found singly in a human body shall be equivalent to the value of *diyat*.
Explanation.—Nose and tongue are included in the organs which are found singly in a human body.

337-R *Arsh for organs in pairs*—The *arsh* for causing *itlaf* of organs found in a human body in pairs shall be equivalent to the value of *diyat* and if *itlaf* is caused to one of such organs the amount of *arsh* shall be one half of the *diyat*:
Provided that, where the victim has only one such organ or his other organ is missing or has already become incapacitated the *arsh* for causing *itlaf* of the existing or capable organ shall be equal to the value of *diyat*.
Explanation.— Hands, feet, eyes, lips and breasts are included in the organ which are found in a human body in pairs.

337-S. *Arsh for organs in quadruplicate.*—(1) The *arsh* for causing *itlaf* of organs found in a human body in a set of four shall be equal to:

(a)   one-fourth of the *diyat*, if the *itlaf* is one of such organs:
(b)   one-half of the *diyat*, if the *itlaf* is of two of such organs:

(c)   three-fourths of the *diyat*, if the *itlaf*, is of three of such organs: and
(d)   full *diyat*, if the *itlaf* is of all the four organs.
    Explanation.—Eyelids are organs which are found in a human body in a set of four.

337-T. *Arsh for fingers*—(1) The *arsh* for causing *itlaf* of a finger of a hand or foot shall be one-tenth of the *diyat*.

    (2)   The *arsh* for causing *itlaf* of a point of a finger shall be one-thirtieth of the *diyat*:
    Provided that where the *itlaf* is of a joint of a thumb, the *arsh* shall be one-twentieth of the *diyat*.

337-U. *Arsh for teeth.*—(1) The *arsh* for causing *itlaf* of a tooth other than a milk tooth shall be one-twentieth of the *diyat*.
    Explanation.— The impairment of the portion of a tooth outside the gum amounts to causing *itlaf* of a tooth.

    (2)   The *arsh* for causing *itlaf* of twenty or more teeth shall be equal to the value of *diyat*.

    (3)   Where the *itlaf* is of a milk tooth the accused shall be liable to *daman* and may also be punished with imprisonment of either description for a term which may extend to one year;
    Provided that, where *itlaf* of a milk tooth impedes the growth of a new tooth, the accused shall be liable to *arsh* specified in sub-section (1)

337-V. *Arsh for hair.*—(1) Whoever uproots.—

(a)   all the hair of the head, beard, moustaches, eyebrow, eyelashes or any other part of the body shall be liable to *arsh* equal to *diyat* and may also be punished with imprisonment of either description for a term which may extend to three years as *ta'zir*.

(b)   one eyebrow shall be liable to *arsh* equal to one-half of the *diyat* and

(c)   one eyelash shall be liable to *arsh* equal to one-fourth of the *diyat*.

    (2)   Where the hair of any part of the body of the victim are forcibly removed by any process not covered under sub-section (1), the accused shall be liable to *daman* and imprisonment of either description which may extend to one year.

337-W. *Merger of arsh.-* (1) Where an accused causes more than one hurt, he shall be liable to the *arsh* specified for each hurt, separately;

    Provided that, where—

    (a)   hurt is caused to an organ, the accused shall be liable to *arsh* for causing hurt to such organ and not for *arsh* for causing hurt to any part of such organ; and

    (b)   the wounds join together and form a single wound, the accused shall be liable to *arsh* for one wound.

Illustrations

(i)   A amputates Z's fingers of the right hand and then at the same time amputates that hand from the joint of his wrist. There is separate *arsh* for hand and for fingers. A shall, however, be liable to *arsh* specified for hand only.

(ii)   A twice stabs Z, on his thigh. Both the wounds are so close to each other that they form into one wound. A shall be liable to *arsh* for one wound only.

(2)   Where, after causing hurt to a person, the offender causes death of such person by committing qatl liable to *diyat arsh* shall merge into such *diyat*;
Provided that the death is caused before the healing of the wound caused by such hurt.

337-X. *Payment of arsh.*—(1) The *arsh* may be made payable in lump sum or in installments spread over a period of three years from the date of the final judgment.

(2)   Where a convict fails to pay *arsh* or any part thereof within the period specified in sub-section (1), the convict may be kept in jail and dealt within the same manner as if sentenced to simple imprisonment until *arsh* is paid in full or may be released on bail if he furnishes security equal to the amount of *arsh* to the satisfaction of the court for payment of the *arsh*.

(3)   Where a convict dies before the payment of *arsh* or of part thereof, it shall be recovered from his estate.

337-Y. *Value of daman*—(1) The value of *daman* may be determined by the court keeping in view—

(a)   the expenses incurred on the treatment of the victim;

(b)   loss or disability caused in the functioning or power of any organ; and

(c)   the compensation for the anguish suffered by the victim.

(2)   In case of non-payment of *daman* it shall be recovered from the convict and until *daman* is paid in full to the extent of his liability, the convict may be kept in jail and dealt with in the same manner as if sentenced to simple imprisonment or may be released on bail if he furnishes security equal to the amount of *daman* to the satisfaction of the court for payment of the *daman*.

337-Z. *Payment of arsh or daman.*—The *arsh* or *daman* shall be payable to the victim or if the victim dies, to his heirs according to their respective shares in inheritance

338   *Isqat-i-haml.* Whoever causes a woman with child whose organs have not been formed to miscarry if such miscarriage is not caused in good faith for the purpose of saving the life of the woman or providing necessary treatment to her, is said to cause '*isqat-i-haml*'.
Explanation.—A woman who causes herself to miscarry is within the meaning of this section.

338-A. *Punishment for isqat-i-haml.*—Whoever causes *isqat-i-haml* shall be liable to punishment as *ta'zir.*

    (a)   with imprisonment of either description for a term which may extend to three years if *isqat-i-haml* is caused with the consent of the woman; or

    (b)   with imprisonment of either description for a term which may extend to ten years if *isqat-i-haml* is caused without the consent of the woman:
    Provided that, if as a result of *isqat-i-haml* any hurt is caused to the woman or she dies, the convict shall also be liable to the punishment provided for such hurt or death, as the case may be

338-B *Isqat-i-Janin.*—Whoever, causes a woman with child some of whose limbs or organs have been formed, to miscarry, if such miscarriage is not caused in good faith for the purpose of saving the life of the woman, is said to cause *isqat-i-janin.*
    Explanation.—A woman who causes herself to miscarry is within the meaning of this action.

338-C. *Punishment for isqat-i-janin.*—Whoever causes *isqat-i-janin* shall be liable to—

    (a)   one-twentieth of the *diyat* if the child is born dead:

    (b)   full *diyat* if the child is born alive but dies as a result of any act of the offender; or

    (c)   punishment as *ta'zir* with imprisonment of either description for a term which my extend to seven years if the child is born alive but dies otherwise than as a result of any act of the offender:

        Provided that, if there are more than one child in the womb of the woman the offender shall be liable to separate *diyat* or *ta'zir*, as the case may be, for every such child:

        Provided further that if, as a result of isqat-in-janin any hurt is caused to the woman or she dies the offender shall also be liable to the punishment provided for such hurt or death, as the case may be.

338-D. *Confirmation of sentence of death by way of qisas or ta'zir etc.*—A sentence of death awarded by way of *qisas* or ta'zir or sentence of *qisas* awarded for causing hurt, shall not be executed, unless it is confirmed by the High Court.

338-E. *Waiver or compounding of offences*—Subject to the provision of this Chapter and notwithstanding any thing contained in section 345 of the Code of Criminal Procedure, 1898, all offences under this Chapter may be waived or compounded and the provisions of section 309 and 310 shall mutatis mutandis, apply to the waiver or compounding of such offences:
    Provided that where an offence has been waived or compounded, the court may, in its discretion having regard to the facts and circumstances of the case acquit of award ta'zir to the offender according to the nature of the offence.

338-F. *Interpretation.*—In the interpretation and application of the provisions of this Chapter and in respect of matters ancillary or akin thereto, the court shall be guided by the Injunctions of Islam as laid down in the Holy Quran and Sunnah.

338-G.*Rules*.—The Government may, in consultation with the Council of Islamic Ideology, by notification in the official Gazette, make such rules as it may consider necessary for carrying out the purposes of this Chapter.

338-H.*Saving*.—(1) Nothing in this Chapter, except sections 309, 310 and 338E, shall apply to cases pending before any court immediately before the commencement of the Criminal Law (Second Amendment) Ordinance, 1990 (VII of 1990), or to the offence committed before such commencement."; and

(2)   After section 338H. substituted as aforesaid, the following new heading shall be inserted, namely:

"CHAPTER XVIA"

5.   **Amendment of section 337, Act V of 1988.**—In the Code of Criminal 1898 (Act V of 1898), hereinafter referred to as the aforesaid Code, in section 337 in sub-section (I) for the full stop at the end a colon shall be substituted and thereafter the following proviso shall be added, namely:—

"Provided that no person shall be tendered pardon who is involved in an offence relating to hurt or *qatl* without permission of the victim or, as the case may be, of the heirs of the victim".

6.   **Amendment of section 338, Act V of 1898.**—In the aforesaid Code, in section 338 for the full stop at the end a colon shall be substituted and thereafter the following proviso shall be added, namely:—

"Provided that no person shall be tendered pardon who is involved in an offence relating to hurt or *qatl* without permission of the victim or, as the case may be, of the heirs of the victim."

7.   **Amendment of section 381, Act V of 1898.**—In the aforesaid Code, in section 381, for the full stop at the end a colon shall be substituted and hereafter the following proviso shall be added, namely:—

"Provided that the sentence of death shall not be executed if the heirs of the deceased pardon the convict or enter into compromise with him even at the last moment before execution of the sentence."

8.   **Amendment of Schedule 11, Act V of 1899.**—In the aforesaid Code, in Schedule 11, for the figures "302 to 338" occurring column 1 and the entries relating thereto in columns 2 to 8 the following shall be substituted, namely:—

(For schedule see next page)

Section	Offence	Whether the Police may arrest without warrant or not	Whether a warrant or a summons shall ordinarily issue in the first instance	Whether bailable or not	Whether compoundable or not	Punishment under the Pakistan Penal Code	By what court triable
1	2	3	4	5	6	7	8
302	*Qatl-i-amd*	May arrest without warrant.	Warrant	Not bailable.	Compoundable.	*Qisas* or death, imprisonment up to 25 years	Court of Session
302 (a)	*Qatl* under *ikrah-i-tam*.	...	...	...	...	Imprisonment of either description for 25 years but not less than 10 years	...
... (b)	Causing of *ikrah-i-tam* for commission of *qatl*.	...	...	...	...	Punishment provided for the kind of *qatl* committed.	...
... (c)	*Qatl* under *ikrah-i-naqis*.	...	...	...	...	Punishment provided for the kind of *qatl* committed.	...
... (d)	Causing *ikrah-i-naqis* for the commission of *qatl*.	...	...	...	...	Imprisonment of either description for 10 years.	...
308	*Qatl-i-amd* not liable to *qisas*.	...	...	...	...	*Diyat*, and imprisonment for either description for 14 years.	...
311	*Qatl-i-amd* when waived compounded	...	...	...	...	Imprisonment of either description for 10 to 14 years.	...
312	*Qatl-i-amd* after compounding of *qisas*.	...	...	...	...	*Qisas*, or *diyat*.	...
316	*Qatl-Shibh-i-amd*.	...	...	...	...	*Diyat*, and imprisonment for either description for 14 years.	...

Section	Offence		Bailable or not	Compoundable or not	Punishment	Court by which triable
319	*Qal-i-Khata.*	...	...	...	*Diyat*, and imprisonment for either description for 5 years.	...
320	*Qal-i-Khata* by rash or negligent driving.	...	...	...	*Diyat*, and imprisonment for either description for 10 years.	...
322	*Qal-bis-sabab.*	...	...	...	*Diyat.*	...
324	Attempt to *qatl-i-amd.*	...	...	...	Imprisonment of either description for 10 years and fine qisas, or arsh in case of hurt and imprisonment up to 7 years.	...
325	Attempt to commit suicide	...	Bailable.	Not compoundable.	Simple imprisonment for one year, or fine, or both.	Magistrate of the 1st or 2nd class.
327	Being a thug.	...	Not bailable.	...	Imprisonment for life and fine.	Court of Session.
328	Exposure of a child under 12 years of age by parent or person having care of it with intention of wholly abandoning it.	...	Not bailable.	...	Imprisonment of either description for 7 years, or fine, or both.	Court of Session or Magistrate of the 1st class.
329	Concealment of birth by secret disposal of dead body.	...	Bailable.	...	Imprisonment of either description for 2 years, or fine, or both.	Magistrate of the 1st class.
334	*Itlaf-i-udw.*	...	Not bailable.	Compoundable.	*Qisas*, or *arsh*, and imprisonment for either description for 10 years.	Court of Session.
336	*Itlaf-i-salahiyyat-i-udw.*	...	...	...	*Qisas*, or *arsh*, and imprisonment of either description for 10 years.	...

Section	Offence						Court
337A (i)	*Shajjah-i-khafifah.*	Shall not arrest without warrant.	Summons	Bailable.	Compoundable.	*Daman,* and imprisonment of either description for 2 years.	Magistrate of the 1st class.
... (ii)	*Shajjah-i-mudihah.*	May arrest without warrant.	Warrant	Not bailable.	...	*Qisas,* or *arsh,* and imprisonment of either description for 10 years.	Court of Session or Magistrate of the 1st class.
... (iii)	*Shajjah-i-hashimah.*	...	...	...	...	*Arsh,* and imprisonment of either description for 7 years.	...
... (iv)	*Shajjah-i-munaqqilah.*	...	...	...	...	*Arsh,* and imprisonment of either description for 10 years.	...
... (v)	*Shajjah-i-ammah.*	...	...	...	...	*Arsh,* and imprisonment of either description for 10 years.	...
... (vi)	*Shajjah-i-damighah.*	...	...	...	...	*Arsh,* and imprisonment of either description for 14 years.	...
337D	*Jaifah.*	...	...	...	...	*Arsh,* and imprisonment of either description for 10 years and punishment provided for *Itlaf-i-udw* or *Itlaf-i-salahiyyat-i-udw,* if caused.	...
337F (i)	*Damiyah.*	Shall not arrest without warrant.	Summons	Bailable.	Compoundable.	*Daman,* and imprisonment of either description for 1 year.	Magistrate of the 1st class.
... (ii)	*Badi'ah.*	May arrest without warrant.	Warrant	Not bailable.	...	*Daman,* and imprisonment of either description for 3 years.	...
... (iii)	*Mutalahimah.*	...	...	...	...	*Daman,* and imprisonment of either description for 3 years.	...
... (iv)	*Mudihah.*	...	...	...	...	*Daman,* and imprisonment of either description for 5 years.	Court of Session or Magistrate of the 1st class.

Section	Offence	May arrest without warrant.	Warrant	Bailable or not.	Punishment	Court by which triable.
... (v)	*Hashimah.*	...	...	Not bailable.	*Daman*, and imprisonment of either description for 5 years.	Court of Session or Magistrate of the 1st class.
... (vi)	*Munaqqilah.*	...	...	...	*Daman*, and imprisonment of either description for 7 years.	...
337G	Hurt by rash or negligent driving.	...	...	...	*Arsh*, or *daman*, and imprisonment of either description for 5 years.	...
337H	Hurt by rash or negligent act.	...	...	...	*Arsh*, or *daman*, and imprisonment of either description for 3 years.	Magistrate of the 1st class.
337I	Hurt by mistake (*khata*).	...	...	...	*Arsh*, or *daman* for the kind of hurt caused.	...
337J	Hurt by poison.	...	...	...	*Arsh*, or *daman*, provided for the kind of hurt caused and imprisonment of either description for 10 years.	Court of Session.
337K	Hurt for extorting confession, etc.	...	...	...	*Qisas, arsh,* or *daman,* provided for the kind of hurt caused and imprisonment of either description for 10 years.	...
337L (a)	Hurts other than specified in section here-to-before.	...	...	...	*Daman*, and imprisonment of either description for 7 years.	Court of Session or Magistrate of the 1st class.
... (b)	Other hurts not covered here-to-before.	...	...	...	*Daman*, and imprisonment of either description for 2 years, or with both.	Magistrate of the 1st class.
337M	Hurt not liable to *qisas*.	...	...	...	*Arsh, ta'zir* and punishment provided for the kind of hurt caused.	...

337N	Hurt where *qisas* cannot be enforced.	...	...	*Arsh, ta'zir* and punishment provided for the kind of hurt caused.	Court of Session or Magistrate of the 1st class.
338A (a)	*Iqusat-i-haml.*	...	...	Imprisonment of either description for 3 years and punishment provided for the kind of hurt or death, if caused.	...
... (b)	*Iqusat-i-haml* without.	...	...	Imprisonment of either description for 3-10 years and punishment provided for the kind of hurt or death, if caused.	...
338C	*Iqusat-i-janin.*	...	...	*Diyat, ta'zir* and imprisonment of either description for 7 years and punishment provided for the kind of hurt or death, if caused".	...

The Criminal Law (Amendment) Ordinance
(IV of 1990)

Preamble: And whereas the National Assembly is not in session and the President is satisfied that circumstances exist which render it necessary to take immediate action;

Now, therefore, in exercise of the powers conferred by clause (1) of Article 89 of the Constitution of the Islamic Republic of Pakistan, the President is pleased to make and promulgate the following Ordinance:—

1. **Short title and commencement**: (1) This Ordinance may be called the Criminal Law (Amendment) Ordinance, 1990.

   (2)   It shall come into force at once.

2. **Amendment of Section 54, Act XLV of 1860**: In the Pakistan Penal Code (Act XLV of 1860), in Section 3 referred to as the said Code, in Section 54, for the full-stop at the end a colon shall be substituted and thereafter the following proviso shall be added, namely:—

   "Provided that, in a case in which sentence of death shall have been passed against an offender convicted for an offence of murder, such sentence shall not be commuted without the consent of the heirs of the victim."

3. **Amendment of Section 55, Act XLV of 1860**: In the said Code, in Section 55, for the full-stop at the end a colon shall be substituted and thereafter the following proviso shall be added, namely:—

   "Provided that, in a case in which sentence of imprisonment for life shall have been passed against an offender convicted for an offence punishable under Section 302, 303, 304, 305, 307, 326 or 329 such sentence shall not be commuted without the consent of the victim or, as the case may be, of his heirs."

4. **Amendment of Section 345, Act V of 1898**: In the Code of Criminal Procedure, 1898 (Act V of 1898), hereinafter referred to as the said Code, in section 345, in sub-section (2), in the table,—

   (a)   before the entries relating to the offence punishable under Section 324 of the Pakistan Penal Code, the following new entries shall be inserted namely:—

"Murder	302, 303	By the heirs of the victim.
Culpable homicide not amounting to murder	304	By the heirs of the victim.
Death by negligence	304-A	By the heirs of the victim.
Abetment of suicide	305, 306	By the heirs of the victim.
Attempt to murder ...	307	The person against whom the offence was committed
Attempt to commit culpable homicide	308	The person against whom the offence was committed"; and

(b)   after the entries relating to the offence punishable under Section 325 of the Pakistan Penal Code, the following new entries shall be inserted, namely:—

"Voluntarily causing grievous hurt by dangerous weapons:	326	The person to whom hurt is caused.
Voluntarily causing hurt to extort property, etc.:	327	Do.
Causing hurt by means of poison:	328	Do.
Voluntarily causing grievous hurt to extort property, etc.:	329	Do.
Voluntarily causing hurt to extort confession, etc.:	330, 331	Do.
Voluntarily causing hurt to deter public servant from performing his duties:	332, 333	Do."

5.   **Insertion of new Section 402-C, Act V of 1898**: In the said Code, in Chapter XXIX, after Section 402-B, the following new section shall be added, namely:—

"402-C, Remission or commutation of certain sentences not to be without consent: Notwithstanding anything contained in Section 401, Section 402, or Section 402-A, the Provincial Government or the President shall not, without the consent of the victim or, as the case may be, of his heirs, suspend, remit or commute any sentence passed under any of the sections of the Pakistan Penal Code hereinafter specified that is to say, 302, 303, 304, 304-A, 305, 306, 307, 308, 323, 324, 325, 326, 327, 328, 329, 330, 331, 332, 333, 334, 335, 337 and 338."

6.   **Amendment of second schedule, Act V of 1898**: In the said Code, in the second schedule in column 6.-

(a)   for the entry relating to Section 302, the entry "Compoundable by the heirs of the victim when permission is given by the Court before which a prosecution is pending" shall be substituted;

(b)   for the entry relating to Sec. 307 the entry "Compoundable by the victim when permission is given by the Court before which a prosecution is pending" shall be substituted;

(c)   for the entry relating to Section 309 the entry "Not compoundable" shall be substituted;

(d)   for the entry relating to Section 326 the entry "Compoundable by the victim when permission is given by the Court before which a prosecution is pending" shall be substituted;

(e)   for the entry relating to Section 329 the entry "Compoundable by the victim when permission is given by the Court before which a prosecution is pending" shall be substituted; and

(f)   for the entry relating to Section 336 the entry "Compoundable by the victim when permission is given by the Court before which a prosecution is pending" shall be substituted.

Appendix III:
Text of the Enforcement of *Shari' ah* Act, 1991

(AS PASSED BY THE NATIONAL ASSEMBLY)
A
BILL

for the enforcement of the Shari' ah

WHEREAS sovereignty over the entire Universe belongs to Almighty Allah alone, and the authority to be exercised by the people of Pakistan through their chosen representatives within the limits prescribed by Him is a sacred trust;

AND WHEREAS Islam has been declared to be the State religion of Pakistan and it is obligatory for all Muslims to follow the Injunctions of the Holy Quran and Sunnah to regulate and order their lives in complete submission to the Divine law;

AND WHEREAS the Objectives Resolution has been incorporated in the Constitution of the Islamic Republic of Pakistan as a substantive part thereof;

AND WHEREAS it is one of the fundamental obligations of the Islamic State to protect the honour, life, liberty and the fundamental rights of the citizens as guaranteed under the Constitution and to ensure peace and provide inexpensive and speedy justice to people through an independent Islamic system of justice without any discrimination.

AND WHEREAS Islam enjoins establishment of social order based on the Islamic values of bidding what is right and forbidding what is wrong (amr bil Ma'roof wa nahi anil Munkar);

AND WHEREAS in order to achieve the aforesaid objectives and goals, it is necessary to give to these measures constitutional and legal backing;

It is hereby enacted as follows:

1 .   **Short title, extent and commencement.**- (1) This Act may by called the Enforcement of Shari'ah Act, 1991.

(2)   It extends to the whole of Pakistan.
(3)   It shall come into force at once.
(4)   Nothing contained in this Act shall affect the personal laws, religious freedom, traditions, customs and way of life of the non-Muslims.

2 .   **Definition.**- In this Act "Shari'ah" means the Injunctions of Islam as laid down in the Holy Quran and Sunnah.

Explanation.- While interpreting and explaining the Shari'ah the recognized principles of interpretation and explanation of the Holy Quran and Sunnah shall be followed and expositions and opinions of recognized jurists of Islam belonging to prevalent Islamic schools of jurisprudence may be taken into consideration.

3 .   Supremacy of Shari'ah.- (1) The Shari'ah that is to say, the injunctions of Islam as laid down in the Holy Quran and Sunnah, shall be the supreme law of Pakistan.

(2)   Notwithstanding anything contained in this Act, the Judgement of any court or any other law for the time being in force, the present political system, including the Majlis-e-Shoora (Parliament) and Provincial Assemblies and the existing system of Government, shall not be challenged in any court, including Supreme Court, the Federal Shariat Court or any authority or tribunal;

Provided that nothing contained herein shall affect the rights of the non-Muslims guaranteed by or under the Constitution.

4 .   Laws to be interpreted in the light of Shari'ah.- For the purpose of this Act-

(a)   while interpreting the statute-law, if more than one interpretation is possible, the one consistent with the Islamic principles and jurisprudence shall be adopted by the Court; and
(b)   where two or more interpretations are equally possible, the interpretation which advances the Principles of Policy and Islamic provisions in the Constitution shall be adapted by the Court.

5 .   Observance of Shari'ah by Muslim citizens.- All Muslim citizens of Pakistan shall observe Shari'ah and act accordingly and in this regard the Mailis-e-Shoora (Parliament) shall formulate code of conduct for Government functionaries.

6. Teaching of, and training in, Shari'ah etc.- The State shall make effective arrangements-

(a)   for the teaching of, and training in, the Shari'ah, Islamic jurisprudence and all other branches of Islamic law at appropriate levels of education and professional training;

(b)   to include courses on the Shari'ah in the syllabi of the law colleges;

(c)   for the teaching of the Arabic language; and

(d)   to avail the services of persons duly qualified in Shari'ah, Islamic jurisprudence and Ifta in judical system.

7. Islamization of education.- (1) The State shall take necessary steps to ensure that the educational system of Pakistan is based on Islamic values of learning, teaching and character building.

(2)   The Federal Government shall, within thirty days from the commencement of this Act, appoint a Commission consisting of educationists, jurists, experts, ulema and elected representatives as it may deem fit and appoint one of them to be its Chairman.

(3)   The functions of the Commission shall be to examine the educational system of Pakistan to achieve the objectives referred to in sub-section (1) and make recommendations in this behalf.

(4)   A report containing the recommendations of the Commission shall be submitted to the Federal Government which shall cause it to be placed before both the Houses of Mailis-e-Shoora (Parliament).

(5)   The Commission shall have the power to conduct its pro-ceedings and regulate its procedure in all respects as it may deem fit.

(6)   All executive authorities, institutions and local authorities shall act in aid of the Commission.

(7)   The Ministry of Education in the Government of Pakistan shall be responsible for the administrative matters relating to the Commission.

8.   Islamization of economy.- (1) The State shall take steps to ensure that the economic system of Pakistan is constructed on the basis of Islamic economic objectives, principles, and priorities.

(2)   The Federal Government shall, within thirty days from the commencement of this Act, appoint a Commission consisting of economists, bankers, jurists, ulema, elected representatives and such other persons as it may deem fit and appoint one of them to be its Chairman.

(3)   The functions of the Commission shall be-

(a)   to recommend measures and steps, including suitable alternatives, by which the economic system enunciated by Islam could be established;

(b)   to recommend the ways, means and strategy for such changes in the economic system of Pakistan so as to achieve the social and economic well being of the people as envisaged by Article 38 of the Constitution;

(c)   to undertake the examination of any fiscal law or any law relating to the levy and collection of taxes and fees or banking or insurance law or practice and procedure to determine whether or not these are repugnant to the Shari'ah and to make recommendations to bring such laws, practices and procedure in conformity with the Shari'ah; and

(d)   to monitor progress in respect of the Islamization of economy, identifying lapses and bottlenecks if any and suggest alternatives to remove any difficulty.

(4)   The Commission shall oversee the process of elimination of *riba* from every sphere of economic activity in the shortest possible time and also recommend such measures to the Government as would ensure the total elimination of *riba* from the economy.

(5)   The Commission shall submit its reports on a regular basis and at suitable intervals to the Federal Government which shall place the same before both the Houses of Mailis-e-Shoora (Parliament) and shall also respond to any queries sent to it by the Federal Government in respect of establishment of the Islamic economic order.

(6)   The Commission shall have the power to conduct its pro-ceedings and regulate its procedure in all respects as it may deem fit.

(7)   All executive authorities, institutions and local authorities shall act in aid of the Commission.

(8)   The Ministry of Finance in the Government of Pakistan shall be responsible for the administrative matters relating to the Commission.

9.   Mass media to promote Islamic values.- (1) The State shall take steps to promote Islamic values through the mass media.

(2)   The publication and promotion of programmes against or in derogation to the Shari'ah, including obscene material shall be forbidden.

10.   Protection of life, liberty, property, etc.- In order to protect the life, honour, liberty, property, and the rights of the citizens, the State shall take legislative and administrative measures to-

(a)   introduce administrative and police reforms;

(b)   prevent acts of terrorism and sabotage and disruptive activities; and

(c)   prevent the possession and display of illicit arms.

11.   Elimination of bribery and corruption.- The State shall take legislative and administrative measures to eliminate bribery, corruption and malpractices and provide for example punishment for such offences.

12.   Eradication of obscenity, vulgarity, etc.- Effective legal and administrative measures shall be taken by the State to eradicate obscenity, vulgarity and other moral vices.

13.   Eradication of social evils.- The State shall take effective measures for enactment of law eradicating social evils and promoting Islamic virtues on the principles of amr bil Ma'roof wa nahi'anil Munkar as laid down in the Holy Quran.

14.   Nizam-i-adl.- The State shall take adequate measures for the Islamisation of the judicial system by eliminating laws delays, multiplicity of proceedings in different courts, litigation expenses and ensuring the quest for truth by the court.

15.   Bait-ul-Mal (Welfare Fund).- The State shall take steps to set up a Bait-ul-Mal for providing assistance to the poor, needy, helpless, handicapped, invalids, widows, orphans and destitute.

16.   Protection of the ideology of Pakistan, etc.- The State shall enact laws to protect the ideology, solidarity and integrity of Pakistan as an Islamic State.

17.   Safeguard against false imputations, etc.- The State shall take legislative and administrative measures to protect the honour and reputation of the citizens agaist false imputations, character assassination and violation of privacy.
18.   International financial obligations, etc.- Notwithstanding anything contained in this Act or any decision of any court, till an alternative economic system is introduced, financial obligations incurred and contracts made between a National

Institution and a Foreign Agency shall continue to, remain, and be, valid, binding and operative.

   Explanation.- In this section, the expression "National Institution" shall include the Federal Government or a Provincial Government, a statutory corporation, company, institution, body, enterprise or any person in Pakistan and the expression "Foreign Agency" shall include a foreign government, a foreign financial institution, foreign capital market, including a bank and any foreign lending agency, including an individual and a supplier of goods and services.

19.   Fulfilment of existing obligations.- Nothing contained in this Act or any decision made thereunder shall affect the validity of any financial obligations incurred, including under any instruments, whether contractual or otherwise, promise to pay, or any other financial commitments made by or on behalf of the Federal Government or a Provincial Government or a financial or statutory corporation or other institution to make payments envisaged therein, and all such obligations, promises and commitments shall be valid, binding and operative till an alternative economic system is evolved.

20.   Rights of women not to be affected.- Notwithstanding anything contained in this Act, the rights of women as guaranteed by the Constitution shall not be affected.

21.   Laws to be enacted by Majlis-e-Shoora (Parliament) and Provincial Assembly only.- Notwithstanding anything contained in this Act or the judgement of any court, including the Supreme Court, all laws shall be enacted exclusively by the Mailis-e-Shoora (Parliament) and the Provincial Assembly, as the case may be, and no law shall be made or be deemed to have been made unless it is made in the manner laid down in the Constitution.

22.   Rules. The Federal Government may, by notification in the official gazette, make rules for carrying out the purposes of this Act.

STATEMENT OF OBJECTS AND REASONS

Having regard to the will of the people of Pakistan to make the country a truly Islamic State wherein, amongst other things

(a)   adjust social order shall be established ensuring equality between citizens, a society free from exploitation, protection of the life, liberty, property and rights of the citizens and availability of inexpensive and speedy justice to all manner of people through an independent Islamic system of justice;

(b)   adequate provisions are made according to Shari'ah to eliminate bribery, corruption and malpractices; and

(c)   obscenity, immorality and other social evils are eradicated;

this Bill declares that the Shari'ah, that is to say, the Injunctions of Islam as laid down in the Holy Quran and Sunnah shall be the supreme law of Pakistan, requires all Muslim citizens of Pakistan to faithfully observe the Shari'ah and casts upon the State the duty to-

(a)   Make effective arrangements for the teaching of and training in, the Shariah and Islamic jurisprudence;

(b)   take adequate measures toensure an Islamic system of justice and to save the people from the necessity of resorting to several courts;

(c)   bring about police reforms to ensure that the life, honour, liberty, property and rights of the citizens are protected;

(d)   make effective provisions by law to combat the offences of corruption of all sorts;

(e)   take steps to set up a Bait-ul-Mal for providing assistance to the poor, needy, widows, orphans and the destitute;

(f)   take effective legal and administrative measures to eradicate obscenity, vulgarity and other moral vices;

(g)   enact laws to protect the ideology, solidarity and integrity of Pakistan;

(h)   undertake legal measures to prevent the possession and display of illicit arms;

(i)   take steps to ensure that the economic system of Pakistan is constructed on the basis of Islamic economic principles, values and priorities and appoint a Commission consisting of economists, bankers, jurists, ulema and elected representatives with the duty to recommend measures and steps, including suitable alternatives, by which the Islamic economic system could be established and to monitor progress in respect of the Islamisation of the economy and oversee the whole process of elimination of Riba from every sphere of economic activity within a shortest possible time;

(j)   take steps to promote Islamic values through the mass media;

(k)   take steps to ensure that the educational system of Pakistan is based on Islamic values of learning, teaching and character building and to appoint a Commission consisting of educationists, jurists, experts, ulema and elected representatives to make recommendations for the purpose;

(l)   take effective measures for enactment of laws eradicating social evils and promoting Islamic values on the principles of *"Amr-bil-Ma'aruf Wa Nahi' Anil Munkar"* as laid down in the Holy Quran.

2.   In order to prevent the disruption of the economic system of Pakistan and to honour sanctity of agreements, the Bill seeks to protect the validity of the financial obligations and contracts between a national institution and a foreign agency until an alternative economic system is introduced.

CH. AMIR HUSSAIN
Minister-in-Charge